BLOCKBUSTER
ENTERTAINMENT
TM
GUIDE TO
TELEVISION
ON VIDEO

GUIDE TO TELEVISION ON VIDEO

POCKET BOOKS
New York London Toronto Sydney Tokyo Singapore

Unless otherwise indicated, all photographs are courtesy of Personality Photos, Inc., P.O. Box 50, Midwood Station, Brooklyn, NY 11230.

An *Original* Publication of POCKET BOOKS

POCKET BOOKS, a division of Simon & Schuster Inc.
1230 Avenue of the Americas, New York, NY 10020

ISBN: 0-671-52902-1

First Pocket Books printing December 1996

10 9 8 7 6 5 4 3 2 1

POCKET and colophon are registered trademarks of Simon & Schuster Inc.

Printed in the U.S.A.

EDITORIAL STAFF

Writers

Alvin H. Marill
Peter Napolitano

Blockbuster Entertainment™

Tom Aucamp
Gordon K. Smith
Steve Menke
Marlene Gordon

The Philip Lief Group, Inc.

Gary M. Krebs
Emily Fraser
Philip Lief

Simon & Schuster

Tom Miller
Amanda Reid
Dan Slater

CONTENTS

INTRODUCTION

Television at Age Fifty

As commercial television reaches the big Five-O, it is instructive to reflect on how it has influenced American culture and society. Television did not, as some naysayers in the 1950s predicted, kill the art of conversation, ruin everybody's eyesight, or corrupt anyone's mind. Instead, we have a legacy of programs that either have endeared themselves to viewers or have become certified classics, to be watched over and over again until fans know the lines better than the original actors from the shows.

Many of television's earliest programs, unfortunately, are gone forever. Staged live, they did not benefit from later technology that would have preserved them for future viewing. In the early 1950s, it was Desi Arnaz who championed filming shows live in front of three cameras, thereby ensuring their survival. The advent of videotape and its growing use by the end of that decade meant that not only would these shows be captured for all time but the quality of the images would improve, allowing the shows to be enjoyed visually by future generations.

In the 1980s home video rentals exploded. And audiences didn't just want feature films on tape, they also wanted television shows on video. Yet why television shows on video when many of these programs could be seen on syndicated cable or network television?

There are several reasons. Primarily, of course, many people want to *own* their favorite shows so they can build a private collection. Secondly, fans who have seen a program several times don't want to suffer through interminable commercials—or even less favorite scenes, which can easily be fast-forwarded on a tape. A tape of a TV show may contain one or two *original* commercials, but these have now become campy, nostalgic, and fun. Thirdly, an individual's favorite television shows tend to appear at the most inconvenient hours and days on cable, often moving around channels and time slots so frequently one can't keep up.

There is yet another distinct advantage to video that cable and network television do not have: uncut and unedited shows. Few people are aware that television programs today are shorter than they used to be—both half-hour sitcoms and hour-long dramas—which means that older shows such as *The Twilight Zone* are cut and edited down to allow additional time for commercials. Many videos not only have sequences unseen on television since the programs were first aired, they also offer special outtakes, interviews, and other bonuses.

The *Blockbuster Entertainment™ Guide to Television on Video* explores a retrospective of nearly 150 classic shows in distinct TV genres—situation comedy, drama, science fiction, and variety—from the early 1950s to the mid-1990s. All of the shows included are available on cassette in selected episodes or in complete series runs.

The aforementioned four categories are fairly self-explanatory. Situation comedy includes those shows that involve a fairly steady group of regular characters who confront humorous problems or issues in each episode. Drama is a somewhat broader section, encompassing westerns, action-adventures, prime-time soaps, miniseries, and some other assorted television productions. Science fiction comprises programs set in the future—often involving aliens and robots—as well as horror and fantasy shows. Variety shows offer a mix of entertainment from stand-up comedy, to humorous sketches, to musical performers, to various novelty acts.

Each entry begins with identification of network(s), year(s) of original air time, number of episodes (where available), a cast list (including characters played), as well as names of significant creators, producers, and principal directors and writers. The summaries of the shows are intended to provide the reader with background on their histories, describe their general premises, point out why the shows were successful (or not), and offer insights into the shows' significance (if any) today. The summaries are followed by headings for Emmy Awards won, interesting trivia tidbits, and video availability. Cassettes of these shows can be rented at certain video rental outlets, or purchased through mail-order houses such as Columbia House, Time-Life Video, and Reader's Digest Video. Some offer Collector's Editions with an ongoing series of additional episodes to selected shows—usually one to four episodes per cassette.

This guide will hopefully entertain and inform, introducing timeless old shows to new fans and welcoming back original faithful viewers. As Jackie Gleason used to say, "And awaaaaayyy we go!"

SITUATION COMEDY SERIES

Archie Bunker. Rob Petrie. Lucy Ricardo. Ralph Kramden. Samantha Stephens. Maxwell Smart. Jeannie-in-a-bottle. Hawkeye Pierce. To the civilized world, these names, though fictional, require no further identification. They are as recognizable as any character from classic literature and as famous as any historical personage. Through countless reruns they are known to every generation since their respective "births" and will continue to delight audiences on videocassettes for decades to come. These characters and their confederates may need no introduction, but perhaps it's fitting to pause a moment to consider their popularity and that of the medium that created them. For, like most good friends, comic characters are often taken for granted.

Sitcoms an art form?

The situation comedy may be one of the few truly American art forms. Begun on radio and perfected for television, it continues a history broad enough to encompass series as diverse as *The Dick Van Dyke Show* and *All in the Family; The Honeymooners* and *Bewitched; Get Smart* and *I Love Lucy.* There have been successful sitcoms about monsters, doctors, taxi drivers, spies, rock groups, policemen, battlefront doctors, prisoners of war, barflys, cabbies, and Martians. Horses have talked, cars have gossiped, nuns have flown, hillbillies have become millionaires, and millionaires have been shipwrecked after a three-hour cruise for which they brought along three years' worth of wardrobe. There have been so-called brainless sitcoms like *The Brady Bunch* and *Three's Company* sharing network schedules with such socially relevant series as *Room 222* and *Barney Miller.* Popular sitcom stars have run the gamut from the easygoing, casual Bill Cosby to the pop-eyed, frenetic Don Knotts; from the sweetness of Florence Henderson to the sarcasm of Roseanne. One constant theme runs through all of these shows, however: the depiction of a "family," be it traditional (the Bradys), or not (the "FYI" crew of *Murphy Brown*). Indeed, the establishment of a solid family of characters with its own family values has always been a cornerstone of the situation comedy.

The earliest sitcoms in the 1950s were transplanted radio shows such as *The George Burns and Gracie Allen Show* and *The Goldbergs,* usually sentimental or zany idealizations of family life. But as television audiences grew in numbers (and variety), so did sitcoms and their stars. Lucille Ball, Jackie Gleason, Phil Silvers, and Danny Thomas were the pioneers who created raucous, physical slapstick grounded in believable, sometimes touching characters. Coexisting with these whirlwinds of energy were the more benign families found in *Father Knows Best, The Adventures of Ozzie and Harriet, The Donna Reed Show,* and *Leave It to Beaver.*

The 1960s introduced two new trends in sitcoms: fantasy and the workplace. Witches, genies, and superheroes were incorporated into the sitcom formula, while *The Dick Van Dyke Show* proved that a show could split its focus between *two* families, one at home and one at work. This innovation found new variations in the best shows of the 1970s and 1980s, including *The Mary Tyler Moore Show* and *Taxi. Cheers* went even further by not being set in either a home or traditional work environment, but rather in a pub; yet it still achieved a strong sense of family. Fantasy shows continued, albeit fewer in number, such as *Mork & Mindy* and *Alf,* though some would say that the Bradys' world was as much a fantasy as either.

Meanwhile, *All in the Family* and *M*A*S*H* proved that a sitcom could extend its range to subject matter that was previously thought only suitable to drama. In the past twenty years, shows like *The Golden Girls,*

Designing Women, and *The Cosby Show* integrated important messages into their comedy on a regular basis.

Today sitcoms run the gamut from the hip, cosmopolitan *Seinfeld* and *Friends* to the working-class *Roseanne.* They can be relatively benign *(Home Improvement)* or on the cutting edge (the successful British import *Absolutely Fabulous*). One thing they all share is a core group of characters struggling to maintain their existence as a family.

Common conventions

Most sitcoms follow a strict formula that is so familiar to us that we hardly notice it. Each episode generally runs for twenty-seven minutes (including commercials) and usually is divided into two acts, often with a short prologue and/or epilogue (known, respectively, in the trade as a "teaser" and a "kicker"). A family of characters continue from week to week, but individual episodes most often are self-contained. The first act sets up a basic problem; the second reaches a resolution.

Ideally, each episode presents a clever variation of an oft-seen conflict. Lucy will plot one more time to break into show business. Sam will keep pursuing Diane. Archie will have another difference of opinion with "Meathead," his liberal son-in-law, or tell Edith to "Stifle!" Gilligan and fellow castaways will try yet again to get off that island. We watch not so much to see *what* happens but *how* it happens. The successful sitcoms have characters (and actors) so amusing and interesting that we don't mind seeing them fight the same sort of battles each week. When we do, the series has run dry, and usually ends.

Other common sitcom conventions include the laugh track (the humor of what we view is reinforced by the sound of an audience laughing, either live, "sweetened" or fabricated); the theme song/credit music (sometimes more famous than any specific episode and often fondly remembered long after the series has gone to rerun heaven); the recurring characters (those inhabitants of a sitcom's world who appear only occasionally, like imperious Mrs. Trumble in *I Love Lucy,* befuddled Aunt Clara in *Bewitched,* troublemaking Ernest T. Bass on *The Andy Griffith Show,* or eccentric backwoods brothers Larry, Darryl, and Darryl on *Newhart*); the guest stars who pop up for variety (and increased ratings), often in defiance of all logic (*Gilligan's Island* is notable for this); and the repeated catchphrase or piece of comedy business that becomes part of our language and defines the character with whom it's associated (Ralph Kramden's "Baby, you're the greatest!" or Fred Flintstone's "Yabba dabba doo!").

Perpetual pleasure

The very familiarity of these elements is what makes watching a situation comedy a satisfying, even comforting experience. We return as viewers because we know what to expect; we know and love these families as well as our own, whether it's the bucolic community of Mayberry, RFD or the midtown Manhattan cab garage or the 4077th Mobile Army Surgical Hospital in a remote battle zone or the peculiar house at 1313 Mockingbird Lane. Of course, it helps when the show is as warm as *The Andy Griffith Show,* as endearing as *Taxi,* as profound as *M*A*S*H,* or as daffy as *The Munsters.* But, most of all, we watch these series for one simple reason—because they're *funny.*

All of the classic sitcoms create unique, often hilarious worlds that we never tire of visiting. Archie holds court in his armchair, Max talks into his shoe, and Samantha twitches her nose, perpetually giving us pleasure. Now, thanks to video, we can rent these sitcoms and we can own them, uncut and in pristine condition, relishing them for the national treasures they are and always will be.

THE ABBOTT AND COSTELLO SHOW

Syndicated, 1952–54, 52 episodes

CAST

Bud	Bud Abbott
Lou	Lou Costello
Mr. Fields	Sidney Fields
Hillary	Hillary Brooke
Mike the Cop	Gordon Jones
Stinky Davis	Joe Besser
Mr. Bacciagalupe	Joe Kirk

PRODUCERS: Alex Gottlieb, Pat Costello
DIRECTOR: Jean Yarbrough
WRITERS: Eddie Forman, Sidney Fields, Clyde Bruckman, Felix Adler, Jack Townley

"Hey Abb-otttttt! . . ."

. . . remains one of the memorable identifying lines in film and television comedy. The words, of course, were invariably screamed by roly-poly Lou Costello, the perennial patsy, to his angular partner, Bud Abbott, the sharpie. Bud and Lou, the premier movie comedy team of the 1940s, brought their basic brand of humor, honed in vaudeville and burlesque during the previous decade, to television following the phenomenal early 1950s popularity of their generational successors, Dean Martin and Jerry Lewis. Throughout fifty-two filmed episodes, Bud and Lou, basically playing themselves but as unemployed actors, lived at the boardinghouse run by second banana

Mr. Bacciagalupe (Joe Kirk) presents a wide-eyed Lou Costello with a towering cake in a scene from *The Abbott and Costello Show.* Kirk was Costello's real-life brother-in-law. COURTESY OF PERSONALITY PHOTOS, INC.

Sidney Fields, a model of exasperation. They always had trouble paying their rent—which was just seven bucks a week—and were desperate for any jobs that came along, whether it be as delivery boys for a hat company, as discount roller skates salesmen, as inept pest exterminators, as dense soda jerks, or as door-to-door salesmen selling No Peddlers Allowed signs.

"I'm a baaaaad boy!"

Bud was the one concocting the weekly harebrained schemes; Lou took the brunt of the abuse—both verbal and gently physical—from Bud, their landlord Mr. Fields (or many of the characters he played, such as druggists, lawyers, ice cream vendors, pet shop owners), or Mike the Cop, the local flatfoot plagued by Lou's well-intentioned antics. Onetime B-movie actress Hillary Brooke, who was in a number of Abbott and Costello films, was the only female regular on the show, invariably turning up in one job or another as Lou's statuesque girlfriend. Joe Besser (later to become one of the Three Stooges) was Stinky, the mischievous thirty-year-old "kid" who was always pestering Lou to play games.

The premise of the series was to string together, within a flimsy plot, as many of the classic knockabout Abbott and Costello routines as possible—those that had made the team immensely popular in radio and films and virtually saved Universal Pictures from near bankruptcy in the 1940s. Bud would invariably buffalo Lou into loaning him whatever few dollars the latter had gotten through a fifty-fifty split, and then through convoluted arithmetic would have Lou convinced that he owed even more money. Or he'd have Lou buy bananas at five cents each or at a special deal of three for a quarter.

Not long after finishing the series, Bud Abbott and Lou Costello decided to break up the team. Bud retired more or less to pursue another passion—playing the ponies—while making an occasional solo dramatic appearance on television. Lou continued on with a nightclub act, playing Las Vegas and Reno, and made one movie on his own before dying of a heart attack at fifty-three in March 1959. (He'd been plagued for years with rheumatic fever.) Bud's final work was doing his own voice for a syndicated cartoon version of *The Abbott and Costello Show* in the mid-1960s. Stan Irwin provided the voice of Lou.

VIDEO AVAILABILITY

Six volumes of *The Abbott and Costello Show* (plus a box set of the first three volumes) are currently available in certain rental outlets. Each black-and-white collection, running approximately 110 minutes, contains four episodes. In addition, there is a volume *The Best of Abbott and Costello Live,* which is a sampler of the team's routines as performed on television in the early 1950s. It runs fifty-eight minutes.

TRIVIA TIDBITS

- *The Abbott and Costello Show* was television's first syndicated sitcom.
- Bud Abbott and Lou Costello made their TV debuts on NBC's *Colgate Comedy Hour* in late 1951 (along with vaudeville pals Sidney Fields and Joe Besser). Their last appearance together was on Ralph Edwards's *This Is Your Life,* a tribute to Bud Abbott, in 1957.
- Producer Pat Costello was Lou's brother; Joe Kirk, who played Mr. Bacciagalupe, was Lou's real-life brother-in-law.
- On the series, Bud and Lou lived at Fields Rooming House at 214 Brookline Avenue in Hollywood.
- The theme music for the show was written by Raoul Kraushaar, a journeyman B-movie composer of the 1940s through the 1960s, who also provided the score to *Abbott and Costello Meet Captain Kidd* (1952) and Lou's one solo effort, *The 30-Foot Bride of Candy Rock* (1959).

ABSOLUTELY FABULOUS

Comedy Central, 1994–95, 18 episodes

CAST

Edina	Jennifer Saunders
Patsy	Joanna Lumley
Saffron	Julia Sawalha
Bubble	Jane Horrocks
Mother	June Whitfield

PRODUCER: Jon Plowman
DIRECTOR: Bob Spiers
PRINCIPAL WRITER: Jennifer Saunders

Politically incorrect

When the outrageous British sitcom *Absolutely Fabulous* was offered to the three major television networks and PBS for American broadcast, all four declined. The series was too controversial, too outspoken, and not politically correct. The show would probably offend audiences and, being British, certainly wouldn't attract high ratings. Finding an American home on cable's Comedy Central, *AbFab* (its hip nickname) quickly achieved a strong cult following that motivated superstar Roseanne to plan a stateside version, although CBS seemed to have beaten her to the punch with its own American cousin wanna-be, *High Society,* with Jean Smart and Mary McDonnell. Whether that version or Roseanne's succeeds or not, one thing seems clear: The networks underestimated their audience's ability to find basically unlikable characters indulging in "immoral behavior" funny. They also conveniently forgot the success of similar series, *All in the*

Booze, cigarettes, sex, and fashion: Patsy (Joanna Lumley, left) and Edina (Jennifer Saunders) take New York City's Central Park by storm in an episode from the cutting-edge British series *Absolutely Fabulous*. COURTESY OF PERSONALITY PHOTOS, INC.

Family and *Sanford and Son,* both based on British series, and *Married . . . With Children.*

Bad habits

Edina (pronounced "Edwina") and Patsy are spoiled, self-indulgent children with monstrous appetites, uncontrollable tempers, and various bad habits. They also happen to be over 40. Thus, instead of dolls and Legos, their toys are alcohol, cocaine, marijuana, and men. Instead of disapproving parents, they are chided by Edina's square teenage daughter, Saffron, who finds her mother's self-destructive behavior repulsive. Ostensibly owner of a fashion agency, Edina hardly ever goes to work, and when she does, her assistant, the aptly named Bubble, makes sure a large bottle of wine is ever handy. When not inebriated (which isn't often), she's ranting about her weight, her bodily functions, her lack of a sex life, and daughter Saffron's inability to understand her. Her partner in crime, Patsy, models herself after Ivana Trump, with a fondness for cocaine that rivals Edina's love for a good chablis. Patsy "works" too, as an editor for a fashion magazine. However, in the one episode in which she goes to the office, she needs a map to get there!

This topsy-turvy universe sounds sad and sordid, but the series is so well written (by its costar, Jennifer Saunders), and performed in such a savage, over-the-top style, that one can't possibly believe it is real. This frees the viewer to laugh, long and hard, at these aging veterans of British counterculture. Like *Road Runner* cartoon characters, Patsy and Edina always bounce back from their binges, as they blithely plow their way through modern London life. Nothing is sacred here. In an episode simply titled "Fat," Edina dreads the arrival of an old nemesis, whom she is sure will humiliate her about her pouchy figure. When the character appears and is revealed to be blind, Edina's response is one of comic elation that her weight will go unobserved—not empathy for the woman's misfortune.

For an adult audience

A literal-minded audience might think that Saunders is glorifying alcoholism and drug use, just as some early viewers of *All in the Family* thought that show was glorifying bigotry. But, in the time-honored tradition of British satire, the show presents its heroines as caricatures of self-involvement and lack of self-control, oblivious to the social and economic conditions of modern-day London. Whether this can translate to an American locale in Roseanne's version (with, possibly, Carrie Fisher and Barbara Carrera) remains to be seen. But the eighteen original episodes could be rerun ad infinitum to great success, rivaling the track record of *Fawlty Towers* (see separate entry). It may not be for children or for the masses, but for an educated adult audience, *Absolutely Fabulous* is naughty, delicious fun.

VIDEO AVAILABILITY

Absolutely Fabulous is available through BBC Home Video and from Fox Home Video. Each volume of the six volumes, running approximately ninety minutes, contains three episodes.

TRIVIA TIDBITS

- The series' theme song, "This Wheel's on Fire," written by Simon Brint (and made famous by The Band), is performed by Julie Driscoll and Adrian Edmondson.
- Indian-born model-turned-actress Joanna Lumley was previously best known to American audiences as John Steed's fourth female partner, Purdy, in *The New Avengers* (1978–79) and before that in 1969 as one of the Bond girls in *On Her Majesty's Secret Service*. She also starred on such hit British series as *Coronation Street* and *Steptoe and Son* (the model for *Sanford and Son*).

THE ADDAMS FAMILY

ABC, 1964–66, 64 episodes

CAST

Gomez Addams	John Astin
Morticia Frump Addams	Carolyn Jones
Uncle Fester	Jackie Coogan
Lurch	Ted Cassidy
Wednesday Addams	Lisa Loring
Pugsley Addams	Ken Weatherwax
Grandmama Addams	Blossom Rock
Cousin Itt	Felix Silla (voice: Tony Magro)

CREATOR/EXECUTIVE PRODUCER: David Levy
PRODUCER: Nat Perrin
DIRECTORS: Jean Yarbrough, Sidney Lanfield, Sidney Miller, Jerry Hopper, Nat Perrin, Arthur Hiller
PRINCIPAL WRITERS: Harry Winkler, Hannibal Coons, Sloan Nibley, Jameson Brewer, Bill Lutz, Seamon Jacobs, Ed James, Phil Leslie, George Tibbles

"They're creepy and they're kooky . . ."

A newlywed suburban couple has been invited by their neighbors for an evening of bridge. As the two approach the door of 000 Cemetery Ridge, they pass a hemlock bush and a rose garden that's nothing but stems and thorns. The doorbell sounds like a foghorn and is answered by a seven-foot-tall butler, who escorts them into a living room adorned with a bearskin rug that growls, a mounted fish with a leg sticking out of its mouth, a painting of a giraffe in a tuxedo, and a noose dangling from the ceiling. Their host and hostess enter in the midst of

Morticia (Carolyn Jones) and Gomez Addams (John Astin) ogle a gargoyle in a scene from *The Addams Family.* COURTESY OF PERSONALITY PHOTOS, INC.

a fencing match. Introducing their guests to the rest of the family, the host, in a smoking jacket, and his gracious lady of the house, dressed in flowing black, are surprised at the guests' reactions of horror upon seeing a disembodied hand and a walking pile of hair. The hostess inquires politely of the visiting couple, "Do you mind if I smoke?" Relieved at this bit of normalcy, they reply, "Why, no." The hostess folds her arms and wisps of smoke curl out of her body. As her screaming guests flee in panic, she turns to her husband and wonders how seemingly civilized people could be so rude.

In the world of *The Addams Family,* nonconformity reigns supreme. Behavior that seems perverse to others is perceived as perfectly normal by the Addams clan—madly in love Morticia and Gomez and sinister-minded son Pugsley and deceptively sweet daughter Wednesday. Morticia and Gomez were probably the only sitcom couple of the mid-1960s who openly lusted after one another. It would not be unusual to find bald-as-a-billiard Uncle Fester wrestling live alligators because "it wouldn't be too sporting to wrestle a dead one" or riding a motorcycle through the house because "the children love to see him do it." In the context of the 1960s, *The Addams Family* was a mainstream reflection of a growing revolt against the cookie-cutter behavior patterns of the 1950s. The show was a fantasy, but its subversive message was real.

Far more sophisticated than *The Munsters,* CBS's superficially similar series (see separate entry), *Addams* became a cult hit, a show appreciated by audiences who understood that this family wasn't monstrous at all, just "different."

Out of the inkwell

The show was inspired by a series of famous cartoons by Charles Addams that appeared in *The New Yorker* magazine in the 1940s and in subsequent best-selling book collections. When producer David Levy decided to turn these macabre, single-panel, often wordless drawings into a television series, he asked the artist to come up with names and personalities for his characters. Thus, Gomez, Morticia, Lurch, Thing (the disembodied hand with its own personality), Uncle Fester, Wednesday, and Pugsley were christened and fleshed out—so to speak—for the series. The morbid, gruesome aspects of the drawings were toned down in favor of a more genial eccentricity, yet the sitcom version is still quite daring for its time. Boldly breaking the mold of nearly every family sitcom since *I Love Lucy,* this was no idyllic Cleaver or Nelson household.

The creepy and kooky Addams clan, from left: John Astin (Gomez), Lisa Loring (Wednesday), Carolyn Jones (Morticia), Jackie Coogan (Uncle Fester), Ted Cassidy (Lurch), and Blossom Rock (Grandmama). Where is Pugsley, we wonder? Has his sister left him to rot in a torture chamber? COURTESY OF PERSONALITY PHOTOS, INC.

Lasting effect

Although the show was canceled after only two seasons, its afterlife is a good example of the lasting effect a television series can have on American culture. There was an animated Saturday morning version of the show (on NBC) from Hanna and Barbera (1973–75), and as new generations went through their own rebellions, *The Addams Family* thrived in reruns. Eventually, in 1991, it became a hugely successful motion picture followed by a sequel *(Addams Family Values)* two years later, both of which starred Anjelica Huston and Raul Julia (who died not long after the second was released). The movies retained many of the gags and character traits created for the series, but returned to the morbid, more death-obsessed quality of the classic Charles Addams cartoons. What they all have in common, however, is a delightful, wicked sense of humor that continues to "thrive and gloom" on home video.

VIDEO AVAILABILITY

Ten volumes of *The Addams Family* are currently available on videocassette in certain rental outlets. Each black-and-white collection, running roughly forty-five minutes, contains two episodes.

TRIVIA TIDBITS

- Thing, that five-fingered wonder, was actually Ted ("Lurch") Cassidy's right hand. During scenes in which Lurch and Thing appeared together, associate producer Jack Vogelin lent a hand.
- Gomez's three affectionate names for Morticia were "Tish," "Cara mia," and "Querida." His favorite food: eye of newt.
- Wednesday's favorite doll is Marie Antoinette, who, of course, is missing her head.
- The Addams family pet was a lion named Kit Kat. Other animals included Pugsley's octopus, Aristotle, and Wednesday's spider, named, appropriately enough, Homer.
- The late Carolyn Jones was nominated for a Best Supporting Actress Oscar in 1956 for *The Bachelor Party,* and was married to producer Aaron Spelling from 1953 through 1964. Occasionally, she did double duty on the series as Morticia's blond sister, Ophelia.

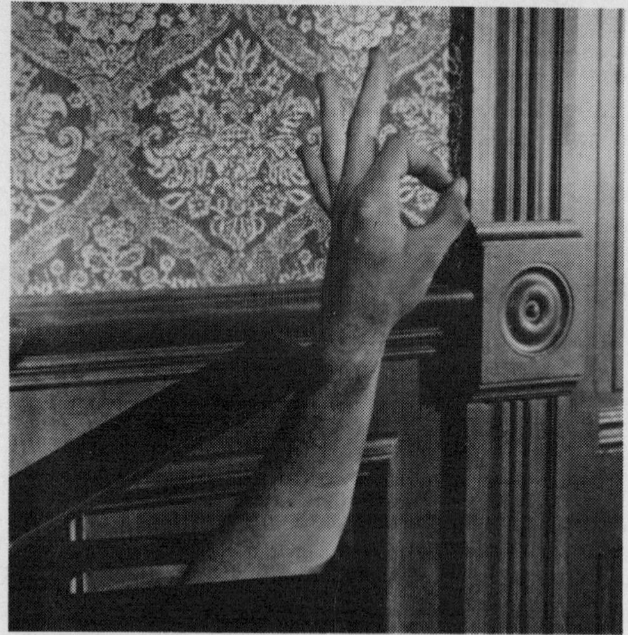

The infamous Thing gives the *okee-dokee* sign in this scene from *The Addams Family.* Ted Cassidy (aka Lurch) lent a hand to this plumb role. COURTESY OF PERSONALITY PHOTOS, INC.

- Lisa Loring ("Wednesday") became a soap star, appearing in *As The World Turns* during the 1980s.
- Jackie Coogan ("Uncle Fester") had an acting career dating back to Charlie Chaplin's *The Kid* (1921), which made him a highly recognized child star.
- Blossom Rock ("Grandmama") was the real-life sister of MGM musical star Jeanette MacDonald, and her husband was Clarence W. Rock. Thus her real name *was* Blossom Rock.
- Margaret Hamilton, forever remembered as the Wicked Witch of the West in *The Wizard of Oz,* ap-

peared as Morticia's mother, Esther Frump, in the episode "Morticia's Romance (Part 1)."

- Ellen Corby, later John-Boy's loving grandmother on *The Waltons,* played Mother Lurch on occasional episodes.
- In the series' animated spin-off, Ted Cassidy and Jackie Coogan returned to voice Lurch and Uncle Fester, while Pugsley was voiced by actress Jodie Foster.
- A reunion TV movie, *Halloween with the Addams Family,* was produced in 1977 with the original cast (minus Blossom Rock, who was ill and died soon after).
- The jaunty, finger-snapping "Addams Family Theme Song" was written by Vic Mizzy.

THE ADVENTURES OF OZZIE AND HARRIET

ABC, 1952–66, 435 episodes

CAST

Ozzie	Ozzie Nelson
Harriet	Harriet Nelson
David	David Nelson
Ricky	Ricky Nelson
"Thorny" Thornberry (1952–58)	Don DeFore
Darby (1955–61)	Parley Baer
Joe Randolph (1956–66)	Lyle Talbot
Clara Randolph (1956–66)	Mary Jane Croft
Wally (1957–66)	Skip Young
Doc Williams (1954–65)	Frank Cady
Connie Edwards (1960–64)	Constance Harper
Fred (1958–64)	James Stacy
Ginger (1962–65)	Charlene Sanders
June (Mrs. David Nelson) (1961–66)	June Blair Nelson
Kris (Mrs. Rick Nelson) (1964–66)	Kristin Harmon Nelson

CREATOR AND PRODUCER: Ozzie Nelson
DIRECTOR: Ozzie Nelson
WRITERS: Ozzie Nelson, Don Nelson

Feel-good fifties

The granddaddy of TV sitcoms and the longest running of them all—it spanned the last few months of the Truman administration, all of the Eisenhower administration, the Kennedy administration, and the first half of the Johnson administration—was *The Adventures of Ozzie and Harriet.* As has often been pointed out, "Adventures" is an exaggeration, unless it refers to Harriet (always in heels and pearls, even when wearing an apron in the kitchen) serving up warm milk and cookies while Ozzie (in his trademark cardigan and no discernible job other than raking leaves) looked over her shoulder. This was warm, cozy—and minimalist—television that audiences cherished. The Nelsons were the ideal family in the early days of TV, as they had been on radio since 1944.

Audiences watched their two neatly pressed sons, David and Ricky, grow up: one to become a fictional lawyer on the series; the other a real-life teen idol and rock star. As part of the show, they simply grew up as everyday (if somewhat idealized) kids. There was no screaming, no shouting, just a touch of brotherly roughhousing, and lots of love. Dialogue on the show seldom went beyond the mundane "Hi, Mom," "Hi, Dave," and "Hi, Pop." They were America's favorite WASP family in the feel-good 1950s, doing things together, as long as they didn't have to leave the front yard. (Later, of course, the show expanded to David and Ricky's squeaky clean social life.) The Nelsons were one step beyond the close-knit Norwegian-American clan of *Mama* and the lower Manhattan East Side Jews of *The Goldbergs,* but not quite *Father Knows Best* or *Leave It to Beaver* or *The Donna Reed Show.*

Fact or fiction?

Ozzie Nelson, who had been a bandleader in the 1930s, discovered vocalist and budding actress Harriet Hilliard and made her singer of his band. They married and had two boys, David and Ricky. The entire family—later with David and Ricky's wives—played themselves on the show, although the parallels between reality and fiction were only superficial. As Ricky evolved into Rick the singer—on-screen and off—Ozzie (who, as it turned out, was something of a real-life Svengali behind that ingratiating smile) gave him the weekly spotlight to promote his latest hit record. Behind the scenes, Ozzie managed Rick's career nearly to the point of stopping it dead.

Following the fourteen-season run of *The Adventures of Ozzie and Harriet,* Ozzie reworked the long-proven concept with a short-lived syndicated show in 1973 called *Ozzie's Girls,* in which Ozzie and Harriet took in a couple of college coeds as boarders, now that their sons had married and moved away. After Ozzie's death in 1975, Harriet more or less retired. There also was the devastation of Rick's New Year's Eve 1985 death in a plane crash. Harriet came out of retirement briefly to play a nun on *The Father Dowling Mysteries* in order to work with Rick's daughter, Tracy Nelson. Rick's twin sons, Gunnar and Matthew, are also rock musicians like their dad, working under the single name Nelson. David Nelson went on to a minor acting career and occasionally directs film and television. Harriet died in 1994 at age eighty-five.

VIDEO AVAILABILITY

Nineteen *Ozzie and Harriet* collections are available at certain video outlets. Each tape runs about fifty-six minutes and contains two episodes.

TRIVIA TIDBITS

- Ozzie, Harriet, David, and Ricky starred together in one film, *Here Come the Nelsons* (1952), which was a trial run for their TV series.
- Ozzie also directed Rick and his wife, Kris, in the 1965 movie *Love and Kisses,* which he rewrote for them from a moderately successful Broadway comedy.
- Ozzie and Harriet guest-starred together on several *Love, American Style* episodes, *Bridget Loves Bernie,* and Rod Serling's *Night Gallery* (in "You Can Come Up Now, Mrs. Millikan" in 1972).

- David Nelson's first wife, June, who starred with him in the series, was a onetime Playboy playmate.
- In 1987 David directed a Disney Channel special entitled *A Brother Remembers,* a warm reminiscence about the family and an affectionate tribute to Rick.

ALL IN THE FAMILY

CBS, 1971–83 (including *Archie Bunker's Place*), 207 episodes plus 89 in revamped series

CAST

Archie Bunker	Carroll O'Connor
Edith Bunker (1971–80)	Jean Stapleton
Gloria Bunker Stivic (1971–78)	Sally Struthers
Mike Stivic (1971–78)	Rob Reiner
George Jefferson (1973–75)	Sherman Hemsley
Louise Jefferson (1971–75)	Isabel Stanford
Lionel Jefferson (1971–75)	Mike Evans
Henry Jefferson (1971–73)	Mel Stewart
Maude Findley (1971–72)	Beatrice Arthur
Walter Findley (1971–72)	Bill Macy
Carol Findley (1971–72)	Marcia Rodd
Bert Munson (1972–77)	Billy Halop
Barney Heffner (1973–83)	Allen Melvin
Irene Lorenzo (1973–75)	Betty Garrett
Frank Lorenzo (1973–74)	Vincent Gardenia
Teresa Betancourt (1976–77)	Liz Torres
Bartender Harry Snowden (1977–83)	Jason Wingreen
Hank Pivnik (1977–81)	Danny Dayton
Stephanie Mills (1978–83)	Danielle Brisebois
Mr. Van Ranseleer (1978–83)	Bill Quinn
Murray Klein (1979–81)	Martin Balsam
Veronica Rooney (1979–82)	Anne Meara

CREATORS/EXECUTIVE PRODUCERS: Norman Lear, Bud Yorkin

BASED ON THE BRITISH SERIES *Till Death Us Do Part,* created by Johnny Specht

PRODUCERS: Mort Lachman, Hal Kanter, Woody Kling, Don Nicholl

PRINCIPAL DIRECTORS: John Rich (nearly every one of the first 85 episodes), Bob LoHendro, H. Wesley Kenney, Paul Bogart

PRINCIPAL WRITERS: Norman Lear, Len Weinrib, Don Nicholl, Philip Mishkin, Rob Reiner, Bryan Joseph, Burt Styler, Lee Kalcheim, Michael Ross, Bernie West, Mel Tolkin, Susan Harris

Those were the days

All in the Family stands as one of the most influential sitcoms in television history. Although laced with racial slurs, bedroom humor, and bathroom jokes, it became a revolutionary series by dealing with such relevant issues as women's liberation, integration, prejudice, abortion, birth control, menopause, and wife-swapping. It was peopled with memorable, three-dimensional characters: a fiftyish bigoted, blue-collar, ultraconservative father; his devoted if somewhat "Dingbat" wife ("Stifle, Edith," he'd order her when she tried to offer an opinion); his sweet, modern-minded, miniskirted daughter ("Little girl," he called her); and his liberal Polish-American "Meathead" son-in-law, a wisecracking, perpetual student with a big appetite and a big mouth who lived with the Bunkers and, representing everything that Archie hates, relished baiting him.

Basically a one-set show with a small cast at its core and only on rare occasions a guest star, *All in the Family* emerged as the first sitcom that, through comedy, forced its audience (both in-studio where it was taped live and at home in their living rooms) to reevaluate its own situations as Archie, Edith, Gloria, and Mike muddled their way through domestic concerns, generational clashes, and political differences. Loudmouth Archie initially was dock foreman at the Prendergast Tool and Die Company by day and "king" by night at his home at 704 Hauser Street in Queens, New York. As the series progressed, he was laid off from his job on the loading dock, drove a

Archie (Carroll O'Connor) sits in his favorite chair, while his wife, Edith (Jean Stapleton), refuses to stifle. *All in the Family* broke social barriers for a network sitcom, but at the same time always managed to provide a laugh and a tear. COURTESY OF PERSONALITY PHOTOS, INC.

cab for a while, and then bought Kelsey's Bar, turning it into Archie Bunker's Place, a bar/restaurant.

Hey, Arch!

Creator Norman Lear's liberal sensibilities became the foundation on which this series, pivotal in television history, was built. It was punctuated with screaming matches on social issues between Archie and Meathead. One hilarious moment was a big fat kiss on bigoted Archie's cheek by guest star Sammy Davis Jr. (in an episode written by comedian Bill "José Jimenez" Dana). In the early days of the show, Archie provided humor through his defense of Richard Nixon: "Well I'll tell you one thing about President Nixon. He should keep Pat home. Which was where Roosevelt should have kept Eleanor. Instead, he let her run around loose until one day she discovered the colored. We never knew they were there. She told them they were gettin' the short end of the stick and we been having trouble ever since."

Antihero Archie's popularity stemmed from his basic lovability, which shone through his innate ignorance and ideological buffoonery. He truly loved his family—and even came to tolerate Mike Stivic, as they both mellowed. After Gloria and Mike moved out, first next door and then to California, Archie and Edith were alone until her nine-year-old niece came to live with them, and the old grouse became somewhat grandfatherly.

When Jean Stapleton decided to leave the series in 1980, the producers made an unprecedented move by "killing off" (between seasons) one of the beloved figures in American television, and Archie Bunker began the new season with a moving episode, grieving over the loss of Edith, who had died suddenly of a stroke. But he went on with his life, becoming more involved with his venture at Archie's Place with, for a time, a partner (Martin Balsam), and raising his niece.

In 1983 Carroll O'Connor decided it was time to move on. The actors returned in 1990 for a reunion special. The enduring popularity of *All in the Family*, however, was illustrated when in the spring and summer of 1991, after years of syndication, CBS aired selected reruns in prime time, and they all landed in the Top Ten in the ratings.

VIDEO AVAILABILITY

Several collections, each containing four half-hour episodes, are available through Columbia House. The 1990

All in the Family 20th Anniversary Special, featuring Archie and Edith, Mike and Gloria, and the rest of the crew, plus producer/creator Norman Lear, and running about seventy-five minutes, is available at certain video outlets.

EMMY AWARDS

1970–71 *All in the Family,* Outstanding Comedy Series
Jean Stapleton, Outstanding Actress in a Comedy

1971–72 *All in the Family,* Outstanding Comedy Series
Carroll O'Connor, Outstanding Lead Actor in a Comedy
Jean Stapleton, Outstanding Lead Actress in a Comedy
Sally Struthers, Outstanding Supporting Actress in a Comedy
John Rich, Outstanding Directorial Achievement in Comedy Series
Burt Styler, Outstanding Writing Achievement in Comedy Series

1972–73 *All in the Family,* Outstanding Comedy Series
Michael Ross, Bernie West, and **Lee Kalcheim,** Outstanding Writing Achievement in Comedy Series

1973–74 **Rob Reiner,** Outstanding Supporting Actor in a Comedy

1976–77 **Carroll O'Connor,** Outstanding Actor in a Comedy

1977–78 *All in the Family,* Outstanding Comedy Series
Carroll O'Connor, Outstanding Actor in a Comedy
Jean Stapleton, Outstanding Actress in a Comedy
Rob Reiner, Outstanding Supporting Actor in a Comedy
Paul Bogart, Outstanding Directorial Achievement in Comedy Series

Bob Weiskopf, Bob Schiller, Barry Harman, and Harve Broston, Outstanding Writing Achievement in Comedy Series

1978–79 **Carroll O'Connor,** Outstanding Actor in a Comedy

Sally Struthers, Outstanding Supporting Actress in a Comedy

TRIVIA TIDBITS

- It was the number one ranked show for five straight seasons (1972–1976).
- Archie Bunker's well-worn armchair now occupies a prominent spot in the Smithsonian Institution in recognition of the show's influence on popular culture during the 1970s.
- Other than *Archie Bunker's Place* (which was actually a continuation of the original show with a new name), *All in the Family* spun off three other series: *The Jeffersons, Maude,* and *Gloria.*
- There were two unaired pilots to *All in the Family,* both with Carroll O'Connor and Jean Stapleton: *Those Were the Days* (with Kelly Jean Peters as Gloria and Tim McIntire as Mike) and *All in the Family* (with Candace Azzara as Gloria and Chip Oliver as Mike).
- The Bunkers were the inspiration for a 1972–73 Saturday morning cartoon series called *The Barkleys,* a family of dogs (Dad's a loudmouth, opinionated bus driver).
- Rob Reiner, son of comedy great Carl Reiner, is today director of several highly successful films, including *This Is Spinal Tap, Stand by Me,* and *When Harry Met Sally.*
- The opening theme song, sung by Archie and Edith, was called "Those Were the Days." It was written by Broadway composers Lee Adams and Charles Strouse, who were responsible for *Bye Bye Birdie, Golden Boy,* and many other musicals.
- The closing theme was written and played by pianist Roger Kellaway.

THE ANDY GRIFFITH SHOW

CBS, 1960–68, 249 episodes

CAST

Sheriff Andy Taylor	Andy Griffith
Deputy Barney Fife	Don Knotts
Opie Taylor	Ronny Howard
Aunt Bee	Frances Bavier
Helen Crump	Aneta Corsaut
Thelma Lou	Betty Lynn
Otis Campbell	Hal Smith
Howard Sprague	Jack Dodson
Floyd Lawson	Howard McNear
Gomer Pyle	Jim Nabors
Goober Pyle	George Lindsey
Ernest T. Bass	Howard Morris

EXECUTIVE PRODUCERS: Sheldon Leonard, Danny Thomas
PRODUCERS: Aaron Ruben, Richard O. Linke, Bob Ross
DIRECTORS: Bob Sweeney, Don Weis, Gene Reynolds, Earl Bellamy, Richard Crenna, Alan Rafkin, Jeffrey Hayden, Coby Ruskin, Howard Morris, Sheldon Leonard, Theodore J. Flicker, Lee Philips, Peter Baldwin
PRINCIPAL WRITERS: Jack Elinson & Charles Stewart, Jim Fritzell & Everett Greenbaum, John Fenton Murray, Paul Henning, Benedict Freeman, Harvey Bullock, Aaron Ruben, Arthur Stander, John Whedon, Bill Idelson & Sam Bobrick, Art Baer & Ben Joelson

Mayberry's pride and joy

Audiences recognize immediately from the opening of each *Andy Griffith Show* episode—in which Andy and

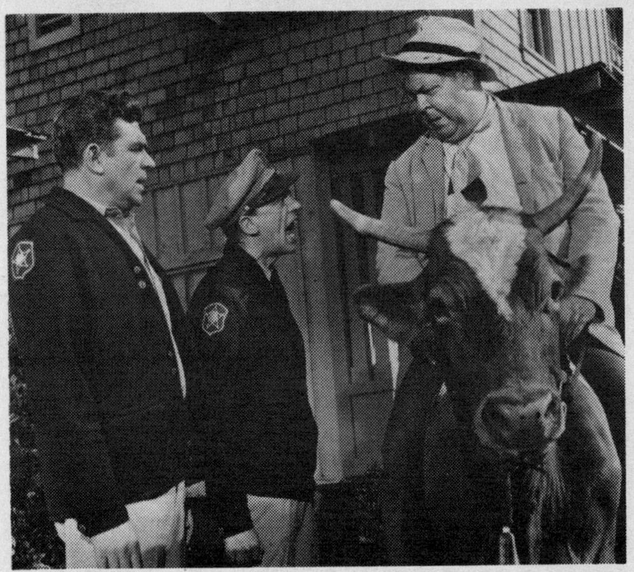

Sheriff Andy Taylor (Andy Griffith, left) and his agitated deputy, Barney Fife (Don Knotts), tend to the town drunk, Otis Campbell (Hal Smith), in a scene from *The Andy Griffith Show.* COURTESY OF PERSONALITY PHOTOS, INC.

Opie Taylor, father and son, amble to the old fishing hole, poles over their shoulders, as the title theme is whistled—that they are in for one of the kindest and gentlest series in all of television history. The entire cast, led by low-key, onetime southern humorist and guitarist and sometimes movie actor Andy Griffith as a widowed small-town sheriff, was to become family to Monday-night viewers over the show's eight-season run.

Andy was the quiet reactor to the doings around him—sometimes gentle, sometimes whirlwind (particularly where the hyper Don Knotts doing his stock-in-trade nervous man was concerned)—while raising his small son or quietly enforcing the law in his totally crime-free town, where jaywalking seems to be the legal system's greatest concern.

The homespun show was filled with little joys week in and week out: from having gangly Barney Fife (as Andy's somewhat rash deputy, he was allowed but one bullet, which he has to keep in his shirt pocket) lazing on Andy's front porch and trying to decide how the day should be spent; to young Opie nursing several small birds after accidentally killing their mother with his slingshot; to Aunt Bee falling in love with an expensive bed jacket she spotted in a local shop and throwing hints to Andy that she'd like it for her birthday.

Friends and neighbors

Andy and Barney had their perennial, incredibly patient girlfriends, Helen Crump and Thelma Lou, and interacted with the other Mayberry locals: Floyd, the fussy barber; Otis Campbell, the town drunk; Howard Sprague, the good-natured town clerk; Gomer Pyle, who pumped gas at the service station; Goober Pyle, his cousin; Emmett, the fix-it man; and the Darling family, mountaineers. Theirs was a feel-good world untouched by national and international events, where the little pleasures of life were offered to the viewer, and where one of the notable film directors on the contemporary scene literally grew up before our eyes (Ron Howard as Opie).

The Andy Griffith Show ended in the spring of 1968, but in effect continued for another three seasons as *Mayberry, RFD*, produced by Griffith and his manager and partner, Richard O. Linke. Andy Taylor married Helen Crump and moved away with Opie, leaving Aunt Bee behind—along with several others from the old show—to become the new housekeeper for Sam Jones (Ken Berry), a widower, gentleman farmer, single dad, and town councilman. In *Return to Mayberry*, a TV-movie produced nearly twenty years later, Andy returned to

Mayberry with Helen to visit Opie (now the editor of the town newspaper) and to run once again for sheriff, unaware that Barney, who still hadn't popped the question to Thelma Lou, was campaigning for the job. All things remained as they had been, except that everyone had grown a little older.

VIDEO AVAILABILITY

Episodes of *The Andy Griffith Show* are available at certain video outlets. There are thirteen volumes, each running thirty minutes, as well as a special set including the first five episodes, running 125 minutes. Also available are six compilation volumes—two dealing with Barney Fife, and one each dealing with cantankerous mountain man Ernest T. Bass, Floyd the barber, mischievous young Opie, and the hillbilly clan, the Darlings. Each has three episodes and runs ninety minutes.

EMMY AWARDS

1960–61 **Don Knotts,** Outstanding Performance in a Supporting Role by an Actor or Actress in a Series

1961–62 **Don Knotts,** Outstanding Performance in a Supporting Role by an Actor

1962–63 **Don Knotts,** Outstanding Performance in a Supporting Role by an Actor

1965–66 **Don Knotts,** Outstanding Performance by a Supporting Actor in a Comedy

1966–67 **Don Knotts,** Outstanding Performance by a Supporting Actor in a Comedy
Frances Bavier, Outstanding Performance by a Supporting Actress in a Comedy

TRIVIA TIDBITS

- *The Andy Griffith Show* began as a pilot episode of *The Danny Thomas Show,* in which Danny and family find themselves stranded temporarily in a small south-

Is this *Make Room for Daddy* or *The Andy Griffith Show?* Actually, it's a scene from the former—which happened to serve as the pilot for the latter. In the hilarious episode, Sheriff Andy Taylor (Andy Griffith) arrests Danny Williams (Danny Thomas) and his wife Margaret (Jean Hagen) for speeding! COURTESY OF PERSONALITY PHOTOS, INC.

ern town while heading for vacation after being arrested for speeding. Andy and Opie were in this episode, but not Barney Fife. Frances Bavier played a different character.

- When it was canceled in 1968 following a change in CBS management, *The Andy Griffith Show* was one of only two shows in TV history to end its run at Number

Deputy Barney Fife (Don Knotts) and Gomer Pyle (Jim Nabors) look like they've seen a ghost in this scene from *The Andy Griffith Show.* Nabors, of course, would go on to star in his own goofy spin-off, *Gomer Pyle, U.S.M.C.* He would be replaced on *The Andy Griffith Show* by his cousin, Goober Pyle (George Lindsey). COURTESY OF PERSONALITY PHOTOS, INC.

One. The other was *I Love Lucy* (see separate entry). It soon went into syndicated reruns as *Andy of Mayberry.*

- The 1986 reunion TV movie, titled *Return to Mayberry,* brought together the entire original cast, except for Howard McNear (Floyd, the barber), who had passed away, and Frances Bavier (Aunt Bee), who was living in retirement in Siler City, North Carolina, and too ill to appear. It was the highest rated TV-movie of the season.
- In 1993 an *Andy Griffith Show Reunion* was aired on CBS, bringing together all of the surviving members to reminisce about their favorite episodes.

- Don Knotts was with Andy in the stage and screen versions of *No Time for Sergeants.* Later, he briefly joined Griffith on his 1986–95 show *Matlock* portraying Ben Matlock's busybody neighbor. The late Aneta Corsaut (as a housekeeper) and Betty Lynn (as a judge) also were invited by Griffith to play recurring roles on *Matlock.*
- Jim Nabors, as naive gas station attendant Gomer Pyle, went on to star in the successful spin-off *Gomer Pyle, U.S.M.C.* (1964–70).
- Ron Howard had tremendous success as star of *Happy Days* (1974–84). Presently, he is one of Hollywood's most sought-after film directors, having hits such as *Splash, Cocoon, Backdraft,* and *Apollo 13*—for which he won the Directors Guild of America award.
- Earle Hagen wrote the show's catchy theme. Andy Griffith later made a recording of it with lyrics.

ARE YOU BEING SERVED?

PBS, 1972–85 (U.K.), 1987–92 (U.S.), 69 episodes

CAST

Mr. Wilberforce Clayborne Humphries	John Inman
Mrs. Betty Slocombe	Mollie Sugden
Capt. Stephen Peacock	Frank Thornton
Mr. James Lucas	Trevor Bannister
Mr. Harry Goldberg	Alfie Bass
Miss Shirley Brahms	Wendy Richard
Mr. Cuthbert Rumbold	Nicholas Smith
Mr. Beverley Harmon	Arthur English
Young Mr. Grace	Harold Bennett
Old Mr. Grace	Kenneth Waller
Mr. Ernest Grainer	Arthur Brough
Mr. Bert Spooner	Mike Berry
Miss Blakewell	Penny Irving
The Nurse	Vivienne Johnson

CREATORS/WRITERS: Jeremy Lloyd, David Croft
PRODUCERS: David Croft, Harold Snoad, Gordon Elsbury, Bob Spiers, Martin Shardlow
DIRECTORS: David Croft, Ray Butt, Bob Spiers, Gordon Elsbury, John Kilby, Martin Shardlow
WRITERS: Jeremy Lloyd, David Croft, Michael Knowles

Natty and naughty

This slightly bawdy and very British 1970s sitcom set in a London department store called Grace Brothers was to become the surprise hit of American public broadcasting in the 1990s. The show concerned idiosyncratic staff, each of whom knew his or her place. Through its long run in Great Britain in the seventies and eighties, the zany *Are You Being Served?* became a viewing tradition.

The quirky cast who were with the show during its entire run included: John Inman as the mincing, white-haired, gap-toothed Mr. Humphries, Sales Assistant in Gentlemen's Ready-to-Wear; Mollie Sugden as the outrageous, unintimidated, man-chasing, garishly coiffed (partial, apparently, to royal blue hair) Mrs. Slocombe, Senior Saleswoman in Ladies' Separates and Underwear; Frank Thornton as Captain Peacock, the stuffy floorwalker, strutting around and, living up to his name, paying constant attention to his plumage; Wendy Richard as Miss Brahms, Mrs. Slocombe's sharp-tongued Cockney assistant who knows how to keep her lusting male colleagues at bay; and Nicholas Smith as Mr. Rumbold, the long-suffering store manager and go-between with dotty Young Mr. Grace, the elderly owner/son of the even more elderly founder.

The ribald series was known—and quite appreciated—for its nearly nonstop laughs generated by double entendre, sexual innuendos, snide observations, low comic pratfalls, and Mrs. Slocombe's chameleonlike appearance, at least from the eyebrows up. The popularity of the show in Great Britain prompted not only a feature-length *Are You Being Served?* movie but also a 1976 stage version that toured the provinces. And when the Grace Brothers' closing sale was announced in a front-page headline in *The Express* in London in February 1985, fans went into mourning. It would be seven years before the staff of Grace Brothers returned for a brief new series called *Grace and Favour* (shown in this country as *Are You Being Served? Again!*).

VIDEO AVAILABILITY

A number of volumes of *Are You Being Served?*, each running about ninety minutes and containing three episodes, are available at certain video outlets.

TRIVIA TIDBITS

- An Americanized *Are You Being Served?*, produced by Garry Marshall and called *Beane's of Boston*, was aired as a pilot by CBS in 1979. It starred Alan *(Laugh-In)* Sues as Mr. Humphries, John Hillerman as Mr. Peacock, Charlotte Rae as Mrs. Slocombe, and Lorna Patterson as Miss Brahms, along with Tom Poston as the store's owner, Mr. Beane.
- John Inman had a hit record in Great Britain in 1975 with "Are You Being Served, Sir?" in his guise of Mr. Humphries.
- Joanna Lumley, ex-wife of series creator Jeremy Lloyd and today Patsy Stone in *Absolutely Fabulous* (see separate entry), made a memorable appearance during the sixth season as a glamorous perfume company representative in the show's very funny "His and Hers" episode.

THE BEVERLY HILLBILLIES

CBS, 1962–71, 274 episodes
(the first 106 in black and white)

CAST

Jed Clampett	Buddy Ebsen
Daisy Moses ("Granny")	Irene Ryan
Elly May Clampett	Donna Douglas
Jethro Bodine	Max Baer Jr.
Milburn Drysdale	Raymond Bailey
Margaret Drysdale	Harriet MacGibbon
Jane Hathaway	Nancy Kulp
Cousin Pearl Bodine (1962–63)	Bea Benaderet

CREATOR: Paul Henning
EXECUTIVE PRODUCER: Al Simon
PRODUCERS: Paul Henning, Joseph DePew, Mark Tuttle
DIRECTORS: Robert Leeds, Richard Whorf
WRITERS: Paul Henning, Mark Tuttle

"Come 'n listen to my story . . ."

An instantaneous hit when it first appeared and the number one show on television during its first two seasons, this beloved rural sitcom followed the weekly misadventures of Jed Clampett and his kin (who, according to the memorable theme song, would always "thank you for droppin' in"). Jed and the backwoods Clampetts had struck it rich when they struck oil on their Ozark property. They immediately packed up their old crate of a pickup, plopped moonshine-guzzlin' Granny in the rocker, which was tied to the truck's bed, and headed to California. The stories involve the family's cornball

The Clampetts throw a party, while Granny gets in a few winks. From left: Buddy Ebsen (Jed), Irene Ryan (Granny), Max Baer Jr. (Jethro), and Donna Douglas (Elly May). COURTESY OF PERSONALITY PHOTOS, INC.

struggles to survive in sunny Beverly Hills, where they had to put up with indoor plumbing, an Olympic-size swimming pool, petty politicians, sharpies out to con them, and all the fancy trappings of modern-day living in the big city.

The clan: mountaineer Jed, a slow-as-molasses widower who longed for life the way it was before coming into $25 million; Granny, his ornery mother-in-law; oh-so-innocent Elly Mae, his pretty, blond, tight-jeaned daughter who could never find a steady beau; and hulking

Jethro Bodine, his goofy nephew with a sixth-grade education and a yen for a sweetheart. Once in a while Jethro's sister, Jethrene, would pay a visit. (Both were played by Max Baer Jr.) Other characters included Milburn Drysdale, the grouchy banker, and his uptight, thin-lipped assistant, Jane Hathaway.

The Beverly Hillbillies and CBS sitcom country cousins *Petticoat Junction* (also created by Paul Henning) and *Green Acres* (coproduced by Henning) found great favor in mid-1960s middle America, and name stars were falling over each other to make guest appearances. In the nine prime-time years that Jed Clampett and kin resided in the hills of Beverly, many big names were "kindly droppin' in," including Sammy Davis Jr. playing an Irish cop; John Wayne saddlin' up; Phil Silvers pulling a con; and Pat Boone, Leo Durocher, Soupy Sales, Gloria Swanson, and Charlie Ruggles (as Mrs. Drysdale's crotchety father, Lowell Reddings Farquhar).

The Beverly Hillbillies and other popular rural shows disappeared from prime-time television in 1971, when new programming executives at CBS took over and decided that American viewers really wanted something hipper and more cosmopolitan. The decision may have been shortsighted, since *The Beverly Hillbillies* and similar countrified sitcoms have met with great success in syndication.

The Clampetts were back briefly in the 1981 TV reunion movie, *Return of the Beverly Hillbillies,* and in the 1993 CBS retrospective, *The Legend of the Beverly Hillbillies.*

VIDEO AVAILABILITY

Thirteen collections are available at certain video outlets. Each tape, running about fifty-one minutes, contains two episodes. Also available are a special four-episode collection, running about 104 minutes, and *The Legend of the Beverly Hillbillies,* the retrospective show with clips from various episodes and interviews with the stars. It runs about forty-eight minutes.

TRIVIA TIDBITS

- Buddy Ebsen, a song and dance man in 1930s vaudeville and on the Broadway stage, played hicks in films until being chosen to be the Tin Man in *The Wizard of Oz*—only to lose the role to Jack Haley when he turned out to be allergic to the silver-based makeup being painted on him for the part.
- Ebsen's earlier TV role was George Russell, sidekick to Davy Crockett (Fess Parker). Later he had one other hit television series, countrified L.A. private detective *Barnaby Jones.* In fact, when *The Beverly Hillbillies* was made into a big-screen feature (with Jim Varney as Jed and Cloris Leachman as Granny) in 1993, Buddy Ebsen turned up briefly in his guise as Barnaby Jones.
- Max Baer Jr. is the son of the colorful 1930s boxing champion. He has left acting for directing. Donna Douglas also has left acting.
- *The Beverly Hillbillies* won an Emmy nomination after its second season for Outstanding Program Achievement in the Field of Humor (but lost to *The Dick Van Dyke Show*). Irene Ryan was twice nominated for Outstanding Continued Performance for an Actress in a Series, and Nancy Kulp received a nomination in 1966–67 as Outstanding Supporting Actress. Neither won.
- Although she did some episode work (including *Hillbillies* knockoff, *Petticoat Junction,* in her Granny role), Irene Ryan never did another TV series. She subsequently costarred on Broadway in the 1980s revival of *Irene.* She has since died, as have Nancy Kulp, Raymond Bailey, and Bea Benaderet (who starred in *Petticoat Junction*).
- Actress Sharon Tate, director Roman Polanski's wife, who was the most prominent victim of Charles Man-

son's cult, was a starlet at the time the series went on the air on CBS and appeared for seasons two and three as Drysdale's secretary, Janet Trego.

- Nancy Kulp eventually left show business for politics, returned home to Pennsylvania, and ran unsuccessfully for Congress.
- The popular theme song "The Ballad of Jed Clampett" was written by creator Paul Henning, strummed by bluegrass legends Lester Flatt and Earl Scruggs—who turned up on the show once in a while as themselves—and sung by Jerry Scoggins.

BEWITCHED

ABC, 1964–72, 254 episodes

CAST

Samantha Stephens	Elizabeth Montgomery
Darrin Stephens	Dick York (1964–1969)
	Dick Sargent (1969–1972)
Endora	Agnes Moorehead
Maurice	Maurice Evans
Larry Tate	David White
Louise Tate	Irene Vernon (1964–1966)
	Kasey Rogers (1966–1972)
Gladys Kravitz	Alice Pearce (1964–1966)
	Sandra Gould (1966–1972)
Abner Kravitz	George Tobias
Aunt Clara (recurring)	Marion Lorne (1964–1968)
Esmeralda (recurring)	Alice Ghostley (1969–1972)
Uncle Arthur (recurring)	Paul Lynde (1965–1972)
Dr. Bombay (recurring)	Bernard Fox (1967–1972)

CREATOR: Sol Saks

EXECUTIVE PRODUCER: Harry Ackerman

PRODUCERS: William Froug, Danny Arnold, Jerry Davis, William Asher

PRINCIPAL DIRECTORS: Richard Kinon, William Asher, E. W. Swackhamer, Seymour Robbie, Jerry Davis, Richard Michaels

PRINCIPAL WRITERS: Ed Jurist, Michael Morris, Sol Saks, Danny Arnold, James Henerson, Lila Garrett, Rick Mittleman, Howard Morris, Peggy Chantler Dick

Has Endora (Agnes Moorehead, right) turned poor Durwood (Darrin, not pictured) into a mule again? Samantha (Elizabeth Montgomery), the star of *Bewitched,* looks on with astonishment. COURTESY OF PERSONALITY PHOTOS, INC.

I married a witch

Samantha and Darrin Stephens are an attractive, upwardly mobile suburban couple who seem to have the perfect marriage, with one hitch: he's a straight-arrow advertising executive, she's a comely modern-day witch. As one of the best fantasy sitcoms, *Bewitched* spawned a multitude of imitators (e.g., *My Mother the Car, The Ghost and Mrs. Muir, I Dream of Jeannie*), but few matched this series' imaginative approach, clever scripts, expert special effects, sparkling ensemble cast, and high ratings, at least for the first five seasons.

Underneath its fluffy sitcom stylings, *Bewitched* touched on a topic that would soon burst into mainstream politics: the changing role and gradual empowerment of women in American society. Virtually the same conflict recurred in every episode: Will unfailingly perky Samantha keep her promise to dullard Darrin and refrain from using her magic powers, or will she give in to pressure from her ever-present family (and her own inclinations) and "zap" herself and her husband out of every jam, usually by twitching her nose? Samantha is thus endowed with talents which, if unleashed, could easily subvert the traditional husband-wife roles: male domination over female. In the context of the mid-1960s, Samantha always chose submission to Darrin, but a modern-day liberated woman can take solace in the fact that it's the witchcraft that drives the show and makes Samantha's family far more interesting than Darrin and his mortal friends.

A magical cast

Whether its social subtext was evident or not proved to be irrelevant. The show was phenomenally popular and established then third-place ABC as a network with which to contend. Much of this was due to the then-novel special effects and a fine cast. Elizabeth Montgomery played her role with a matter-of-fact charm that made all the whimsy credible. She is so immensely likable in the role, one often wishes she'd take her mother's advice and leave "Durwood." (Ironically, despite Montgomery's charm and her adeptness at comedy, when *Bewitched* finally left prime-time television, she never again chose to play comedy in the medium, and never did another series—just a number of consistently high-rated dramatic TV movies.)

Played by Agnes Moorehead, Endora stylishly embodies the antagonistic, meddlesome mother-in-law who can't be bothered to remember her son-in-law's name, let alone respect his position as head of his household. This fine dramatic actress (her films include Orson Welles's *The Magnificent Ambersons* and *Citizen Kane*) surprisingly carries off a role as broad as the mascara streaked across her face. Numerous episodes focus on spells Endora casts to humiliate or punish Darrin, such as turning him into an eight-year-old, or forcing him to tell the truth for a day.

An effective counterpoint to the sophisticated Endora was bumbling Aunt Clara, played to a dithering fare-thee-well by the marvelous, Emmy-winning Marion Lorne. She was one of several recurring relatives, including a riotous Paul Lynde as practical joker Uncle Arthur; the famed Shakespearean actor Maurice Evans as Samantha's father (Maurice); and Elizabeth Montgomery herself, doubling as Samantha's mischievous look-alike cousin (Serena). Still more relatives were deliriously played by Estelle Winwood, Jane Connell, and Reta Shaw, among others. Also a standout was Bernard Fox as a literal "witch doctor" (Dr. Bombay). Samantha's suburban bliss was also threatened by the mortals around her, who often came perilously close to exposing her, including Darrin's manipulating boss and his wife, nicely played by David White and Irene Vernon (replaced by Kasey Rogers). The gifted comedienne Alice Pearce stole many episodes as nosy neighbor Gladys Kravitz, also winning an Emmy for her hysterical double takes as furniture flew, elephants appeared, and infants talked. (Sadly, Pearce passed away during the show's third season.)

How these special effects were achieved seems primitive by today's standards. When an object disappeared, the cameras would stop rolling, and every actor had to freeze in their exact position until the object was removed. Then the filming would begin again, causing the object to disappear. Most of the pressure was on Montgomery to keep her hands completely still during this process. According to the actress, she most dreaded the scenes in which entire rooms would magically clean themselves by a wave of her hands. In reality, she had to keep her arms lifted until a stage crew could change the set, causing muscle pains no nose-twitching could dispel.

Switching husbands

As the witchcraft novelty began to wear thin, *Bewitched* added a Stephens infant to the mix with baby Tabitha, who was "born" at the beginning of the third season. Eventually the child proved to be as endowed as her mother. A mortal son, Adam, followed in 1969. By then, the untimely deaths of both Marion Lorne and Alice Pearce had seriously weakened the show's ensemble. (Their respective replacements, Alice Ghostley and Sandra Gould, were barely adequate.) The most startling cast change occurred at the beginning of the show's sixth season when Dick York was replaced by Dick Sargent with nary an explanation. So Endora got her wish after all!

Less eccentric than York, Sargent entered the series shortly after the show switched from black and white to color, curiously marking a definite downward turn in both the ratings and the quality of the series. Still, it lasted for three more seasons, proving to be one of the most enduring and delightful sitcoms of the 1960s and one of the rare long-running programs that never had a "reunion" show. Montgomery's death in 1995 makes this now an impossibility, especially since all of the other principal players are gone as well.

VIDEO AVAILABILITY

Bewitched is available from Columbia House. Each volume contains four twenty-four-minute episodes.

EMMY AWARDS

1965–66 **William Asher,** Outstanding Directorial Achievement in Comedy
Alice Pearce, Outstanding Performance by an Actress in a Supporting Role in a Comedy

1967–68 **Marion Lorne,** Outstanding Performance by an Actress in a Supporting Role in a Comedy

TRIVIA TIDBITS

- Elizabeth Montgomery, who was married to writer/producer/director William Asher, earned close to $6 million from *Bewitched,* making her one of the highest-paid TV performers of the time. Arguably the top female star in television after Lucille Ball, she never really cottoned to the big screen, starring in only three movies (*The Court-Martial of Billy Mitchell* with Gary Cooper, *Who's Been Sleeping in My Bed?* with Dean Martin, and as a gun-toting moll in *Johnny Cool,* directed by William Asher).
- Three sets of twins played Baby Tabitha because California labor laws limited a baby's shooting schedule to two hours per day.
- The jaunty *Bewitched* theme was written by Howard Greenfield and Jack Keller.
- The Stephenses lived at 1164 Morning Glory Circle in Westport, Connecticut. Darrin worked at the McMann and Tate Advertising Agency in Manhattan.
- When playing Serena, Samantha's cousin, Elizabeth Montgomery was billed as Pandora Spocks.
- *Bewitched* was the second most highly rated series in its first season, bested only by *Bonanza.*
- The *Bewitched* spin-off, *Tabitha* (1977–78), made a TV star of Lisa Hartman, as a bright young witch who inherited her mother's nose-twitching powers and had a job as a television production assistant at a California station.

THE BLACK ADDER

Arts & Entertainment, 1986–87 (several multipart series aired on BBC in the mid-1970s)

CAST

Edmund Blackadder	Rowan Atkinson
(In various roles)	Tony Robinson
	Miranda Richardson
	Hugh Laurie

PRODUCER: John Lloyd
DIRECTOR: Martin Shardlow
WRITERS: Rowan Atkinson, Richard Curtis, Ben Elton

Forsooth . . . and all that rot

This hilarious British comedy had a highly original hook: Each series of episodes was set in a completely different historical time period. Cowriter and star Rowan Atkinson referred to the lampoons as "situation tragedies," while others described them as the fifteenth-century equivalent of the Hitler diaries. In all installments, no matter what the time frame, Rowan Atkinson plays the sniveling, scheming Edmund Blackadder with a wry finesse that is unprecedented in TV sitcom history.

In one series, set in medieval times, Prince Edmund, Duke of Edinburgh, is second in line to his father's throne in England and forever plotting to wear the crown ("I pour ice cubes down the vest of fate"). Outrageous in the British manner, he stoops to deeds of unspeakable but hilarious treachery to seize power with the help of his two henchmen, Percy and Baldrick.

In another *Blackadder,* Atkinson brings his spiky venom and cringing servility to the tale of an adviser to a befuddled, whiny-voiced Queen Elizabeth I (played by Miranda Richardson). In a third, he turns up as the avaricious, quick-witted manservant to the rather dense Prince of Wales in merrie olde England of the late 1700s. Another series of three episodes finds him on the Western Front in World War I, helping his men do anything to avoid the taste of combat. In a fourth, he inadvertently decapitates Sir Francis Drake and voyages to New Zealand in pursuit of potatoes. And in a Christmas send-up of Dickens's *A Christmas Carol,* told in reverse, Blackadder is a genuinely nice guy who over the course of events turns into a Scrooge.

VIDEO AVAILABILITY

Eight volumes of this historical spoof, each running about ninety minutes and containing three episodes, along with *Blackadder's Christmas Carol,* running about forty-five minutes, are available at certain video outlets.

TRIVIA TIDBITS

- Rowan Atkinson, long a household name in Great Britain because of his earlier BBC series, *Not the 9 O'Clock News,* is an Oxford graduate with a degree in electrical engineering. Broadway fans recall him from his 1986 hit one-man show, *Rowan Atkinson at the Atkinson.*
- Atkinson's wacky pantomime style—from the Jacques Tati school by way of Jerry Lewis—later became evident to American audiences all over again through his subsequent British series, *Mr. Bean,* of the late 1980s.

THE BOB NEWHART SHOW

CBS, 1972–78, 142 episodes

CAST

Robert Hartley	Bob Newhart
Emily Hartley	Suzanne Pleshette
Howard Borden	Bill Daily
Dr. Jerry Robinson	Peter Bonerz
Carol Kester Bondurant	Marcia Wallace
Margaret Hoover (1972–73)	Patricia Smith
Ellen Hartley (1974–76)	Pat Finley
Cliff Murdock	Tom Poston
Elliott Carlin	Jack Riley
Lillian Bakerman	Florida Friebus
Miss Larson (1972–73)	Penny Marshall
Emil Peterson (1973–78)	John Fiedler
Dr. Bernie Tupperman (1972–76)	Larry Gelman
Michelle Nardo (1973–76)	Renee Lippin
Larry Bondurant (1975–77)	Will Mackenzie

CREATORS: David Davis, Lorenzo Music

EXECUTIVE PRODUCERS: Tom Patchett, Jay Tarses

PRODUCERS: Glen and Les Charles, Gordon and Lynne Farr, Martin Cohan

PRINCIPAL DIRECTORS: Jay Sandrich, Alan Rafkin, Jerry London, Rick Edelstein, Peter Bonerz, Michael Zinberg, Dick Martin

PRINCIPAL WRITERS: David Davis, Lorenzo Music, Martin Cohan, Jerry Mayer, Tom Patchett, Jay Tarses, Charlotte Brown, Gordon and Lynne Farr, Hugh Wilson, Sy Rosen, Gary David Goldberg

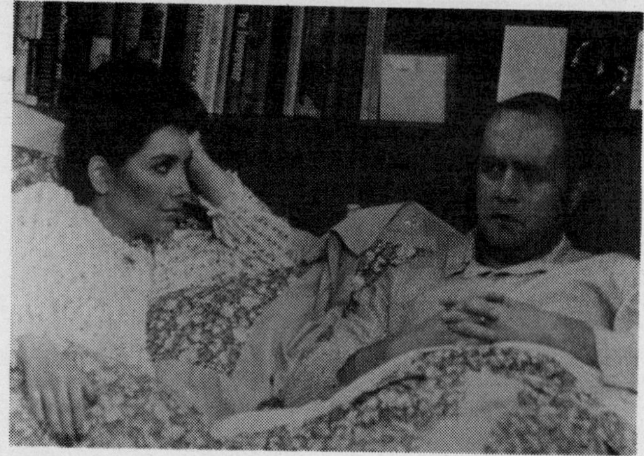

Is this *The Bob Newhart Show* or the brilliant famed last episode from *Newhart?* You decide. Dr. Robert Hartley (Bob Newhart) and Emily Hartley (Suzanne Pleshette) conduct a private therapy session. COURTESY OF PERSONALITY PHOTOS, INC.

Doctor Bob

Low-key Bob Newhart, accountant turned deadpan stand-up comic who developed into one of the great reactors in television comedy (second perhaps only to Jack Benny), starred as an amiable Chicago psychologist who shares a high-rise apartment with his warm, supportive, beautiful wife, Emily, a third-grade teacher, and office space with children's orthodontist Jerry Robinson, who together share a smart-mouth receptionist, Carol Kester. Bob and Emily's space is constantly being invaded by a well-meaning but mooching neighbor, Howard Borden, a divorced 747 navigator who during the early part of the series was Bob's sister's boyfriend.

Dr. Bob Hartley, a rational Everyman, finds himself surrounded by absurd logic, as personified by money-chasing Jerry, the nearly clairvoyant Carol (of the Radar O'Reilly of *M*A*S*H* school of efficiency), and the quirky cases, from paranoid Elliott Carlin and incredibly timid Emil Peterson to kindly, knitting Lillian Bakerman and neurotic Ms. Nardo.

In one episode, following a group session with his patients, Bob accompanies Mr. Carlin to the elevators in the reception area. They chat momentarily about schizophrenia, which Carlin feels might be another of his psychoses. Then both elevator doors open simultaneously, giving him a choice as Bob stands nonplussed awaiting his patient's impossible decision. This particularly funny sight gag was reworked in another episode that has Bob concerned about his mortality after sitting through a rather depressing session with the group, and being greeted at the elevator by the Grim Reaper, a dour man with a long beard, dressed in a white sheet and holding a long scythe in one hand.

One of the Christmas shows had Bob foolishly attempting to raise sagging holiday spirits by inviting his group to his and Emily's apartment for an impromptu Yule party—which depresses one and all. And on another occasion, Bob wondered whether he should accept an expensive gift from his newest patient, a recently paroled ex-con (played by a pre-Fonz Henry Winkler) who served time for armed robbery.

Bob stands—or generally sits—in the eye of a hurricane reacting to the insanity that sometimes continues swirling around him on the home front as neighbors and relatives pop up in daffy appearances. But there's always comforting, understanding, equally rational Emily. Bob plodded hilariously through it all for six humorous TV seasons until he and Emily were dispatched by the peerless *Newhart* writers to Oregon in the final episode, where it was announced he had moved to take a college teaching job.

VIDEO AVAILABILITY

The Bob Newhart Show is available in five tape collections at certain video outlets. Each runs about fifty minutes and contains two episodes, including the 1972 premiere and a pair of Christmas shows.

TRIVIA TIDBITS

- Bob Newhart also starred in an earlier *Bob Newhart Show,* a half-hour variety show that ran on NBC during the 1961–62 season.
- The theme for *The Bob Newhart Show* was written by cocreator Lorenzo Music and his wife, Henrietta. Music went on to greater fame as the intercom voice of the never-seen Carlton Your Doorman on Valerie Harper's *Rhoda* sitcom, as well as the character's own animated *Carlton Your Doorman* Saturday morning children's favorite of the 1980s.
- Bob Newhart, as Dr. Hartley, made a gag appearance on *Murphy Brown* in the early 1990s to retrieve Marcia Wallace—his longtime receptionist, Carol Kester Bondurant—who had taken a job as Murphy's "secretary of the week."
- Longtime Newhart buddy Tom Poston became a semi-regular as Bob Hartley's backslapping college chum Cliff ("The Peeper") Murdock and would also be a prominent cast member in *Newhart,* Bob's subsequent hit series.
- Bill Daily, who previously had a role similar to Howard Borden as Roger Healey in *I Dream of Jeannie,* moved on to three short-lived series in the 1980s but has not done much since. Peter Bonerz (Jerry the orthodontist) has become a sitcom director much in demand.
- Among the guest stars on the series were Ralph Bellamy, Morgan Fairchild, Henry Winkler, Martha Scott, Ann Rutherford, Loni Anderson and Howard Hesseman (both before hitting it big on *WKRP in Cincinnati*), Keenan Wynn, and Howard Morris.
- Newhart pal Dick Martin (of the comedy team of Rowan and Martin) became the principal director during the show's final seasons.

THE BRADY BUNCH

ABC, 1969–74, 117 episodes

CAST

Mike Brady	Robert Reed
Carol Brady	Florence Henderson
Alice Nelson	Ann B. Davis
Greg	Barry Williams
Marcia	Maureen McCormick
Peter	Christopher Knight
Jan	Eve Plumb
Bobby	Michael Lookinland
Cindy	Susan Olsen

CREATORS: Sherwood Schwartz, Lloyd J. Schwartz
EXECUTIVE PRODUCER: Sherwood Schwartz
PRODUCERS: Lloyd J. Schwartz, Howard Leeds
PRINCIPAL DIRECTORS: Peter Baldwin, Leslie H. Martinson, John Rich, Hal Cooper, Bruce Bilson, Russ Mayberry, Jerry London, Oscar Rudolph, Jack Arnold
PRINCIPAL WRITERS: Sherwood Schwartz, Lloyd J. Schwartz

Here is a story about a man named . . .

Rumor has it that in American culture community singing is an activity that has gone the way of knickers and silent movies. Yet, if one begins to hum the theme song to *The Brady Bunch* at a party, chances are anyone over thirty will break into song and finish it *en masse*. It is among the most famous of sitcom theme songs, corny and catchy at the same time. That may also be said about the show itself, which presented a picture of idealized family life amidst the turbulent era of the late 1960s and early 1970s.

Before Mike Brady's hair became curly and before Marcia broke her nose: The ever-campy Bradys pose on their familiar staircase. From left: Susan Olsen (Cindy), Michael Lookinland (Bobby), Eve Plumb (Jan), Christopher Knight (Peter), Maureen McCormick (Marcia), Barry Williams (Greg), Ann B. Davis (Alice), Florence Henderson (Carol), and Robert Reed (Mike). COURTESY OF PERSONALITY PHOTOS, INC.

As recounted in the song, Mike Brady was a widower with three preteen sons who marries Carol Martin, a widow with three preteen daughters. The two families become one and, along with architect Mike's perpetually cheery housekeeper named Alice, settle into a crowded four-bedroom, two-bathroom home at 4222 Clinton Avenue in Los Angeles. The concept was inspired by two popular 1968 films: Lucille Ball's *Yours, Mine & Ours* and Doris Day's *With Six, You Get Eggroll.* It was a clever conceit, providing the newlyweds with a large family while avoiding such messy subjects as pregnancy or birth control.

A world of their own

In the world of the Bradys, current social issues such as Vietnam, drug abuse, student protest, the sexual revolution, feminism, etc., were ignored in favor of domestic crises like "Will Marcia get rid of her pimple before the spring dance?" or "Will the destroyer of Mom's favorite vase confess to his or her crime?"

The Brady parents, played by Robert Reed (who died in 1993) and onetime Broadway musical star Florence Henderson, were attractive, youthful, ever-supportive authority figures. Anger and resentment seldom surfaced in the Brady household, although Mike could show irritation, as when he installed a pay phone to curtail the youngsters' personal calls. Sibling rivalry did often lead to harmless skirmishes, refereed by the all-knowing housekeeper. Played by Ann B. Davis (formerly of *Love That Bob*), Alice was never too busy to meddle in the family's domestic intrigues, managing to cook and clean for eight people, and take care of several pets without ever getting dirty or looking tired—or even asking for a raise! Alice was also the clown of the show and wasn't above taking an occasional pratfall or two.

Even though its head was in the political/social sand, *The Brady Bunch* did, however, attempt to recognize the popular appeal of rock music and current fashions. Eldest son Greg aspired to become a pop singer and, with his brothers and sisters, formed a group known as The Brady Six. Their type of music, often referred to as bubblegum rock, was bland and inoffensive like that of their TV rivals, *The Partridge Family.* Their plaid, multicolored clothes were suburban versions of "mod" fashions, with polyester the prevailing fabric. As the children grew older, the boys' hair became longer, but never so long as to suggest that Greg was becoming a hippie.

From camp to cult

The show, like creator Sherwood Schwartz's earlier *Gilligan's Island,* was critically panned and ignored during most of its original run in favor of a new breed of realistic sitcom exemplified by CBS's *All in the Family.* The Bunkers and the Bradys may have shared the same airwaves in the early 1970s, but they were truly in different universes. Every unpleasant truth about family life that *The Brady Bunch* ignored was embraced by *All in the Family.* Soon the Nielsen ratings proved to the networks that American viewing tastes had changed and the Bunch disappeared, almost unnoticed by press and public alike.

However, time has been good to the Bradys. Spawning several spin-offs, a cartoon series, a couple of TV movie reunions, an Off Broadway show, and in 1995 a hit feature film starring Shelley Long and Gary Cole (another, *A Very Brady Sequel,* was released in 1996), the family has continued to thrive long after its prime-time cancellation in 1974. Although the Bunkers may have won the Emmys and the critical praise, the Bradys are the cult favorite for millions who grew up in the early 1970s and will always cherish some of the show's snippets of timeless dialogue, such as "Marcia, Marcia, Marcia!" and "Mom always told us not to play ball in the house." Whether it's a taste for "camp" or a nostalgic yearning to return to a time that never existed, *The Brady Bunch* continues to entertain and hold an ever-growing audience.

VIDEO AVAILABILITY

The Brady Bunch is available from Columbia House and certain video outlets. Each volume, running approximately fifty minutes, contains two episodes.

TRIVIA TIDBITS

- Through the years, the Brady household often resembled a menagerie with Tiger, the family dog; Romeo and Juliet, Cindy's pet rabbits; Bobby's pet parakeet, Bird; and Greg's white mouse, Myron. In the pilot episode the girls have a cat named Fluffy, but the feline is never again mentioned.
- *The Brady Bunch* theme song was written by Frank DeVol and Sherwood Schwartz. It was performed during the first season by the Peppermint Trolley Car Company and by the Brady Kids thereafter.
- The famous title sequence features the family in a tic-tac-toe-type configuration. The order from left to right is: (top row) Marcia, Carol, Greg; (middle row) Jan, Alice, Peter; and (bottom row) Cindy, Mike, Bobby.
- In one episode, Robert Reed and Florence Henderson played Mike's own grandfather and Carol's own grandmother. In another, Ann B. Davis played Alice's look-alike cousin, Emma. And in still another, Imogene Coca turned up as Mike's Aunt Jenny.
- Among the guests on the series were Vincent Price, the Monkees' Davy Jones, football star Joe Namath, baseball star Don Drysdale, Desi Arnaz Jr. (son of Lucy and Desi), Jay ("Tonto") Silverheels, Jackie Coogan (from *The Addams Family*), and Jim Backus (from *Gilligan's Island*).
- There were five series spin-offs to the original one: *The Brady Kids* (an animated version that ran for twenty-two episodes from 1972 to 1974); *The Brady Bunch Hour* (nine episodes in 1977); *The Brady Girls Get Married* (three episodes in 1981); *The Brady Brides* (seven episodes in 1981); and *The Bradys* (four episodes in 1990). Between the last two came a pair of reunion movies on television: *The Brady Girls Get Married* in 1981 (an edited version of the brief series earlier in the year) and *A Very Brady Christmas* in 1988. The following season, the bunch appeared on the

NBC sitcom *Day by Day* in an episode entitled "A Very Brady Episode."

- Barry Williams (Greg Brady) not only wrote a book about his days as a Brady (titled *Growing Up Brady*) but also put together in the early 1990s the successful Off Broadway show *The Real Live Brady Bunch*, using original scripts from the popular series.

CAR 54, WHERE ARE YOU?

NBC, 1961–63, 60 episodes

CAST

Officer Gunther Toody	Joe E. Ross
Officer Francis Muldoon	Fred Gwynne
Lucille Toody	Beatrice Pons
Capt. Martin Block	Paul Reed
Officer Leo Schnauser	Al Lewis
Sylvia Schnauser	Charlotte Rae
Officer O'Hara	Albert Henderson
Officer Anderson	Nipsey Russell
Officer Antonnucci	Jerome Guardino
Officer Steinmetz	Joe Warren
Officer Kissel	Bruce Kirby
Officer Ed Nicholson	Hank Garrett
Officer Wallace	Frederick O'Neal
Desk Sergeant Sol Abrams	Nathaniel Frey

CREATOR AND PRODUCER: Nat Hiken
DIRECTORS: Nat Hiken, Stanley Prager
PRINCIPAL WRITER: Nat Hiken

"There's a holdup in the Bronx . . ."

This comedy cop show, which initially aired on Sunday nights opposite the last half hour of Ed Sullivan's program, can be seen as something of a precursor to the next decade's *Barney Miller*. It teamed short, garrulous ex-vaudevillian Joe E. Ross, with his hangdog expression and his "Ooh! Ooh! Ooh!" exclamations, and tall, intellectual, deep-voiced Shakespearean actor Fred Gwynne and placed them in a squad car as Keystone Kops-like

Officers Toody (Joe E. Ross, left) and Muldoon (Fred Gwynne) on the beat in *Car 54, Where Are You?* COURTESY OF PERSONALITY PHOTOS, INC.

Officers Toody and Muldoon. The duo was assigned to New York's 53rd precinct, and their beat was a run-down area in the Bronx. The men of the 53rd caught more abuse from their wives than the local criminals, and although most of the lawbreakers on the series were portrayed as lovable bumblers, the weekly culprits were nabbed invariably because of their own stupidity. The cops were not much brighter, from laconic, somber-faced Muldoon and excitable Toody; to their ever-flustered captain Martin Block (not, of course, the disc jockey of New York radio); and to their fellow officers Schnauser (whose name was an inside joke reference to a character named Sergeant Doberman from Nat Hiken's earlier *Sergeant Bilko*), Nicholson, and Steinmetz.

Among the nutty predicaments in which the boys from the 53rd (and loved ones) found themselves over the show's two wacky seasons: Toody making a plaster cast of Sergeant Abrams's feet to give him orthopedic shoes for his twenty-fifth anniversary as a cop; the entire precinct entering a barbershop quartet singing contest; Schnauser's wife, Sylvia, trying to publish a book about her love life; and Toody, after seeing *The Taming of the Shrew* in Central Park, trying to tame his wife, Lucille. And, of course, somewhat goofy Muldoon and his crazy partner, Toody tooling around in the ever-errant Car 54. Years after leaving prime-time television, they and their incompetent pals in blue would find themselves back in the hearts of their fans and new converts as one of the most popular shows on Nick at Nite.

VIDEO AVAILABILITY

Eight volumes of *Car 54, Where Are You?* are available at certain video outlets. Each tape runs about fifty-five minutes and contains two episodes.

EMMY AWARD

1961–62 **Nat Hiken,** Outstanding Directorial Achievement in Comedy

TRIVIA TIDBITS

- Fred Gwynne and Al Lewis, Officers Muldoon and Schnauser, went on, of course, to team on *The Munsters.*
- Creator Nat Hiken's other best known show was his earlier *Sergeant Bilko,* in which *Car 54*'s Joe E. Ross and Bea Pons also played a mismatched married couple, Rupert and Emma Ridzik.
- The show's famous theme was written by Nat Hiken and John Strauss.
- *Car 54, Where Are You?* joined the growing list of well-remembered TV shows being remade for the big screen. The 1994 incarnation starred David Johansen as Toody and John C. McGinley as Muldoon, along with a number of big names in cameos and even Al Lewis (the original Schnauser), and Nipsy Russell.
- Among the guest stars on the series were Maureen Stapleton, Molly Picon, Wally Cox, Larry Storch, Tom Bosley, Ossie Davis, Sugar Ray Robinson, Rocky Graziano, Margaret Hamilton, and Alice Ghostley (as Muldoon's girlfriend Bonnie Calsheim).
- The show was filmed on location in the Bronx. The fictional 53rd Precinct was the old Biograph studio, first used by pioneer moviemaker D. W. Griffith.
- In order to ensure that local citizens and real cops would not be confused during filming, the squad cars of *Car 54* were painted red and white to differentiate them from the NYPD's blue-and-whites. Of course, viewers would not know this since the series was done in black and white.

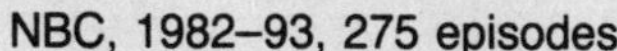

CHEERS

NBC, 1982–93, 275 episodes

CAST

Sam Malone	Ted Danson
Diane Chambers (1982–87)	Shelley Long
Carla Tortelli LeBec	Rhea Perlman
Ernie "Coach" Pantusso (1982–85)	Nicholas Colasanto
Norm Peterson	George Wendt
Cliff Clavin	John Ratzenberger
Dr. Frasier Crane (1984–93)	Kelsey Grammer
Nick Tortelli (1984–86)	Dan Hedaya
Woody Boyd (1985–93)	Woody Harrelson
Rebecca Howe (1987–93)	Kirstie Alley
Dr. Lilith Sternin (1986–93)	Bebe Neuwirth
Evan Drake (1987–88)	Tom Skerritt
Eddie LeBec (1989–91)	Jay Thomas
Robin Colcord (1989–91)	Roger Rees
Kelly Gaines (1989–93)	Jackie Swanson
Paul (1991–93)	Paul Willson

CREATORS/EXECUTIVE PRODUCERS: Glen and Les Charles, James Burrows

PRODUCERS: Ken Levine, David Isaacs, Cheri Eichen, Bill Steinkeller, Phoef Sutton, David Lee, David Angell, Andy Ackerman, Mert Rich, Tim Berry, Dan O'Shannon

DIRECTOR: James Burrows (nearly every episode)

PRINCIPAL WRITERS: Glen Charles, Les Charles, Earl Pomerantz, Ken Estin, Ken Levine, David Isaacs, Heidi Perlman (Rhea's sister), David Lloyd, David Angell, Tom Reeder

Everyone knows the names of the original *Cheers* cast, from left: George Wendt (Norm), Shelley Long (Diane), Ted Danson (Sam), Rhea Perlman (Carla), Woody Harrelson (Woody), and John Ratzenberger (Cliff). Dr. Frasier Crane (Kelsey Grammer) was unavailable for the photo; perhaps he was toning his radio voice for his next show, *Frasier.* COURTESY OF PERSONALITY PHOTOS, INC.

Pour one for us

There were other well-remembered sitcoms that were set in a bar: *Duffy's Tavern,* a longtime radio favorite that was made into an all-star, but not too successful, film before becoming a TV series for about thirteen weeks in 1954; *Archie Bunker's Place,* a revamped extension of *All in the Family,* which stayed around for another four seasons; and *Love and War* in the early 1990s, in which a gang of regulars boozed it up in a bar masquerading as a trendy restaurant. None had the impact or the cleverness of *Cheers,* a Boston watering hole where, as the song goes, everybody knows your name. It was populated with servers and drinkers who came to be family to each other and, for eleven years, to millions of viewers.

Everybody knows their name

Cheers was run by Sam Malone, a former Boston Red Sox pitcher turned alcoholic (but carefully staying on the wagon) who pictured himself as the quintessential womanizer whose most prized possession, other than the bar, is his little black book. His bartender, Coach, was his dense but lovable baseball coach who had been put out to pasture. Carla Tortelli was the diminutive, plain Jane razor-tongued barmaid who has been unlucky in love and has a brood of kids to show for it. Into the mix wandered brainy but incredibly insecure Diane Chambers, a teaching assistant who took a job as a waitress, withstood Carla's unending barrage of barbs, and parried sexually with Sam for several years—even finally walking down the aisle with him but getting cold feet at the altar—before leaving to find herself. The two bar regulars were postman Cliff Clavin, a know-it-all mama's boy, and beer-bellied Norm Peterson, an unemployed accountant who sat on the corner stool (which now resides in the Smithsonian Institution) and guzzled his way through the day while complaining about his never-seen wife, Vera.

Others who wandered into the place over the years and stayed until the last call were: Rebecca Howe, a smoky-voiced temptress who took Diane's place (and for a while even owned the joint) and kept looking for Mr. Right, as long as he was a millionaire; Frasier Crane, a neurotic psychiatrist who dispensed bar-side advice; Woody Boyd, a huggable hayseed hired to tend bar after Coach's death and who provided rural humor; and Lilith Sternin, an erudite ice queen and fellow psychiatrist who turned

Frasier on and subsequently married him and then left him.

When the last call finally came in 1993 and it was time to turn the lights out in Cheers, NBC orchestrated an event and generated huge ratings. It all ended with Sam, alone in the place, simply telling a patron rushing up to the door for one last one, "Sorry, we're closed."

VIDEO AVAILABILITY

Cheers is available at certain video outlets in two-episode cassettes, each running about fifty minutes.

EMMY AWARDS (twenty-eight in all, including eight technical awards)

1982–83 *Cheers,* Outstanding Comedy Series
Shelley Long, Outstanding Lead Actress in a Comedy Series
James Burrows, Outstanding Directing in a Comedy Series
Glen and Les Charles, Outstanding Writing in a Comedy Series

1983–84 *Cheers,* Outstanding Comedy Series
Rhea Perlman, Outstanding Supporting Actress in a Comedy Series
David Angell, Outstanding Writing in a Comedy Series

1984–85 **Rhea Perlman,** Outstanding Supporting Actress in a Comedy Series

1985–86 **Rhea Perlman,** Outstanding Supporting Actress in a Comedy Series

1986–87 **John** *(Monty Python)* **Cleese,** Outstanding Guest Performer in a Comedy Series

1988–89 *Cheers,* Outstanding Comedy Series
Woody Harrelson, Outstanding Supporting Actor in a Comedy Series
Rhea Perlman, Outstanding Supporting Actress in a Comedy Series

1989–90 **Ted Danson,** Outstanding Lead Actor in a Comedy Series
Bebe Neuwirth, Outstanding Supporting Actress in a Comedy Series
1990–91 *Cheers,* Outstanding Comedy Series
Kirstie Alley, Outstanding Lead Actress in a Comedy Series
Bebe Neuwirth, Outstanding Supporting Actress in a Comedy Series
James Burrows, Outstanding Directing in a Comedy Series
1992–93 **Ted Danson,** Outstanding Lead Actor in a Comedy Series

TRIVIA TIDBITS

- The premiere episode of *Cheers* on September 30, 1982 ranked seventy-seventh among the top seventy-seven TV shows.
- *Cheers* ended up receiving a record 119 Emmy nominations over its twelve seasons.
- Much-married Carla's full name was Carla Maria Victoria Angelina Teresa Appollonia Lozupone Tortelli LeBec.
- *The Tortellis,* starring Dan Hedaya, who was Carla's slimy ex-husband, was the first spin-off from *Cheers* (it lasted about thirteen weeks in early 1987). The much more successful *Frasier* is the second, with Frasier Crane now a pompous, know-it-all radio psychiatrist in Seattle, bedeviled on occasion by a "guest" visit from ex-wife Lilith or from Diane, who stood him up at the altar on *Cheers.*
- Cheers bar was located at 112½ Beacon Street in Boston. Its inspiration (and opening establishing shot under the opening credits) was Boston's Bull & Finch bar on Beacon Street, just down the street from the Massachusetts State House.
- The *Cheers* theme song, "Where Everybody Knows Your Name," was written by Judy Hart Angelo and Gary Portnoy and was sung by Portnoy.

THE DICK VAN DYKE SHOW

CBS, 1961–66, 158 episodes

CAST

Rob Petrie	Dick Van Dyke
Laura Petrie	Mary Tyler Moore
Sally Rogers	Rose Marie
Buddy Sorrell	Morey Amsterdam
Richie Petrie	Larry Matthews
Mel Cooley	Richard Deacon
Jerry Helper	Jerry Paris
Millie Helper	Ann Morgan Guilbert
Alan Brady	Carl Reiner

CREATOR: Carl Reiner

EXECUTIVE PRODUCERS: Sheldon Leonard, Danny Thomas

PRODUCERS: Carl Reiner, Ronald Jacobs, Bill Persky & Sam Denoff

PRINCIPAL DIRECTORS: John Rich, Robert Butler, James Komack, Jerry Paris, Hal Cooper, Alan Rafkin, Sheldon Leonard, Howard Morris, Lee Philips, Claudio Guzman, Stanley Z. Cherry, Theodore J. Flicker, Peter Baldwin

PRINCIPAL WRITERS: Carl Reiner, Bill Persky & Sam Denoff, Garry Marshall & Jerry Belson, Dale McRaven & Carl Kleinschmitt, Ben Joelson & Art Baer, Rick Mittleman, Joseph Bonaduce

Cream of the crop

The Dick Van Dyke Show remains one of the most highly praised comedy series in television history. Its witty, inventive writing, its superb ensemble cast, its ability to be

Obviously someone didn't get the joke: Comedy writer Rob Petrie (Dick Van Dyke) explains things to his wife, Laura (Mary Tyler Moore), from behind bars. *The Dick Van Dyke* show remains one of the funniest, most influential sitcoms of all time. COURTESY OF PERSONALITY PHOTOS, INC.

outrageously funny while never sacrificing its link to reality were qualities that not only won the series fifteen Emmys and consistently high ratings but also had a lasting influence on the development of situation comedy. Yet, it almost didn't happen.

It began in the fertile comedy mind of Carl Reiner, who filmed a pilot in 1959 called *Head of the Family* (financed by Peter Lawford and father-in-law Joseph Kennedy!) with himself as comedy writer Rob Petrie and Barbara Britton as his comely wife, Laura. Nightclub comic Morty Gunty and actress Sylvia Miles were cast as Rob's writing partners Buddy Sorrell and Sally Rogers. Reiner had little luck selling this to the networks as a series, but CBS aired the one-shot in the summer of 1960 before it went to the unsold pilot graveyard. Sheldon Leonard, former movie tough guy turned successful producer and partner of Danny Thomas, then produced a new pilot from a new script by Reiner, brought in a new cast, and *The Dick Van Dyke Show* was born.

The enduring series that set the standards for sitcoms (like today's *Frasier*) revolved around the star's interaction at the workplace and at home: with wisecracking fellow writers Sally and Buddy, who worked with him on *The Alan Brady Show*; with Brady, who was loudly heard in the first few seasons but not seen until later on; with pompous, balding, bespectacled producer Melvin Cooley (who held his job only because he was Brady's brother-in-law); and at home with loving homemaker Laura and son Richie, and neighbors Jerry and Millie Helper.

Although the show languished in the wrong time slot for the first thirteen weeks before being moved and finally discovered, Van Dyke and company (no, not Dick's later unsuccessful variety hour of that name) created television magic, working their ensemble way through crackerjack and consistently hilarious scripts, mainly by Carl Reiner for the first several seasons (Reiner wrote forty-one of the first sixty-three shows) and by several up-and-coming writing teams who followed.

"Oh, Rob!"

The chemistry between the pair of lovebird leads has lasted through the years, and they remain linked as pals through the pantheon of television. Whether the camera was on the lithe Dick with his expressive face and peerless double takes or on beauteous Mary with her flair for keeping the home front spotless and for saying "Oh, Rob!" in endless variations (whether in surprise or in mock anger, lovingly or dishearteningly), there was a spark that made them TV's perfect twosome. In fact, in

Mary Tyler Moore's classic series that followed, the initial idea of making her character a divorcée was quickly discarded for fear that America would think that ideal couple Laura and Rob Petrie had gone splitsville.

As one astute writer once noted about the show, Rob and Laura shared a physical attraction that was remarkably frank for television, but in five years, they rarely uttered the words "I love you" on screen. Perhaps that was because audiences everywhere already knew they did.

VIDEO AVAILABILITY

The Dick Van Dyke Show is available through Columbia House in a collector's edition with four half-hour episodes per videocassette.

EMMY AWARDS

1961–62 **Carl Reiner,** Outstanding Writing Achievement in Comedy

1962–63 *The Dick Van Dyke Show,* Outstanding Program Achievement in the Field of Humor
John Rich, Outstanding Directorial Achievement in Comedy
Carl Reiner, Outstanding Writing Achievement in Comedy

1963–64 *The Dick Van Dyke Show,* Outstanding Program Achievement in the Field of Comedy
Dick Van Dyke, Outstanding Continued Performance by an Actor in a Comedy Series (Lead)
Mary Tyler Moore, Outstanding Continued Performance by an Actress in a Comedy Series (Lead)
Jerry Paris, Outstanding Directorial Achievement in Comedy
Carl Reiner, Sam Denoff, Bill Persky, Outstanding Writing Achievement in Comedy or Variety

1964–65 *The Dick Van Dyke Show,* Outstanding Program Achievement in Entertainment
Dick Van Dyke, Outstanding Continued Performance by an Actor in a Comedy Series (Lead)

1965–66 *The Dick Van Dyke Show,* Outstanding Comedy Series
Dick Van Dyke, Outstanding Continued Performance by an Actor in a Comedy Series (Lead)
Mary Tyler Moore, Outstanding Continued Performance by an Actress in a Comedy Series (Lead)
Sam Denoff and Bill Persky, Outstanding Writing Achievement in Comedy

TRIVIA TIDBITS

- Dick Van Dyke came to the series having just won a Tony for starring on Broadway in *Bye Bye Birdie.*
- Although then unknown, Mary Tyler Moore would subsequently find even greater fame in her own series, *The Mary Tyler Moore Show* (see separate entry). Dick Van Dyke made a few successful films (e.g., *Mary Poppins, Bye Bye Birdie,* and *Chitty Chitty Bang Bang*), but floundered in his attempts to return to television. Late in life he found a niche on TV as crime-solving Dr. Mark Sloan in *Diagnosis: Murder.*
- Rob and Laura met at the Camp Crowder Air Base in Joplin, Missouri, where he was a sergeant and she was part of a USO troupe.
- Rob, Laura, and young Richie Petrie made their home in New Rochelle, New York, on Bonnie Meadow Road. (The address is alternately given as 148 and 485.)
- Jerry Paris left acting to become a successful director of sitcoms, most notably on *The Mary Tyler Moore Show* and *Happy Days,* and dozens of TV movies. He died in 1986 at age sixty.

- Three decades after *The Dick Van Dyke Show* left the air, Carl Reiner recreated his Alan Brady character in a hilarious episode of *Mad About You*—and won an Emmy.
- Rose Marie and Morey Amsterdam put in a joint appearance in 1996 as senior citizens sharing a Manhattan apartment in an episode of *Caroline in the City.*
- The show's jaunty theme was written by Earle Hagen, composer of "Harlem Nocturne."

DINOSAURS

ABC, 1991–94

VOICES

Earl Sinclair	Stuart Pankin
Fran Sinclair	Jessica Walter
Robbie Sinclair (age 14)	Jason Willinger
Charlene Sinclair (age 12)	Sally Struthers
Baby Sinclair	Kevin Clash
Grandma Ethyl	Florence Stanley
Roy Hess	Sam McMurray
B.P. Richfield	Sherman Hemsley

CREATORS: Jim and Brian Henson
EXECUTIVE PRODUCERS: Brian Henson, Michael Jacobs
PRODUCERS: Bob Young, Mark Brull
DIRECTORS: Bill Dear, Tom Trbovich
WRITERS: Bob Young, Michael Jacobs, Dava Savel

The really big monsters next door

Conceived by Jim Henson before his death and brought to life at Henson Productions' Creature Shop in London by his son Brian, this animated sitcom using sophisticated puppetlike figures focused on the modern-day life and foibles of a domesticated family of dinosaurs living in the year 60,000,003 B.C. The character names of family and friends were derived from present-day oil companies (presumably because of the popular Sinclair Oil dinosaur). The show revolved around a blustery, henpecked megalosaurus—part Fred Flintstone and part Homer Simpson—who smoked cigars and worked for a development company that leveled forest for suburban tract

Domesticity, dinosaur style: Robbie and his mother, Fran, in a scene from *Dinosaurs.* COURTESY OF PERSONALITY PHOTOS, INC.

homes for his fellow creatures, and his wife, a ten-ton allosaurus who ran both his home and his life and kept various "things" from the dinosaur world in the family refrigerator. There also were three kids—a rebellious teenage son, a shop-happy daughter, and a recently hatched smart-mouthed brat of a baby—along with a nagging mother-in-law, a tyrannical boss, and Earl's best friend, a swinging bachelor. These were the elements of the everyday TV sitcom, like *The Flintstones*, to which *Dinosaurs* resembles a kissing cousin (substituting puppet figures for cartoon characters).

VIDEO AVAILABILITY

At least a dozen tape collections of *Dinosaurs* are available at certain video outlets. Each runs about forty-five minutes and contains two episodes.

TRIVIA TIDBITS

◆ Among those supplying voices for *Dinosaurs* were two cast members of *All in the Family:* Sally (Gloria Bunker Stivic) Struthers and Sherman (George Jefferson) Hemsley, playing, respectively, Earl Sinclair's daughter and his blowhard employer.

- This prime-time series was crafted by those who created the Muppets and the Teenage Mutant Ninja Turtles, using a complex process called Audio-Animatronics.

FAWLTY TOWERS

BBC, 1975–79, 12 episodes

CAST

Basil Fawlty	John Cleese
Sybil Fawlty	Prunella Scales
Manuel	Andrew Sachs
Polly	Connie Booth
Major Gowen	Ballard Berkeley
Miss Tibbs	Gilly Flower
Miss Gatsby	Renee Roberts
Terry	Brian Hall

CREATORS AND WRITERS: John Cleese and Connie Booth
PRODUCERS: Douglas Argent, John Davies
DIRECTOR: Bob Spiers

To sir, with gall

John Cleese—the former Monty Python trouper with the silly walks—plays Basil Fawlty, the snobbish, devious manager of the worst-run hotel in England who bootlicks wealthy guests and acts insufferably rude to others. His overcoiffed, overbearing wife, Sybil, played by Prunella Scales, is always on his case; his hopeless but ever hopeful bellboy-waiter, Manuel (Andrew Sachs), has difficulty speaking and understanding English; and his chef, Terry (Brian Hall), is forever concocting delicacies like "filigree Siberian hamster," which turns out to be rat. The only staff member with any real competence is Polly, the calm and capable would-be artist housekeeper struggling—usually in vain—to keep her boss out of trouble. She is played by Connie Booth, at the time Cleese's wife and

Another ill-conceived plot put in motion: Basil Fawlty (John Cleese) oozes smugness as he stands in front of his hotel—which is without question the worst in Great Britain. Only twelve episodes of *Fawlty Towers* were created, but all are classics of the highest order. COURTESY OF PERSONALITY PHOTOS, INC.

also cowriter for the show. And then there is the stream of abused hotel guests.

In one of the outrageous episodes, "Gourmet Night," duck has been ordered by one of the diners, and ultimately Basil, in his "Mein Herr" mode, wheels in the serving cart and, sharpening his knife with panache, discovers on taking off the tray cover not a duck but a large ornate pink trifle. He slams the cover down, then lifts it a little and peers disbelievingly beneath. Whipping the lid off, he then looks around the room for the escaped duck. It's not there, or is it on the lower shelf of the trolley? Basil finally plunges both hands into the trifle and ransacks it madly, to the horror of those at the table but to the glee of those viewing. John Cleese's brilliance for madcap brand of humor turns material such as this into howlingly funny routines.

The idea for the series came, according to Cleese, from a Monty Python tour of the British hinterlands in the early 1970s. "[We] had the misfortune to stay in a seaside establishment in Devon which gave [us] a somewhat jaundiced view of the catering industry. The manager was so rude he was fascinating. He thought the guests were sent along to annoy him and prevent him from running the hotel."

VIDEO AVAILABILITY

All of the show's twelve episodes, individually (three to a ninety-minute tape) and as a boxed set, are available at certain outlets.

TRIVIA TIDBITS

- For his Basil Fawlty, John Cleese won Britain's *TV Times* Award as Funniest Man on Television.
- Cleese and Booth authored the book *The Complete Fawlty Towers*, a collection of the show's scripts.
- An American version of *Fawlty Towers*, called *Snavely*, was aired as a pilot on ABC in 1978. Harvey Korman and Betty White starred in the John Cleese and Prunella Scales roles as Henry and Gladys Snavely, proprietors of Snavely Manor.
- A second attempt to Americanize *Fawlty Towers* was 1983's short-lived *Amanda's* on ABC. Bea Arthur had the John Cleese role as proprietor of problem-fraught Amanda's-by-the-Sea, and Kevin McCarthy, as her brother-in-law, had the revamped Prunella Scales part.

THE FLINTSTONES

ABC, 1960–66, 166 episodes

VOICES

Fred Flintstone	Alan Reed
Wilma Flintstone	Jean VanderPyl
Barney Rubble	Mel Blanc
Betty Rubble (1960–64)	Bea Benaderet
Betty Rubble (1964–66)	Gerry Johnson
Dino the Dinosaur	Mel Blanc
Pebbles Flintstone (1962–66)	Jean VanderPyl
Bamm Bamm Rubble (1963–66)	Don Messick

PRODUCERS/DIRECTORS: William Hanna, Joseph Barbera

The good old (really old) days

The Flintstones, always considered by TVphiles to be an animated version of *The Honeymooners,* was a prime-time cartoon parody on modern suburban life set in the Stone Age. Rather than Ralph Kramden's bus driver and Ed Norton's sewer worker, there was Fred Flintstone as the operator of a dinosaur-powered crane at a quarry cave outside his town of Bedrock in 1,000,072 B.C. with his pal, next-cave neighbor, and fellow lodge member, Barney Rubble. Loudmouth Fred's hearty "Yabba dabba doo!" became a national catchphrase.

During its six-season run, far longer than any other prime-time cartoon show of its time, *The Flintstones* maintained its witty, contemporary spin on prehistoric living, with Fred and Wilma (born Slaghoople) residing quite comfortably in their split-level cave with its Stoneway piano; its hi-fi set (a turntable and a long-

Like Ralph and Alice Kramden, these two require little introduction: Fred and Wilma Flintstone of *The Flintstones.* © Hanna-Barbera. COURTESY OF PERSONALITY PHOTOS, INC.

beaked "stylus" bird doing its things as—what else—a stylus, providing Fred with his "rock" music); its garbage disposal with a buzzard under the sink; and its living lawnmower. The family pet, Dino, was a six-foot purple-spotted Snarkasaurus. Fred (with his natty caveman outfit and bow tie) even had a sporty car equipped with steamroller wheels (although all passengers had to get the car started with their feet). Fred and Wilma's bundle of joy, whom they named Pebbles, came along during the show's third season; for a playmate, Barney and Betty adopted a son named Bamm Bamm. Periodic guests lent their voices to characters drawn to their likenesses and given takeoffs on their names: Ann-Margret played Ann-Margrock, Gina Lollobrigida was Lollobrickida, Tony Curtis was Stoney Curtis, and Elizabeth Montgomery was Samantha the Witch.

VIDEO AVAILABILITY

Eight tape collections of *The Flintstones* are available at certain video outlets. Each runs approximately fifty minutes and contains two classic episodes.

TRIVIA TIDBITS

- In addition to the spin-off series with the kids as teenagers, *Pebbles and Bamm Bamm* with voices by Sally *(All in the Family)* Struthers and Jay *(Dennis the Menace)* North, that aired briefly on CBS in 1971–72, there were several other Flintstone shows over the years: *The Flintstone Comedy Hour* (1972–74), *The New Fred and Barney Show* (Feb.–Sept. 1979), *Flintstone Family Adventures* (1980–81), *The Flintstones* (new version, 1981 and 1982, although only four episodes), *The Flintstone Funnies* (1981–84), and *The Flintstone Kids* (1986–88, and again briefly during 1990). Two other prime-time animated specials aired on ABC in 1993: *Yabba Dabba Doo* and *Hollyrock-a-Bye Baby,* each running two hours.
- Fred and Barney were lodge brothers in The Royal Order of Water Buffalos.
- A feature-length cartoon version, *The Man Called Flintstone,* a Stone Age superspy spoof, was released theatrically in 1966. A live-action film, starring John Goodman and Elizabeth Perkins as Fred and Wilma, and Rick Moranis and Rosie O'Donnell as Barney and Betty, was released in 1994. Even Elizabeth Taylor returned to films to play Fred's nagging mother-in-law.
- Veteran animators Hanna and Barbera, flush with the success of *The Flintstones,* reworked the concept in 1962 with *The Jetsons,* moving the cartoon family and best friends from the very distant past to the very distant future.

THE GEORGE BURNS AND GRACIE ALLEN SHOW

CBS, 1950–58, 239 episodes

CAST

Himself	George Burns
Herself	Gracie Allen
Himself	Harry Von Zell
Himself	Ronnie Burns
Blanche Morton	Bea Benaderet
Harry Morton	Hal March, John Brown, Bob Sweeney, Fred Clark, Larry Keating
Bonnie Sue McAfee	Judi Meredith
Ralph Grainger	Robert Ellis
Mr. Beasley	Rolfe Sedan
Chester Vanderlip	Grandon Rhodes

CREATOR: George Burns
PRODUCERS: Fred DeCordova, Al Simon, Ralph Levy, Rod Amateau
DIRECTORS: Fred DeCordova, Ralph Levy, Rod Amateau
WRITERS: William Burns, Harvey Helm, Keith Fowler, Norman Paul, Sid Dorfman, Jesse Goldman

Say hello, Gracie

One of the most legendary husband-and-wife acts in show business history, George Burns and Gracie Allen headlined in vaudeville in the 1920s, on radio and then in films in the 1930s and 1940s, and on television in the 1950s (until Gracie retired in 1958). In the TV series, which

Who is the stronger? Gracie Allen draws her own conclusions between a muscle builder (Steve Reeves, a future Hercules) and her husband (on *The George Burns and Gracie Allen Show,* as well as in real-life)—the future Grand Old Man of Comedy, George Burns. COURTESY OF PERSONALITY PHOTOS, INC.

spanned nearly the entire decade, George, with his ever-present cigar, acted as a Greek chorus of sorts, an on-screen narrator who then stepped into the scene to be straight man to wife Gracie and act bemused but unflappable by her harebrained schemes and ditsy comments, often about her (unseen) family. He'd then step out of the scene, do a monologue, and discuss with the live audience his take on what flibbertigibbet Gracie was doing. Just as Lucy and Desi had the Mertzes as their comedy buddies and foils, George and Gracie had the Mortons—Blanche and her accountant husband, Harry—to accompany them on Gracie's crazy escapades.

George and Gracie brought their show virtually intact, theme song and all, from radio to TV with the same cast. The only change was that Harry Von Zell succeeded the original announcer, Bill Goodwin. They did the program live before an audience from New York during the first two seasons, but then moved to Hollywood where the series became a weekly filmed fixture.

Along with lifelong pals Jack Benny and Mary Livingstone and good friends Jim and Marian Jordan (aka Fibber McGee and Molly), George and Gracie were among the premier husband-and-wife comedy teams in show business. In this case, as everyone knows, Gracie had all the funny lines—virtually all of which were concocted for her by George, only proving his own genius—letting her do all the work while he stood around puffing on his cigar and reacting. Invariably, he would bring Gracie out to meet the audience at the end of each show, chat briefly with her, and then instruct her to "Say goodnight, Gracie"—to which she'd dutifully respond, "Goodnight, Gracie."

When Gracie decided to hang it up as a performer (she died in 1964), George went right on trouping until he was in his late nineties. He continued the TV show with the remaining cast for a year after Gracie's retirement, and then took his act to nightclubs. For a while, he used Carol Channing, then Connie Stevens as his foil, doing Gracie's part and reading the lines he'd written for Gracie. And he discovered Ann-Margret along the way. In 1975 he returned to movies—his first one in thirty-six years—*The Sunshine Boys,* which earned him an Academy Award. More films, TV specials, commercials, recordings, and public appearances followed, making Burns truly the Grand Old Man of Comedy. His long-standing contract to perform at the London Palladium on his 100th birthday in January 1996, however, had to be canceled because of various infirmities. George Burns died at the age of 100 years and two months.

VIDEO AVAILABILITY

Several Burns and Allen collections are available at certain outlets. One contains three approximately thirty-minute episodes: three feature two episodes each; and there are a pair of Christmas sets—one a single thirty-minute tape of their 1951 Christmas show and one containing their holiday shows from 1955 and 1956.

TRIVIA TIDBITS

- On their television show, George and Gracie lived in Suite 2216 of the St. Moritz Hotel while in New York. When they moved to the West Coast, they resided at 312 Maple Street in Beverly Hills.
- George's chum, Jack Benny, was to have had the *Sunshine Boys* role that resurrected Burns's movie career. But Benny died prior to filming. So Burns' solo career began at nearly 80. Already a show biz deity, George then went on to play God three times on film.
- George and Gracie's adopted son, Ronnie, played himself on both *The George Burns and Gracie Allen Show* and its continuation, *The George Burns Show.*
- "Love Nest," one of the handful of truly memorable theme songs from both radio and the early days of television, was George and Gracie's musical signature, which they adopted while in vaudeville. It was written in by Louis A. Hirsch and Otto Harbach for producer George M. Cohan's long-forgotten 1920 Broadway musical, *Mary,* starring Jack McGowen.

GET SMART

NBC, 1965–69; CBS, 1969–70; 138 episodes

CAST

Maxwell Smart/Agent 86	Don Adams
Agent 99	Barbara Feldon
The Chief	Edward Platt
Conrad Siegfried	Bernie Kopell
Shtarker	King Moody
Agent Larrabee	Robert Karvelas
Agent 13	Dave Ketchum
Agent 44	Victor French
Hymie the Robot	Dick Gautier
Harry Hoo	Joey Foreman
Admiral Hargrade	William Shallert

CREATORS: Mel Brooks, Buck Henry
EXECUTIVE PRODUCER: Leonard B. Stern
PRODUCERS: Daniel Melnick, Jay Sandrich
PRINCIPAL DIRECTORS: Don Richardson, Paul Bogart, Bruce Bilson, Gary Nelson, Earl Bellamy, James Komack, Richard Donner, Don Adams, Alan Rafkin, Jay Sandrich
PRINCIPAL WRITERS: Stan Burns, Mike Marmer, Gerald Gardner, Dee Caruso, Mel Brooks, Buck Henry, Arne Sultan, Marvin Worth, Pat McCormick, Leonard Stern, Chris Hayward, Allan Burns

"And . . . loving it!"

Maxwell Smart (aka Agent 86)—the bumbling but supremely confident secret agent who talked into a shoe phone—battled the heinousness of archenemy KAOS,

Keeping the world safe from KAOS spies and oversize keyholes: the dim-witted Maxwell Smart (Don Adams) and the fetching Agent 99 (Barbara Feldon) from *Get Smart*. COURTESY OF PERSONALITY PHOTOS, INC.

conferred with his beleaguered CONTROL superior in a faulty Plexiglas "cone of silence," worked with one perfect colleague who happened to be a robot, and partnered the woman known only as Agent 99, a beautiful spy who was inexplicably head over her five-inch heels in love with him. The show provided inspired, Keystone Kops lunacy and a passel of popular catchphrases ("Sorry about that, Chief," "I asked you not to tell me that," "Would you believe . . .") that entered the American lexicon of the 1960s. Concocted by comic writers Mel Brooks and Buck Henry, *Get Smart* set the standard for spy spoofs in the wake of the popularity of the Ian Fleming, John Le Carre, and Len Deighton books turned movies. Its popularity, strangely, never pushed the series into the Top Ten during its five-season, Emmy-winning run. As Maxwell Smart would have put it, the show "missed it by *that* much!"

"Would you believe . . . ?"

Max, 99, and company's weekly adventures were generally parodies of popular movies. There were "House of Max," "Ice Station Siegfried," "Witness for the Execution," "The Mess of Adrien Listenger," "The Not-So-Great Escape," and "The Treasure of C. Errol Madre," among others. Smart, a terminal clod, would find some way to look stupid seemingly every three minutes; he accidentally ate a list of enemy agents scrawled on a piece of paper hidden in his sandwich and hid the microfilm plans for a nuclear reactor in the teeth of a convict being sent up the river. Agent 99, his perfect partner, would inevitably bail him out of any tight spot.

Mention should also be made of a fellow agent, a four-footed one: Max's dog, Fang (code name Morris), a lethargic mutt who rarely followed commands and constantly fled danger. Fang was CONTROL's top canine spy and Max's intellectual equal; the two were graduated from spy school in the same class. On the other side there was sinister, heel-clicking, fiercely conceited KAOS kingpin, Siegfried, who had convinced himself that he was smarter than Smart but remained stymied and continually outsmarted by his incompetent nemesis.

Max and 99 totally frustrated KAOS with their ability to evade every trap that could be concocted, just as much as 86 frustrated the Chief with his inability to do even the simplest of tasks right. Somehow everyone muddled through, often hilariously, for five seasons.

VIDEO AVAILABILITY

Get Smart is available through Columbia House, with four half-hour episodes per cassette. Also available in certain video outlets are the TV movie *Get Smart Again!* and the theatrical Maxwell Smart feature, *The Nude Bomb.*

EMMY AWARDS

1966–67 **Don Adams,** Outstanding Continued Performance by an Actor in a Leading Role in a Comedy Series

1967–68 *Get Smart,* Outstanding Comedy Series
Don Adams, Outstanding Continued Performance by an Actor in a Leading Role in a Comedy Series
Bruce Bilson, Outstanding Directorial Achievement in Comedy ("Maxwell Smart, Private Eye" episode)

1968–69 *Get Smart,* Outstanding Comedy Series
Don Adams, Outstanding Continued Performance by an Actor in a Leading Role in a Comedy Series

TRIVIA TIDBITS

- Maxwell Smart and Agent 99 were married on the episode of November 16, 1968.
- Don Adams starred in the 1980 film *The Nude Bomb* (aka *The Return of Maxwell Smart*), which unwisely did not bring back any other original cast members.
- The only TV movie reunion was *Get Smart Again!* on ABC in February 1989, which brought together all of the living original members. (Edward Platt passed away in 1974.)
- During the 1993–94 season, Don Adams and Barbara were called back to service as Maxwell Smart and wife Agent 99 (her real name was never revealed) for a short-lived new *Get Smart* series on the Fox network, in which their klutzy son became the bumbling agent.
- Before Don Adams became Max, Mel Brooks had considered playing the part himself; then the name of Orson Bean came up (he recently portrayed crotchety Loren Bray, owner of the general store on *Dr. Quinn, Medicine Woman*); and next under consideration was Tom Poston.
- Of the 138 *Get Smart* episodes, the first, entitled "Mr. Big" and featuring Michael Dunn as an evil KAOS dwarf, was the only one filmed in black and white. It was written by Mel Brooks and Buck Henry, directed by Howard Morris, and shot in New York. (The setting of the series was then moved to Washington.)

- Among the guest stars who turned up on the series were Vincent Price, Leonard Nimoy, Martin Landau, Bob Hope, Carol Burnett, Julie Newmar, Don Rickles, Danny Thomas, Bill Dana, James Caan, Steve Allen, Milton Berle, and Broderick Crawford.
- The *Get Smart* Theme was written by Irving Szathmary, musician brother of Don Adams's longtime pal and performing partner, Bill "José Jimenez" Dana.

GILLIGAN'S ISLAND

CBS, 1964–67, 98 episodes (first 36 in black and white)

CAST

Gilligan	Bob Denver
The Skipper (Jonas Grumby)	Alan Hale Jr.
Thurston Howell III	Jim Backus
Lovey Wentworth Howell	Natalie Schafer
Ginger Grant	Tina Louise
The Professor (Roy Hinkley)	Russell Johnson
Mary Ann Summers	Dawn Wells

CREATOR/EXECUTIVE PRODUCER: Sherwood Schwartz
PRODUCERS: Jack Arnold, Robert L. Rosen
PRINCIPAL DIRECTORS: John Rich, Richard Donner, Stanley Z. Cherry, Jack Arnold, Hal Cooper, Jerry Hopper, Ida Lupino, Leslie Goodwins, Tony Leader
PRINCIPAL WRITERS: Lawrence J. Cohen, Fred Freeman, Austin Kalish, Elroy Schwartz, Sherwood Schwartz, Al Schwartz, David P. Harmon, Joanna Lee, Brad Radnitz, Gerald Gardner, Dee Caruso

A three-hour tour

Two things can be safely said about *Gilligan's Island.* For the three seasons it ran on CBS, it was one of the most critically abused programs in the history of television. "Inept," "moronic," "a new low in the networks' estimate of public intelligence," was the common consensus, and, in most TV histories, that still holds. It also was, and remains, one of the most popular programs among younger viewers and is fondly remembered by many baby boomers as an integral part of their childhood. Yes, it's

Stranded—again? The hapless survivors of the wreck of the S. S. *Minnow,* from left: Russell Johnson (the Professor), Alan Hale Jr. (the Skipper), Bob Denver (Gilligan), Dawn Wells (Mary Ann), Tina Louise (Ginger), Jim Backus (Thurston Howell III), and Natalie Schafer (Lovey Howell). COURTESY OF PERSONALITY PHOTOS, INC.

silly and often makes no logical sense. But as low comedy with an undeniable appeal to children, it *works* and survives long after many of its more highly praised contemporaries have disappeared.

Like most fantasy/gimmick sitcoms, its premise is simple. Seven people representing a cross-section of recognizable comic stereotypes board the S.S. *Minnow,* a small pleasure craft, for a three-hour tour off the coast of California. There is a storm and a shipwreck, and our hapless castaways are stuck on a remote island that gets more guest star visitors than *Fantasy Island!*

In addition to the cheery, rotund Skipper and his bumbling first mate, Gilligan, the stranded company includes:

a Marilyn Monroe-type movie star (Ginger); a bookworm professor (who can devise homemade record players and program robots, but can't build a boat!); an eccentric billionaire (Thurston Howell III); his featherbrained wife (Lovey); and an eternally peppy general store clerk from Kansas (Mary Ann). Most episodes brought the group to the brink of rescue, only to have their hopes dashed, usually by Gilligan's ineptitude or their own greed and/or stupidity.

Live-action cartoon

Children love this show, and one can see why. It's really a live-action cartoon with broadly drawn characters that date back to silent movies. The relationship between Gilligan and the Skipper harks back to classic thin man/fat man comic teams ranging from Laurel and Hardy to Abbott and Costello to Carney and Gleason. Yet, while most of the spare plots seem contrived, the actual shows are, for the most part, quite funny and cleverly executed. As for being moronic, it is interesting to note that in one episode (guest-starring Phil Silvers), there are references to *Hamlet, Carmen, Tales of Hoffman,* and *The Trojan Women!* True, they are silly references, but how many other sitcoms that appeal to children can claim the same?

VIDEO AVAILABILITY

Gilligan's Island is available from Columbia House. The first thirty-six episodes are in black and white, the remaining sixty-two in color. Each volume, running about seventy-five minutes, contains three episodes.

TRIVIA TIDBITS

- Gilligan's first name was never revealed, but producer Sherwood Schwartz and star Bob Denver decided that, if one was ever needed, it would be Willy.

- The later animated version, called *The New Adventures of Gilligan* (1974–77), had all of the original actors, except Tina Louise (who wanted nothing further to do with the show and has never had anything good to say about it) and Dawn Wells, voicing their famous characters. Another animated spin-off, *Gilligan's Planet* (1982–83), had them all back again, this time including Dawn Wells, who voiced both Ginger and Mary Ann.
- There were three reunion movies: *Rescue From Gilligan's Island* (1978), *The Castaways on Gilligan's Island* (1979), and *The Harlem Globetrotters on Gilligan's Island* (1981). Judith Baldwin played Ginger in the first two; Constance Forsland took the role in the third.
- "The Ballad of Gilligan's Island" was written by George Wyle and Sherwood Schwartz. It initially was performed by the Wellingtons. After the first season it was rerecorded by the Eligibles, and the lyrics were altered to include the characters of the Professor and Mary Ann, who were originally referred to as "the rest."
- Among the shipwrecked guests who turned up on the island and later managed to get off: Hans Conried (several times as Wrongway Feldman), Henny Backus (Jim's wife), Zsa Zsa Gabor, Phil Silvers, Mike Mazurki, Sterling Holloway, and football star Roman Gabriel.
- Bob Denver's next TV series, *Dusty's Trail,* was really *Gilligan's Island* in the Old West. Forrest Tucker was his exasperated foil in place of Alan Hale Jr.
- The role of Ginger was originally created with Jayne Mansfield in mind, but she turned the part down.
- A big-screen version of *Gilligan's Island* has been announced as "a coming attraction."

HAZEL

NBC, 1961–65; CBS, 1965–66; 154 episodes

CAST

Hazel Burke	Shirley Booth
George Baxter (1961–65)	Don DeFore
Dorothy Baxter (1961–65)	Whitney Blake
Harold Baxter	Bobby Buntrock
Steve Baxter (1965–66)	Ray Fulmer
Barbara Baxter (1965–66)	Lynn Borden
Susie Baxter (1965–66)	Julia Benjamin
Rosie Hamicker	Maudie Prickett
Harvey Griffin	Howard Smith
Deidre Baxter Thompson (1961–65)	Cathy Lewis
Harry Thompson (1961–65)	Robert P. Lieb
Harriet Johnson (1961–65)	Norma Varden
Herbert Johnson (1961–65)	Donald Foster
Miss Scott	Molly Dodd

CREATED BY: William Cowley, Peggy Chantler
EXECUTIVE PRODUCER: Harry Ackerman
PRODUCER: James Fonda
PRINCIPAL DIRECTORS: William D. Russell, Charles Barton, Hal Cooper, E. W. Swackhamer
PRINCIPAL WRITERS: William Cowley, Peggy Chantler, Robert Riley Crutcher, Ted Sherdeman, John McGreevey

Housekeeping for Mr. B

Based on the popular cartoon by Ted Key that was a regular *Saturday Evening Post* feature during the 1940s and 1950s, *Hazel* was the lovable, unflappable live-in maid who worked for—and meddled in the business affairs of—long-suffering attorney George Baxter ("Mr. B" is how she invariably referred to him) and his family. Played by Broadway star Shirley Booth, Hazel, with her broad Queens accent (though not nearly as broad as Fran Drescher's *Nanny* of the 1990s), went through her weekly misadventures while running the Baxter household for four successful seasons. Then, in a revised format, she did the same for George Baxter's younger brother Steve after George is transferred to the Middle East, meaning that actor Don DeFore decided to leave the show.

VIDEO AVAILABILITY

Two Christmas shows featuring 1960s America's favorite maid are available on a single collection at certain video outlets. Running forty-five minutes, it teams "Just 86 Shopping Minutes Left Until Christmas," in which Hazel plays Santa Claus, and "Hazel's Christmas Shopping," with her cracking a shoplifting case.

EMMY AWARDS

1961–62 **Shirley Booth,** Outstanding Continued Performance by an Actress in a Series

1962–63 **Shirley Booth,** Outstanding Continued Performance by an Actress in a Series

TRIVIA TIDBITS

- Shirley Booth, a veteran Broadway actress whose film career was limited to just five 1950s movies, won a Tony and an Oscar (for both the stage and screen versions of *Come Back, Little Sheba*) as well as two Emmys. She later starred in one other TV series, the short-lived *A Touch of Grace* (ABC, 1973), although she did other work on variety shows and dramatic programs.
- Know-it-all Hazel, Mr. B, and the Baxter family resided at 123 Marshall Road in the fictional Hydsberg, New York.

- Whitney Blake is the mother of TV star Meredith Baxter (of *Bridget Loves Bernie, Family,* and *Family Ties,* as well as loads of television movies). She also was the first defendant on *Perry Mason* in 1957, and, with husband Alan Mannings, later created the TV sitcom *One Day at a Time.*
- A young Ann Jillian became a *Hazel* regular during the show's final season, playing Millie Ballard, Steve Baxter's secretary.
- Dick Sargent, who would go on to be the second Darrin Stephens on *Bewitched,* had a recurring role on *Hazel* as the nephew of Harvey Griffin, one of George Baxter's clients.

HOGAN'S HEROES

CBS, 1965–71, 168 episodes

CAST

Col. Bob Hogan	Bob Crane
Col. Wilhelm Klink	Werner Klemperer
Sgt. Hans Schultz	John Banner
Cpl. Louis LeBeau	Robert Clary
Cpl. Peter Newkirk	Richard Dawson
Sgt. James Kinchloe (1965–70)	Ivan Dixon
Sgt. Richard Baker (1970–71)	Kenneth Washington
Sgt. Alexander Carter	Larry Hovis
Helga (1965–66)	Cynthia Lynn
Hilda (1966–70)	Sigrid Vardis
Colonel Crittenden	Bernard Fox
Marya	Nita Talbot
Major Hockstedder	Howard Caine

PRODUCER: Edward H. Feldman
PRINCIPAL DIRECTORS: Robert Butler, Irving J. Moore, Gene Reynolds, Ivan Dixon, Howard Morris
PRINCIPAL WRITERS: Laurence Marks, Gene Reynolds

The good life

"If you liked World War Two, you'll love *Hogan's Heroes!*" So went the promotional spot designed by Stan Freberg on commission from CBS, which was so appalled, it junked the whole campaign for the series that intended to prove that life in a Nazi POW camp could be fun. The popular sitcom was set in Stalag 13, where strutting, inept Colonel Klink and his bumbling, gullible Sergeant Schultz were manipulated by U.S. Air Force

One was never too sure who was running the camp on *Hogan's Heroes*—prisoner Hogan (Bob Crane, right) or his gullible nemesis, Colonel Klink (Werner Klemperer). COURTESY OF PERSONALITY PHOTOS, INC.

colonel Hogan and his fellow American, French, and British prisoners. Every week for five seasons, Hogan's men made fools of their captors by conducting spy missions for the Allies from behind the barbed wire of their compound, shuttling Allied fugitives in and out of the camp, and securing top-secret information for their superiors.

The unwitting and reluctant accomplice to most of their brazen schemes was portly Sergeant Schultz, a quivering tub of Jell-O who hid behind a gruff facade and feared being betrayed to his sputtering, slow-burning commandant and dispatched to the Russian front. Continually he professed, "I see nothing. I know nothing."

One might think that a sitcom set in a Nazi POW camp would have incited storms of protest—but there seemed to have been none. What sank the show finally was a plagiarism suit by the creators of the Broadway play (and subsequent movie) *Stalag 17,* which dealt on a much more serious level with the same concept.

VIDEO AVAILABILITY

Hogan's Heroes is available through Columbia House in a collector's edition, with four half-hour episodes on each videocassette.

EMMY AWARDS

1967–68 **Werner Klemperer,** Outstanding Performance by an Actor in a Supporting Role in a Comedy

1968–69 **Werner Klemperer,** Outstanding Continued Performance by an Actor in a Supporting Role in a Series

TRIVIA TIDBITS

- Never previously aired, the pilot episode of *Hogan's Heroes* finally saw the light on Nick at Nite's TV Land channel in spring 1996 in a special all-night marathon of first episodes of classic series. The pilot, which had Leonid Kinskey among the regular cast members as a Russian prisoner, was a direct rip-off of *Stalag 17,* which is probably why it was never aired as part of the series.
- Werner Klemperer, the balding, monocled Klink, is the son of noted symphony conductor Otto Klemperer and is himself a famed musician. Although a Jew from Austria, he (like Otto Preminger in *Stalag 17*) specialized in playing Nazis, both comic and serious, and was previously known for his portrayal of Adolf Eichmann in *Operation Eichmann,* the 1961 movie about the Nazi leader.

- Diminutive Robert Clary was a Holocaust survivor who became a musical comedy performer after the war in France and was "discovered" on Broadway in *New Faces of 1952* with his signature song, "I'm in Love With Miss Logan." Clary went on to join the cast of the long-running afternoon soap, *Days of Our Lives.* He was also entertainer Eddie Cantor's son-in-law.
- John Banner, like Werner Klemperer, was an Austrian Jew who fled the Nazis and was permanently typed by his *Hogan's Heroes* character. He jumped into another CBS series, *The Chicago Teddy Bears,* virtually the day after hanging up his camp uniform in 1971.
- Ivan Dixon has become a respected actor and stage, screen, and television director.
- Richard Dawson went on to host the TV game show *Family Feud* and played Arnold Schwarzenegger's unctuous nemesis in the film *The Running Man* (1987).
- Bob Crane, who earlier was a regular on *The Donna Reed Show,* subsequently starred in the short-lived *The Bob Crane Show.* He was bludgeoned to death under bizarre circumstances in 1978. The case is still unsolved.

THE HONEYMOONERS

CBS, 1955–56, 39 episodes
(the 13 "Lost" Episodes: 1956–57)

CAST

Ralph Kramden	Jackie Gleason
Ed Norton	Art Carney
Alice Kramden	Audrey Meadows
Trixie Norton	Joyce Randolph

CREATORS: Joe Bigelow, Harry Crane, Jackie Gleason
EXECUTIVE PRODUCER: Jack Philbin
PRODUCER: Jack Hurdle
DIRECTOR: Frank Satenstein
WRITERS: Marvin Marx & Walter Stone, A.J. Russell & Herbert Finn, Leonard Stern & Sydney Zelinka

The Great One and pals

The honeymoon is never over between the self-styled Great One and his adoring audiences. It officially began in a TV sketch on October 5, 1951 and was in full bloom between 1955 and 1957 as it chronicled the wedded (though somewhat loud) bliss between Ralph Kramden and his long-suffering Alice and their friendship with the neighbors in the upstairs flat, Ed and Trixie Norton. Usually set in the highly charged universe of the Kramden's walk-up at 328 Chauncey Street in Brooklyn, *The Honeymooners* might well be the most beloved sitcom in television history. The simplicity of the show's formula, as has been pointed out by assorted observers, is exceeded only by its execution—usually in a single take with flubs

After over four decades of syndication, *The Honeymooners* continues to make repeat viewers laugh at lines known by heart. From left, three brilliant comic performers: Jackie Gleason (Ralph), Art Carney (Norton), and Audrey Meadows (Alice). COURTESY OF PERSONALITY PHOTOS, INC.

left in. Virtually every show is concerned either with Ralph's comically frustrating attempts to better his situation or equally doomed ones to assert authority over Alice. "One of these days, Alice . . . one of these days," he invariably bellows in an empty threat, "Pow! Right in the kisser!" Of course, there's the perennial closing, in which Ralph and Alice fall into each other's arms after she forgives him for his pig-headed ways and he admits to her, "Baby, you're the greatest!"

"Hey there, Ralphie boy!"

Along with the sarcastic bickering with Alice, there is the other indestructible relationship: blustering Ralph's Laurel-and-Hardy rapport with Norton, the always accommodating sewer worker pal (nearly always dressed in his casual open vest, T-shirt, and porkpie hat). Their relationship is as much of a center in *The Honeymooners* as Ralph's marriage to Alice. Pals to the end, lodge brothers at the International Order of Loyal Raccoons, they had their own honeymoon with one dreaming the big dream and the other backing him up, no matter how outrageous his schemes became. Later, *The Flintstones* would give an almost identical, unabashed, Fred-and-Barney cartoon twist to their fellowship.

The timeless themes of *The Honeymooners,* enacted by its tight-knit cast, have kept the classic series fresh, despite the four decades that have elapsed since they first convulsed TV audiences. Certain themes recur throughout, as Donna McCrohan chronicled in *The Honeymooners Companion* and *The Honeymooners Lost Episodes.* Bombastic Ralph Kramden, the dreamer, devises ill-fated, harebrained get-rich-quick schemes in "Better Living Through TV," "Ralph Kramden, Inc.," and "A Dog's Life." The bonds of love and marriage are tested time after time in episodes such as "A Woman's Work Is Never Done," "'Twas the Night Before Christmas," and "A Matter of Record." And in "The $99,000 Answer," "A Man's Pride," and "Young Man With a Horn," it is Ralph, the Everyman, flailing against the world. And then there are themes involving Ralph's deceptions, jealousies, and all-around bad temper.

When Gleason produced this series of filmed *Honeymooners* episodes—the "Classic 39"—in the mid-1950s, he used the new technology of the Electronicam, which allowed production personnel to follow the action from monitors during rehearsals and actual filming. With this process, each episode was directed and shot as if live, much as later sitcoms (like *All in the Family*) were taped before an audience. Notorious for keeping rehearsal time to a minimum, Gleason shot these without retakes and refreshingly marked by ad-libs and flubs.

VIDEO AVAILABILITY

All *Honeymooners* episodes from 1955 onward are available in various combinations (two to a cassette) at certain video outlets. There are thirty-nine individual volumes as well as a special boxed set that includes Vols. 29–39 plus *The Honeymooners: History of the Lost Episodes.*

EMMY AWARD

1955–56 **Art Carney,** Best Supporting Actor in a Regular Series

TRIVIA TIDBITS

- *The Honeymooners* began life in late 1951 in periodic sketches on *Cavalcade of Stars,* which Jackie Gleason headlined on the long-defunct DuMont Network. Pert Kelton was the initial Alice on the DuMont show and with the Gleason troupe that toured theaters during the summer of 1952.
- The "Lost" Episodes, long out of syndication, were actually sketches of varying lengths (10–37 minutes) on *The Jackie Gleason Show,* which began in September 1956.
- Four hour-long *Honeymooners* reunion specials were broadcast on ABC between February 1976 and December 1978.
- *The Honeymooners* theme song, "You're My Greatest Love," was written by Gleason.
- Art Carney also won Supporting Actor Emmys as Jackie Gleason's second banana in 1953 and 1954, and Individual Achievement awards in 1966–67 and 1967–68. Audrey Meadows won a Supporting Actress Emmy in 1954.

- *Honeymooners* musical specials in the early 1970s featured Sheila MacRae as Alice and Jane Kean as Trixie.
- Gleason and Carney also acted together in 1953 in the *Studio One* drama, "The Laugh Maker" and later worked together for one last time in the 1985 TV movie, *Izzie and Moe.*

I DREAM OF JEANNIE

NBC, 1965–70, 139 episodes (first 39 in black and white)

CAST

Jeannie	Barbara Eden
Captain/Major Tony Nelson	Larry Hagman
Roger Healey	Bill Daily
Dr. Alfred Bellows	Hayden Rorke
General Peterson	Barton MacLane
Amanda Bellows	Emmaline Henry

CREATOR/EXECUTIVE PRODUCER: Sidney Sheldon
PRODUCER: Claudio Guzman
PRINCIPAL DIRECTORS: Gene Nelson, Claudio Guzman, Hal Cooper, E. W. Swackhamer, Alan Rafkin, Michael Ansara
PRINCIPAL WRITERS: Sidney Sheldon, James Henerson, Dick Bensfield, Tom Waldman, Frank Waldman, Peggy Chantler

Daughter of Bewitched?

A handsome young man lives with a beautiful blond who has magic powers. Sound familiar? When it premiered, *I Dream of Jeannie* was dismissed by most critics as a thinly disguised, inferior clone of the previous season's hit sitcom, *Bewitched.* No one expected the show to run more than a season or two, and it wouldn't have, if those naysayers had been right. But comely *Jeannie* fooled them, blinking its way into a five-year initial run and a perpetual afterlife in syndication. It is probably every bit as famous as its nose-twitching forerunner and, if not quite as good by critical standards, is certainly funny

Jeannie (Barbara Eden) spoon-feeds her master (and future husband) Major Tony Nelson (Larry Hagman). The debate over who is more powerful, Jeannie or Samantha from *Bewitched*, continues unabated. COURTESY OF PERSONALITY PHOTOS, INC.

enough in its own right to merit a warm place in any sitcom lover's heart.

Aside from the initial premise of having a female character with magical powers, the two shows actually don't have much in common. In *Jeannie*, astronaut Tony Nelson finds a bottle on a deserted island, containing a lovely young woman in harem pants who proclaims him her master. He agrees to let her "serve" him with her magic powers and takes her and the bottle back to Florida with him. Over the next five years, ever-sunny Jeannie desperately tries to convince Captain (later Major) Nelson to see her as something more than a genie-in-waiting, while trying to avoid discovery by his exasperated boss. She uses her magical powers to thwart her master's love life and keep him indebted to her. In *Bewitched,* Darrin constantly pressures his witch wife, Samantha, not to use her powers, but Tony Nelson's delighted when Jeannie folds her arms and magically blinks his house clean. It's only when Jeannie refuses to submit to his will that his complaints begin.

An out-of-the-bottle charmer

During its fifth and final season, Jeannie finally got to marry her astronaut in a highly promoted wedding. It was both the series climax and its death knell: The sexual tension that kept the series interesting was spent. But, the four and a half seasons of magical courtship that preceded it are more than enough to keep *Jeannie* a perennial charmer on video.

Although it never became a Top Ten ratings hit, *I Dream of Jeannie* did have a loyal, large audience. Yet it was a headache to the NBC censors, who were constantly concerned about the show's suggestive premise. That's why early episodes often show Jeannie disappearing into her bottle near the end, implying that her bed was definitely behind brass, so to speak. Then there was the case of Barbara Eden's navel. As most TV fans know, Jeannie's belly button is never seen, even though she wears a midriff-exposing outfit. One can also notice a preponderance of camouflaging veils during the first two seasons, but, as the show progressed, the censors relaxed to the point of letting Jeannie drop a veil or two, à la Salome. However, the offensive navel remained hidden until a couple of TV movie reunions (sans Larry Hagman, who was "away" orbiting Earth), years later.

VIDEO AVAILABILITY

I Dream of Jeannie is available through Columbia House and in certain rental outlets. There are currently twenty-two volumes in release, each running approximately fifty minutes and containing two episodes.

TRIVIA TIDBITS

- Jeannie was born on April 1, 64 B.C. in Baghdad. She was turned into a genie when she refused to marry evil genie Blue Djinn (played by Barbara Eden's then-husband, Michael Ansara, who also directed a number of the episodes).
- Tony Nelson lives at 1020 Palm Drive in Cocoa Beach, Florida. Other addresses given during the show's run are 1137 Oak Grove Street and 811 Pine Street, although the house always remained the same.
- During the course of the show, Barbara Eden played her character's own sister, Jeannie II, and her mother, unnamed. Her dog was named Djinn Djinn.
- The famous "I Dream of Jeannie Theme," written by Hugo Montenegro, Buddy Kaye, and Richard Weiss, premiered in the second season. The first, forgettable theme song was written by Weiss.
- Series creator Sidney Sheldon later became a best-selling novelist *(The Other Side of Midnight).*
- Barbara Eden ironically had starred opposite Tony Randall in the 1964 big-screen comedy *The Brass Bottle,* which also dealt with a genie in a bottle. However, the genie was not a shapely girl but a chubby Burl Ives.
- Larry Hagman and Barbara Eden later worked together in the TV movie drama *A Howling in the Woods* (1971). During the 1990–91 season of the series *Dallas,* Eden signed on for several episodes as wealthy, manipulative LeeAnn De La Vega, who reenters the life of nasty J. R. Ewing (Hagman), years after he jilted her in college, and is determined to buy Ewing Oil from under him.
- Larry Hagman made his directorial debut with one episode of *Jeannie:* "The Birds and the Bees Bit."
- Among the *Jeannie* guests over the years were Milton Berle, Bob Denver (as a klutzy genie wannabe who

can't get the magical powers thing straight), Farrah Fawcett (twice), and *Laugh-In* stars Judy Carne, Arte Johnson, Gary Owens, and producer George Schlatter. In one of the classic shows, guest star Sammy Davis Jr. finds himself being duplicated by Jeannie to help Tony impress General Peterson.

- There were two reunion movies, in which Eden at last exposed her navel. First came the 1985 *I Dream of Jeannie—15 Years Later,* with Bill Daily and Hayden Rorke reprising their roles and Wayne Rogers coming in to play Tony Nelson. (Hagman had gone on to become J. R. Ewing and was not available.) Then, six years after that, came *I Still Dream of Jeannie,* with Daily (now a colonel) but not Rorke (who had passed away). Astronaut Larry Hagman was not around (he was on an "extended secret mission"), but Ken Kercheval was to become Jeannie's temporary master for convoluted reasons.

I LOVE LUCY

CBS, 1951–57, 179 episodes

THE LUCY-DESI COMEDY HOUR

CBS, 1957–60, 13 episodes

CAST

Lucy Ricardo	Lucille Ball
Ricky Ricardo	Desi Arnaz
Ethel Mertz	Vivian Vance
Fred Mertz	William Frawley

PRODUCERS: Desi Arnaz, Jess Oppenheimer
PRINCIPAL DIRECTORS: Marc Daniels, William Asher, James V. Kerns
PRINCIPAL WRITERS: Jess Oppenheimer, Madelyn Pugh, Bob Carroll Jr., Bob Schiller, Bob Weiskopf

Who doesn't love Lucy?

Maybe there are some misguided souls in the world who don't love Lucy, or, perish the thought, don't *like* her, but it's impossible that there are many people who don't know her. Since the show first hit the small screen on October 15, 1951, it has never really left. For forty-five

When the Ricardos and the Mertzes went to California, autograph hound Lucy managed to sneak up on a host of major Hollywood stars. In this memorable episode, William Holden was her victim. COURTESY OF PERSONALITY PHOTOS, INC.

years, through countless reruns all over the world, millions of viewers have laughed at the antics of New York housewife Lucy Ricardo, her Cuban bandleader husband, Ricky, and their best friends and landlords, Fred and Ethel Mertz. They have watched Lucy in Japanese, Spanish, Italian, French, etc. They have picketed stations that have dared pull the redheaded comedienne off the air. Baby boomers have grown up with Lucy, watching her in the morning when they were children, and now revisiting her through the cable network Nick at Nite as adults.

Lucy lovers get into furious debates over which is the *very* best episode. Is it Lucy and Ethel in the chocolate factory? Lucy in the wine vat? Lucy with Harpo Marx as mirror images? What they (and we) all can agree on is one thing: *I Love Lucy* has become an inescapable, intrinsic part of American culture. It virtually created the situation comedy, as we know it; it reflected (and still reflects) on basic conflicts involving marriage and friendship; and it shows no signs of ever disappearing. But, most of all—it's sidesplittingly funny four decades later, too!

They wouldn't believe it

In 1950 Lucille Ball was a movie star who never quite made it to the top rung and who was currently performing in a weekly CBS radio comedy series entitled *My Favorite Husband* opposite Richard Denning. Married for nearly ten years to touring Cuban bandleader Desi Arnaz, Lucy was tired of the constant periods of separation caused by their conflicting schedules, which made raising a family virtually impossible. When CBS expressed interest in turning *Husband* into a television series, Lucy agreed, but on one condition: that Desi would become her new costar. At first the network and potential advertisers balked, claiming that American audiences would not believe that she was married to Desi. Lucy's famous response was, "What do you mean nobody'll believe it? We *are* married!"

After Lucy and Desi toured the country in a vaudeville act designed to convince the network that they had middle-American appeal, the powers that be relented long enough to let a pilot be filmed.

Meanwhile, Desi was making some important business decisions that would affect not only the show but all of television. He devised a system of filming the show in front of a live audience using three cameras simultaneously, thus winding up with a product that could be rerun over and over. Most sitcoms in the ensuing four decades have used the same system. The technique was more expensive than traditional methods, so, in order to make up the difference, the stars agreed to cut their salary by $1,000 per week in exchange for outright ownership of the show. Shortsighted CBS agreed. Seven years later,

Lucy and friend do a fancy dance in a wine vat in one of the funniest scenes in television history. COURTESY OF PERSONALITY PHOTOS, INC.

that concession would cost the network over $5 million when they bought back the now blockbuster show.

Finally, after all of the haggling and foot-dragging, *I Love Lucy,* with its supporting cast of film veteran William Frawley and stage actress Vivian Vance, was ready for its premiere broadcast. Getting excellent reviews, it scored in the Top Ten its first time out and would stay there for most of its six-year run.

Sublime slapstick, delicious discord

The formula or basic "situation" of *Lucy* is a deceptively simple one. Lucy Ricardo is a happily married Manhattan housewife, or would be, if her harebrained schemes didn't constantly get her into trouble. Whether about Lucy's trying to get a job in show business or simply about her attempts to possess a new hat, each episode focuses on something Lucy wants but can't have—at least not until she figures out a crazy way to get it.

The initial obstacle is usually her husband, Ricky. He won't give her the money ("We canafordit!") or won't let her "get into the act," so to speak. Before the first commercial, Lucy gets her brilliant idea and usually enlists the aid of best friend, Ethel, to pull it off. By the second commercial, Lucy's scheming has backfired to such an extent that *another* scheme is needed to set *that* right. The upshot is that everything goes horribly, hilariously wrong and is "fixed" only when Ricky discovers the schemes and either "teaches Lucy a lesson" or capitulates or both.

The strength of the show's structure is that it provides Lucy and her writers room to constantly top themselves with more elaborate schemes and brilliantly timed slapstick routines, such as the aforementioned candy factory sequence. Each of these broadly comic routines has an inner logic. They seem impossible, yet, they *could* happen. For example, take Lucy's struggles with an enormous errant headdress during one of the Hollywood episodes. Her every descent down the staircase presents an increasingly outrageous variation of the same routine, until we are quite convinced that it's the prop that's controlling the performer and not the other way around, when, of course, quite the opposite is true.

The relationships among the four characters have a similar consistency. Lucy will always talk Ethel into helping her. Their friendship and constant bickering is one of the joys of the series, a woman-to-woman relationship that has spawned countless variations (Mary and Rhoda of *The Mary Tyler Moore Show, Laverne & Shirley, The Golden Girls, Cybill,* Patsy and Edina of *Absolutely Fabulous,* etc.). Just as Ralph Kramden and Ed Norton of *The*

Honeymooners have a love-hate relationship, so do Lucy and Ethel.

Yet their sisterly rivalry is secondary to the show's main concern: marital relations. Rooted in the customs of the 1950s, Lucy Ricardo is the epitome of the frustrated housewife who refuses to just mind the house and play bridge. That she'll never completely win is a given. But, thankfully, she'll never give up trying, either.

I Love Lucy was remarkably successful at keeping its high quality throughout its run. Luck had something to do with it, at least when it came to the phenomenon of Lucy's real-life/on-screen pregnancy. Until Lucy Ricardo, having a baby was something that television was not prepared to deal with. Lucy and Desi's shrewd decision to incorporate their own child into their fictional counterparts' lives cemented the close relationship not only between themselves and their characters but between the characters and their audience. The nation felt as if their best friends were having a baby, and 92 percent of the television audience tuned in on January 19, 1953 to watch. That same night, Lucille Ball had her own baby by caesarean section, as illusion and reality came together in one bold stroke.

By 1957, Lucille Ball and Desi Arnaz had decided that *I Love Lucy* was taking up too much of their energy and hurting their marriage. In an effort to stay together, they decided to reduce their workload to monthly hour-long specials, known as *The Lucy-Desi Comedy Hour.* By its final airdate, Lucy had already filed for divorce.

The thirteen hour-long *Lucy-Desi Comedy Hour* episodes vary in quality, but the best of them unite Lucy with name guests from TV and the screen capable of holding their own with the sitcom diva. Our picks of the best are:

1. "THE CELEBRITY NEXT DOOR"

Lucy tries to get theater star/neighbor Tallulah Bankhead to appear in a PTA show. In a role written for Bette Davis, flamboyant Tallulah's throaty insults and withering stares make for a high-camp classic.

2. "LUCY MAKES ROOM FOR DANNY"

The Ricardos are sorry they rented their home to the Danny Williams family (from Danny Thomas's hit sitcom, *Make Room for Daddy*), forcing them to live with the Mertzes. This show has a terrific script that utilizes all three couples and the children to maximum advantage.

3. "MILTON BERLE HIDES OUT AT THE RICARDOS"

The king and queen of TV comedy go at it with gusto in this clever show about mistaken identity that gives Uncle Miltie a chance to perform in drag and both stars the opportunity to do some memorable physical comedy while dangling from a building together!

4. "LUCY TAKES A CRUISE TO HAVANA"

Hollywood gossip columnist Hedda Hopper gets Lucy to relate how she and Ricky met. Flash back twenty years: Lucy, as a young New York stenographer, takes a Havana cruise with pal Ann Sothern (as Susie MacNamara, her *Private Secretary* character) and aboard ship meets newlyweds Fred (with hair!) and Ethel Mertz, "his charming child bride of 1934." Also on board is singer Rudy Vallee. At dockside, Lucy and Susie meet a couple of locals, Ricky Ricardo and Carlos Garcia (played by Cesar Romero), who run a taxi service. Lucy and Ricky (who also performs at a local nightclub) quickly hit it off, and she pesters Rudy Vallee into giving Ricky a job with his band. The two couples get involved in a series of comic brawls and Lucy even manages to get drunk at one point. The episode is significant for the number of name guest stars who are woven into the plot.

5. "LUCY GOES TO ALASKA"

After she and the Mertzes accompany Ricky to Nome,

where his band is scheduled to appear on *The Red Skelton Show,* Lucy finds herself stuck in the middle of the Alaskan wilderness with television's other great redhead of the era (with whom Lucy had costarred in several 1940s films) and a bunch of Eskimos. The two find that their only way back to civilization is to fly a plane by themselves.

More than half of the episodes in this series, spread over three TV seasons, were directed by Desi Arnaz. Other guest stars who were featured: Fred MacMurray and wife June Haver; Betty Grable and husband Harry James; Ernie Kovacs and Edie Adams; Ida Lupino and husband Howard Duff; and Fernando Lamas, Maurice Chevalier, Paul Douglas, and Bob Cummings.

Columnists of the time speculated that the Arnazes' real-life breakup would forever ruin the illusion of Ricardo nuptial bliss, and that *I Love Lucy*'s rerun life would be hurt accordingly. On the contrary, the make-believe world of *Lucy* became even more precious when its flesh-and-blood counterpart had ceased to exist.

Regardless of their portrayers' real-life troubles, the magic of Lucy and Ricky continued throughout the 1960s and lives on today. By watching the restored, uncut episodes on videocassette, one can relish cherished routines for the umpteenth time. One can chortle with pleasure as Ethel tries yet again to contact a ghost ("Ethel to Tillie . . . Ethel to Tillie . . . Come in, Tillie!"). One can marvel at the technical mastery of Lucy getting high on health tonic. And, most importantly, one can whisper a prayer of thanks to Desi Arnaz and those three cameras for preserving a legacy of laughter that will continue well into the next century.

VIDEO AVAILABILITY

Episodes of *I Love Lucy* are available in most rental outlets from CBS Home Video. The Hollywood episodes are available in two gift packages of three cassettes each.

Father and child or man and wife? Ricky once again berates Lucy for one of her harebrained schemes. COURTESY OF PERSONALITY PHOTOS, INC.

Columbia House offers a "Collector's Edition," currently up to twenty-four volumes, with each tape containing three half-hour episodes.

EMMY AWARDS

1952 **Best Situation Comedy**
Lucille Ball, Best Comedienne
1953 **Best Situation Comedy**
Vivian Vance, Best Series Supporting Actress
1955 **Lucille Ball,** Best Actress in a Continuing Performance

TRIVIA TIDBITS

- Lucille Ball's original choices for the parts of Fred and

Another classic scene from *I Love Lucy:* Ethel (Vivian Vance) communicates with a spirit named Tillie, while Lucy, Jay Novello, and Ricky attempt to concentrate. COURTESY OF PERSONALITY PHOTOS, INC.

Ethel Mertz were Gale Gordon (who would later play Mr. Mooney on *The Lucy Show*) and Bea Benadaret (who later starred in *Petticoat Junction*). Both were committed to other series at the time.

- The Ricardos and the Mertzes lived at 623 East 68th Street, which would put Fred and Ethel's building somewhere in the middle of the East River!
- Lucy's mother, Mrs. MacGillicuddy, was played by Kathryn Card. Mrs. Trumbull was played by Elizabeth Patterson.
- The *I Love Lucy* theme music is by Eliot Daniel. The lyrics (which were heard in "Lucy's Last Birthday," #60) are by Harold Adamson. Desi's recording of the song was a pop chart hit in 1953, with "There's a Brand New Baby at Our House" on the "B" side.
- "Little Ricky" was played at various times by twins Richard Lee and Ronald Lee Simmons, twins Michael and Joseph Mayer, and Keith Thibodeaux (who changed his name to Ricky Keith).

- Vivian Vance's contract for the show included a "fat clause" which stated that she must be twenty pounds heavier than Lucille Ball during shooting periods, to make her look older than Lucy. She actually was a year younger.
- A complete list of celebrity guest stars who appeared on *I Love Lucy* are: Tennessee Ernie Ford (three times), golf pro Jimmy Demaret, William Holden, Eve Arden, Richard Crenna, fashion designer Don Loper, Sheila MacRae, Hedda Hopper, Cornel Wilde, Rock Hudson, Van Johnson, Harpo Marx, Richard Widmark, John Wayne, Charles Boyer, Bob Hope, Orson Welles, George "Superman" Reeves, and the wives of Holden, Dean Martin, Van Heflin, Forrest Tucker, Alan Ladd, and Richard Carlson.
- In Episode #119, "Don Juan Is Shelved," MGM studio head Dore Schary is played by Philip Ober, Vivian Vance's husband at the time. Schary was supposed to play himself as a stunt, but changed his mind at the last minute.

I MARRIED JOAN

NBC, 1952–55, 98 episodes

CAST

Joan Stevens	Joan Davis
Judge Bradley Stevens	Jim Backus
Minerva Parker	Hope Emerson
Beverly Grossman	Beverly Wills
Mabel	Geraldine Carr
Charlie	Hal Smith
Janet Tobin	Sheila Bromley
Kerwin Tobin	Dan Tobin
Mildred Webster	Sandra Gould

PRODUCERS: P.J. Wolfson, Dick Mack, Al Simon
DIRECTORS: Hal Walker, Marc Daniels, Ezra Stone, John Rich
WRITERS: Phil Sharp, Sherwood Schwartz, Jesse Goldstein, Hugh Wedlock, Howard Snyder, Frank Tarloff, Ben Starr, Arthur Stander

Tell it to the judge

Veteran (though long neglected) comedienne Joan Davis was one of the most popular performers in films and on radio in the 1930s and 1940s. She came to television in *I Married Joan* to play—in the tradition of Lucille Ball and Gracie Allen—a scatterbrained housewife named Joan Stevens, full of dreams and schemes. The show also had the put-upon straight-man husband, à la Desi Arnaz and George Burns, in this case a domestic relations court judge played by Jim Backus. Around this time Backus was making myopic Mr. Magoo a national rage, although it would be several years before he would be stranded as Thurston Howell III on *Gilligan's Island.* Joan Stevens tried her best to be a good housewife and to maneuver the household funds to balance the budget, but she invariably messed up. Of course, she could not resist shopping for a bargain (she became known to salespeople as "one of those yo-yo dames"). To long-suffering husband Judge Bradley Stevens she was "lover." He'd open each show from the bench where he'd just heard a domestic relations case, and then start explaining how he dealt with a similar situation with his own wacky wife. The show would fade in to the harried home front at 345 Laurel Drive—and Joan would begin her weekly misadventure.

VIDEO AVAILABILITY

Five volumes of *I Married Joan* episodes are available at certain video outlets. Each runs about seventy-five minutes and contains three shows from the wacky series, including the pilot episode. Also available is a package containing all five volumes as a complete set.

TRIVIA TIDBITS

- *I Married Joan* was Joan Davis's only TV series.
- Beverly Wills, who played Joan's look-alike sister on the show, was actually her real-life daughter.
- The theme song for *I Married Joan* was performed by the prestigious Roger Wagner Chorale.
- Joan Davis reportedly was the comedienne whom Fanny Brice once said she wanted to play her in the movies.

THE JACK BENNY SHOW

CBS, 1950–64, 304 episodes; NBC, 1964–65, 39 episodes

CAST

Himself	Jack Benny
Herself	Mary Livingstone
Rochester	Eddie Anderson
Himself	Don Wilson
Himself	Dennis Day
Lois Wilson	Lois Corbett
Harlow Wilson	Dale White
Professor LeBlanc (and other roles)	Mel Blanc
Miss Gordon	Maudie Prickett
Miss Adrian	Iris Adrian
Himself	Fred DeCordova
Mr. Kitzel	Artie Auerbach
Yes Man	Frank Nelson

EXECUTIVE PRODUCER: Irving Fein
PRODUCERS: Hilliard Marks, Ralph Levy, Norman Abbott, Fred DeCordova
DIRECTORS: Don Weis, Fred DeCordova, Seymour Burns, Ralph Levy, Norman Abbott, Bud Yorkin
WRITERS: Al Gordon, Hal Goldman, George Balzer, Sam Perrin, Milt Josefsberg, John Thackaberry

Jack—of all trades

Jack Benny, one of the most beloved comedians in all of show business, starred as his own penny-pinching, self-deprecating, thirty-nine-year-old self with the family he had built up on radio in the 1930s and 1940s—and developed on television one of the longest-running sitcoms.

The incomparable Jack Benny, with his valet/chauffeur Rochester (Eddie Anderson). Benny could squeeze a ten-minute laugh from an audience with an effortless stare. COURTESY OF PERSONALITY PHOTOS, INC.

The idol of generations of comics and assorted funnymen, Benny set the standard for greatness. His television show transcended the sitcom label, mixing in stand-up routines, variety, sketches of varying lengths, and appearances from a host of entertainment greats, all of whom appeared genuinely thrilled to be working with Benny. Among those turning up were Humphrey Bogart, Ernie Kovacs, Kirk Douglas, George Burns, and Harry S. Truman! Even the likes of Jimmy Stewart agreed to be semi-regulars on the show. (Stewart and wife, Gloria—in real-life close friends of Jack and Mary Livingstone Benny—played Jack's put-upon neighbors who reluctantly got involved in his side-splitting misadventures.)

Many of Benny's wonderfully crafted radio routines were transferred to his TV show: occasional trips to his underground money vault, protected by a crocodile-filled moat and ear-piercing alarms; violin lessons with exasperated Professor LeBlanc (Mel Blanc); the famous encounter with a holdup man and Jack's hilariously agonizing decision about the mugger's demand, "Your money or your life!"; a spin with Rochester in his beloved but decrepit Maxwell auto; a memorable violin duet with Gisele McKenzie; the uproarious airport exchange with a Mexican traveler named Cy (Mel Blanc again); his run-ins with stuffy floorwalkers, surly ticket agents, smug maitre d's, condescending florists, etc., regularly played by Frank Nelson, who'd confront Jack with an ever identifiable "Yes!"; and so many more. How well these made the transition from aural to visual was a tribute not only to Benny but also to his longtime writers.

Mary Livingstone remained the eternal "girlfriend" of Jack, who fancied himself a bon vivant; tenor Dennis Day, his bright-eyed sycophant; Don Wilson, his long-suffering announcer; Rochester, his insouciant valet/chauffeur; and incredibly versatile Mel Blanc as just about everyone else (including the voice of Jack's smart-mouthed parrot and the sickly motor of Jack's Maxwell).

With his masterful timing, his jaunty gait, his identifiable stance (one arm across his chest, the other perpendicular with his elbow resting on that arm and his cupping his jaw and cheek), his Bennyisms like "Well!" and "Now cut that out!" he became in inspiration for generations of comics—Johnny Carson and Rich Little, in particular, whose impersonations of him mirrored the original.

Benny and his company of regulars (minus Phil Harris, a radio pal who became busy with his own show with his wife, Alice Faye) were truly members of everyone's family.

VIDEO AVAILABILITY

Fifteen collections from *The Jack Benny Show* and other Benny specials are available at certain outlets. Most run about sixty minutes and contain two complete Benny shows.

EMMY AWARDS

1957 **Jack Benny,** Best Continuing Performance (Male) in a Series by a Comedian, Singer, Host, MC, Announcer, Narrator, Panelist, or Any Person Who Essentially Plays Himself

Jack Benny, Trustees' Award, for his significant contributions to the television industry as a showman.

1958–59 *The Jack Benny Show,* Best Comedy Series

Jack Benny, Best Actor in a Leading Role (Continuing Character) in a Dramatic Series

Sam Perrin, George Balzer, Hal Goldman, Al Gordon, Best Writing of a Single Program of a Comedy Series

1959–60 **Ralph Levy and Bud Yorkin,** Outstanding Directorial Achievement in Comedy

Sam Perrin, George Balzer, Hal Goldman, Al Gordon, Outstanding Writing Achievement in Comedy

1960–61 *The Jack Benny Show,* Outstanding Program Achievement in the Field of Humor

TRIVIA TIDBITS

- Benny, who conquered every aspect of show business in his extraordinary career, made his initial foray into TV in 1950 with a series of specials before gradually increasing his appearances to a weekly sitcom format.
- As Benny's longtime valet from the mid-1930s onward, Eddie "Rochester" Anderson was in effect the first black star on radio and worked with his "boss" for more than thirty years. Robert Guillaume's later character Benson on *Soap* (see separate entry) and on the subsequent *Benson* series was a tribute to Rochester.
- In addition to being the voice of Bugs Bunny and so many other screen cartoon characters, Mel Blanc, with his assorted characters and voices, established a reputation on Benny's shows as, in baseball parlance,

an indispensable utility player—whether playing music teachers, train conductors, or Mexican tourists, or being the voices of parrots, cars, or railroad dispatchers announcing: "Train leaving on track five for Anaheim, Azusa, and Cucamunga" (the last hilariously drawn out halfway through the word—sometimes as long as five minutes). His other famous television roles after *The Jack Benny Show* include the voice of Barney Rubble in *The Flintstones* (see separate entry) and of the robot Twiki in *Buck Rogers in the 25th Century* (see separate entry).

◆ For Benny's contribution to American culture, on his death on the day after Christmas 1974, *Variety* honored him with one of the longest, most comprehensive obituaries it had ever published—dividing it among the various sections in the paper: vaudeville, stage, radio, screen, and television.

LOVE THAT BOB
(THE BOB CUMMINGS SHOW)

NBC, Jan.–Sept. 1955; CBS, Sept. 1955–Sept. 1957; NBC, Sept. 1957–July 1959; 173 episodes

CAST

Bob Collins	Bob Cummings
Margaret MacDonald	Rosemary DeCamp
Charmaine "Shultzy" Shultz	Ann B. Davis
Chuck MacDonald	Dwayne Hickman
Pamela Livingston	Nancy Kulp
Paul Fonda	Lyle Talbot
Collette DuBois	Lisa Gaye
Harvey Helm	King Donovan
Francine Williams	Diane Jurgens
Ruth Helm	Mary Lawrence
Mary Beth Hall	Gloria Marshall
Shirley Swanson	Joi Lansing
Olive Sturgess	Carol Henning

CREATORS/EXECUTIVE PRODUCERS: Al Simon, Paul Henning
PRODUCER: Bob Mosher

Watch the birdie!

Perennially clean-cut Bob Cummings (the George Hamilton of his day) starred in this popular comedy following the weekly romantic—often leaning toward the smutty—misadventures of a suave, swinging bachelor/photographer living in Hollywood with his widowed sister and his envious teenage nephew. Always there to oversee his private model-filled life was his faithful, if smart-mouthed, assistant (played by Ann B. Davis), who had a secret crush on her playboy boss but couldn't compete with the shapely competition. His sister never quite understood his social life, and his nephew was forever around taking mental notes on skirt-chasing from "the master." Occasionally, wolf Bob would fly home to Joplin, Missouri (Cummings's real hometown) to play his own grandfather, who also had an eye for the ladies.

Dwayne Hickman later wrote in his 1993 memoirs, *Forever Dobie,* that he could not have had a better teacher than Bob Cummings, who took him under his wing and explained the intricacies of light comedy. (See *My Hero* for information on Cummings's earlier series.)

VIDEO AVAILABILITY

Four collections of *Love That Bob* are available at certain video outlets. Each runs about fifty minutes and contains two episodes.

EMMY AWARDS

1957–58 **Ann B. Davis,** Best Continuing Supporting Performance by an Actress in a Dramatic or Comedy Series

1958–59 **Ann B. Davis,** Best Supporting Actress (Continuing Character) in a Comedy Series

TRIVIA TIDBITS

- Many of the cast members later went on to star in other classic TV series: Dwayne Hickman in *Dobie Gillis,* Ann B. Davis in *The Brady Bunch,* Nancy Kulp in *The Beverly Hillbillies,* Rosemary DeCamp in *That Girl*—and even Bob Cummings in *The New Bob Cummings Show* and *My Living Doll.*
- Guest stars ranged from George Burns and Gracie Allen (in a crossover episode) to Zsa Zsa Gabor, Alan Ladd, Ozzie Nelson, Steve Allen, Art Linkletter, and Don Knotts.

- Cummings, known more formally as Robert in his movie star days, was a versatile light comedian in films of the 1930s and 1940s, but also did dramatic turns, especially for Alfred Hitchcock in *Saboteur* (1942) and *Dial M for Murder* (1954).
- Bob Cummings's only Emmy Award came for his dramatic performance in the original *Twelve Angry Men,* a role Henry Fonda later played on the screen.
- Cummings starred as a character coincidentally named Bob Collins in the 1945 film *You Came Along,* directed by John Farrow, Mia's dad.

THE LUCY SHOW

CBS, 1962–68, 157 episodes

CAST

Lucy Carmichael	Lucille Ball
Vivian Bagley (1962–65)	Vivian Vance
Mr. Barnsdale (1962–63)	Charles Lane
Theodore J. Mooney (1963–68)	Gale Gordon
Chris Carmichael (1962–65)	Candy Moore
Jerry Carmichael (1962–66)	Jimmy Garrett
Sherman Bagley (1962–65)	Ralph Hart
Harry Connors (1962–64)	Dick Martin
Mary Jane Lewis (1965–68)	Mary Jane Croft
Harrison Cheever (1965–68)	Roy Roberts
Bob Mooney (1964–66)	Eddie Applegate
Ted Mooney Jr. (1964–67)	Michael J. Pollard

EXECUTIVE PRODUCERS: Lucille Ball, Desi Arnaz
PRODUCERS: Elliott Lewis, Jack Donahue, Tommy Thompson
DIRECTORS: Jack Donahue, Maury Thompson
WRITERS: Bob Carroll & Madelyn Pugh Martin, Bob Schiller & Bob Weiskopf, Milt Josefsberg, Garry Marshall & Jerry Belson

Forever Lucy

The Lucy Show, Lucille Ball's first sitcom AD (after Desi), came in two forms. For the initial four seasons, the first lady of American television was the widowed mother of two children living in Connecticut with her pal Vivian Vance, a divorcée with a son. Together they attempted weekly harebrained schemes to acquire money and snag new husbands. In the process, they became the bane of cantankerous banker Barnsdale's (Charles Lane) existence. The show's format was revised in season five, and Lucy—minus kids or Vivian (who had retired, but paid an occasional visit from back East)—was transplanted to San Francisco, where she became scatterbrained secretary to imperious Theodore J. Mooney (Gale Gordon), a bank vice president (he had replaced Barnsdale in Connecticut). Veteran radio/television actress Mary Jane Croft came aboard as Lucy's new pal and unwitting coconspirator in zaniness. Those dropping by occasionally included Ethel Merman (in a classic two-part episode in which Lucy has the temerity to teach Ethel—Merman, not Mertz—as look-alike Agnes Schmidlapp a thing or two about singing), George Burns, Carol Burnett, Danny Kaye, Arthur Godfrey, and John Wayne.

In 1968 *The Lucy Show* was transformed once again overnight by CBS into *Here's Lucy,* with Lucille Ball and Gale Gordon continuing for another six seasons as sister-in-law and brother-in-law; they had new names and new characters but the same hilarious interaction as she worked as secretary for his employment agency. Mary Jane Croft continued from the previous show. Joining this version were Lucille Ball's real-life children, Lucie Arnaz and Desi Jr. This variation of the ongoing Lucille Ball sitcom tradition was notable for its parade of guest stars—particularly Elizabeth Taylor and Richard Burton in September 1970—turning up under improbable circumstances.

VIDEO AVAILABILITY

Three episodes of *The Lucy Show,* each running thirty minutes, are available at certain video outlets: the 1968 episode in which she tries to convince Jack Benny to move his money out of his underground vault and into the bank where she works; the 1964 one in which she and Vivian try their hand at plumbing (Benny and Hope turn up on this one); and the 1962 one in which the two of them join a barbershop quartet.

EMMY AWARDS

1966–67 **Lucille Ball,** Outstanding Continued Performance by an Actress in a Leading Role in a Comedy Series

1967–68 **Lucille Ball,** Outstanding Continued Performance by an Actress in a Leading Role in a Comedy Series

TRIVIA TIDBITS

- It was Desi Arnaz who urged Lucille Ball to return to sitcoms following her interlude on Broadway in the musical *Wildcat,* where she met and later married Gary Morton. (Lucy and Desi had divorced in 1960, but remained partners at Desilu Productions.)
- Ann Sothern, an old Lucille Ball movie colleague (they were chorus girls together) and star of *Private Secretary* and *My Mother, the Car,* turned up several times as the Princess, a daffy would-be socialite.
- William Frawley, the erstwhile Fred Mertz, returned to the fold one last time in late 1965 in "Lucy and the Countess Have a House Guest" as his final acting appearance.
- Gale Gordon, who was so associated with Lucille Ball during her last twenty years, had been the original choice for what became the Fred Mertz role in *I Love Lucy,* but was committed to another project at the time.

MAKE ROOM FOR DADDY

ABC, 1953–57; CBS, 1957–64 (as *The Danny Thomas Show*); 336 episodes

CAST

Danny Williams	Danny Thomas
Margaret Williams (1953–56)	Jean Hagen
Kathy Williams ("Clancey")(1957–64)	Marjorie Lord
Rusty Williams	Rusty Hamer
Terry Williams (1953–58)	Sherry Jackson
Terry Williams (1959–60)	Penney Parker
Linda Williams (1957–64)	Angela Cartwright
Louise (1953–64)	Amanda Randolph
Horace (1953–54)	Horace McMahon
Benny (1953–57)	Ben Lessy
Liz O'Neal	Mary Wickes
Jesse Leeds (1955–57)	Jesse White
Uncle Tonoose (1958–64)	Hans Conried
Phil Arnold (1959–61)	Sheldon Leonard
Pat Hannigan (1959–60)	Pat Harrington Jr.
Gina (1959)	Annette Funicello
"Uncle Charley" Halper (1959–64)	Sid Melton
Bunny Halper (1961–64)	Pat Carroll

CREATOR: Danny Thomas, Mel Shavelson, Louis F. Edelman

EXECUTIVE PRODUCERS: Sheldon Leonard, Danny Thomas

PRODUCERS: Louis F. Edelman, Charles Stewart, Jack Elinson, Ronald Jacobs

DIRECTORS: Sheldon Leonard, William Asher

WRITERS: Mel Shavelson, Charles Stewart, Jack Elinson, Jim Fritzell, Bill Manhoff, Larry Burns, Peggy Chantler, Arthur Stander

Danny Williams (Danny Thomas, right), the star of *Make Room for Daddy,* and his beloved sitcom family, from left: Rusty Hamer (Rusty), Jean Hagen (Margaret), and Sherry Jackson (Terry). COURTESY OF PERSONALITY PHOTOS, INC.

Uncle Daddy

Danny Thomas, like many of the sitcom stars of the early 1950s, played a character loosely based on himself: a nightclub entertainer attempting to balance a showbiz career with a normal family life. As several critics pointed out, at last here was a sitcom dad who wasn't stupid: Danny Thomas was a warm, endearing performer who injected his TV alter ego (Danny Williams) with his real-life personality. Initially, there was a wife plus an eleven-year-old daughter and a seven-year-old son, and he was given to bellow—although lovingly—at their "bratty" ways. His performing often took him away from the family, and, when he was home, the kids had to shift bedrooms and "make room for Daddy" (hence the original title). After the third season, Danny Williams became a widower, at which point he began dating his son's nurse, Clancey.

Daddy Danny

Danny and Clancey didn't marry, however, until the start of the sixth season when the show changed networks and titles, and a five-year-old stepdaughter was added to the clan. At this point the show leaped to the Top Ten, where it stayed for the remainder of *Make Room for Daddy*'s prime-time life. As Danny Williams continued to prosper both in his career and in his happy home, the children grew and went off to school, and new characters were added to the mix (the most notable, Danny's blustery Lebanese Uncle Tonoose). Lots of guests turned up on the show over the years: Dean Martin, Bob Hope, Milton Berle, Tennessee Ernie Ford, Jimmy Durante, Shirley Jones, Tony Bennett, and even Lucille Ball and Desi Arnaz as Lucy and Ricky Ricardo. (Lucy and Desi's Desilu Productions produced the show.) One episode turned out to be the pilot to *The Andy Griffith Show* (see separate entry), in which Danny found himself under arrest for speeding in the town of Mayberry while heading south with the family for vacation. Ultimately, a weary Danny Thomas—by now he had entered the ranks of the show-biz "beloved," working tirelessly for a personal cause, St. Jude's Hospital for children in Memphis—decided to call it quits, and the show ended in 1964—for a while, at least. The cast was reassembled on occasion, focusing on son Rusty, newly graduated from college and marrying the daughter of his Army CO. In 1971 *Make Room for Granddaddy* took to the airwaves with basically the same cast, but only for one season on ABC.

VIDEO AVAILABILITY

Ten *Danny Thomas Show* collections of the show (with Marjorie Lord) are available at certain video outlets, as well as two special sets of five volumes each. Each individual collection, running approximately seventy-five minutes, contains three episodes. Also available is one half-hour episode from the early years with Jean Hagen, under the show's original title.

EMMY AWARDS

1953	*Make Room for Daddy,* Best New Program
1954	*Make Room for Daddy,* Best Situation Comedy Series
	Danny Thomas, Best Actor Starring in a Regular Series
1956	**Sheldon Leonard,** Best Direction in Comedy
1960–61	**Sheldon Leonard,** Best Directorial Achievement in Comedy

TRIVIA TIDBITS

- Danny Thomas, who originally had misgivings about television after earlier occasionally hosting NBC's *All Star Revue,* became one of the medium's most important executives during the 1950s and 1960s. With partner Sheldon Leonard, he produced such shows as *The Andy Griffith Show, The Dick Van Dyke Show, Gomer Pyle, USMC,* and *The Mod Squad.*
- Jack Benny guest-starred on the first show, "Love in Las Vegas," along with Peter Lind Hayes and his wife, Mary Healy.
- Danny's daughter, Marlo Thomas, first made a name on *That Girl,* became a major TV star, and married TV talk show host Phil Donahue.
- Danny's son, Tony, became an influential TV writer/producer and, with partner Paul Junger Witt, created such shows as *The Golden Girls* and *Empty Nest.*
- Jean Hagen, one of the stars of the film *Singin' in the Rain,* became one of the first stars to be "killed off" on series television after she decided to leave the show.
- Marjorie Lord is the mother of actress Anne Archer.

MARRIED . . . WITH CHILDREN

Fox, 1987—

CAST

Al Bundy	Ed O'Neill
Peggy Bundy	Katey Sagal
Kelly Bundy	Christina Applegate
Bud Bundy	David Faustino
Steve Rhoades (1987–90)	David Garrison
Marcy Rhoades D'Arcy	Amanda Bearse
Jefferson D'Arcy (1991–)	Ted McGinley

CREATED BY: Ron Leavitt, Michael G. Moye
EXECUTIVE PRODUCERS: Ellen L. Fogle, Arthur Silver
CREATIVE CONSULTANTS: Richard Gorman, Katherine Green, Kevin Curren
PRODUCER: Stacie Lipp

Marriage (and love)?

This domestic comedy, with an amazingly long and successful life both in prime time and in simultaneous syndication, offered the hilariously dark side of marriage in the mode of radio's The Bickersons. There was Dad: a hapless couch potato who toiled as a shoe salesman was a henpecked chauvinist with a prized collection of *Playboy* magazines stashed in the garage (the "Bundy legacy"), and endless get-rich-quick schemes. There was Mom: a vision in spandex, teased hair, and too much makeup, who lolled around the house waiting for hubby to come home so she could alternately belittle him or entice him into hanky-panky in the bedroom. There was the airhead teenage daughter: a mall shopper who dressed like a

TV chauvinism didn't end with Archie Bunker. Three Bundys from the popular series *Married . . . With Children,* from left: Katey Sagal (Peggy), David Faustino (Bud), and Ed O'Neill (Al). COURTESY OF PERSONALITY PHOTOS, INC.

tramp and tolerated Dad enough to wheedle more of an allowance from him. And there was the semi-delinquent, smart-mouthed, budding con man son who was forever at Sis's throat. Even the family dog, Buck, put up with his master only reluctantly.

The sexually charged, weekly familial sniping on this show tickled the funny bones of millions of viewers who made it the cornerstone of the newly established Fox

Network and one of the most durable sitcoms well into the 1990s. The ironic theme song—Frank Sinatra's "Love and Marriage"—said it all, as the opening titles froze to ice and became icicles.

VIDEO AVAILABILITY

Married . . . With Children: It's a Bundyful Life, the show's Christmas special, spoofed the famed Frank Capra/Jimmy Stewart movie, with a scruffy "guest" guardian played by Sam Kinison. Available at certain video outlets, it runs about fifty minutes.

TRIVIA TIDBITS

- Katey Sagal, formerly one of the Harlettes, Bette Midler's backup vocal group, is the older sister of twins Liz and Jean Sagal, stars of the mid-1980s NBC series *Double Trouble.* Their father was the late Boris Sagal, noted TV director; their stepmom is Marge Champion, the former dancer.
- Amanda Bearse, initially the Bundys' next-door neighbor, left acting to become one of the show's principal directors (although she occasionally puts in an appearance in front of the camera on the show).
- The Bundys lived at 9674 Jeopardy Lane in Chicago.

THE MARY TYLER MOORE SHOW

CBS, 1970–77, 168 episodes

CAST

Mary Richards	Mary Tyler Moore
Lou Grant	Ed Asner
Ted Baxter	Ted Knight
Murray Slaughter	Gavin MacLeod
Rhoda Morgenstern (1970–74)	Valerie Harper
Phyllis Lindstrom (1970–74)	Cloris Leachman
Georgette Franklin (1973–77)	Georgia Engel
Sue Ann Nivens (1973–77)	Betty White

CREATORS/EXECUTIVE PRODUCERS: James L. Brooks, Allan Burns

PRINCIPAL DIRECTORS: Jay Sandrich, Alan Rafkin, Jerry Paris, Peter Baldwin, Jerry Belson, James Burrows

PRINCIPAL WRITERS: James L. Brooks, Allan Burns, Bob Ellison, Treva Silverman, Ed. Weinberger, Stan Daniels, David Lloyd, Lorenzo Music

On her own

When *The Mary Tyler Moore Show* premiered on Saturday, September 19, 1970, the first image audiences saw was an attractive young woman behind the wheel of a car, driving down a highway, as the words "How will you make it on your own?" were sung to a plaintive melody. As the theme sequence continued, the mood changed to an upbeat montage of friendship, activity, and finally elation, ending with a now-famous freeze-frame shot of the same woman on a Minneapolis sidewalk, tossing her hat in the air.

Ted (Ted Knight, left) consoles his grouchy but lovable boss, Lou (Ed Asner), in this scene from *The Mary Tyler Moore Show.* In the news room, Mary Richards (Mary Tyler Moore), was something of a Snow White to her male dwarfs. Many consider the show to be the finest of the 1970s. COURTESY OF PERSONALITY PHOTOS, INC.

Over twenty-five years later, *The Mary Tyler Moore Show* remains one of the most beloved sitcoms in television history, famous for its brilliant writing, near-perfect ensemble acting, and groundbreaking subject matter.

After a decade of fantasy-filled 1950s and 1960s sitcoms such as *Bewitched* and *I Dream of Jeannie* and family-oriented fare such as *The Andy Griffith Show,* here in the 1970s was something new: a mature show about a single working woman making her way in a new environment with only the support of her friends both in the workplace and at home. As Mary Richards would tearfully pronounce in the famous closing episode of the series, these friends had become her "family." This acknowledgment crystallizes much of the appeal and significance of the show. The sensibilities of family life in America were changing—i.e., women had become more independent—and *The Mary Tyler Moore Show* was one of the first TV series to reflect this new era.

Mary's "seven dwarfs"

Mary Richards's "family" consisted of seven imperfect people with distinct personalities that developed and deepened during the show's seven-season run. At her job as assistant editor (and later producer) in the newsroom of local television station WJM-TV, there's Lou Grant, her gruff, hard-drinking boss who's a pussycat at heart; newswriter Murray Slaughter, whose amiable manner and biting wit function as defense mechanisms for his basic insecurity; and vain, pompous anchorman Ted Baxter, who's blessed with the emotional maturity (and IQ) of a ten-year-old. Later in the show's run, a new character emerges at the station: back-stabbing Sue Ann Nivens, sex-obsessed home-and-cooking-show star. Meanwhile, back at her modest studio apartment, Mary's social life involves: her best friend Rhoda Morgenstern, a resilient, wisecracking single Jewish woman from New York who imagines a weight problem; her bossy, neurotic landlady, Phyllis Lindstrom; and, eventually, Rhoda's coworker, Georgette Franklin, whose sunny disposition, little-girl voice, and Stan Laurel intellect catch Ted's romantic eye. At the center of this group of wonderfully conceived characters, Mary Richards emerges as a modern-day Snow White in search of a prince who will never come. Intelligent, attractive, career-driven but a touch prudish, Mary doesn't know how to say no to her friends, throws disastrous parties, and seems doomed to date an endless parade of Minneapolis bachelors in the pursuit of an ever-elusive "Mr. Right."

It is a testament to the show's cast and writers that each of these characters became beloved friends to millions of viewers on a weekly basis, both on *The Mary Tyler Moore Show* and, in several cases, later on their own series. As they interact, confronting situations that put their friendships to the test, mutual respect and understanding shine through the temporary irritations and discord that occur in every episode. Each relationship becomes more complex as the show continues, so that, unlike most earlier sitcoms, the characters don't seem "frozen" in eternally repetitious behavior. Despite running gags, such as Murray's insulting jokes about Ted and Sue Ann, and Rhoda's self-deprecating put-downs, each episode manages to be fresh and unique, telling us a little more about these people. Maintaining an extraordinarily high level of quality and humor throughout, the series made one grateful that its "powers that be" decided to end the show at its artistic peak, with a classic episode that reunited the entire cast, past and present.

As Mary walks through the double doors of the newsroom for the last time after the station has been sold and all but one of them has been terminated, she turns, smiles one final sad, wistful smile, then switches off the lights, and departs with pride. She did, after all, "make it on her own"—if with a little help from her friends.

VIDEO AVAILABILITY

Ten volumes of *The Mary Tyler Moore Show* are currently available in certain video outlets. Each volume runs approximately fifty minutes and contains two episodes. There is also a special single-episode volume, featuring the classic "Chuckles Bites the Dust," which runs twenty-five minutes.

EMMY AWARDS

1970–71 **Ed Asner,** Best Supporting Actor (Comedy)
Valerie Harper, Best Supporting Actress (Comedy)
Jay Sandrich, Best Director (Comedy)
James L. Brooks & Allan Burns, Best Comedy Writing

1971–72 **Ed Asner,** Best Supporting Actor (Comedy)
Valerie Harper, Best Supporting Actress (Comedy)

1972–73 **Mary Tyler Moore,** Best Actress (Comedy)
Ted Knight, Best Supporting Actor (Comedy)
Valerie Harper, Best Supporting Actress (Comedy)
Jay Sandrich, Best Director (Comedy)

1973–74 **Mary Tyler Moore,** Best Actress (Comedy)
Cloris Leachman, Best Supporting Actress (Comedy)
Treva Silverman, Best Comedy Writing

1974–75 **Best Comedy Series**
Ed Asner, Best Supporting Actor (Comedy)
Betty White, Best Supporting Actress (Comedy)
Cloris Leachman, Best Single Performance by a Supporting Actress (Comedy)
Ed. Weinberger & Stan Daniels, Best Comedy Writing

1975–76 **Best Comedy Series**
Mary Tyler Moore, Best Actress (Comedy)
Ted Knight, Best Supporting Actor (Comedy)
Betty White, Best Supporting Actress (Comedy)
David Lloyd, Best Comedy Writing

1976–77 **Best Comedy Series**
Allan Burns, James L. Brooks, Ed. Weinberger, Stan Daniels, David Lloyd & Bob Ellison, Best Comedy Writing

TRIVIA TIDBITS

- Mary's apartment in Minneapolis during the first five seasons was at 119 North Weatherly.
- Reportedly, Mary was to have been a divorced woman, but CBS was concerned that audiences would be upset that she and Rob Petrie (from *The Dick Van Dyke Show*) had called it quits!

- Chuckles the Clown, whose death was the premise for perhaps the most famous episode ("Chuckles Bites the Dust"), was played by two actors during the show's run: Mark Gordon and Richard Schall.
- Nancy Walker, who played Rhoda's meddling mother, Ida Morgenstern, in several episodes, starred in Broadway musicals for almost twenty years (*On the Town, Do Re Mi,* etc.), was a regular on the mystery series *McMillan & Wife,* and later directed the cult flop movie *Can't Stop the Music.* She is perhaps best remembered, however, as Rosie, the "quicker picker-upper" waitress, in the Bounty towel commercials.
- Mary Richards's parents were named Dotty and Walter and were played by Nanette Fabray and Bill Quinn.
- In the extended family of WJM-TV, occasional characters and the actors who played them were: weatherman Gordie Howard (John Amos); Lou's wife, Edie, who divorced him (Priscilla Morrill); Murray's wife, Marie (Joyce Bulifant); Phyllis's daughter, Bess (Lisa Gerritsen); sportscaster Andy Rivers (John Gabriel); and Mary's Aunt Flo (Eileen Heckart).
- Mary Tyler Moore—for whom the MTM production empire with its pussycat logo was named by Grant Tinker, then her husband—made her directorial debut with the November 1974 episode "A Boy's Best Friend." One other cast member, Nancy Walker, also directed an episode.
- Former First Lady Betty Ford made a much-publicized appearance at the end of an episode. Other celebrity cameos featured Walter Cronkite and Johnny Carson.
- Future TV series stars who had small roles during the show's run included Penny Marshall, Henry Winkler, Mary Frann, Craig T. Nelson, and Linda Kelsey (who also appeared on *Lou Grant* in a different role).
- Rhoda (Valerie Harper), Phyllis (Cloris Leachman),

and Lou (Ed Asner) all went on to have their own spin-off shows. Gavin MacLeod ended up as Captain Stubbings on *The Love Boat.*

- "Love Is All Around," the show's theme song, was written and performed by Sonny Curtis.

M*A*S*H

CBS, 1972–83, 251 episodes

CAST

Capt. Benjamin Franklin Pierce (Hawkeye)	Alan Alda
Capt. John McIntyre (Trapper John) (1972–75)	Wayne Rogers
Maj. Margaret Houlihan (Hot Lips)	Loretta Swit
Maj. Frank Burns (1972–75)	Larry Linville
Cpl. Walter O'Reilly (Radar) (1972–79)	Gary Burghoff
Lt. Col. Henry Blake (1972–75)	McLean Stevenson
Father John Mulcahy	William Christopher
Cpl. Maxwell Klinger (1973–83)	Jamie Farr
Col. Sherman Potter 1977–83)	Harry Morgan
Capt. B. J. Hunnicut (1975–83)	Mike Farrell
Maj. Charles Emerson Winchester (1977–83)	David Ogden Stiers
Lt. Maggie Dish (1972)	Karen Philipp
Spearchucker Jones (1972)	Timothy Brown
Maj. Sidney Freedman	Allan Arbus

CREATORS: Larry Gelbart, Gene Reynolds

EXECUTIVE PRODUCERS: Burt Metcalfe, John Rappaport

PRODUCERS: Gene Reynolds, Larry Gelbart, Burt Metcalfe, Allan Katz, Don Reo, John Rappaport, Jim Mulligan, Thad Mumford, Dan Wilcox, Dennis Koenig

PRINCIPAL DIRECTORS: Gene Reynolds, Hy Averback, William K. Jurgenson, Don Weis, Jackie Cooper, Alan Alda, Charles S. Dubin, Earl Bellamy, Joan Darling, Harry Morgan

PRINCIPAL WRITERS: Larry Gelbart, Laurence Marks, Alan Alda, Bob Klane, Carl Kleinschmitt, Linda Bloodworth, Mary Kay Place, Everett Greenbaum, Jim Fritzell, Burt Prelutsky, Ken Levine, David Isaacs, Thad Mumford, Dan Wilcox, David Pollock, Elias Davis

All hail the 4077th

A landmark seriocomic television smash spanning 11 seasons and 251 sometimes hilarious, sometimes poignant episodes, *M*A*S*H* set many standards—particularly in writing and in execution—that have been incorporated into the production of medical shows such as *St. Elsewhere* in the 1980s and *Chicago Hope* and *E.R.* in the 1990s. Following the exploits of the often irreverent but always dedicated doctors and nurses of the 4077th Mobile Army Surgical Hospital on the front lines during the Korean War, *M*A*S*H* was basically about how they retained their sanity amid the insanity of war. Though constantly breaking military rules and regulations, they (medical officers, NCOs, and grunts) use hijinks to relieve the tensions of war, skirt orders, pursue nurses, make hootch, scrounge supplies, and bedevil their uptight CO. Except for an occasional wisecrack, the surgeons are all business in the operating tent, where the saving of human life is uppermost.

The icons of the 4077th are quick-witted, skilled surgeons Hawkeye Pierce—the natural leader—and Trapper John McIntyre (and later, when Trapper John is rotated back to the States, family man B. J. Hunnicut). Writer and series cocreator Larry Gelbart once said of Alan Alda, the show's "Hawkeye": "He's the linchpin. The cast can change, but the starting pitcher is always there. Alan Alda has come to represent *M*A*S*H*."

Then there is pompous and humorless Maj. Frank Burns, whose self-righteous ploys to maintain military order are always thwarted by Hawkeye and Trapper John. Meanwhile, Burns frequently engages in hanky-

The second crew from *M*A*S*H,* from left: Mike Farrell (B. J. Hunnicut), William Christopher (Father Mulcahy), Harry Morgan (Col. Potter), Alan Alda (Hawkeye Pierce), Loretta Swit (Maj. Houlihan), Jamie Farr (Cpl. Klinger), and David Ogden Stiers (Maj. Winchester). Although the series was persistently funny, the show also took on serious overtones and used techniques that have influenced medical shows such as *E.R.* COURTESY OF PERSONALITY PHOTOS, INC.

panky with army brat head nurse Hot Lips Hoolihan, who is alternately hated and lusted after. Attempting to run the unit is Lt. Col. Henry Blake, an addle-brained but lovable CO, who is constantly second-guessed by his company clerk, clairvoyant Radar O'Reilly. Hustler Corporal Klinger adds drag humor to the show by wearing dresses and pearls in order to obtain a Section 8. Father

Mulcahy, the padre—whose hobbies include boxing—was the 4077th's guiding spirit from the first episode to the last. During the show's final five years, Col. Sherman Potter, a pragmatic cavalry veteran with a deep respect for his men (and their antics), became the CO. The last regular added to the show was stuffy Harvard-bred Maj. Charles Emerson Winchester III, who came in as a replacement surgeon for Frank Burns—and proved to be an even worthier adversary to Hawkeye and B.J.

War's hell, M*A*S*H *innovative*

*M*A*S*H* producers used a number of offbeat touches, such as adding a low-key laugh track that was so toned down, it's said viewers were almost completely unaware of it. (In Great Britain the laugh track was eliminated.) In one unusual episode, Hawkeye, injured in a jeep accident and suffering from a concussion, babbles (in a twenty-minute monologue) to a non-English speaking Korean family to keep himself awake. *M*A*S*H* tackled devices and concepts then unheard of in comedy, including: shooting episodes in black and white using a documentary approach; the death of a beloved character, Henry Blake, killed in a chopper crash; and filming an episode in "real time," with a wounded soldier requiring lifesaving surgery within twenty-five minutes, which was almost exactly the running time of the compressed episode. These distinctive moves kept this classic show fresh and set it apart from anything else on the air at that time.

The series ended in a marathon two-and-one-half-hour episode that was both cheerful and tearful as one by one the *M*A*S*H* personnel took their leave. It was a true television event, the most watched entertainment program in the history of the medium.

VIDEO AVAILABILITY

*M*A*S*H* is available through Columbia House on a continuing series of cassettes, each featuring three half-hour episodes

EMMY AWARDS (91 nominations total)

1973–74 *M*A*S*H*, Outstanding Comedy Series
Alan Alda, Outstanding Lead Actor in a Comedy Series
Jackie Cooper, Outstanding Directing in Comedy Series

1974–75 **Gene Reynolds,** Outstanding Directing in Comedy Series

1975–76 **Gene Reynolds,** Outstanding Directing in Comedy Series

1976–77 **Gary Burghoff,** Outstanding Continuing Performance by a Supporting Actor in a Comedy Series
Alan Alda, Outstanding Directing in a Comedy Series

1978–79 **Alan Alda,** Outstanding Writing in a Comedy Series

1978–79 **Harry Morgan,** Outstanding Supporting Actor in a Comedy Series
Loretta Swit, Outstanding Supporting Actress in a Comedy Series

1981–82 **Alan Alda,** Outstanding Lead Actor in a Comedy Series
Loretta Swit, Outstanding Supporting Actress in a Comedy Series

TRIVIA TIDBITS

- *M*A*S*H* began life as a novel, written under the pseudonym Richard Hooker, by Dr. Richard Hornberger, who spent a year and a half as a surgeon in a M*A*S*H unit in Korea. The book had seventeen rejections before being published and becoming a best-seller.
- Alan Alda, Loretta Swit, and William Christopher (except for the pilot episode) were the only cast members who played the entire run of the series.
- Gary Burghoff, as Radar O'Reilly, was the only actor who played his role in both the 1970 Robert Altman

movie and in the series, which he left early in the eighth season. Jamie Farr, as Klinger, was the only member of the cast to have actually fought in Korea.

- *M*A*S*H* lasted nearly four times longer than the Korean War itself.
- Alan Alda wrote and/or directed thirty-two episodes (including the final one) and became the only TV star to date to win Emmys for acting, directing, and writing on a single series.
- Harry Morgan (who appeared in one episode earlier in the series as a no-nonsense general) directed eight episodes, David Ogden Stiers two, and Jamie Farr one. Mike Farrell wrote and/or directed seven.
- McLean Stevenson, the show's Henry Blake, died in February 1996, one day before Roger Bowen, who played Henry Blake in the film.
- Among the guest stars turning up on the show were: Timothy Brown and G. Wood, both of whom were in the Altman film; Ed Flanders; Leslie Nielsen; Joan Van Ark; Teri Garr; Pat Morita; Ned Beatty; Philip Ahn; Keye Luke; Susan Saint James; Patrick Swayze; Blythe Danner; Edward Herrmann; Shelley Long; Gwen Verdon; Judy Farrell (then Mike's wife, who also wrote a couple of episodes); and Robert Alda and Antony Alda, Alan's dad and younger brother, respectively.
- *M*A*S*H* spawned two spin-off series: *Trapper John, M.D.*, with Pernell Roberts in the role Wayne Rogers had originated—twenty-eight years later (it lasted for seven seasons), and *AfterMASH*, with three members of the original show (Harry Morgan, Jamie Farr, and William Christopher) reunited Stateside on the staff of a VA hospital. This series played sporadically over a season and a half in the mid-1980s. There was a little-remembered 1984 TV pilot for a show called *Walter*,

with Gary Burghoff returning to his Radar O'Reilly character, now a rookie cop in Kansas.

- Johnny Mandel wrote the *M*A*S*H* theme song, subtitled "Suicide Is Painless," which was written for the movie version.

THE MUNSTERS

CBS, 1964–66, 69 episodes

CAST

Herman Munster	Fred Gwynne
Lily Munster	Yvonne DeCarlo
Grandpa	Al Lewis
Marilyn	Beverly Owen (1964) Pat Priest (1964–66)
Eddie Munster	Butch Patrick

CREATORS/PRODUCERS: Bob Mosher, Joe Connelly

PRINCIPAL DIRECTORS: Norman Abbott, Seymour Burns, Jerry Paris, Earl Bellamy, Gene Reynolds, Joseph Pevney, Charles Barton, Lawrence Dobkin, Charles R. Rondeau

PRINCIPAL WRITERS: Joe Connelly, Bob Mosher, George Tibbles, Norm Liebman, Tom Adair, Richard Baer

Ghoul in the family

In September 1964 an odd thing happened on network television. Well, *two* odd things: both *The Munsters* and *The Addams Family* (see separate entry) premiered during the same week, on CBS and ABC, respectively. Both were fantasy sitcoms about macabre, ghoulish families living in the midst of middle-class suburbia. Both ran for only two seasons, would be compared to each other, and would continue to thrive in syndication and future reincarnations. But, in reality, no two series could be less alike.

The Munsters has provided silly fun for kids since the mid-1960s. From left: Fred Gwynne (Herman), Yvonne DeCarlo (Lily), Butch Patrick (Eddie), Al Lewis (Grandpa), and Beverly Owen (Marilyn). COURTESY OF PERSONALITY PHOTOS, INC.

Maliciously clever, *The Addams Family* had an appeal to adult audiences and was rooted in subtle, subversive humor that was ahead of its time. There was nothing subtle about *The Munsters.* Created by the same team responsible for *Leave It to Beaver,* its formula was simple: take a typical sitcom family and immerse them in typical sitcom plots—only make them monsters modeled after the most famous creatures in horror film history. Since Universal Studios, which owned the rights to such 1930s classics as *Dracula* and *Frankenstein,* produced the series, each character was instantly recognizable: Frankenstein's monster became bumbling Herman Munster; Herman's father-in-law, Grandpa, was a photocopy of Dracula; Lily, Herman's wife, was a female vampire straight out of horror comic books; and Herman and Lily's son, Eddie, was a miniature Wolfman. The only "normal" member of the family was Lily's niece, Marilyn, a beautiful young woman who, of course, was considered an "ugly duckling." The Munsters' house, at 1313 Mockingbird Lane in the small town of Mockingbird Heights, was a gothic monstrosity that put *Psycho*'s Bates Motel to shame.

Sweet and silly

While Herman, Lily, and family garnered a quick reputation for inadvertently scaring the wits out of any hapless neighbor who encountered them, there was nothing frightening about *The Munsters.* Completely oblivious to their effect on others, they strived for a family lifestyle that, despite the elaborate makeup, was as wholesome as Beaver's. Lily's house may be festooned with cobwebs and her dinner table may have featured cream of vulture soup, but she tended to her home with the sanitized cheerfulness of a Donna Reed. Herman, played brilliantly by Fred Gwynne, may have been seven foot three, with bolts sticking out of his neck, but he behaved like an innocent child, trusting everyone and incapable of harming others.

The show appealed primarily to children because of this striking juxtaposition between gruesome exteriors and silly sitcom behavior. Like *Gilligan's Island* and *Mr.*

Ed, it was critically reviled, but much of its sweet, goofy humor remains intact. In one episode, for example, Grandpa (played with relish by former vaudevillian Al Lewis) needs to remove Marilyn from the house temporarily, so he decides to cast a spell: "Don't let time or space detain ya—off you go to Transylvania!" The living room fills with dense smoke. Herman calls out, "Grandpa! It worked! Grandpa! Grandpa?" When the smoke clears, the telephone rings, and, sure enough, it's Grandpa, Lily, Eddie, and Marilyn, calling from a motel room in Kansas City!

Exactly how loved *The Munsters* was became obvious when a misguided TV revival, *The Munsters Today,* starring John Schuck and Lee Meriwether, premiered in 1988. Though completely humorless, it managed to run in first-run syndication for three years. One hopes that it hasn't scared off contemporary audiences from viewing the funny goings-on at Mockingbird Lane. Perhaps another of Grandpa's spells would do the trick: "Abracadabra and asee dosee, alakazam and Bela Lugosi!"

VIDEO AVAILABILITY

Ten volumes of *The Munsters* are currently available in certain video outlets, each in black and white, running roughly fifty minutes and containing two episodes. There is also a special volume, *The Munsters: The Lost Episode,* which features the previously unaired color pilot, as well as behind-the-scenes clips.

TRIVIA TIDBITS

- Prior to cancellation of the series, a color feature film, *Munster, Go Home!* was released in 1966, starring the TV cast. A reunion TV movie, *The Munsters' Revenge,* was made in 1981, with Gwynne, DeCarlo, and Lewis reprising their roles. Yet another TV movie, *Here Come the Munsters,* turned up on Halloween night 1995 on Fox, with Edward Herrmann, Veronica Hamel, and Robert Morse, as Herman, Lily, and Grandpa. In one restaurant scene, the original surviving Munsters—DeCarlo, Lewis, Butch Patrick, and Pat Priest (Fred Gwynne died in 1993)—had amusing cameos.

- The original Marilyn, Beverly Owen, left the show after only thirteen episodes because of "artistic differences." Her replacement, Pat Priest, was the daughter of former United States Treasurer Ivy Baker Priest.
- Fred Gwynne and Al Lewis previously were teamed in another classic TV sitcom, *Car 54, Where Are You?* (see separate entry).
- The family pets were Spot, a dragon living under the staircase; Igor the bat; Kitty Kat, a feline who roars like a lion; Eddie's snake named Elmer; and an unnamed raven in a clock, which popped out every hour to shriek "Nevermore!"
- Herman worked at the Gateman, Goodbury & Graves funeral parlor.
- Lily's costume and makeup were based on that of Carol Borland in *Mark of the Vampire,* MGM's 1935 imitation of Universal horrors.
- Eddie's middle name was Wolfgang, and his werewolf doll's name was Woof Woof.
- Guest stars who appeared on *The Munsters* include Harvey Korman, Don Rickles, John Carradine, Dom DeLuise, Bonnie Franklin, Louis Nye, Leo Durocher, and Paul Lynde (three stints as Dr. Dudley).
- The show's theme music, "At the Munsters," was written by Jack Marshall.
- An original Munsters *TV Guide* cover (January 2, 1965) has become a collectible, fetching $40. Also commanding a good price is a talking Herman doll which says, "You must come over and meet my mummy."

MY HERO

NBC, 1952–53, 33 episodes

CAST

Robert S. Beanblossom	Bob Cummings
Julie Marshall	Julie Bishop
Willis Thackery	John Litel

PRODUCER: Mort Green
DIRECTOR: Marc Daniels
WRITERS: Norman Paul, Jack Ellinson, Bob Cummings

Cummings and goings

In the first of his four television sitcoms, ever youthful, playboy-confident Bob Cummings portrayed Robert S. Beanblossom, a carefree, easygoing, but somewhat inept real estate agent working for the Thackery Realty Company in Los Angeles. The single-season sitcom, also known as *The Bob Cummings Show* (not to be confused with *The Bob Cummings Show* [see separate entry] of the early 1960s), had affable Bob stumbling through assorted real estate deals, with his ever-loyal secretary/girlfriend, Julie Bishop, managing to straighten out his weekly misadventures and protect him from the wrath of his slow-burning boss, John Litel.

My Hero represented the bare-bones sitcom of the early 1950s. Take a popular light comedian whose star was waning on the big screen, surround him with several equally competent but lesser names, concoct a humorous basic situation, and let him turn on the charm while making a fool of himself for about twenty-five minutes a week.

Saturday night viewers took to the show, which still holds up well on video more than four decades later.

VIDEO AVAILABILITY

Four collections of *My Hero* are available at certain video outlets, each running about sixty minutes and containing two episodes. In addition, there is another episode in a package teaming *My Hero* with *The Mickey Rooney Show* of 1954.

TRIVIA TIDBITS

- Bob Cummings began his career by lying his way into showbiz as Blade Stanhope Conway, Englishman, and then broke into films as southern-drawling Brice Hutchens, Texan.
- Cummings received an Emmy nomination for Best Actor in a Regular Series, but lost to Danny Thomas for *Make Room for Daddy* (see separate entry).
- Julie Bishop was a B actress at Warner Bros. in the 1940s who landed several starring roles.
- Cummings and Julie Bishop—who starred earlier opposite Bogart in *Action in the North Atlantic* and Errol Flynn in *Northern Pursuit* and spent the early part of her film career acting under the name Jacqueline Wells—appeared together in the 1945 film comedy *You Came Along*.
- John Litel, a sturdy, dependable veteran character actor who appeared in a wide range of roles in some 200 films, was a much-decorated World War I hero before embarking on a show business career. *My Hero* was his only TV series.

MY LITTLE MARGIE

CBS, 1952–53; NBC, 1953–55; 126 episodes

CAST

Margie Albright	Gale Storm
Vern Albright	Charles Farrell
Freddie Wilson	Don Hayden
Roberta Townsend	Hillary Brooke
George Honeywell	Clarence Kolb
Clarissa Odettes	Gertrude Hoffman
Charlie	Willie Best

PRODUCERS: Hal Roach Jr., Roland Reed
DIRECTORS: Walter Strenge, Hal Yates

Daddy dearest

Hollywood veteran Gale Storm starred as beautiful, unpredictable Margie Albright, who lived in Fifth Avenue digs in New York City with her investment counselor widowed dad—played by the venerable Charlie Farrell, one of the top leading men in Hollywood as film was finding its voice. Margie's job in life became matchmaking, which stemmed from her desire to save her eligible, womanizing dad from the machinations of grasping women who found him—and presumably his money—irresistible. He in turn felt a fatherly obligation to maintain parental control of her, despite the fact that she was twenty-one years old.

Others with regular roles in the series were Margie's boyfriend, Freddie Wilson; Roberta Townsend, Vern's frequent lady friend; George Honeywell, vice president of the firm where Vern worked; Clarissa Odettes, Margie and Vern's kindly neighbor; and Charlie, the handyman and elevator operator.

The misadventures of Margie and Vern Albright—she to keep him out of the clutches of gold diggers; he to keep her at arm's length from the opposite sex—entertained viewers for three seasons on two networks while running concurrently on CBS radio with the same two leads (not a simulcast but different shows with a different cast).

VIDEO AVAILABILITY

One collection of *My Little Margie,* running sixty minutes and containing two complete episodes, is available at certain video outlets.

TRIVIA TIDBITS

- *My Little Margie* initially was a summer replacement for *I Love Lucy* (see separate entry).
- The show began its run on radio *after* becoming a TV hit. (It premiered on CBS television in June 1952 and on radio the following December.)
- Although playing a twenty-one-year-old on the show, Gale Storm at the time was a rather mature thirty.
- Among the recurring characters on the show was then-unknown Fess Parker—a couple of years away from playing Davy Crockett—as one Lenny Crutchmeyer, Mrs. Odettes's nephew.
- Gale Storm went on to star in one other series, *Oh! Susanna* (aka *The Gale Storm Show*) in the late 1950s. Likewise, Charlie Farrell (the longtime real-life mayor of Palm Springs) had one other 1950s series, playing himself as the owner of the Racquet Club in Palm Springs, California, in *The Charlie Farrell Show.*

MYSTERY SCIENCE THEATER 3000

The Comedy Channel, 1990–91, 26 episodes; Comedy Central, 1991–96, 102 episodes

CAST

Joel Robinson (1990–94)	Joel Hodgson
Mike Nelson (1994–96)	Michael J. Nelson
Dr. Clayton Forrester	Trace Beaulieu
Dr. Larry Erhardt (1990–91)	Josh Weinstein
TV's Frank (1991–95)	Frank Conniff
Mrs. Pearl Forrester (1995–96)	Mary Jo Pehl
Gypsy	voice of Jim Mallon
Tom Servo	voice of Josh Weinstein (1990–91)
	voice of Kevin Murphy (1991–96)
Crow T. Robot	voice of Trace Beaulieu

CREATED BY: Joel Hodgson
PRODUCER: Jim Mallon
EXECUTIVE PRODUCERS: Jim Mallon, Joel Hodgson (1990–94)
PRINCIPAL DIRECTORS: Jim Mallon, Kevin Murphy, Trace Beaulieu
PRINCIPAL WRITERS/CONTRIBUTORS: Michael J. Nelson, Trace Beaulieu, Frank Conniff, Joel Hodgson, Kevin Murphy, Jim Mallon, Mary Jo Pehl, Paul Chaplin, Bridget Jones, David Sussman, Josh Weinstein, Colleen Henjum

In the not too distant future . . .

Mystery Science Theater 3000 (or *MST3K,* its official abbreviation) began as a no-budget local program on KTMA in Minneapolis in 1989, the brainchild of stand-up comic

The show that features characters poking fun at cheesy movies can at last be rewound and played back on video. The hilarious movie hecklers, from left: Crow T. Robot (voice by Trace Bealieu), Mike (Michael J. Nelson), and Tom Servo (voice by Kevin Murphy). COURTESY OF MCA-UNIVERSAL HOME VIDEO/UNIVERSAL CITY STUDIOS INC. PHOTO BY MICHAEL KIENITZ.

Joel Hodgson—to make a comedy series out of a common American pastime: razzing that stinker on the tube or at the drive-in with your buddies over a couple of cold ones. Here *MST3K*'s premise was formulated with many of the creative and performing personnel that would continue through the show's seven seasons. As the opening segment musically informs us, "in the not too distant future . . ." Joel, the janitor at Gizmonics Institute, has been shot into space aboard the SOL (Satellite of Love) by mad scientist Clayton Forrester and his assistant, Dr. Erhardt (later, TV's Frank). From their laboratory in Deep 13, Dr. Forrester subjects Joel and his puppet robot pals, Crow T. Robot, Tom Servo, Gypsy, and Cambot, to a cruel experiment: forcing them to watch the worst movies ever made and monitoring the effect on their brains via the inventions they concoct in their spare time. In between the "host segments," Joel and company, seen in silhouette at the bottom of the screen, maintain a running commentary on whatever bad movie they're screening, replete with peanut-gallery puns, in-jokes, and arcane movie/TV references. The carefully chosen films thus analyzed have included (badly) dubbed monster slugfests such as *The Robot vs. The Aztec Mummy* and *Gamera vs. Gaos,* Eurotrash muscleman epics like *Hercules and the Captive Women,* exploitation classics like Ed Wood's *The Sinister Urge,* and even the occasional big-name turkey like Gregory Peck's *Marooned* (aka *Space Travelers*). Shorter films have been paired with campy short subjects and serial "chapters" equally ripe for ribbing.

After twenty-one shows (and a local sensation) at KTMA, a thirteen-episode deal was made at HBO's newly emerging Comedy Channel. The show's trademark door-slamming tracking shot sequence was created at MST's "Best Brains" Studios in Eden Prairie, Minnesota, where all episodes have been taped. The first film to be skewered, on show #101, was *The Crawling Eye*—a tacky 1958 sci-fi featuring Forrest Tucker and a *lot* of giant mobile peepers from outer space.

As The Comedy Channel morphed into Comedy Central at the beginning of season three, the show's cult grew like "The Amazing Colossal Man" (the subject of show #309) into the phenomenal fan network it remains today.

Hodgson left the series after show #512 to pursue further TV opportunities and was replaced by Mike Nelson as a new victim of the evil Dr. Forrester. No stranger to the Satellite of Love, Nelson was already a writer and performer on the show, and thereafter did double duty as the head writer, as well. Likewise, as a look at any episode's end credits reveals, most of the *MST3K* gang wore multiple hats on both sides of the camera.

The end of the experiment

Citing supposedly slipping ratings (attributed to Hodgson's absence, among other things), the new head honchos at Comedy Central limited season seven to six episodes, and subsequently declined to renew the show that had been the cable network's number one original production for years. Loyal "MSTies" (as fans have dubbed themselves) are fearing not, as they have kept the show alive with fan clubs and live convention appearances (at which the cast will "do" a movie live onstage before an interacting audience). As of this writing, the show's producers are shopping around for a new cable network home, with The Sci Fi Channel as a likely new orbit for the SOL.

VIDEO AVAILABILITY

Three classic episodes have been released on Rhino Video and are available at select video stores: #301 *(Cave Dwellers),* #309 (*The Amazing Colossal Man*) and #512 (*Mitchell,* the final Hodgson episode); seventeen more are planned for video release through 1997.

TRIVIA TIDBITS

- *Mystery Science Theater 3000-The Movie* was finally released in the spring of 1996 after a year of production and delays. It features Mike and the 'bots lambasting a condensed version of the 1955 Universal sci-fi cult fave *This Island Earth,* and more elaborate "wraparound" segments. A video release is scheduled by the end of '96.

- Dr. Clayton Forrester's name is taken from Gene Barry's character in the 1953 classic *War of the Worlds.*
- The Official *MST3K* newsletter is called *The Satellite News.*
- *The Mystery Science Theater 3000 Amazing Colossal Episode Guide,* by the *MST3K* writers and performers, was published concurrent with the film, and contains typically wacky overviews of the series episodes and personalities.
- In 1993 thirty favorite episodes were re-edited into one-hour shows for syndication under the title *The Mystery Science Theater Hour,* hosted by Mike Nelson doing a remarkable send-up of A&E's Jack Perkins.
- Over the course of its run the show received a 1993 Peabody Award for Excellence in Broadcasting, numerous Cable Ace Award nominations, and Emmy nominations in 1993 and 1994 for Outstanding Writing for a Comedy or Variety Show (losing both times to Dennis Miller).
- The campy theme music, "The MST Love Theme," contains lyrics by Joel Hodgson and Josh Weinstein and music by Charlie Erickson and Joel Hodgson.

NEWHART

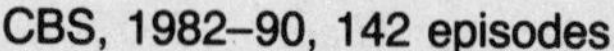

CBS, 1982–90, 142 episodes

CAST

Dick Loudon	Bob Newhart
Joanna Loudon	Mary Frann
Kirk Devane (1982–84)	Steven Kampmann
George Utley	Tom Poston
Leslie Vanderkellen (1982–83)	Jennifer Holmes
Stephanie Vanderkellen (1983–90)	Julia Duffy
Cindy Parker Devane (1984)	Rebecca York
Michael Harris (1984–1990)	Peter Scorlari
Larry	William Sanderson
Darryl #1	Tony Papenfuss
Darryl #2	John Voldstad
Jim Dixon	Thomas Hill
Chester Wanamaker	William Lanteau
Harley Estin (1984–85)	Jeff Doucette
Constable Shifflett (1985–89)	Todd Susman

EXECUTIVE PRODUCER: Barry Kemp
PRODUCER: Sheldon Bull
PRINCIPAL DIRECTORS: John Rich, Will Mackenzie, Dick Martin, Michael Zinberg, Rod Daniel
PRINCIPAL WRITERS: Barry Kemp, Sheldon Bull, Barton Dean, Earl Pomerantz, Emily Marshall, Miriam Trogdon

Green Mountain innkeeper

The second of Bob Newhart's memorable sitcoms (see *The Bob Newhart Show* entry; the third, *Bob,* was a later miss in 1992–93) again put the star and an extraordinarily

Dick Loudon (Bob Newhart) plays it straight to a chicken, as his wife, Joanna (Mary Frann), looks on, aghast, in a scene from *Newhart.*
COURTESY OF PERSONALITY PHOTOS, INC.

patient, lovely wife amid a bunch of colorful, individualistic zanies. This time, Bob (as writer Dick Loudon) ran an out-of-the-way inn with his wife in a rustic Vermont town, having left the New York rat race. For most of the series, he was a successful author/local radio show host, whose life was being assaulted by his crusty, slow-thinking handyman; three scrungy wilderness brothers (two of whom, each with the same name, never uttered a word through the entire series until just before the finale); a self-infatuated, poor-little-rich-girl housekeeper (actually two of them, cousins, when one actress was replaced by another); a trendy, insecure young program director who laid his pretentious world on Bob's shoulders; and assorted local old-timers.

The great reactor

As with his earlier sitcom, Newhart did his unique, low-key, always calm, somewhat bemused everyman routine with his usual finesse. One of his episodes had him—because of a clause in his contract with the local TV station—playing second banana to a newly hired, obnoxious talk show host (played by Don Rickles, one of Bob Newhart's closest real-life friends) and become the butt of his acidic humor. In another, Dick and Joanna Loudon are shamed into giving a dollar-a-mile pledge for weird brothers Larry, Darryl, and Darryl's "Save a Swamp" walkathon. On a particular occasion, the innkeeping Loudons are befriended by a fun-loving couple who announce they have bought the place next door and are turning it into formidable competition for Dick and Joanna; it becomes the darling of travel and restaurant critics, and it even has a terrific handyman and maid who outdo their own George Utley and Stephanie Vanderkellen.

The show, which managed to be both successful and hilarious without having to rely on more than a handful of big-name guest stars, ended after eight seasons with one of television's all-time surprise sight gags, keeping with the sophistication and cleverness which the writers set as standards. In the final episode, Dick Loudon is bopped on the head by a golf ball; in the last few minutes of the show, wakes up in bed not next to Mary Frann—Joanna on the show—but next to Suzanne Pleshette, Emily Hartley from Bob's previous TV series. Momentarily confused, he concludes that the entire eight years as an innkeeper had been a dream!

VIDEO AVAILABILITY

Seven collections of *Newhart* are available at certain video outlets. Each runs about fifty minutes and includes two episodes.

TRIVIA TIDBITS

- Although nominated a number of times for Emmy Awards, including Outstanding Comedy Series during each of its first three seasons, neither *Newhart* nor its star ever won.
- The show was filmed during its first season and taped for the remaining seven.
- Dick and Joanna Loudon ran the Stratford Inn, built in 1774 in Norwich, Vermont, at 28 Westbrook Road, where the flying squirrel was the town bird.
- Beautiful Mary Frann's wardrobe for every one of the 142 episodes included a designer sweater.
- Jerry Van Dyke was the original choice for the role of handyman George Utley.
- Henry Mancini wrote the show's main theme.

THE ODD COUPLE

ABC, 1970–75, 114 episodes

CAST

Felix Unger	Tony Randall
Oscar Madison	Jack Klugman
Murray Greshner	Al Molinaro
Speed (1970–74)	Garry Walberg
Vinnie	Larry Gelman
Roger (1973–74)	Archie Hahn
Roy (1970–71)	Ryan McDonald
Cecily Pigeon (1970–71)	Monica Evans
Gwendolyn Pigeon (1970–71)	Carol Shelly
Dr. Nancy Cunningham (1970–72)	Joan Hotchkis
Gloria Unger (1971–75)	Janis Hansen
Blanche Madison	Brett Somers
Myrna Turner (1971–75)	Penny Marshall
Miriam Welby (1972–74)	Elinor Donahue

CREATOR: Neil Simon
EXECUTIVE PRODUCERS: Jerry Belson, Garry Marshall, Harvey Miller, Sheldon Keller
PRODUCERS: Jerry Davis, Tony Marshall, Phil Mishkin
PRINCIPAL DIRECTORS: Jerry Paris, Mel Ferber, Frank Buxton, Jay Sandrich, Jerry Belson, Bob Birnbaum, Hal Cooper, Charles R. Rondeau
PRINCIPAL WRITERS: Mark Rothman, Lowell Ganz, Buz Cohan, Garry Marshall, Bill Angelos, Ben Joelson, Art Baer, Bob Brunner, John Rappaport

To Oscar—F.U.

Neil Simon's howlingly funny play *The Odd Couple* has been arguably his most creative vehicle—first as a Broad-

Before she was one of Hollywood's top film directors and before she was Laverne on *Laverne and Shirley,* Penny Marshall played Oscar Madison's dour secretary Myrna Turner on *The Odd Couple.*
COURTESY OF PERSONALITY PHOTOS, INC.

way smash with Walter Matthau and Art Carney, then as the hit 1968 movie with Matthau and Jack Lemmon, and as the classic TV series with Tony Randall and Jack Klugman (who went on the road with it in summer stage tours in the mid-1970s). The concept brought together in one apartment two mismatched friends who have only one thing in common: They were both divorced by their wives. As the announcer asks at the show's opening, "Can two divorced men share an apartment without driving each other crazy?" Sports columnist Oscar Madison, a gambling, beer-drinking slob, lives in a pig sty of a Park Avenue apartment. Portrait photographer Felix Unger, the compulsive neat freak and ultimate neurotic, moves in with Oscar and the two clash—with hysterical results.

Friends and family

Felix and Oscar got on each other's nerves from the opening moment, but maintained a love-hate relationship through five hilarious seasons of misadventures and characters. There are their ex-wives, Blanche and Gloria, who remain in their lives to pester them; the saucy, flighty Pigeon sisters from England who live upstairs; the pals who assemble for Oscar's weekly—and messy—poker game: Murray, the chubby cop, Speed, Vinnie, and Roger; and Oscar's whining secretary, Myrna Turner (who constantly tells her not especially interested boss about her unseen brother, Werner Turner, and sister, Verna Turner).

Howlingly funny was Felix's obsessiveness as a housekeeper: from vacuuming up potato chips the boys were dropping while munching their way through the Thursday poker games; to even disinfecting the cards they were using—while they were using them; to berating Oscar for the whirlwind of a kitchen he'd leave behind. For his part, Oscar would growl, "You want the brown juice or the green juice?" Felix would then ask, "What's the difference?" Oscar's response: "Two weeks." On another laugh-packed occasion, in which the two managed to find themselves on retreat at a religious commune, Felix stared at an anthill for five hours while Oscar organized a crap game among the monks. One episode was a reworking of the classic film *Roman Holiday,* with guest star Jean Simmons as royalty out to see Manhattan on her own and running into a surprisingly tender Oscar Madison, who insists on showing her the sights, despite Felix's urging that only cultural stops befit the lady.

But for all the yelling and bellowing, the endless conflicts between hotheaded Oscar and fussy Felix show that they really are, almost begrudgingly, best friends—most like a married twosome than either would admit. For un-

Tony Randall (left) and Jack Klugman will forever be known to generations of TV viewers as Felix and Oscar. *The Odd Couple* offers something for everyone's funny bone: from Felix's honking to clear his nasal passages, to Oscar's three-week-old tuna fish sandwiches.
COURTESY OF PERSONALITY PHOTOS, INC.

fathomable reasons, the show was not a huge hit in prime time but has become a cult classic in syndication.

VIDEO AVAILABILITY

The Odd Couple Collector's Edition is available through Columbia House, with each cassette containing four half-hour episodes.

EMMY AWARDS

1970–71 **Jack Klugman,** Outstanding Continued Performance by an Actor in a Leading Role in a Comedy Series

1972–73 **Jack Klugman,** Outstanding Continued Performance by an Actor in a Leading Role in a Comedy Series

1974–75 **Tony Randall,** Outstanding Lead Actor in a Comedy Series

TRIVIA TIDBITS

- Tony Randall and Jack Klugman played Felix and Oscar on Broadway for a sold-out benefit performance of Randall's National Actors Theatre in 1991, and became the summer hits of the London stage with the show in 1996.
- Klugman first played Oscar as Walter Matthau's replacement on Broadway and then led the London company of the show for a year. Randall first played Felix opposite Mickey Rooney in the late 1960s in Las Vegas and then for two summers in Chicago.
- During one of their summer tours of *The Odd Couple,* Randall and Klugman briefly switched roles, but the audiences were not receptive.
- *The Odd Couple: Together Again,* a 1993 reunion TV movie, brought together once more much of the original cast, including Penny Marshall (now a big-screen director).
- An ABC Saturday morning cartoon series, *The Oddball Couple* (1975–77), turned Oscar into a canine slob, Felix into a perfectionist cat, with a receptionist named Goldie Hound.
- *The New Odd Couple* on ABC (1982–83) reworked the original series with a racially mixed cast, including African-American actors Ron *(Barney Miller)* Glass and Demond *(Sanford and Son)* Wilson as Felix and Oscar.
- Carol Shelley and Monica Evans, who played the Pigeon Sisters, had the same roles on stage, on TV, and on the big screen.
- Brett Somers, who played Oscar's ex-wife, was Jack Klugman's real-life wife (and, during the show's run, real-life ex-wife).

- Felix and Oscar coexisted in Apartment 1102 at 1049 Park Avenue in Manhattan.
- The theme song by Neal Hefti was written originally for the movie version.

POLICE SQUAD!

ABC, 1982, 6 episodes

CAST

Det. Lt. Frank Drebin	Leslie Nielsen
Capt. Ed Hocken	Alan North
Ted Olson	Ed Williams
Johnny	William Duell
Norberg	Peter Lupus
Abraham Lincoln	Rex Hamilton

EXECUTIVE PRODUCERS/CREATORS: David Zucker, Jim Abrahams, Jerry Zucker
PRODUCER: Robert K. Weiss
DIRECTORS: Z.A.Z., Peter Krasny, Joe Dante, Reza Badiyi, Georg Stanford Brown
PRINCIPAL WRITERS: Nancy Steen, Neil Thompson, Robert Wuhl, Pat Proft, Tina Insana

Cigarette? Yes, it is

Two years after reinventing slapstick satire with their smash hit *Airplane!*, the comedy team of Zucker, Abrahams, and Zucker (originally known as Kentucky Fried Theatre and later just as ZAZ) tried to do to the standard TV cop show what they had done to airplane disaster movies, sending up not only the clichés but the familiar faces and the structure of those shows they had grown up watching on the tube. The result, with the similarly generic title of *Police Squad!*, was in the ratings cellar from the beginning and canceled after only six episodes. Over a decade later, however, the show not only has a fervent following that considers it the funniest half hour in TV history but it has spawned a hit film series and has turned a familiar TV actor into a bona fide comedy superstar.

For Lt. Drebin, ZAZ again cast the actor who had already gleefully parodied his TV image in *Airplane!*: Leslie Nielsen. This time, ZAZ spoofed Nielsen's countless TV tough-cop roles, especially in Quinn Martin productions such as *Cannon* and *The F.B.I.* After the opening announcement of "POLICE SQUAD, IN COLOR!" each episode would segue into an opening credit sequence, wherein the cast would blaze away at no one in particular (save for Abe Lincoln shooting back at John Wilkes Booth, his sole appearance each time!), followed by a "special guest star" (William Shatner, Robert Goulet, Lorne Greene, et al.) who was *immediately* killed off, and a typically pretentious QM-type title, such as "tonight's episode—'Testimony of Evil!'" (while the title on screen actually reads, "The Dead Don't Laugh"). Drebin and crew would bungle their crime-solving way through two acts and an epilogue, in which he would invariably pronounce the show's culprit a new resident of "Stateville Prison," followed by Drebin and Hocken imitating a freeze frame ending while the set collapsed around them or a bystander stood there in total confusion.

You had to watch

So why did the concept work like gangbusters on the big screen but not on the little one? Even ZAZ admitted that *Police Squad!* failed to click on prime time because "you had to *watch* it." Those used to doing more TV *listening* than *watching* over dinner or the evening paper missed most of the show's brilliant sight gags—such as the extra pair of hands on the wheel in Drebin's car, the squad car glove box stuffed with various kinds of gloves, or squad member Al, who was so tall that his head was always unseen above the frame. Since there wasn't a laugh track to cue those not paying attention—and ZAZ's cast was entirely straight-faced—the gags and malaprops were wasted on those used to the obviousness of most sitcom jokes. Luckily, the guys tried the concept again six years later on the big screen, and it found its widest audience with the box office hit *The Naked Gun: From the Files of Police Squad!* and its sequels, *The Naked Gun 2½: The Smell of Fear* (1991) and *The Naked Gun 33⅓: The Final Insult* (1994)—all of which have recycled some gags from the original series. And, thanks to *Police Squad!*'s home video release, that audience can watch it again and again—this time, to be sure to catch everything.

VIDEO AVAILABILITY

All six episodes are available on tape in select video stores, on two volumes: *Police Squad! Help Wanted!* and *More! Police Squad!*, each containing three episodes.

TRIVIA TIDBITS

- Prior to *Airplane!*, Leslie Nielsen had long been a favorite with sci-fi fans for starring in the 1956 cult classic, *Forbidden Planet*.
- John Belushi filmed one of the "special guest star" cameo gags, but after his sudden death the bit was cut and reshot with another actor before airplay.
- Nielsen, of course, repeated the role of Frank Drebin in the *Naked Gun* films, but Hocken was played by George Kennedy and Norberg by O. J. Simpson; only Ed Williams also repeated his role from the series, as forensic scientist Ted Olson, a wicked "Mr. Science" parody.
- Ira Newborn's *Police Squad!* theme was also used in the three movies.
- The members of ZAZ split up in the '90s to pursue more varied TV and film work. Jerry Zucker has had

the most success, as director of the Oscar-winning megahit *Ghost* and in 1995, *First Knight*.

- During the summer of 1991, with the second *Naked Gun* film raking it in at the box office, CBS reran the original series. It has since also been seen on Comedy Central.

SLEDGE HAMMER!

ABC, 1986–88, 41 episodes

CAST

Deputy Inspector Sledge Hammer	David Rasche
Sergeant Dori Doreau	Anne-Marie Martin
Captain Trunk	Harrison Page
Officer Mayjoy	Leslie Morris
Officer Daley	Patti Tippo
Coroner Norman Blates	Kurt Paul

CREATOR/EXECUTIVE PRODUCERS: Alan Spencer, William P. D'Angelo
PRODUCERS: Thomas Kane, Ron Friedman
PRINCIPAL DIRECTORS: Martha Coolidge, Jackie Cooper, James Sheldon, David Wechter, Chuck Braverman, Bruce Bilson, Bill Bixby, Reza Badiyi, Dick Martin
PRINCIPAL WRITERS: Chris Ruppenthal, Mark Curtiss & Rod Ash, Alan Spencer, Jim Fisher & Jim Staahl, Mert Rich & Brian Pollack

Hammered and hammered again

Square-jawed, totally self-confident, sartorially incorrect, insufferably macho Sledge Hammer was the ultimate cop in this spoof of Dirty Harry tough lawmen. He had no mercy for wimps, lowlifes, the scum of the earth, and jaywalkers and loved to use excessive force to collar perps and miscreants (at least one of whom he forced to slap himself silly). According to his book, even litterers deserved to be shot. His one true love and confidant: his giant, pearl-handled .44 Magnum. He called this weapon "Gun." Like the Royal Canadian Mounties, he invariably got his man, usually through bumbling—and the savvy proficiency of his female partner—to the relief of their commanding officer, the bellowing, migraine-ridden Captain Trunk.

At the end of the first season, things looked so glum for Sledge that the producers actually had him blown up while trying to defuse a nuclear device. When the network reversed itself and renewed the spoof for another season, Sledge was miraculously resurrected—no questions asked!

The obvious model for this cop show/movie send-up was the now legendary *Police Squad!* with Leslie Nielsen (which later evolved into the hugely successful *Naked Gun* flicks).

VIDEO AVAILABILITY

Two multi-episode collections, *Hammered: The Best of Sledge, Vols. 1 & 2,* are available at certain video outlets. Vol. 1 runs about 105 minutes and contains four episodes; Vol. 2 runs 75 minutes and contains three.

TRIVIA TIDBITS

- David Rasche, with his broad shoulders, deep blue eyes, and John Barrymore profile, had been a regular on the soap *Ryan's Hope* in the mid-1970s, and more recently had a recurring role as editor Mary McDonnell's pliant boss on CBS's *High Society* in 1995.
- Guest-starring as villains were Ray Walston, Bernie Kopell, John Vernon, Bill Dana, Robin Leach, Bill Bixby (who also directed a half-dozen episodes), rock star Adam Ant, and Davy Jones of the Monkees.

SOAP

ABC, 1977–81, 93 episodes

CAST

Jessica Tate	Katherine Helmond
Mary Campbell	Cathryn Damon
Chester Tate	Robert Mandan
Burt Campbell	Richard Mulligan
Corinne Tate (1977–80)	Diana Canova
Eunice Tate	Jennifer Salt
Billy Tate	Jimmy Baio
Danny Dallas	Ted Wass
Jodie Dallas	Billy Crystal
Benson DuBois (1977–79)	Robert Guillaume
Sanders	Roscoe Lee Brown
The Godfather (1977–78)	Richard Libertini
The Major	Arthur Peterson
Chuck/Bob Campbell	Jay Johnson
Peter Campbell (1977)	Robert Urich
Dutch (1978–81)	Donnelly Rhodes
The Godfather (1978–79)	Richard Libertini
Father Timothy Flotsky (1978–79)	Sal Viscuso
Detective Donahue (1978–80)	John Byner

CREATOR: Susan Harris

EXECUTIVE PRODUCERS: Paul Junger Witt, Tony Thomas, Susan Harris

PRODUCERS: Susan Harris, Dick Clair, Jenna McMahon

DIRECTORS: Jay Sandrich, J. D. Lobue

WRITERS: Susan Harris, Dick Clair, Jenna McMahon, Danny Jacobson, Tony Lang, Stu Silver, Barry Vigon

Come clean with a smirk

This controversial spoof of afternoon soaps chronicling the lives of two sisters, wealthy Jessica Tate and not-so-rich Mary Campbell, and their zany families in the fictional Connecticut town of Dunns River, provided outrageous viewing that offended more people than Norman Lear's *All in the Family* and his own soap opera send-up, *Mary Hartman, Mary Hartman,* combined. *Soap,* a wacky, highly original farce, was way ahead of its time dealing with such subjects as transsexualism, impotence, murder, extramarital affairs, cults, organized crime, banana republic revolutionaries, insanity, possessed babies, extraterrestrials, and everything else under the sun.

Meet your everyday families

There were the filthy-rich Tates: Jessica, a free-thinking socialite convicted of murder during the first season; Chester, her pompous, philandering husband who suddenly confesses to the crime; one lusty, sex-obsessed daughter (Corinne) who ultimately seduces a priest; her embarrassingly conservative sister, Eunice; their bratty teenage brother, Billy; a dotty old veteran grandfather who is unaware that World War II is over; and the family's delightfully insolent butler/cook/retainer, Benson DuBois.

And there were the blue-collar Campbells: Mary, a ditsy but lovable wife; Burt, her nutty second husband, who is captured by Martians; Danny, a macho son involved with the Mob; Jodie, his homosexual brother who longs for a sex-change operation; and a third son, Peter, a bed-hopping tennis pro whose womanizing ways get him bumped off. Wisecracking at the family is stepson Bob, a ventriloquist who has no control over what his dummy (Chuck) says.

Over *Soap*'s four prime-time seasons, and multiple, comically convoluted, and increasingly bizarre plot

The Tates, the Campbells—and wisecracking Benson in the middle: *Soap* offended many viewers during its four-year run, but the soap opera spoof was ahead of its time in dealing with controversial issues. From left: Katherine Helmond (Jessica Tate), Robert Mandan (Chester Tate), Robert Guillaume (Benson), Richard Mulligan (Burt Campbell), and Cathryn Damon (Mary Campbell). COURTESY OF PERSONALITY PHOTOS, INC.

twists, the voices of a number of ethnic and religious groups—including the National Council of Churches—tried intimidating ABC into shutting the lid on its *Soap* dish by picketing affiliates and boycotting the show's sponsors. The onslaught ultimately caused the network to cave, and *Soap*—which in its last few months had expanded to an hour—left for syndication heaven with a number of odd story lines unresolved.

VIDEO AVAILABILITY

Soap is available on tape through Columbia House in a collector's edition, with four half-hour episodes in each cassette.

EMMY AWARDS

1978–79	**Robert Guillaume,** Outstanding Supporting Actor in a Comedy, Comedy-Variety or Music Series
1979–80	**Richard Mulligan,** Outstanding Lead Actor in a Comedy
	Cathryn Damon, Outstanding Lead Actress in a Comedy

TRIVIA TIDBITS

- ◆ Robert Guillaume re-created his character of family butler Benson DuBois, the only sane member of the Tate household, in *Soap*'s sole spin-off show, *Benson* (1979–86).
- ◆ Billy Crystal made his splash with this series, playing Jodie Campbell, the gay son, before moving on to *Saturday Night Live* (see separate entry), a big-time stand-up career, and movie stardom in films like *When Harry Met Sally . . .* and *City Slickers.* Many of the others in the cast became notable names in television: Richard Mulligan, *(Empty Nest),* Katherine Helmond *(Who's the Boss?),* Ted Wass *(Blossom),* Diana Canova *(I'm a Big Girl Now),* and Robert Urich *(Spenser: For Hire).* Cathryn Damon starred briefly on *Webster,* but died soon after.
- ◆ The last five hour-long episodes from the spring of 1981 have been edited into thirty-minute segments to match the others in length for syndication.
- ◆ George Aliceson Tipton wrote the music to *Soap.*

TAXI

ABC, 1978–82; NBC, 1982–83; 112 episodes

CAST

Alex Reiger	Judd Hirsch
Louie DePalma	Danny DeVito
Elaine Nardo	Marilu Henner
Bobby Wheeler (1978–81)	Jeff Conaway
Tony Banta	Tony Danza
Latka Gravis	Andy Kaufman
"Reverend" Jim Ignatowski (1979–83)	Christopher Lloyd
Simka Gravis (1981–83)	Carol Kane
John Burns (1978–79)	Randall Carver

CREATOR/EXECUTIVE PRODUCERS: James L. Brooks, Stan Daniels, Ed. Weinberger, David Davis

PRODUCERS: Glen Charles, Les Charles, Ian Praiser, Richard Sakai, Howard Gerwitz

PRINCIPAL DIRECTORS: James Burrows, Ed. Weinberger, Will Mackenzie, Noam Pitlik, Michael Zinberg, Michael Lessac, Danny De Vito, Richard Sakai, Joan Darling

PRINCIPAL WRITERS: Barry Kemp, Earl Pomerantz, Glen Charles, Les Charles, Ken Estin, Ian Praiser, Howard Gerwitz, David Lloyd

Hailing the cabbies

Like *The Mary Tyler Moore Show,* this sitcom—created by four former staffers of that classic show—was a glib ensemble comedy set around a workplace, the Sunshine Cab Company in Manhattan. The happy but perennially grumbling blue-collar gang included glum-looking career cabbie (and father confessor) Alex Reiger and other driv-

Do you remember the character of John Burns (Randall Carver, top left)? The original cast of *Taxi,* circa 1978, from left: Marilu Henner (Elaine Nardo), Carver, Andy Kaufman (Latka Gravis), Jeff Conaway (Bobby Wheeler), Judd Hirsch (Alex Reiger), Tony Danza (Tony Banta), and Danny DeVito (Louie DePalma). COURTESY OF PERSONALITY PHOTOS, INC.

ers: struggling boxer Tony Banta; would-be actor Bobby Wheeler; lost soul John Burns (first season only); and aspiring art dealer and single mom Elaine Nardo. There was also mechanic Latka ("Tenk you veddy much") Gravis, a befuddled, childlike immigrant from a fictional country who spoke a fractured English (and, on occasion, revealed a superstud alter ego, Vic Ferrari), and later his featherbrained, ditzy girlfriend (and subsequently wife) Simka from "the old country." Into the mix came "Reverent Jim," a burned-out 1960s hippie who was ordained in the Church of the Peaceful. All were supposedly under the thumb of a little Napoleon dispatcher, the lecherous, self-loathing Louie DePalma, who threw his diminutive weight around from a wire cage in the center of the garage.

Hack tales

"See that guy over there," Alex tells Elaine, who has just become a cabbie. "He's an actor. And the one behind him, he's a boxer. And that girl—she's a beautician. And that other guy—he's a writer. I'm the only cabdriver in the place." There are the wonderfully punctuated grousing comments and well-timed zingers as the gang whiles away the time bemoaning the life of a hack driver. Frequently hilarious situations arose regularly out of sad-sack Alex's put-downs of his ex-wife (played on occasion by Louise Lasser of *Mary Hartman, Mary Hartman*); Reverend Jim's ruminating over his favorite lunch, SpaghettiOs and herring, and later, after making a killing at the track, buying the winning horse to take home as a pet; Louie's perennial insults, like "I hope somebody slams the cab door on your nose and your head explodes"; shy Latka's observation when Alex (wearing a ridiculous "old country" outfit) proposes to Simka on his behalf: "It's usually the village idiot, but you'll do in a pinch"; Bobby being stunned when an inexperienced actor fresh off the bus lands a plum role in his very first audition; Elaine envisioning herself belting out Broadway showstoppers in the dreary garage; Tony getting a job lead from his seafaring dad to be a deckhand on a Chinese freighter; and the cabbies planning to hobnob with the stars after crashing what they assume is Woody Allen's masquerade ball.

When it comes down to a single-word description, in *Taxi* it would probably be friendship. The show celebrated the optimism of dreamers, losers, outcasts, and eccentrics with both warmth and biting humor. Even tyrannical Louie secretly yearned to be "one of the boys," as Elaine was. In one episode, the gang had a chance to pursue other avenues when the Sunshine Cab Company briefly closed down. Dour-faced Alex became a night watchman, Louis a Wall Street stockbroker, Elaine an executive secretary, Tony a bookie's collector, Bobby an entertainer at kiddies' parties, and Reverend Jim a door-to-door encyclopedia salesman. But it would always be in the garage between shifts where, despite their grumbling, they would blossom and live out their deceptively rich lives.

VIDEO AVAILABILITY

Taxi: The Collector's Edition is available through Columbia House and features four half-hour episodes per cassette.

EMMY AWARDS

1978–79 *Taxi,* Outstanding Comedy Series
Ruth Gordon, Outstanding Lead Actress in a Comedy Series (Single Performance)

1979–80 *Taxi,* Outstanding Comedy Series
James Burrows, Outstanding Directing in a Comedy Series

1980–81 *Taxi,* Outstanding Comedy Series
Judd Hirsch, Outstanding Lead Actor in a Comedy Series
Danny DeVito, Outstanding Supporting Actor in a Comedy Series
James Burrows, Outstanding Directing in a Comedy Series
Michael Lessac, Outstanding Writing in a Comedy Series

1981–82 **Carol Kane,** Outstanding Lead Actress in a Comedy Series
Christopher Lloyd, Outstanding Supporting Actor in a Comedy Series
Ken Estin, Outstanding Writing in a Comedy Series

1982–83 **Judd Hirsch,** Outstanding Lead Actor in a Comedy Series
Carol Kane, Outstanding Supporting Actress in a Comedy, Variety or Music Series
Christopher Lloyd, Outstanding Supporting Actor in a Comedy, Variety or Music Series

TRIVIA TIDBITS

- Andy Kaufman, brilliant but bizarre stand-up comic, died of lung cancer in 1984 at thirty-four.
- Danny DeVito and Christopher Lloyd both made their major feature debuts in the film *One Flew Over the Cuckoo's Nest.* DeVito and Judd Hirsch had worked together earlier Off Broadway in *Line of Least Existence.* (DeVito played Hirsch's dog!)
- In later episodes, Rhea Perlman became a semiregular as Danny DeVito's girlfriend, Zena. In real life, they had lived together for eleven years and married during the run of *Taxi.*
- Broadway actor Judd Hirsch went on to star in *Dear John* for several seasons beginning in 1988 before returning to the stage and winning Tonys for both *I'm Not Rappaport* and *Conversations with My Father.* Actress Marilu Henner moved on to star as Burt Reynolds's wife in *Evening Shade,* and then in 1995 hosted her own daytime TV talk show. Christopher Lloyd scored later on the big screen as the wild-eyed inventor in the three *Back to the Future* movies. Tony Danza had a TV hit after *Taxi* with *Who's the Boss?,* which ran for ten seasons.
- Danny DeVito moved on to become a prominent Hollywood actor/director (*Throw Momma From the Train* in 1987; *The War of the Roses* in 1989; *Hoffa* in 1992; etc.), while wife Rhea Perlman found stardom as sarcastic Carla Tortelli on *Cheers* (see separate entry), the next hit show by *Taxi* cocreator brothers Glen and Les Charles.
- Picking up his second Emmy for playing Alex—after the much-honored series had been turned loose twice, first by ABC and then by NBC—Judd Hirsch brought down the house with his quip, "Don't they know we've been canceled?"
- Aside from Ruth Gordon, who won an Emmy during the show's first season as a free-spirited widow in the

episode "Men Are Such Beasts," guest stars on the series included Tom Selleck (pre-*Magnum PI*), Ted Danson (pre-*Cheers*), Keenan Wynn, Penny Marshall, Tom Hanks, Mandy Patinkin, Martin Short, Joanna Cassidy, Sally Kellerman (as Latka's mom), Jack Gilford, Wally "Famous" Amos, Herve Villechaize, and Eric Sevareid.

- Bob James was the composer of the show's theme song.

WHEN THINGS WERE ROTTEN

ABC, Sept.–Dec. 1975, 12 episodes

CAST

Robin Hood	Dick Gautier
Friar Tuck	Dick Van Patten
Alan-a-Dale	Bernie Kopell
Bertram/Renaldo	Richard Dimitri
Sheriff of Nottingham	Henry Polic II
Maid Marian	Misty Rowe
Little John	David Sabin
Prince John	Ron Rifkin
Princess Isabelle	Jane A. Johnston

CREATOR/EXECUTIVE PRODUCER: Mel Brooks
PRODUCER: Norman Steinberg
DIRECTORS: Jerry Paris, Joshua Shelley, Marty Feldman, Peter H. Hunt, Coby Ruskin
WRITERS: Mel Brooks, John Boni, Pat Proft, Jim Mulligan, E. Jack Kaplan, Bo Kaprall, John Stiles

Mel's merrie maniacs

Mel Brooks's zany satire on Robin Hood—having him played as a complete nitwit with a sexy but shallow Maid Marian—was embraced by the critics when it premiered, but audience reception was not strong enough to keep the show on the air for more than half a season. In Brooks's skewed world, stumblebum Robin and his misfit Merrie Men stole by tradition from the rich and gave to the poor whatever was left after expenses. Among the guests turning up in Sherwood Forest—which Prince John is intent on chopping down for a new housing development for wealthy burghers—in this regrettably short-lived historical send-up were Brooks's onetime boss, Sid Caesar (episode "The French Disconnection") and diminutive British nutcake, Dudley Moore. Much of the half-hour sitcom's humor was based on non sequiturs and historical anachronisms, the hallmark of Brooks's movie work through the years.

VIDEO AVAILABILITY

When Things Were Rotten, Vol. 1, containing three episodes of the series, is available at certain video outlets.

TRIVIA TIDBITS

- *When Things Were Rotten* was Mel Brooks's first series following the classic *Get Smart,* and reunited him with two members of that show's cast: Dick (Hymie the Robot) Gautier and Bernie (KAOS head Conrad Siegfried) Kopell.
- In the wake of several 1990s films about Robin Hood, Brooks reworked his off-kilter *When Things Were Rotten* premise with his 1993 feature, *Robin Hood: Men in Tights.*
- Mel Brooks's only other TV series to date has been *Nutt House* in the late 1980s.
- The theme to *When Things Were Rotten* was written by Artie Butler.

WKRP IN CINCINNATI

CBS, 1978–82, 87 episodes

CAST

Andy Travis	Gary Sandy
Jennifer Marlowe	Loni Anderson
Arthur Carlson	Gordon Jump
Bailey Quarters	Jan Smithers
Johnny Caravella (aka Dr. Johnny Fever)	Howard Hesseman
Les Nessman	Richard Sanders
Herb Tarlek	Frank Bonner
Gordon Sims (aka Venus Flytrap)	Tim Reid
Carmen Carlson	Allyn Ann McLerie
Mrs. Carlson	Carol Bruce
Arthur Carlson Jr.	Sparky Marcus

CREATOR/EXECUTIVE PRODUCER: Hugh Wilson
PRODUCERS: Rod Daniel, Bill Dial, Blake Hunter, Peter Torkovei, Steven Kampmann
DIRECTORS: Jay Sandrich, Michael Zinberg, Asaad Kelada, Hugh Wilson, Rod Daniel, Will Mackenzie, Linda Day
WRITERS: Hugh Wilson, Tom Chehak, Judi Neer, Bill Dial, Michael Filerman, Peter Torkovei, Steven Kampmann, Max Tash

Sleepless in Cincinnati

In the mold of *The Mary Tyler Moore Show,* this popular ensemble series was also set in broadcasting. Here, however, the workplace was a fictional 5,000-watt radio outlet in Cincinnati, the number sixteen station in an eighteen-station market, run by an insecure, middle-aged, flum-

Radio station WKRP employed some very strange individuals (from left): paranoid newsman Les Nessman (Richard Sanders), buxom blond receptionist Jennifer Marlowe (Loni Anderson), hip late-night disc jockey Venus Flytrap (Tim Reid), bashful continuity writer Bailey Quarters (Jan Smithers), scatterbrained station manager Arthur Carlson (Gordon Jump), and plaid-dressed sales manager Herb Tarlek (Frank Bonner). COURTESY OF PERSONALITY PHOTOS, INC.

moxed Arthur Carlson, cowed by his overbearing mother who owned the place and made all the behind-the-scenes decisions. The staff included: eager-beaver program director, Andy Travis; sexy secretary/receptionist Jennifer Marlowe, a blond eyeful who ran the station without actually doing anything; gullible, nerdy news director Les Nessman; deejays Johnny Fever (the spaced-out rock 'n' roller behind the shades) and Venus Flytrap (the hip jazz aficionado); shy continuity writer and sometimes news reporter Bailey Quarters; and smarmy, sartorially incorrect, self-absorbed sales manager Herb Tarlek, a walking riot of checks and plaids who lusts after Jennifer.

The station, a money-loser that needed a facelift, had brought in Andy Travis and a rock format that alienated both its elderly audience and its few sponsors. Carlson, the general manager (called "the Big Guy"), didn't know anything about rock 'n' roll, nor did Les Nessman, whose main concerns were his hog reports (for which he became the proud recipient of the coveted Silver Sow award) and his pretend office, a wall-less corner space with chalk marks where the walls would be. Into the mix came counterculture—1960s survivor Johnny Fever for the morning drive show and at night cool night guy Gordon Sims, who called himself Venus Flytrap. Other than weatherman Skivvy Nelson (who was never seen), no other on-air people seemed to work at WKRP.

Still not number one

The zany goings on that drove the show included: the famous Thanksgiving episode in which the station hatched a sponsor promotion by dropping live turkeys from a plane over a mall, only to have them hit the ground like wet bags of cement; Les Nessman's lofty plans to update the station's news coverage by parking his mobile news scooter and covering Cincinnati in a World War I biplane flown by a crazy war veteran named Buddy; and Herb Tarlek's latest commercial sale, bringing in the business of an undertaking tycoon to advertise his funeral packages—despite the station's groovy rock format and its young audience.

The nutty week-to-week schemes intertwined with the very real relationships that developed among the WKRP staff members, who were always there for one another, endeared this sitcom to viewers not only through the show's four-year prime-time run but also through the subsequent years in syndication. Nearly a decade after the original program left the CBS schedule, *The New WKRP in Cincinnati* turned up, debuting in 1991 and running for a couple of seasons. It was one of the first sitcoms to return to TV with first-run episodes in syndication. Arthur Carlson, Herb Tarlek, and Les Nessman were the only original station employees to return, although Johnny Fever, Venus Flytrap, and Jennifer Marlowe dropped by occasionally for well-publicized guest appearances.

VIDEO AVAILABILITY

Three *WKRP* collections (including the two-part pilot) are available at certain tape outlets. Each runs about fifty minutes and contains two episodes.

TRIVIA TIDBITS

- The Les Nessman character provided a running gag that lasted four seasons: an unexplained Band-Aid that roamed from week to week over every visible part of his body.
- Legendary movie star Sylvia Sidney had the role of Mrs. Carlson in the pilot episode, but chose not to continue.
- Loni Anderson became one of America's top sex symbols of the era. Jan Smithers, on the other hand, married actor James Brolin and left show business when the series ended. Gordon Jump went on to replace veteran actor Jesse White as the Lonely Repairman on the Maytag commercials. Gary Sandy, a former soap star, returned to the Broadway stage briefly and then dropped from sight.
- Cast members Gordon Jump, Frank Bonner, and Howard Hesseman each directed at least one episode of the series. Tim Reid and Richard Sanders wrote several of the episodes.
- Creator Hugh Wilson and Tim Reid later became involved in CBS's offbeat, somewhat eccentric *Frank's Place* (1987–88), critically acclaimed but lacking an audience.
- The *WKRP* theme was written by Tom Wells.

YES, MINISTER / YES, PRIME MINISTER

BBC, 1980–82; Arts and Entertainment, 1982–83;
15 episodes

CAST

James Hacker, MP	Paul Eddington
Sir Humphrey Appleby	Nigel Hawthorne
Bernard Woolley	Derek Fowlds
Annie Hacker	Diana Hoddinott
Frank Weisel	Neal Fitzwilliams
Foreign Secretary	Tenniel Evans
Sir Frederick Stewart (Jumbo)	John Savident

PRODUCER: Sydney Lotterby
CREATORS/WRITERS: Antony Jay, Jonathan Lynn

Comedy corridors of power

This popular early 1980s British series, reportedly Margaret Thatcher's favorite program, takes a skewed look at life at No. 10 Downing Street. The weekly half-hour show that made the stiff upper lips of Britons (to say nothing of discerning Americans) twitch followed the laugh-provoking, ongoing power struggle between cabinet ministers and deferential, fawning civil servants ("Yes, Minister! No, Minister! If you wish it, Minister!"). The cast included Paul Eddington's Right Honorable James Hacker, Minister for Administrative Affairs, and his associates: Nigel Hawthorne's harrumphing Sir Humphrey Appleby, permanent secretary; Derek Fowlds' self-serving Bernard Woolley, the minister's private secretary; and Neal Fitzwilliams's Frank Weisel, the minister's political adviser (at least for the first seven episodes). As the newly appointed minister, Hacker soon finds many of his ideas for reform openly opposed by the civil servants whose job it is to implement them—most notably Sir Humphrey, who became locked in wacky conflict from week to week.

VIDEO AVAILABILITY

Five collections of the series, retitled *Yes, Prime Minister* for video, are available at certain outlets. Each runs about ninety minutes and contains three episodes.

TRIVIA TIDBITS

- Aside from *Yes, Minister,* noted British actor Nigel Hawthorne is best known in the United States for his starring role in *Shadowlands* on Broadway in 1991, which earned him a Tony Award as Outstanding Lead Actor in a Drama; his memorable title performance in *The Madness of King George*, which earned him an Oscar nomination in 1994 as Best Actor; and his Duke of Clarence in Ian McKellen's 1995 film of *Richard III.*
- Paul Eddington, a noted Shakespearean actor and a longtime member of the Old Vic, has starred on the American stage but remains best known for his work on London's West End and in many British TV series.

DRAMA SERIES

Everybody loves a good story. And from time immemorial, stories have been spun verbally. Over the ages they were, successively, carved into walls, put down on paper, performed in town squares and traveling shows, acted out on stage, committed to film, played out on radio, and dramatized on television. Today they are told on audio cassette and available for the reading on CD-ROM. Every story is a drama of sorts, whether lighthearted or serious, frivolous or thought-provoking.

Drama comes in all forms: extraordinary storytelling as in historical or autobiographical documents such as *Roots, Holocaust, The Autobiography of Miss Jane Pittman,* and *The Civil War;* compelling continuing drama such as *I, Claudius* and *Upstairs, Downstairs;* adaptations of great American plays ranging from *Death of a Salesman* to *The Caine Mutiny Court-Martial* to *The Piano Lesson;* and timeless classics in the mold of *King Lear* with Olivier. Television has had the honor of featuring Ingrid Bergman in Henry James's *Turn of the Screw* at the start of her career on TV and playing Golda Meir at the end of it. For stark contrast, television has had the dubious credit of presenting three movies about Amy Fisher and Joey Buttafuocco—all in a period of five days.

Much memorable television drama emerged from the medium's Golden Age of the 1950s. But a great deal of it has been lost, either because it was performed live or possibly captured on kinescope, which was such an unsophisticated process that many shows deteriorated to the point of being unwatchable. Videotape began to be used in the late 1950s, around the time that *Playhouse 90*—arguably the last of the great anthology drama shows of the era—was nearing the end. Another form of popular drama was then taking over the network schedules, the television western (at one point seven of the top ten shows, starting with *Gunsmoke,* were cowboy sagas). Into the mix came cop shows, medical dramas, action/adventure tales, and even the inevitable TV movie-of-the-week—which has evolved from a handful in the late 1960s to more than 200 a season on the major networks, on cable, and in first-run syndication.

Never-ending stories

Although daytime dramas, known affectionately since radio days as soap operas, provided a daily diet for the homebound—from *One Man's Family* to *Days of Our Lives*—their prime-time equivalent found a faithful audience beginning with *Peyton Place* in 1964. Then after a time, they gained a renewed, rather fanatic following in the late seventies with *Dallas, Dynasty, Knots Landing,* and *Falcon Crest.* The tradition continues today with *Beverly Hills 90210, Melrose Place,* and assorted other youth-oriented soaps and their various knockoffs, produced by the contemporary king of the genre, Aaron Spelling.

Cops and robbers

Police files—actual and fictional—have provided a particularly rich source of dramatic, even thoughtful television, whether merely showing dedicated law enforcement officers going through their everyday work—as in Jack Webb's *Dragnet*—or tossing various amounts of action into the plot and giving younger audiences the impression that police duty was adrenaline-pumping and pressure-packed 24 hours a day with tough-talking men and women in blue playing urban cowboys—as in, perhaps, *The Untouchables* and *The Streets of San Francisco.* These shows' legacies continue in today's gripping programs not yet available on video, *Homicide: Life on the Street* and *NYPD Blue.*

Saddle tramps and sodbusters

As durable a dramatic genre as any on film (or video), the western has its roots in movies' earliest days. Whether the western dramas unwind as simple morality plays—basically the good guys versus the bad guys—or as a series of shoot-'em-ups for action's sake, they represent an undying part of Americana that viewers made a television staple in the 1950s and '60s, and have been on a mission of rediscovery in the West (both Old and New) in recent years, beginning with *Lonesome Dove* and continuing through today's *Dr. Quinn, Medicine Woman* and *Walker: Texas Ranger.* To paraphrase that immortal Texas bard, Waylon Jennings, "our heroes have always been cowboys," and cowboys—from Wyatt Earp and Bat Masterson to the Mavericks and the assorted figures from the Louis L'Amour frontier tales—have captured the imagination of viewers who, doubtless, will always look pridefully on the western genre as America's own contribution to pop culture.

Doctors and patients

As much as cop shows and westerns, dramas (both feel-good and provocative) dealing with doctors—from Richard Boone's Konrad Steiner to Jane Seymour's Michaela Quinn—have been beloved and much-watched staples of the medium for more than four decades. There is little more dramatic than having the doctors and nurses dodging crash carts in emergency rooms in shows like *Chicago Hope* and *E.R.;* going through lifesaving routines and assorted surgeries (even if concocted by writers steeped in medical jargon), as in *St. Elsewhere;* or comforting patients old and young, and dispensing prescriptions and prognostications, in the manner of often surly *Ben Casey* or compassionate, kindly *Marcus Welby, M.D.*

Legal eagles

Human emotions are swayed as much in legal dramas as in the doctor shows—in series such as *The Defenders* in one era, *L.A. Law* in another, and *Murder One* in a third—that never fail to capture the viewers' attention. There have been dollops of high drama in these courtroom sagas, whether the spotlight was on Raymond Burr as burly, dogged Perry Mason or Andy Griffith as homey, rumpled Ben Matlock. Their shows, and dozens like them through the decades, dispensed the type of law the average viewer found both accessible and endlessly entertaining and brought him or her back for more season after season, as much for vicariously solving the crime with the wily counselors as for watching the always tidy (though not always reality-based) court proceedings.

Miniseries and movies of the week

The miniseries, in its true dramatic form, was an outgrowth of finding a way to visualize a book on television over a brief period of time, whether it be over several nights in one-, two-, or three-hour segments; or, in the case of "epics" like James Michener's *Centennial* or Herman Wouk's *The Winds of War* and *War and Remembrance,* over a period of months. The ABC "Novel for Television" and NBC's "Best Sellers" series in the 1970s were created for dramatizations of works such as John Steinbeck's *East of Eden,* Ernest Hemingway's *The Sun Also Rises,* F. Scott Fitzgerald's *Tender Is the Night,* and others by Taylor Caldwell, Irwin Shaw, Robert Ludlum, and Conrad Richter, acted by stellar casts. Although the expansive miniseries has been diminished in recent years, the dramatic impact of the best of them has been undeniable, as has been the staple for three decades, the so-called movie of the week—dealing, at its best, with social issues such as racial understanding *(My Sweet Charlie),* the AIDS epidemic *(An Early Frost),* the homeless *(No*

Place Like Home), the Vietnam War aftermath *(To Heal a Nation),* battered spouses *(The Burning Bed),* etc.

Dramatic diversity

Television drama has proven to be a magnet that constantly brings viewers back to the set, luring them with diverse settings and backgrounds; war and warriors (World War II's *Combat* and *The Rat Patrol;* Vietnam's *Tour of Duty* and *China Beach*); Depression-era America *(The Waltons);* small-town America (Rome, Wisconsin of *Picket Fences*); big-city America (*Naked City* and its eight million stories); the frontier (*Little House on the Prairie* and *How the West Was Won*); the inner city (*Nasty Boys* and *Room 222*); comic book action heroes (*Batman, Wonder Woman, The Incredible Hulk, Captain America,* and *The Flash*); and even reality shows such as *Resue 911, America's Most Wanted, Unsolved Mysteries,* and *Cops.*

Although many of the great dramatic anthology shows of the fifties—the Golden Age—are no longer widely available, most of the classic series have enough episodes (some even have a complete run) on tape to offer the viewer an extraordinarily diverse sampling of fair and quality shows. The 66 or so assorted series and dramatic specials included here—all available in certain video outlets in one form or another—will hopefully bring back old memories or develop a taste for programs that passed some viewers by.

THE ADVENTURES OF ROBIN HOOD

CBS, 1955–58, 143 episodes

CAST

Robin of Locksley	Richard Greene
Maid Marian Fitzwater (1955–57)	Bernadette O'Farrell
Maid Marian Fitzwater (1957–58)	Patricia Driscoll
Prince John	Donald Pleasence Herbert Gregg
Sheriff of Nottingham	Alan Wheatley
Friar Tuck/Francis Tucker	Alexander Gauge
Little John/John Little	Archie Duncan Rufus Cruikshank
Will Scarlet/Will of Winchester	Paul Eddington Ronald Howard
Sir Richard the Lionhearted	Ian Hunter
Lady Guinivere	Gillian Sterrett
Jennie (Maid Marian's servant)	Geraldine Hagan
King Arthur	Peter Asher
Queen Eleanor	Jill Esmond

PRODUCER: Hannah Weinstein
DIRECTORS: Bernard Knowles, Lindsay Anderson, Ralph Smart, Terry Bishop

Man of Sherwood Forest

This swashbuckling British series, set in eleventh-century England, relates the legendary adventures of Robin Hood and his Merry Men of Sherwood Forest, robbing from the rich and giving to the poor, and battling the evils of Prince John and his nasty cohort, the Sheriff of Nottingham. The oft-told tale, of course, has been filmed theatrically innumerable times, but this television series with then-popular adventure stalwart Richard Greene (onetime Hollywood hopeful) was the first for the medium. It later was syndicated as *Adventures in Sherwood Forest.* Subsequently, in 1967, there was a futuristic cartoon version of the legend, *Rocket Robin Hood,* in which he and a band of spacemen stationed aboard Sherwood Asteroid in the thirtieth century battled the forces of injustice throughout the universe.

Nearly two decades later, a British movie made for cable, *Robin Hood,* premiered in the U.S. on Showtime, with Michael Praed as the star. It was followed by an eleven-part series in 1984–85. Praed, as Robin Hood, was killed off in the last segment and replaced by Jason Connery (Sean's son) as Robert of Nottingham, who became the new Robin Hood, in a second eleven-part series (1985–86).

VIDEO AVAILABILITY

Five *Robin Hood* collections—including the two-part premiere episode—are available at certain video outlets. Each runs about fifty-two minutes and contains two shows.

TRIVIA TIDBITS

- Mel Brooks's satiric *When Things Were Rotten* (for television) and the later *Robin Hood: Men in Tights* (for the big screen) spoofed the traditional Robin Hood tale, as did the 1984 CBS made-for-TV movie *The Zany Adventures of Robin Hood,* with George Segal and Morgan Fairchild.
- As an American movie star, Richard Greene is best remembered for playing opposite Shirley Temple in *The Little Princess,* getting billed over Basil Rathbone and Nigel Bruce in the first major Sherlock Holmes movie, *The Hound of the Baskervilles,* and starring opposite Spencer Tracy in *Stanley and Livingstone.*

AGATHA CHRISTIE'S MISS MARPLE

PBS "Mystery!", 1985–93 (first American broadcast),
12 multipart episodes

CAST

Jane Marple	Joan Hickson
Inspector Slack	David Horowitch

PRODUCERS: Guy Slater, George Gallaccio
DIRECTORS: Silvio Narizzano, Roy Boulting, David Giles, Guy Slater, John Davies, Mary McMurray, David Tucker, Martyn Friend, Alan Plater, Norman Stone, Christopher Petit
WRITERS: T. R. Bown, Julia Jones, Ken Taylor, Jill Hyem

Sleuthing in sensible shoes

Agatha Christie was twenty-five when she wrote her first detective story in 1916. It would be another dozen or so years before village busybody-turned-amateur-detective Miss Jane Marple of St. Mary Mead made her debut in *The Murder at the Vicarage* and went on to star in twelve novels and nineteen short stories. And it would be veteran British character actress Joan Hickson's knowing performance as the spinsterish sleuth who has proven to be the definitive embodiment of Christie's creation. John Leonard in *New York* magazine wrote: "She is everything a Marple ought to be . . . Nothing escapes her eyes and her needles . . . She believes in evil: It has always been, it will continue to be, and she pursues it in sensible shoes." When the first of the several Miss Marple series *(The Body in the Library)* premiered in Great Britain on Christmas Day 1984, Hickson was 78. The British press described her as being "possibly the oldest actress ever to take a leading role in a TV series."

Joan Hickson personified just about everything about Jane Marple that Agatha Christie described in her autobiography. She was physically like the sweet old lady of Agatha's vision, her character pleasingly quiet and determined. She viewed everything and assessed everyone from the vantage point of her garden in the village of St. Mary Mead and her passions in life with knitting and gossip—not that she spoke much, but she invariably probed gently and encouraged others to tell all.

Before the tweedy, birdlike Joan Hickson put her imprint on the fastidious Marple character, it was jowly, quite ample Margaret Rutherford whom most people pictured as the indomitable sleuth through her lighthearted trio of Marple movies of the 1960s. Interestingly, Hickson played a small role in one of these films, *Muder She Said,* as a charwoman.

The impeccable Hickson Miss Marples that followed *The Body in the Library* are:

The Moving Finger (an outbreak of poison-pen letters in an idyllic East Anglian village)
A Murder Is Announced (games that lead to death)
A Pocketful of Rye (murder in the Home Counties)
Murder at the Vicarage (Marple's first case in the Christie canon)
Sleeping Murder (investigating a woman's vision of a strangled body—actually, Marple's final case)
At Bertram's Hotel (intrigue about family inheritances)
Nemesis (murder on a coach tour of historic homes)
4:50 From Paddington (death on the railway)
A Caribbean Mystery (murder on the sunny isle of St. Honore, where Miss Marple's nephew had sent her on holiday)
They Do It With Mirrors (Christie's fifth Marple novel, written in 1952; with Jean Simmons as Marple's childhood friend, Carrie Louise Serrocold)

The Mirror Crack'd From Side to Side (intrigue when an American film crew shoots a picture at the nearby home of a Marple friend)

A Caribbean Mystery and *They Do It With Mirrors* were both filmed by CBS earlier (the latter retitled *Murder With Mirrors*) with Helen Hayes as Miss Marple. *The Mirror Crack'd* was filmed theatrically in 1980 with Christie's indefatigble sleuth being portrayed by Angela Lansbury, later TV's Jessica Fletcher on *Murder, She Wrote,* Miss Marple in all but name.

VIDEO AVAILABILITY

Many of the twelve Miss Marple tales with Joan Hickson are available on tape at certain video outlets. They run anywhere from 100 to 150 minutes. Also available is a boxed collector's set containing four of the most famous adventures of the septuagenarian sleuth.

TRIVIA TIDBITS

- Agatha Christie took the name from Marple Hall, a spectacular, supposedly haunted house in Cheshire, England, of which she was very fond.
- Joan Hickson, whose acting career spans seven decades, won a Tony Award on Broadway for Alan Ayckbourn's *Bedroom Farce* in 1979.
- The two other Jane Marples—preceding Joan Hickson, Angela Lansbury, Helen Hayes, and Margaret Rutherford—were British film and West End star Barbara Mullen (on stage in *Murder at the Vicarage* in 1949 and again in 1975) and music hall performer-turned-comedienne, singer and actress Gracie Fields (TV's first Miss Marple in *A Murder Is Announced,* 1956).

ANNE OF GREEN GABLES

PBS WonderWorks, 1985, 4 episodes

ANNE OF AVONLEA

Disney Channel; PBS WonderWorks; 1987, 4 episodes

CAST

Anne Shirley	Megan Follows
Marilla Cuthbert	Colleen Dewhurst
Mathew Cuthbert (1985)	Richard Farnsworth
Gilbert Blythe	Jonathan Crombie
Diana Barry	Schuyler Grant
Rachel Lynde	Patricia Hamilton
Miss Stacy	Marilyn Lightstone
Mrs. Barry	Rosemary Radcliffe
John Barry	Robert Collins
Matilda Bluewit (1985)	Samantha Langevin
Mrs. Hammond (1985)	Jayne Eastwood
John Sadler (1985)	Joachim Hanson
Elspeth Allen (1985)	Christine Krueger
Reverend Allen (1985)	Cedric Smith
Amelia Evans (1985)	Jackie Burroughs
Morgan Harris (1987)	Frank Converse
Mrs. Harris (1987)	Dame Wendy Hiller
Miss Brooke (1987)	Rosemary Dunsmore

Jen Pringle (1987)	Suzanna Hoffman
Emmeline Harris (1987)	Genevieve Appleton
Mabel Sloanne (1987)	Kay Hawtrey
Alice Lawson (1987)	Mag Ruffman
Mr. Lawson (1987)	Les Carlson

EXECUTIVE PRODUCER/DIRECTOR: Kevin Sullivan
COEXECUTIVE PRODUCER: Lee Polk
COPRODUCER: Ian McDougall
WRITERS: Kevin Sullivan, Joe Wisenfeld
BASED ON NOVELS BY: Lucy Maud Montgomery

A children's classic

Fiery, redheaded young Anne Shirley, mistreated by a blacksmith's family and returned to the orphanage, comes to the attention of aging spinster Marilla Cuthbert and her bachelor brother Mathew, owners of a farm in the small village of Avonlea on Canada's Prince Edward Island. Although Marilla and Mathew had hoped to adopt a boy from the orphanage to help work the farm, carrot-topped Anne is mistakenly sent and soon captures the heart of shy, retiring Mathew. Even the taciturn Marilla grudgingly accepts the bright and lively girl, whose romantic dreams and penchant for dramatics constantly create problems. Over the course of the two miniseries, spanning eight hours, Anne grows to young womanhood, endears herself to the entire community, falls in love, becomes a teacher, and helps adoptive mother Marilla live out her life happily.

This loving dramatization of Lucy Maud Montgomery's original *Anne of Green Gables* and three subsequent novels—all written in the early part of the twentieth century—were filmed on location on Prince Edward Island. The show proved exceptional television fare for younger viewers and won a slew of awards in Canada and an Emmy on American TV. It also led the way for a long, well-reviewed series called *Tales of Avon-*

lea (with a new, young female lead, Sarah Polley, as the new protagonist, Sara Stanley) and a number of guest stars in period costumes dropping by (Christopher Reeve, Jane Seymour, Michael York, Madeline Kahn, and Christopher Lloyd—in an Emmy-winning performance). It premiered in spring 1990 and continued well into the decade.

VIDEO AVAILABILITY

Both of the original miniseries are available at certain video outlets. Each is a two-set collection running about 220 minutes. In addition, several volumes of *Tales of Avonlea* are available, each running about 100 minutes and containing two episodes of the series.

EMMY AWARD

1985–86 Outstanding Children's Program

TRIVIA TIDBITS

- A musical version of *Anne of Green Gables* was initially staged at the Charlottetown Festival Theatre on Prince Edward Island in 1965 and has become a children's perennial. An operatic production of it was staged in New York at the City Center in 1971.
- The first film version of *Anne of Green Gables* was made in 1919 with silent star Mary Miles Minter as the pigtailed Anne Shirley.
- The only sound film version of the story was made in 1934 with a young unknown named Dawn O'Day as the star. She took the character name of Anne Shirley as her own, and acted from then on under that name. She also starred in the 1940 sequel, *Anne of Windy Poplars.*
- Canadian-born Colleen Dewhurst brought her *Anne of Green Gables* character of Marilla Cuthbert to the *Tales of Avonlea* series on several occasions before her death in 1991.

BEVERLY HILLS 90210

Fox, 1990–

CAST

Brenda Walsh (1990–94)	Shannen Doherty
Brandon Walsh	Jason Priestley
Jim Walsh	James Eckhouse
Cindy Walsh	Carol Potter
Kelly Taylor	Jennie Garth
Steve Sanders	Ian Ziering
Dylan McKay (1990–95)	Luke Perry
Andrea Zuckerman	Gabrielle Carteris
David Silver	Brian Austin Green
Donna Martin	Tori Spelling
Scott Scanlon (1990–91)	Douglas Emerson
Nat	Joe E. Tata
Samantha Sanders (1991–)	Christina Belford
Chris Suiter (1991)	Michael St. Gerard
Henry Thomas (1991–)	James Pickens Jr.
Emily Valentine (1991–)	Christine Elise
Nikki (1992–)	Dana Barron
Meyers (1992–93)	Mark Kiely
Clare Arnold (1993–)	Kathleen Robertson
Valerie Malone (1994–)	Tiffani-Amber Thiessen
Ray Pruit (1994–)	Jamie Walters
Joe Bradley (1995–)	Cameron Bancroft

CREATOR: Darren Star

EXECUTIVE PRODUCERS: Aaron Spelling, E. Duke Vincent, Charles Rosin, Paul Waigner, Steve Wasserman & Jessica Klein

SUPERVISING PRODUCER: John Eisendrath
PRODUCERS: Kenneth Miller, John Whelpley, Dinah Kirgo, Jason Priestley

TV-land's best-known zip code

A particular favorite among younger audiences of the early 1990s, this ensemble prime-time soap revolved initially around twin siblings (played by Shannen Doherty and Jason Priestley) who move from Minneapolis to posh Beverly Hills and adjust to life at West Beverly Hills High with the privileged children of celebrities and tycoons: fast-lane teens who drove Jags, BMWs, and Porsches. An instant hit on the then-struggling Fox Network, and soon to emerge as one of the most popular American television shows of its day internationally, it portrayed issues that concerned young people: safe sex, alcoholism, drugs, date rape, and suicide. As the years went by and the high school kids moved on to college and careers, the shows continued to reflect the problems and interests of Generation X.

Several of the original "newcomers"—like Shannen Doherty and Luke Perry—became media darlings and left for TV movies and other ventures later in the 1990s. But there were more than enough revolving story lines and attractive young actors to fill continuing roles. Among the young stars who found 1990s celebrity status through the stylish *90210* were Jason Priestley (who ultimately became one of the show's producers), Jennie Garth, Tiffani-Amber Thiessen, Cameron Bancroft, Tori Spelling (daughter of Aaron Spelling, the prolific television producer who also was responsible for this hit series), Grant Show, Brian Austin Green, and Gabrielle Carteris (who simultaneously had a brief fling as host of a daytime talk show).

A number of companion shows, such as popular *Melrose Place* and its not-as-well-received East Coast counterpart, *Central Park West* (later retitled *CPW*), at-

The hot kids from *Beverly Hills 90210* (clockwise, from top right): Luke Perry (Dylan), Shannen Doherty (Brenda), Jason Priestley (Brandon), Gabrielle Carteris (Andrea), Tori Spelling (Donna), Brian Austin Green (David), Jennie Garth (Kelly), and Ian Ziering (Steve). COURTESY OF PERSONALITY PHOTOS, INC.

tempted to reach the same 1990s audience, but they simply did not have the same zip code.

VIDEO AVAILABILITY

Several collections of *Beverly Hills 90210* are available at certain video outlets; among them, the pilot to the one-hour series, including twenty-five minutes of footage never previously seen, and the episode dealing with the original cast's high school graduation, with a special interview segment featuring the stars added.

THE BIG VALLEY

ABC, 1965–69, 112 episodes

CAST

Victoria Barkley	Barbara Stanwyck
Jarrod Barkley	Richard Long
Nick Barkley	Peter Breck
Audra Barkley	Linda Evans
Heath Barkley	Lee Majors
Eugene Barkley (1965–66)	Charles Briles
Silas	Napoleon Whiting
Sheriff Steve Madden	Douglas Kennedy

EXECUTIVE PRODUCERS: Jules Levy, Arthur Gardner, Arnold Laven

PRODUCER: Lou Morheim

DIRECTORS: Virgil W. Vogel, Arthur H. Nadel, Lawrence Dobkin, Don Taylor, Charles S. Dubin, Arnold Laven, Paul Henreid, Bernard McEveety, William A. Graham, Norman S. Powell, Richard Sarafian, Ida Lupino, Michael Ritchie

WRITERS: John O'Dea, Arthur Rowe, Jay Simms, Steven W. Carabatsos, Don Ingalls, Ken Pettus, Mel Goldberg, Edward J. Lasko, Lee Erwin

Lady of means—and a gun

White-haired Barbara Stanwyck's portrayal of the wealthy, iron-willed matriarch in a family of cattle ranchers in 1878 marked the acme of her television career (except for her later appearance in the first episode of *The Thorn Birds*) following a long and impressive body

The rugged Barkley clan, led by matriarch Victoria Barkley—played to perfection by screen legend Barbara Stanwyck. From left: Peter Breck (Nick), Stanwyck, Linda Evans (Audra), Lee Majors (Heath), and Richard Long (Jarrod). COURTESY OF PERSONALITY PHOTOS, INC.

of films. Her status in buckskins—overseeing a 30,000-acre spread in California's San Joaquin Valley—put her right up there shoulder to shoulder with the Ponderosa's Ben Cartwright at the head of a brood of stalwart sons (plus a shy, sensitive daughter, played by up-and-coming Linda Evans). Helping Victoria run the spread: level-headed lawyer son Jarrod; hotheaded number two son, ranch foreman Nick; feisty Heath, the illegitimate son of Victoria's deceased husband and his fling with an Indian maiden; and introspective young Eugene, who disappeared without a trace after the show's first season. There also was the family retainer, Silas. With the boys, Victoria stood her ground against the lawless Old West: schemers, murderers, bank robbers, con men (one played by Milton Berle), Mexican revolutionaries, and any number of varmints.

The Big Valley showed the Barkleys as a clan as well as individual characters. There are fights, humor, warmth—and a familial philosophy holding the series together. There were moving episodes such as "Boots With My Father's Name" (Jeanne Cooper, mother of Corbin Bernsen, played an impoverished extortionist attempting to conceal the facts regarding Heath's birthright), thrillers like "A Day of Terror" (Stanwyck faces down a sister matriarch, Colleen Dewhurst, who happens to be a vicious outlaw), and lighthearted ones, "The Great Safe Robbery" in particular, with Warren Oates playing a bumbling thief. The show boasted terrific fights such as those in "The Emperor of Rice" and "The Challenge," and even cliff-hangers with perils rivaling any by Pearl White (the silent screen's "Queen of the Cliff-hangers") in "Four Days to Furnace Hill," in which Stanwyck at sixty did many of her own quite dangerous stunts, like being lassoed around the waist, pulled to the ground, and dragged by the horse of the varmint who has captured her. And, in "Earthquake," she found herself buried in the rubble of a collapsing church.

On her own, however, Barbara Stanwyck, who appeared in all but seven of the 112 episodes and won Emmy nominations in each of the first three seasons of *The Big Valley,* continued to reject the description of Victoria Barkley as "Ben Cartwright in skirts," but simply a self-sufficient woman who made good on the frontier.

The series came to the end of the prime-time trail in 1969, but found great success in its TV afterlife, where, as reported in *Variety* in 1972, "it is consistently at the top of the list of ALL the off-network hour shows in syndication."

VIDEO AVAILABILITY

The Big Valley is available at certain video outlets in two feature-length adventures, each running about ninety minutes; and a double-feature collection—one guest-starring Charles Bronson, the other William Shatner.

EMMY AWARDS

1965–66 **Barbara Stanwyck,** Outstanding Continued Performance by an Actress in a Leading Role in a Dramatic Series.

TRIVIA TIDBITS

- Despite being one of the great ladies of the American screen over a period of four decades with eighty-four films, Barbara Stanwyck never won an Academy Award (although she was nominated four times). She received an Honorary Oscar at the 1982 ceremony.
- An earlier foray into television was as host and occasional star of the single-season half-hour dramatic anthology, *The Barbara Stanwyck Show,* in 1960. Although the show was not successful, its star won an Emmy for Outstanding Performance by an Actress in a Series. (She would win her third Emmy years later for *The Thorn Birds*.)
- One episode, "Rimfire," served as a prospective spin-off for a series with Van ("The Green Hornet") Williams, but the pilot failed to sell.
- Two fellow stars during Stanwyck's days at Warner Bros. in the 1940s—Paul Henreid and Ida Lupino—directed several episodes each of *The Big Valley.*
- Victoria Barkley's horse was named Misty Girl.
- The theme music to *The Big Valley* was written by George Duning.

BONANZA

NBC, 1959–73, 440 episodes

CAST

Ben Cartwright	Lorne Greene
Adam Cartwright (1959–65)	Pernell Roberts
Hoss (Eric) Cartwright (1959–72)	Dan Blocker
Little Joe Cartwright	Michael Landon
Jamie Cartwright (1970–73)	Mitch Vogel
Hop Sing	Victor Sen Yung
Sheriff Roy Coffee (1960–72)	Ray Teal
Deputy Clem Poster (1961–73)	Bing Russell
Mr. Canaday (Candy) (1967–70, 1972–73)	David Canary
Griff King (1972–73)	Tim Matheson
Dusty Rhodes (1970–72)	Lou Frizzell

CREATOR/EXECUTIVE PRODUCER: David Dortort
PRODUCERS: Richard Collins, David Dortort, Robert Blees
PRINCIPAL DIRECTORS: Edward Ludwig, Paul Landres, Christian I. Nyby II, Joseph Kane, John Brahm, Lewis Allen, Arthur Lubin, Robert Altman, Lee H. Katzin, Marc Daniels, Tay Garnett, Jacques Tourneur, William Whitney, Don McDougall, Virgil W. Vogel, Charles R Rondeau, Irving J. Moore, Michael Landon
PRINCIPAL WRITERS: David Dortort, Al C. Ward, Thomas Thompson, Clair Huffaker, Dean Riesner, Gene L. Coon

Men of the Ponderosa

Bonanza was a bonanza for NBC, becoming its longest-running dramatic show—second only to CBS's compet-

Dominance on the homestead—the Cartwright clan guards the Ponderosa. The all-male leads of *Bonanza,* from left: Dan Blocker (Hoss), Pernell Roberts (Adam), Michael Landon (Little Joe), and Lorne Greene (Ben). COURTESY OF PERSONALITY PHOTOS, INC.

ing western, *Gunsmoke,* which ran for twenty years. Set in the vicinity of Virginia City, Nevada, not long after the discovery of the Comstock Silver Lode following the Civil War, *Bonanza* traced the exploits of Ben Cartwright and his three grown sons (each by a different wife). Their massive spread, the Ponderosa, sprawled over a thousand square miles; their stories dealt with mining, banking, and ranching interests—and the ordinary people whose paths they crossed.

Bonanza was a continuing drama about the relationships among the principals and characters (guest stars) who turned up weekly—as opposed to a shoot-'em-up western. The family patriarch was silver-haired, sonorous Ben Cartwright. Adam, his oldest son, was the introspective one, a hardheaded dude with a ready smile; hulking Hoss, the middle one, the somewhat slow-witted, jolly son with the ten-gallon hat; Little Joe, the cute, curly-haired one destined to be a heartthrob to contemporary young audiences. All, of course, were handy with their guns when needed. Not long after Adam decided to strike out for other opportunities and vamoosed from the series, a saddle tramp known as Candy came onto the scene and became in effect an honorary Cartwright, helping to oversee the Ponderosa.

Bonanza was really a he-man's show. Despite the fact that few women were to be seen, these guys kept an immaculate house (with the help of Chinese houseboy/cook Hop Sing). And there were rumblings over the years about having four grown men living together and why the sons never left home. Any woman who happened by and caught the eye of one or another of them was dead or departed by the end of the episode. But Ben Cartwright and sons (in later seasons there was an adopted kid, played by Mitch Vogel) continued on their steady path of helping uphold local law and order, righting wrongs when possible, and running the spread—which never seemed to have more than four ranch hands, despite the Ponderosa's immense size. It ended when Lorne Greene and Michael Landon, the two original cast members left, decided to strike out for other horizons—the former as a contemporary detective on the short-lived *Griff* and then the futuristic *Battlestar Galactica,* the latter finding his path on *Little House on the Prairie* and then *Highway to Heaven.*

VIDEO AVAILABILITY

Episodes of *Bonanza* are available at certain video outlets. Each cassette, running about 100 minutes, contains two episodes.

TRIVIA TIDBITS

- *Bonanza* was the first western broadcast in color on television. (*The Lone Ranger* had episodes filmed in color in anticipation of future color set popularity.)
- The title theme was written by Jay Livingston and Ray Evans, Oscar-winning composers of "Buttons and Bows" and "Mona Lisa." Words were written to the theme, which was sung only once—by the four leads at the opening credits.
- Pernell Roberts left his role as Adam after five seasons to pursue other vistas—like playing Rhett Butler in the musical stage version of *Gone With the Wind*—and, although doing lots of episode work on TV, didn't work in another series for fourteen years until he returned—bearded and sans toupee—to star in *Trapper John, M.D.*
- Dan Blocker's sudden death of a heart attack on the eve of the 1972–73 season of *Bonanza* marked the first blow to the show's continued success. Moving it from its long-held Sunday slot to Tuesday evenings was the second.
- Three made-for-TV movie *Bonanza* follow-ups (in 1988, 1993, and 1995) featured Lorne Greene's daughter and the sons of Michael Landon and Dan Blocker.
- Landon died of pancreatic cancer in 1991.
- Victor Sen Yung was Charlie Chan's #1 son in a number of films in the 1940s.

BRIDESHEAD REVISITED

PBS Great Performances, (first American broadcast) 1982, 2 two-hour episodes, 9 one-hour episodes

CAST

Capt. Charles Ryder	Jeremy Irons
Lord Sebastian Flyte	Anthony Andrews
Julia Flyte	Diana Quick
Lord Marchmain	Laurence Olivier
Lady Marchmain	Claire Bloom
Cara	Stephane Audran
Nanny Hawkins	Mona Washbourne
Father Mowbray	John Le Mesurier
Edward Ryder	John Gielgud
Celia Ryder	Jane Asher
Anthony Blanche	Nickolas Grace
Mr. Samgrass	John Grillo
Lord Brideshead	Simon Jones

PRODUCER: Derek Granger
DIRECTORS: Charles Sturridge, Michael Lindsay-Hogg
WRITER: John Mortimer

Wealth and circumstance

The elegantly mounted, stylishly cast *Brideshead Revisited*—adapted from Evelyn Waugh's 1945 novel and told in flashback—follows the wealthy, aristocratic Marchmain family of English Catholics from the early 1920s to the close of World War II. The "dazzling marathon," as *Variety* called the memorable, multitextured production on its American premiere, is recalled through the reminiscences of Charles Ryder, a Protestant school friend of

The stars of the eleven-part series *Brideshead Revisited,* from top left: Jeremy Irons (Charles Ryder), Diana Quick (Julia Flyte), and Anthony Andrews (Sebastian Flyte). COURTESY OF PERSONALITY PHOTOS, INC.

the Marchmains' youngest son, the charming, profligate Sebastian Flyte. "My theme is memory," Ryder, as narrator, states, "that winged host that soared about me one gray morning of wartime." Here the memory is of the Flyte family at Brideshead Castle.

Topflight performers, superb direction, an outstanding distillation of Waugh by writer John Mortimer, handsome production designs by Peter Phillips, and costumes by Jane Robinson combined to make *Brideshead* truly a place to be revisited. Particularly extraordinary is the impeccable latter-day performance in the final two-hour chapter of Laurence Olivier as the failing marquis, played right up to an unforgettable death scene with imperious disdain. No less impressive are Claire Bloom as the unbending wife Olivier left for a younger woman, John Gielgud as Jeremy Irons's imperious father, Nickolas Grace as effeminate Anthony Blanche, Jane Asher as adulterous Celia Ryder, John Grillo as Sebastian's unctuous advisor, Stephane Audran as Marchmain's Italian mistress, and Mona Washbourne as the alert nanny.

All told, heady television in the grand manner.

VIDEO AVAILABILITY

Brideshead Revisited is available at certain video outlets in six individual volumes (called Books), each running about ninety-eight minutes. The complete miniseries is also available in a deluxe collector's edition.

EMMY AWARD

1981–82 **Laurence Olivier,** Outstanding Supporting Actor in a Limited Series or a Special.

TRIVIA TIDBITS

- Charles and Celia Ryder's children are named, quite coincidentally in Kennedy style, Caroline and John-John—as they were in the original 1940s Waugh novel.
- Laurence Olivier, in his early seventies when he took the role, played Lord Marchmain from age fifty to his late seventies. Nearly three decades earlier, he and fellow *Brideshead* actors Claire Bloom and John Gielgud had costarred in the Olivier film version of *Richard III.*
- Ryder's (Jeremy Irons) first days at Oxford were filmed not only in novelist Evelyn Waugh's old college, Hertford, but in Waugh's own rooms.

- Filming was begun in Malta in 1979 under the direction of Michael Lindsay-Hogg, son of actress Geraldine Fitzgerald, but a labor dispute back in England brought production to a halt some months later. The director was then forced to leave because of other commitments, and Charles Sturridge, a young Waugh specialist, took his place when production resumed later in the year.
- The mythical estate Waugh called Brideshead is the magnificent Castle Howard in Yorkshire.

CENTENNIAL

NBC, 1978–79, 12 chapters (26 hours, later edited to 21 hours)

CAST

Pasquinel	Robert Conrad
Alexander McKeag	Richard Chamberlain
Henry Bockweiss	Raymond Burr
Lise Bockweiss	Sally Kellerman
Clay Basket	Barbara Carrera
Joe Bean	Clint Walker
Lame Beaver	Michael Ansara
Old Sioux	Chief Dan George
Jacques Pasquinel	Stephen McHattie
Mike Pasquinel	Kario Salem
Levi Zendt	Gregory Harrison
Elly Zahm	Stephanie Zimbalist
Oliver Seccombe	Timothy Dalton
Maxwell Mercy	Chad Everett
Sam Purchas	Donald Pleasence
Lucinda McKeag Zendt	Cristina Raines
Hans Brumbaugh	Alex Karas
General Asher	Pernell Roberts
Lt. John McIntosh	Mark Harmon
Col. Frank Skimmerhorn	Richard Crenna
John Skimmerhorn	Cliff De Young
R. J. Poteet	Dennis Weaver
Nate Person	Glynn Turman
Nacho Gomez	Rafael Campos
Amos Calender	Jesse Vint
Mike Lasater	Scott Hylands
Bufe Coker	Les Lannom
Jim Lloyd	William Atherton

Charlotte Seccombe	Lynn Redgrave
Mule Canby	Gregg Mullavey
Axel Dumire	Brian Keith
Finlay Perkin	Clive Revill
Mervin Wendell	Anthony Zerbe
Maude Wendell	Lois Nettleton
Philip Wendell	Doug McKeon
Tranquilino	A Martinez
Morgan Wendell	Robert Vaughn
Lew Vernor	Andy Griffith
Sidney Enderman	Sharon Gless
Cisco Calender	Merle Haggard
Aunt Augusta	Gale Sondergaard
Paul Garrett/Narrator	David Janssen

CREATOR AND EXECUTIVE PRODUCER: John Wilder
PRODUCERS: Howard Alston, Malcolm R. Harding, Alex Beaton, George Crosby
DIRECTORS: Virgil W. Vogel, Paul Krasny, Harry Falk, Bernard McEveety
WRITERS: John Wilder, Jerry Ziegman, Charles Larson

Only the rocks live forever

Centennial, a monumental, all-star dramatic event (to be surpassed in sheer size and length more than a decade later only by *The Winds of War/War and Remembrance*), initially spanned several months in two- and three-hour individually titled chapters, and recounted James Michener's epic 1,100-page novel depicting the evolution of the American West. The rousing tale begins in the middle 1700s in uncharted frontier territory with the alliance of Pasquinel (played by Robert Conrad), a French Canadian trapper, and Alexander McKeag (a heavily bearded Richard Chamberlain), a Scottish fugitive. They become partners and work their way through Indian territory over the next thirty-odd years, during which time their progeny would marry and intermarry.

The miniseries spanned the Indian wars, the Mormon treks of the 1840s, the first great cattle drives from Texas to Colorado, and the range wars of the 1870s. It moved into the twentieth century with the 1930s dust bowl and ended in the contemporary, fictional Colorado town of Centennial. Somehow, amidst all of the events described, the Civil War and World Wars I and II were entirely overlooked.

In terms of scope, there never has been anything as ambitious on television as *Centennial,* covering more than 200 years of history. (*Roots* probably comes the closest.) Michener himself contributed a brief prologue to the miniseries, while David Janssen narrated the tale from the point of view of Paul Garrett, the fictional direct descendant of the trapper Pasquinel and the ultimate owner of the vast Venneford Ranch, the largest in Colorado. Janssen appeared in the final episode, having related the story (through flashback) to Andy Griffith, as a modern-day Michener-like historian.

VIDEO AVAILABILITY

The entire saga of James Michener's *Centennial* is available through Columbia House on twelve two-hour cassettes.

TRIVIA TIDBITS

- Despite the enormity of this miniseries, with its nearly three dozen principal actors, only two Emmy nominations came its way: film editing (chapter 1) and art direction/set decoration (chapter 7). The Emmy season was dominated by *Roots: The Next Generations* and *Backstairs at the White House.*
- The show's $25 million budget—four times that of *Roots*—made this the most expensive television venture up to its time.

- The sweeping score to *Centennial,* available on CD, was composed by John Addison.
- Stephanie Zimbalist acted here with Timothy Dalton. Her later TV work opposite Pierce Brosnan in *Remington Steele* gave her the unique distinction of costarring with two future (and consecutive) James Bonds.

CHEYENNE

ABC, 1956–63, 107 episodes

CAST

Cheyenne Brodie	Clint Walker
Smitty	L. Q. Jones

EXECUTIVE PRODUCER: William T. Orr
PRODUCERS: Arthur Silver, Roy Huggins, Harry Foster
PRINCIPAL DIRECTORS: Herbert L. Stock, George Waggner, William Hale, Douglas Heyes, Leslie H. Martinson, Arthur Lubin, Paul Landers, Stuart Heisler, Jerry Hopper, Jean Yarbrough

Tall man riding

Stalwart Clint Walker rode tall in the saddle as frontier scout Cheyenne Brodie, an adventurer in the post-Civil War West who drifted from job to job along with a side-kick (at least for the first season), and worked his way through tough gunfighters, bank robbers, rustlers, assorted varmints, and beautiful women. This was the first of the famed Warner Bros. television westerns, based rather loosely on the studio's 1947 film starring Dennis Morgan, but it rambled through a somewhat convoluted history. Initially, it was one of three rotating anthologies under the umbrella title *Warner Bros. Presents* (together with a series based on the classic *Casablanca*—with tough guy Charles McGraw in the Bogart role—and one based on another 1940s movie, *Kings Row*). *Cheyenne* quickly emerged as the most popular element, and the other shows fell by the wayside. Strapping (and very tall) Clint Walker became an overnight star in a stock company of TV players that Warners was grooming. These included James Garner (who appeared in several early *Cheyenne* episodes), Jack Kelly, Ty Hardin, Will Hutchins, Efrem Zimbalist Jr., Roger Moore, Robert Conrad, Troy Donahue, Van Williams, Edd "Kookie" Byrnes, Connie Stevens, Dorothy Provine, and Wayde Preston.

By the second *Cheyenne* season, Walker was riding alone without partner Smitty; by the third, he had competition on the airwaves, as Warners launched both *Sugarfoot,* with Will Hutchins and Jack Elam, and the lighthearted *Maverick.* Just before the start of the fourth season of *Cheyenne,* Clint Walker asked for a big pay raise and walked out on his contract. The studio then brought in Ty Hardin to play the part of Bronco Layne, but kept the *Cheyenne* title and the popular *Cheyenne* theme (by William Lava and Stan Jones). The following season, Walker returned to his role, the Bronco Layne character was split off into a *Bronco* series, and, with *Sugarfoot,* the three shows were combined to make *The Cheyenne Hour.*

VIDEO AVAILABILITY

A number of *Cheyenne* episodes are available on videocassette in certain tape outlets, among them adventures with young stars Dennis Hopper and Michael Landon. Each runs approximately fifty minutes. Also available: several episodes of *Bronco,* including one with newcomer Mary Tyler Moore, and another with James Coburn as a rather nasty Jesse James.

TRIVIA TIDBITS

◆ James Garner guest-starred in the premiere episode of *Cheyenne,* entitled "Mountain Fortress." The last show of the first season, "The Dark Rider," was a pilot for *Maverick,* and featured Garner along with Jack Kelly and Diane Brewster (she'd have a recurring role on that show).

- Among the guest stars over the years: Angie Dickinson, Dennis Hopper, John Carradine, Adam (Batman) West, Chad Everett, Sally Kellerman, and Jack Elam.
- Clint Walker made his film debut as "Tarzan" in a gag bit in the 1954 Bowery Boys comedy *Jungle Gents* (billed as "Jett Norman"). Two years later, he was a spear carrier in Cecil B. DeMille's *The Ten Commandments.* Subsequently, he was signed to a seven-year Warner Bros. contract. When it ran out in 1963, he chose to concentrate on big-screen features but starred in only a dozen or so—the most notable being *Send Me No Flowers* (with Doris Day), *Night of the Grizzly,* and *The Dirty Dozen.* In 1975 he starred in his only other TV series, *Kodiak* (not to be confused with *Kolchak,* which premiered the same night, or *Kojak,* which was running at the same time). It was a modern-day action-adventure show set in Alaska and lasted one season.

CHINA BEACH

ABC, 1988–91, 62 episodes

CAST

Lt. Colleen McMurphy	Dana Delany
Pvt. Samuel Beckett	Michael Boatman
Pvt. Frankie Bunsen	Nancy Giles
Dodger	Jeff Kober
Dr. Dick Richard	Robert Picardo
Maj. Lila Garreau	Concetta Tomei
Boonie Lanier	Brian Wimmer
K.C. (Karen Charlene Koloski)	Marg Helgenberger
Laurette Barber (1988)	Chloe Webb
Cherry White (1988–89)	Nan Woods
Wayloo Marie Holmes (1988–89)	Megan Gallagher
Natch Austin (1988–89)	Tim Ryan
Jeff Hyers (1989–90)	Ned Vaughn
Holly Pelegrino (1989–90)	Ricki Lake
Sergeant Pepper (1989–91)	Troy Evans

CREATORS/EXECUTIVE PRODUCERS: William Broyles Jr., John Sacret Young

Nurses in 'Nam

A strong, antiwar look at the horrors of Vietnam through the eyes of an army nurse at China Beach, a U.S. Armed Forces hospital and recreational facility at Da Nang, *China Beach* was one of only two major TV series to date about the war. Dana Delany became a star in her role as triage nurse Colleen McMurphy from Lawrence, Kansas. Also making a name for herself was Marg Helgenberger as K.C., a civilian hooker on the base who plies her trade for $100 an hour. Robert Picardo appeared in the cast as mellow Dr. Dick, McMurphy's true love, but he was married. Tim Ryan was a pilot named Natch, one of the assorted men with whom she had passing affairs. Generally, each episode of the hour-long show would juggle three interlocking story lines, including: one in which a swaggering lieutenant colonel comes to the front line hospital and into the lives of three of the women there, seeing "potential" in all of them; one in which McMurphy reconsiders the fling she's having with Dr. Dick; and one in which a GI leaves the hospital thinking he's Chuck Berry.

Like *M*A*S*H* of another era, the dramatic *China Beach* was laced with black humor to relieve the tensions of war. Some came from sarcastic, street-smart Samuel Beckett, the morgue attendant, and some from chubby Red Cross nurse Holly Pelegrino, known as Holly the Donut Dolly (played by Ricki Lake, the erstwhile roly-poly John Waters favorite in *Hairspray,* who later slimmed down significantly to reemerge as a mid-1990s talk show host).

The much-acclaimed, emotion-packed series interlaced flashbacks and flash-forwards. As *China Beach* wound down to its conclusion, it allowed McMurphy and others, now in the 1980s, to recall with both pride and sorrow their experiences in Vietnam. William Broyles Jr. and John Sacret Young had created some powerful and quite thoughtful television.

VIDEO AVAILABILITY

The feature-length TV-movie pilot to the series, running about ninety-five minutes, is available at certain video outlets.

EMMY AWARDS

1988–89 **Dana Delany,** Outstanding Lead Actress in a Drama Series.

1989–90 **Marg Helgenberger,** Outstanding Supporting Actress in a Drama Series.

TRIVIA TIDBITS

- The site of much of the action was the 510th Evac Hospital, 63rd Division.
- *China Beach* was one of two concurrent series that featured a Samuel Beckett. The other: *Quantum Leap* (Scott Bakula's character).
- One particularly moving episode featured a rare performance by Harold Russell, the World War II veteran who had lost both arms in a training accident and later was cast in the film *The Best Years of Our Lives* (winning two Academy Awards). He then left acting and subsequently became longtime president of AMVETS and chairman of President Lyndon Johnson's Committee on the Hiring of the Handicapped. He returned to the screen in 1980 in *Inside Moves* before accepting a guest role on *China Beach* in 1989.
- The show theme, entitled "Reflections," was performed by Diana Ross and the Supremes.

THE CISCO KID

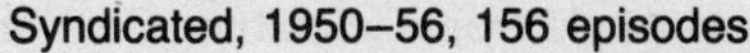

Syndicated, 1950–56, 156 episodes

CAST

The Cisco Kid	Duncan Renaldo
Pancho	Leo Carrillo

PRODUCER: Walter Schwimmer
DIRECTORS: Eddie Davis, Paul Landers, Lambert Hillyer, Leslie Goodwins, Sobey Martin
PRINCIPAL WRITERS: Royal Cole, Irwin Lieberman, Endre Bohem, Sherman Lowe, Gerald Geraghty, Don Brinkley, Betty Burbridge, Elizabeth Breecher, Andre Lamb

"Oh, Pancho!" "Oh, Ceesco!"

This popular, long-running series, the first to be filmed in color, brought O. Henry's legendary "Robin Hood of the Old West" to television (after a long run on radio beginning in 1943) along with the two actors who had ridden together seeking adventure in a dozen or so "B" westerns of the late 1940s. The TV *Cisco Kid* quickly became one of the most popular kids' westerns and one of the most durable—despite the fact that it wasn't on any of the three major networks.

Happy-go-lucky Cisco, a Mexican bandit, and his somewhat slovenly, buffoonish sidekick Pancho had been fractured-English saddle pals since coming out of O. Henry's series of stories that began in 1907 with "The Caballero's Way." The pair scoured the Old Southwest, righting wrongs, and having a gay old time before the days of political correctness when many viewers only saw the racial stereotypes being projected. Through the years, immaculately attired Cisco, oozing with Latin charm, and his fun-loving pal traditionally have been portrayed by Hispanic actors, making light of the image being offered. Only the sound screen's first Cisco Kid, suave Warner Baxter, was an Anglo from Columbus, Ohio, introducing the character in the 1929 movie *In Old Arizona*. He won an Oscar as Best Actor for the role and did two more Cisco Kid movies. At the end of the 1930s, dashing Cesar Romero played Cisco as a smarmy dandy in half a dozen movies, with Chris-Pin Martin as Pancho. It would fall to a lesser name, Duncan Renaldo, who became *the* Cisco Kid in 1945, teamed with Leo Carrillo. (Gilbert Roland also played Cisco in a handful of films in the late 1940s.) Finally, in 1950, Renaldo and Carrillo brought the characters to television. In the eyes of the law, Cisco and Pancho were desperadoes, wanted for unspecified crimes; in the eyes of the poor and downtrodden, the two were do-gooders—Latin Robin Hoods, often acting where inept and unscrupulous lawmen would not.

In 1995 Turner Network Television resurrected *The Cisco Kid* in a "revisionist" made-for-TV movie costarring Jimmy Smits and Cheech Marin (late of Cheech and Chong), complete with their familiar "Oh, Pancho!" "Oh, Ceesco!" as the pair rode into the sunset seeking new adventures, while the pop group War gave its contemporary music take on the familiar Cisco Kid theme.

VIDEO AVAILABILITY

The Cisco Kid rides with jovial sidekick Pancho in nine two-episode collections, each running about fifty-two minutes and available at certain video outlets. In addition, there is an interesting set that pairs a Cisco Kid movie starring Cesar Romero, *The Caballero,* with an episode from the TV series with Duncan Renaldo.

TRIVIA TIDBITS

- Cisco's horse was named Diablo; Pancho rode Loco.

- Years after production finally ended on the ZIV series, Duncan Renaldo continued to tour with the aging Diablo. (He passed away in 1980.) Leo Carrillo retired and died in 1961 at age eighty-one. A beloved screen figure, he has a beach named after him in southern California.
- *The Cisco Kid* theme was composed by Albert Glasser.

COLUMBO

NBC, 1971–78, 44 episodes of 90 and 120 minutes; ABC, 1989–90, 19 two-hour episodes, plus assorted two-hour "movies" through 1996

CAST

Lieutenant Columbo	Peter Falk

CREATORS: Richard Levinson, William Link
EXECUTIVE PRODUCERS: Roland Kibbee, Dean Hargove
PRODUCERS: Edward K. Dodds, Everett Chambers, Richard Alan Simmons, Douglas Benton, Robert F. O'Neill
DIRECTORS: Steven Spielberg, Alf Kjellin, Vincent McEveety, Harvey Hart, Richard Quine, Patrick McGoohan, Robert Douglas, Bernard Kowalski, Edward M. Abroms
WRITERS: Richard Levinson, William Link, Jackson Gillis, Peter S. Fischer, Larry Cohen

Cop in the coat

Durable Lieutenant Columbo of the LAPD, with ratty raincoat, smelly cheroot, and smoke-belching 1960 Peugeot, is by any standard one of the great original creations in television history. After twenty-five years of doggedly tracking down diabolically clever killers in posh southern California, Columbo continues to be a funny, lovable, pesky fellow whenever actor Peter Falk chooses to don the infamous raincoat. Falk's wily, bumbling, ever-so-humble cop had an unfailingly apologetic manner that masked a razor-sharp mind and his relish of cat and mouse games with guest villains convinced they'd committed the perfect crime.

Lieutenant Columbo began his intricate homicide investigations as one element of the umbrella *NBC Mystery Movie* which featured four rotating series. Over the years, his quirky manner befitted the intentionally convoluted story lines. Unlike other mysteries, the smug killer was, with rare exceptions over the years, seen perpetrating the crime, then covering it up. Columbo put in his first appearance exactly eighteen minutes into the show; the viewer was thus challenged to keep up with the intrepid homicide detective as he waded his way through the minutest of clues and the biggest red herrings while methodically solving the crime.

Columbo had no known first name ("Just call me Lieutenant") and never pulled a gun. It's questionable whether he even carried one. He had a loving wife at home who was never seen and a dog called Dog who accompanied him on cases but usually cowered in Columbo's heap of a car. As for that rumpled raincoat, Columbo seldom removed it, even when walking down the beach in Santa Monica amidst bikini-clad sunbathers. Viewers no doubt chuckled when he took it off for the first time during a thunderstorm while everyone else was wearing one or when he was applauded at a masquerade party where all the guests were in costume and Columbo showed up in his normal attire.

Following two TV movie pilots (the first, an adaptation of the play *Prescription: Murder;* the second, *Ransom for a Dead Man*), Columbo began ingratiating himself with audiences as the premiere element of *NBC Wednesday Mystery Movie* (later it became a Sunday mainstay). In "Murder by the Book," Jack Cassidy was the suave, dastardly killer who became our folksy, suppliant hero's first quarry. It was directed by an up-and-coming Universal contract director named Steven Spielberg, then twenty-four. Through the years there was a parade of name "murderers," some turning up two and even three times in various guises: Janet Leigh, Robert Culp, Sal Mineo, Roddy McDowall, Robert Conrad, Vincent Price, Ida

Lupino, William Shatner, Ruth Gordon, and, in recent years, Faye Dunaway (with whom Columbo—still married and talking about the missus—had a rather uncharacteristic, discreet date and even shared a kiss!). Patrick McGoohan (of *The Prisoner*) became a particular Columbo fan and became the arrogant bad guy two separate times, notably as the ruthless martinet heading a military academy who's not above murder in "By Dawn's Early Light." McGoohan won an Emmy for his acting both times. Later, he directed a couple of Columbo episodes.

Just one more thing

No matter how clever the plan, no matter how brilliant the murderer, whom he alternately amused and annoyed to distraction—"Just one more thing," he'd say to the killer—Columbo always outwitted him or her before the final commercial. The show became so popular and profitable that by the end of the initial NBC series in 1978, Falk was commanding an astounding $2 million a season, even when doing only a half-dozen shows. Fearing typecasting, however, Peter Falk walked away from the role. In the late 1980s he was lured back when ABC convinced him he could do the part whenever the moment struck him and still take diverse work elsewhere. When Columbo returned to television, either in occasional TV movies or in a weekly series in 1988–89, it was apparent that the raincoat still had never seen the inside of a dry cleaning establishment. In reality, the producers—one of whom now was graying Peter Falk—maintained a rack of identical rumpled, soiled raincoats that had become part of the character's indelible image.

VIDEO AVAILABILITY

More than two dozen *Columbo* escapades are available on tape—two episodes per cassette—through Columbia

House. Select episodes, including the two-hour *Prescription: Murder,* are available at certain video outlets.

EMMY AWARDS

1971–72	**Peter Falk,** Outstanding Continued Performance by an Actor in a Leading Role in a Drama Series
	Richard Levinson and William Link, Outstanding Writing Achievement in a Drama Series
1973–74	Outstanding Limited Series
1974–75	**Peter Falk,** Outstanding Lead Actor in a Limited Series
	Patrick McGoohan, Outstanding Single Performances by a Supporting Actor in a Comedy or Drama Series
1975–76	**Peter Falk,** Outstanding Lead Actor in a Drama Series
1989–90	**Peter Falk,** Outstanding Lead Actor in a Drama Series
	Patrick McGoohan, Outstanding Guest Actor in a Drama Series

TRIVIA TIDBITS

- Peter Falk was not the first Columbo. Bert Freed introduced the character in "Enough Rope," a 1960 episode of *The Chevy Mystery Show.* Then, in the Levinson-Link 1968 Broadway mystery *Prescription: Murder* (later made into a TV movie with Falk), Thomas Mitchell played the part with his rich Irish brogue.
- Bing Crosby was the first choice to play the role in the series, but at sixty-seven, he relished his golf game and did not want to get tied down to a regular television show.
- Only once, in the two-hour *Last Salute to the Commodore* in 1976 (directed by Patrick McGoohan), was the killer's identity concealed until the closing.

- In the short-lived (February–December 1979) spin-off show, *Kate Columbo* aka *Kate Loves a Mystery,* Mrs. Columbo—the lieutenant's never seen "missus" on his own series—was finally seen. This time, Columbo himself was the invisible spouse. Mrs. Columbo was played by Kate Mulgrew, most familiar to contemporary viewers as Capt. Kathryn Janeway on *Star Trek: Voyager.*
- In addition to Columbo, Richard Levinson and William Link—acknowledged giants of the TV mystery genre—created another sleuth who became a television institution: Jessica Fletcher, who solved 264 murders over twelve seasons on *Murder, She Wrote.*

COMBAT

ABC, 1962–67, 152 episodes

CAST

Lt. Gil Hanley	Rich Jason
Sgt. Chip Saunders	Vic Morrow
PFC Paul "Cage" Lemay	Pierre Jalbert
Pvt. William Kirby (1963–67)	Jack Hogan
Littlejohn (1963–67)	Dick Peabody
Doc Walton (1962–63)	Steve Rogers
Doc (1963–65)	Conlan Carter
Pvt. Braddock (1962–63)	Shecky Greene
Pvt. Billy Nelson (1963–64)	Tom Lowell

EXECUTIVE PRODUCER: Selig J. Seligman

PRODUCERS: Gene Levitt, Robert Altman, William Self, Robert Blees

PRINCIPAL DIRECTORS: Robert Altman, Boris Sagal, Laslo Benedek, Ted Post, Burt Kennedy, Byron Paul, Tom Gries, Vic Morrow, Bernard McEveety, Georg Fenady, Michael Caffey

PRINCIPAL WRITERS: Gene Levitt, Malvin Wald, Robert Altman, Robert Pirosh, James S. Henerson, Burt Kennedy, Art Wallace, William Bast, Anthony Wilson, Gene L. Coon, William Robert Yates

War is heck!

This gritty, mud-spattered series following an infantry platoon across World War II Europe in the wake of D day set a television standard for war series in the days before Vietnam. It also was one of the series that brought Robert Altman to the fore as both writer and director.

Realism was the keynote of this war series—one of the longest of a spate from the early 1960s—with authentic battle footage often used. The various story lines seesawed between straight combat adventure to human interest, with humorous themes featuring the usual company cutups (including nightclub comic Shecky Greene as the resident hustler) thrown in as tension-relievers. Leading the squad were a pair of tough, hard-boiled leaders: suave and swarthy Rick Jason and glowering Vic Morrow, as the no-nonsense lieutenant and his battle-hardened NCO. The two had their most famous TV series roles here. Jason later went on to joint the cast of *The Young and the Restless* in the 1970s, while Morrow began directing series episodes and acting in a variety of TV movies. He later died in the infamous stunt accident on the set of John Landis's segment from the film version of *The Twilight Zone.*

VIDEO AVAILABILITY

Five tape collections of *Combat,* each running about fifty minutes, are available at certain video outlets. They feature such guest stars as Lee Marvin, Charles Bronson, James Coburn, Telly Savalas, Eddie Albert, and Rocky Marciano.

TRIVIA TIDBITS

- Vic Morrow was the father of actress Jennifer Jason Leigh, one of the bright lights of contemporary film.
- Like Morrow, director Boris Sagal (father of Katey Sagal of *Married . . . With Children*) died tragically in a film set mishap involving a helicopter.
- In addition to Robert Altman, a number of the directors of the *Combat* series went on to call the shots on cult films: Tom Gries *(Will Penny),* Burt Kennedy *(Support Your Local Gunfighter),* et al. Laslo Benedek is best known for having directed Marlon Brando's *The Wild One.*

DALLAS

CBS, 1978–91, 356 episodes

CAST

John Ross (J.R.) Ewing Jr.	Larry Hagman
Eleanor Southworth (Miss Ellie) Ewing (1978–84, 1985–80)	Barbara Bel Geddes
Eleanor Southworth (Miss Ellie) Ewing (1984–85)	Donna Reed
John Ross (Jock) Ewing (1978–81)	Jim Davis
Bobby Ewing (1978–85, 1986–91)	Patrick Duffy
Pamela Barnes Ewing (1978–87)	Victoria Principal
Lucy Ewing Cooper (1978–85, 1988–90)	Charlene Tilton
Sue Ellen Ewing (1978–89)	Linda Gray
Ray Krebbs (1978–88)	Steve Kanaly
Cliff Barnes	Ken Kercheval
Willard "Digger" Barnes (1978)	Keenan Wynn
Willard "Digger" Barnes (1979–80)	David Wayne
Valene Ewing (1978–81)	Joan Van Ark
Gary Ewing (1978–79)	David Ackroyd
Gary Ewing (1979–81)	Ted Shackelford
Kristin Shepard (1979–81)	Mary Crosby
Donna Culver Krebbs (1979–87)	Susan Howard
Clayton Farlow (1981–91)	Howard Keel
Jenna Wade (1983–88)	Priscilla Presley
Carter McKay (1988–91)	George Kennedy
LeeAnn De La Vega (1990–91)	Barbara Eden

CREATOR: David Jacobs

EXECUTIVE PRODUCERS: Philip Capice, Lee Rich

PRODUCER: Leonard Katzman

PRINCIPAL DIRECTORS: Irving J. Moore, Barry Crane, Joseph Manduke, Victor French, Leonard Katzman, Robert Day, Patrick Duffy, Larry Hagman, Vincent McEveety, Harry Harris, Alexander Singer, William F. Claxton

PRINCIPAL WRITERS: Leonard Katzman, Arthur Bernard Lewis, Linda Elstad, Howard Lakin, Shimon Wincelberg, Will Lorin, Camille Marchetta

Sex and greed at Southfork

A continuing drama focusing on the drives, ambitions, passions, and conflicts of the oil-and-cattle rich Ewings—owners of the Ewing Oil Company in Dallas and the Southfork Ranch in Braddock, Texas—*Dallas* captured the country's imagination for thirteen seasons. The hugely popular series—the first major prime-time soap opera since *Peyton Place* in the 1960s—became a Top Ten (and occasionally number one) phenomenon and international sensation as it followed the story of the offspring of Texas oil millionaires, Jock Ewing and "Digger" Barnes, whose long-ago partnership had gone sour when one made off with most of the profits and his pal's true love. Much of this setup was recounted in a 1986 made-for-TV movie "prequel" to *Dallas.*

Sex, lies, and oil revenue traced the lives of Jock and Miss Ellie's three sons: family black sheep J. R., whose villainy knew no bounds (*Time* once aptly described him as "that human oil slick"); upright brother Bobby, who married the daughter of his dad's old partner and was a constant thorn in J.R.'s side; and emotionally fragile Gary, the middle son who after three seasons was dispatched with his wife Valene to their own competing series. Unscrupulous men crossed swords with J.R. and his ilk; beautiful females connived their way to the family wealth and made overt plays toward whoever had it at that particular moment. All of deliciously malevolent J.R.'s nasty shenanigans and his unending pursuit of money and power and women finally brought his world down around him in the final months of the series, and it ended with him putting a gun to his head in the last episode. A shot rang out out of camera range and . . . For the worldwide army of fans left hanging, the resolution to this turn of events came in a belated *Dallas* "reunion" movie during the 1996–97 season.

VIDEO AVAILABILITY

Dallas is available on tape through Columbia House, with two hour-long episodes per cassette.

TRIVIA TIDBITS

- The *Dallas* theme was composed by Jerrold Immel.
- Only Larry Hagman and Ken Kercheval remained with the series through its entire thirteen seasons.
- *Knots Landing,* the show's sole spin-off with a cast headed by Ted Shackelford and Joan Van Ark as Gary and Val Ewing, equalled *Dallas* in length of prime-time run.
- *Dallas* was initially conceived as a limited series of five episodes, but hung in there for 351 more.
- The resolution of the famed "Who Shot J.R.?" episode, opening the third season of the show (unscrupulous J. R. Ewing had two bullets pumped into him by, it turned out, his scorned sister-in-law, played by Bing Crosby's sweet-faced daughter Mary), was the highest-rated non-news show in television history to that date following the season-ending cliffhanger. It was later surpassed by the final *M*A*S*H* episode three years later.
- *Dallas* was noted for its creative casting of name stars through the years in continuing roles. In the final season, Barbara Eden was brought aboard to torment her old *I Dream of Jeannie* (see separate entry) costar Larry Hagman.
- In one of the most bizarre programming ploys of its day, an entire season was summarily wiped out when

Patrick Duffy as "good" brother Bobby Ewing came back to the show a year after being killed by a speeding car. The return forced the writers to declare everything that occurred during his absence a dream by Bobby's wife Pam (Victoria Principal).

- Miss Ellie was played initially by Barbara Bel Geddes, then Donna Reed for a season, then Bel Geddes again; Gary Ewing was played first by David Selby, then Ted Shackelford; "Digger" Barnes first by Keenan Wynn, then by David Wayne; and Jenna Wade first by Morgan Fairchild, then by Francine Thacker, and finally by Priscilla Presley.
- The Southfork Ranch set, just outside Dallas, was—and continues to be—an internationally popular tourist attraction.

DANGER MAN / SECRET AGENT

Danger Man: CBS, 1961, 24 episodes
Secret Agent: CBS, 1965–66, 45 episodes

CAST

John Drake	Patrick McGoohan

CREATOR/EXECUTIVE PRODUCER: Ralph Smart
PRODUCERS: Sidney Cole
DIRECTORS: Seth Holt, Terry Bishop, Julian Amyes, Peter Graham Scott, Clive Donner, Anthony Bushell, Charles Frend, Patrick McGoohan
WRITERS: Ralph Smart, Don Ingalls, Brian Clemens, Jo Eisinger, Oscar Brodney, Ian Stuart Black, Michael Pertwee

Before being Number 6

Before Patrick McGoohan found his place in TV cultdom as Number 6 in *The Prisoner* (see separate entry), he was erudite British operative John Drake, special NATO investigator, in three distinct but overlapping series—only two of which were shown in the U.S. in prime time. (A fourth series, in color for the first time, was scheduled to begin production in 1965 but abandoned when McGoohan—then England's highest-paid television star—gave notice that he would not be continuing.)

There's a man who leads a life of danger . . .

Danger Man John Drake refused to carry a gun and avoided violence whenever possible while doing his spying—initially for the North Atlantic Treaty Organization and later for British Intelligence. The first *Danger Man* series, produced in Great Britain for ATV, was done in a half-hour format; the second, retitled *Secret Agent* in the U.S., was an hourly show. For home consumption, *Danger Man* emerged as the most popular show on British television in its time. In the United States the success was not as great—until later generations discovered it in syndication.

In the months before *Dr. No* emerged and Bondmania began, cool, engaging John Drake was the spy to reckon with. (*Danger Man* actually began production in mid-1959.) As Richard Meyers points out in his book *TV Detectives,* "Considering the series had its United States premiere a year before *Dr. No* was released, Drake's outlandish adventures the world over were fairly groundbreaking. He was a suave but extremely dangerous sort, with one of the hardest right crosses on television." His assorted missions had him infiltrating a school for Russian agents; seeking out moles; roping in wayward British agents; etc. When Drake came back several years later as *Secret Agent,* he was a new man, no longer prone toward fisticuffs. His most outlandish gadgetry: a typewriter that incorporated a camera and an electric shaver that was actually a tape recorder. McGoohan and the producers made certain that the action was plentiful and the spy machinery and doodads never outside the realm of possibility.

VIDEO AVAILABILITY

Four *Danger Man* cassettes, each running about thirty minutes, and six *Secret Agent* cassettes, each running about fifty minutes, are available at certain video outlets. Also available is the feature-length *Secret Agent: Koroshi,* with John Drake possibly meeting his match with a fanatical brotherhood in Hong Kong. It runs about 100 minutes.

TRIVIA TIDBITS

- Patrick McGoohan, the quintessential British spy of the 1960s (until out-Bonded), was actually a New Yorker, born in Astoria, Queens.
- McGoohan's later television career found him as a buddy of Peter Falk, writing, guest-starring in, and/or directing a number of *Columbo* shows. For one, "By the Dawn's Early Light," in 1975 he won an Emmy for Outstanding Single Performance by a Supporting Actor in a Comedy or Drama Series. In 1980 he won a second Emmy, Outstanding Guest Actor in a Drama Series, for his performance in "Agenda for Murder."
- The theme, "Secret Agent Man," was composed by P. F. Sloan and Steve Barri, and sung by Johnny Rivers.

DEATH VALLEY DAYS

Syndicated, 1952–75, 558 episodes

HOSTS

Stanley Andrews ("the Old Ranger") (1952–65)
Ronald Reagan (1965–66)
Robert Taylor (1966–68)
Dale Robertson (1968–72)
Merle Haggard (1975)

PRODUCER: Darrell McGowan
DIRECTOR: Stuart McGowan (and others)

Frontier days

Death Valley Days proved to be the most durable anthology series in television history, aside from the daytime soaps. Produced by Gene Autry's Flying A Productions, it offered dramatizations of the Old West and depicted incidents in the lives of various individuals who lived, worked, and journeyed throughout areas of Nevada and California in the late 1800s. About twenty new episodes were filmed every year and were hosted—at least during the first thirteen seasons—by veteran western actor Stanley Andrews (as "The Old Ranger"). Sometimes he played in them, too, along with just about every actor who was on television in those days: Clint Eastwood, Robert Taylor, Robert Blake, Doug McClure, Forrest Tucker, DeForest Kelley, James Caan, Vic Morrow, and Ronald Reagan.

Reagan took over as host for about a year before moving onto the governorship, and acted in at least six entries including "Tribute to a Dog," "No Gun Behind the

Before his political appointments but after his film career, Ronald Reagan was the host of *Death Valley Days,* a durable western anthology series. Reagan also acted in a few of the episodes; here he plays a flamboyant banker named Billy Ralston in "Raid on the San Francisco Mint." COURTESY OF PERSONALITY PHOTOS, INC.

Badge," and "Temporary Warden." Robert Taylor, MGM's onetime Golden Boy, then became host for two years, followed by Dale Robertson, star of such TV Western series as *Tales of Wells Fargo* and *The Iron Horse.*

Death Valley Days has inexorably been tied in with its longtime soap sponsor Twenty Mule Team Borax, and invariably opened with a bugle call and scenes of the mule team hauling Borax wagons out of the desert. The TV show was a holdover from radio, where it had a fifteen-year run beginning in 1930 after being created by a Manhattan ad agency writer named Ruth Woodman. Although she had never laid eyes on Death Valley, she once claimed that there never had been a script without a solid basis in fact.

VIDEO AVAILABILITY

Seven two-episode collections, each running about sixty minutes, and one three-story set, running about eighty-five minutes are available at certain video outlets.

TRIVIA TIDBITS

- Rosemary DeCamp, who had starred in such series as *The Life of Riley* and *Love That Bob,* and later would be a semiregular on *Petticoat Junction,* was the on-camera spokesperson for Borax and also had roles in several *Death Valley Days* episodes.
- Original host Stanley Andrews's "Old Ranger" was based on a real "old ranger" found early on by creator Ruth Woodman, a grizzled desert rat named Wash Cahill who apparently knew his way around Death Valley and everyone there.

DRAGNET

NBC, 1951–59, 1967–70

CAST

Sgt. Joe Friday	Jack Webb
Sgt. Ben Romero (1951)	Barton Yarborough
Sgt. Ed Jacobs (1952)	Barney Phillips
Off. Frank Smith (1952)	Herb Ellis
Off. Frank Smith (1953–59)	Ben Alexander
Off. Bill Gannon (1967–70)	Harry Morgan

CREATOR/EXECUTIVE PRODUCERS: James E. Moser, Jack Webb

PRODUCERS: Jack Webb, Stanley Meyer, Mike Meshekoff, Herman Canfield

DIRECTOR: Jack Webb

WRITER: Richard L. Breen (and others)

Just the facts

Dragnet was a hallmark in television, the prototype of the realistic action series, despite the seeming lack of action and the clipped, matter-of-fact dialogue. The original half-hour black-and-white Jack Webb show was arguably the most innovative program of its time, as well as one of the most popular and probably one of the most imitated. All future cop shows borrowed something from it. Despite his (non) acting, deadpan style which became the target of parodies through the years, Webb's contribution to broadcasting (radio as well as television) has been acknowledged only posthumously. His character, Sgt. Joe Friday, was so scrupulously dedicated to police work, he had mastered the art of patiently solving a puz-

Dum-de-dum-dum! Dragnet's theme has perhaps the most recognizable musical chords in TV history. Sgt. Joe Friday (Jack Webb, left) and Off. Bill Gannon (Harry Morgan) had stiff necks, but always got the criminal—while simultaneously protecting the innocent, of course. COURTESY OF PERSONALITY PHOTOS, INC.

zle, no matter how drudging. Friday and his partner solved the cases usually without drawing their service revolvers.

Generally, Friday and partner(s) worked on cases that were relatively mundane; one week they'd be working out of the bunco squad, the next they'd grill somebody who rolled a drunk or was involved in a hit-and-run or a purse-snatching. Seldom did they have a murder case. Seldom also did Joe Friday even talk about his home life, if he even had any. He was all business.

Ultimately he made lieutenant during the first (black-and-white) series. Eight years after the initial *Dragnet* went off the air, Webb revived the show—this time in color—in the more active 1960s. He had a new partner played with a touch of sardonic humor by Harry Morgan, an unexplained "demotion" back to sergeant, and topical cases involving hippies, the disaffected, student dissidents, and minor drugs. This incarnation of *Dragnet* lasted for two and a half seasons, and, like its predecessor, produced a separate feature-length version.

Only the names have been changed

Both the fifties and sixties versions of *Dragnet* had the same distinctive openings and closings. Each began with Jack Webb, in a voice-over, announcing "This is the city," as a panoramic view of Los Angeles dissolved into various localized shots. Webb, as Friday, would give a brief monologue about an aspect of the work done by the particular division out of which he was working that week, and he'd end with the statement, "I wear a badge." The denouement of the show, usually narrated by George Fenneman, would announce: "The story you have just seen is true. Only the names have been changed to protect the innocent," after which the week's perpetrator was shown, and Fenneman would annouce the judicial decision about his (or her) case.

The same Webb quality was given to his other television projects—many dealing with federal, state, and local government services. His company, Mark VII, was responsible for sixteen TV series (*Emergency* and *Adam 12,* among them), a number of made-for-television movies, a handful of pilots, as well as several theatrical films—in virtually all of which Webb served as producer, director, narrator, or actor. His company's imprint: the sweaty hand of a smithy hammering the Roman numeral VII into steel.

Webb's stylized acting technique as well as his stylized production approach were defined in *Dragnet.* His stone-faced, seemingly humorless manner came to identify him, although it was belied by a very funny, classic routine on Johnny Carson's *Tonight Show* that was invariably included in the latter's anniversary specials. Webb filmed *Dragnet* using a basic approach. Initially there was only a single camera. He set up shots first with Joe Friday's close-ups and then Frank Smith's, then possibly the weekly perpetrator. Group shots were infrequent; violence was rarely if ever depicted. Just the basics. And of course, "Just the facts, ma'am," which became one of the catchphrases among TV viewers of the day.

VIDEO AVAILABILITY

Five two-episode collections of the original *Dragnet* are available at certain video outlets. Each runs about fifty-five minutes. The 1954 theatrical version and the 1987 spoof film also are available.

EMMY AWARDS

1952	Best Mystery, Action, or Adventure Program
1953	Best Mystery, Action, or Adventure Program
1954	Best Mystery or Intrigue Series

TRIVIA TIDBITS

- In 1955, at the height of *Dragnet*'s initial popularity, Jack Webb, who had begun playing Joe Friday on radio in 1949, created a theatrical version with himself and Ben Alexander—the first feature film based on a TV series.
- Joe Friday, badge 714, was promoted from sergeant to lieutenant toward the end of the initial run of the series. *Badge 714* was the syndicated title for the original TV series.
- The second wave of *Dragnet* (1967–70), in which Joe Friday (back to being a sergeant) was joined Officer Bill Gannon (played by Harry Morgan), also spawned a feature-length version that was shown as both a TV movie and a theatrical one.
- Jack Webb and Harry Morgan worked together in several films—on the other side of the law—including *Dark City* (1950) and *Appointment With Danger* (1951).
- The *Dragnet* spoof in 1987 starred Dan Aykroyd as Friday's somewhat dense but dedicated nephew and

Tom Hanks as his freewheeling new partner. Harry Morgan, now promoted to captain, also was part of the big-screen venture as their supervisor.

- *The New Dragnet,* a first-run syndicated series, premiered in 1990. A rather undistinguished, short-lived update of the classic show, it starred Jeff Osterhage and Bernard White as partners Sgt. Vic Daniels and Sgt. Carl Molina, along with Don Stroud as their superior.
- Jack Webb went through three partners in the first few seasons: Barton Yarborough, Webb's sidekick on the radio version who died shortly after the TV pilot episode; Barney Phillips, who sounded too much like Webb in his delivery and had to be replaced; and Ben Alexander, a onetime child actor in films who became a noted character player.
- Raymond Burr played a mad bomber in the first episode; Leonard Nimoy was a juvenile delinquent in one in 1954.
- Composer Walter Schumann's famous "dum-de-dum-dum," possibly the most famous musical notes this side of the start of Beethoven's Fifth, began what would be the opening to the show's stirring march theme.
- Jack Webb based his character on a cop he played in the 1948 film noir *He Walked By Night* (his film debut).
- In 1953 Stan Freberg had a hit parody, "St. George and the Dragonet." Jack Webb lent *Dragnet*'s orchestra to Freberg for the recording.

THE FUGITIVE

ABC, 1963–67, 120 episodes

CAST

Dr. Richard Kimble	David Janssen
Lt. Phillip Gerard	Barry Morse
Fred Johnson (One-armed man)	Bill Raisch

CREATOR: Roy Huggins
EXECUTIVE PRODUCER: Quinn Martin
PRODUCERS: Wilton Schiller, Alan Armer
PRINCIPAL DIRECTORS: Gerald Mayer, Leo Penn, Robert Douglas, Jesse Hibbs, Robert Butler, William A. Graham, Walter Graumann, Richard Donner, Ida Lupino, Laslo Benedek
PRINCIPAL WRITERS: Stanford Whitmore, Alan Caillou, George Eckstein, Richard Levinson, William Link, Robert Pirosh, John Meredyth Lucas, Barry Oringer

In search of a one-armed man

On August 29, 1967, 72 percent of that evening's television audience watched the shooting of a one-armed man atop a water tower in a deserted amusement park. Thus ended fugitive-from-justice Richard Kimble's fictitious four-year pursuit of his wife's true murderer. It was an event that not only illustrates the narrative power of the medium but stands as a testament to *The Fugitive*'s success and its hold over the American viewing public.

Much of the popularity of the show (the first two seasons were shot in black and white, the rest in color) may have been due to a powerful, attention-grabbing premise. As developed by Quinn Martin and dramatized in the

Lt. Philip Gerard (Barry Morse, right) collars convict-on-the-run Dr. Richard Kimble (David Janssen) in the thrilling suspense show *The Fugitive.* The series, which spawned a successful film starring Harrison Ford, was more than a slight homage to Victor Hugo's novel *Les Miserables.* COURTESY OF PERSONALITY PHOTOS, INC.

classic pilot episode, Dr. Richard Kimble is a well-to-do Indiana pediatrician whose wife is violently murdered shortly after the couple quarrel over adopting a child. Kimble sees a one-armed man fleeing the scene of the crime, but the authorities refuse to believe his story. Convicted of murder, Kimble escapes when the train transporting him to death row derails. The accompanying detective, Lt. Philip Gerard, becomes obsessed with Kimble's capture, and the manhunt begins. This story may have been influenced by the true-life murder case of Dr. Sam Shepard, but it has elements that hark back to

Victor Hugo's *Les Miserables,* mixed with Hitchcock's perennial "wrong man" theme.

Whatever the source, this story line kept audiences riveted for four seasons, even though each episode adhered to an essentially repetitious formula. First, new audiences were introduced to the premise through a clever credit sequence that condensed the pilot into two action-packed minutes. Then Kimble, played with a stoic, low-key sensuality by David Janssen, was introduced arriving in a strange town with an assumed identity. Each week he got a new job, a new name, and a new set of acquaintances to interact with. Every episode basically cut back and forth between two focuses: Gerard and/or local police beginning to track down Kimble's latest whereabouts; and the problems of Kimble's new friends, which were usually solved by the fugitive before the authorities made his departure a necessity. Of course, there were necessary variations and occasional gimmicks used throughout the show's run, including Kimble developing amnesia, blindness, pneumonia, and a friendship with Gerard's wife (played by Barbara Rush).

Still on the run

Solving that mystery not only gave *The Fugitive* its record-breaking finale but also gave Quinn Martin and local broadcasters some worries. Would the show be appealing in reruns if everyone knew the outcome? Happily, the answer was yes. Since Kimble's guilt was never really a possibility, the conclusion was almost as preordained as each week's formula. Long after audiences forgot the details of that two-part finale, they were still entertained by the taut scripts and appealing presence of Janssen. Also, the success of the 1993 feature film version, starring Harrison Ford and Tommy Lee Jones, as pursued and pursuer, has rekindled interest in the original. In fact, in a most unusual broadcasting ploy, NBC resurrected the final two-part episode of the 1960s series (entitled "The

Judgment") and rebroadcast it in prime time in the 1990s as the big-screen version was about to premiere.

A prime example of 1960s weekly drama, *The Fugitive,* after thirty years, is still running and still going . . . strong.

VIDEO AVAILABILITY

The Fugitive is currently available in twenty-two volumes at certain video outlets, each cassette running 105 minutes and containing two episodes. Two other cassettes feature the pilot episode (forty-five minutes) and the two-part finale (103 minutes). There are also two collector sets available, each containing five volumes.

EMMY AWARD

1965–66 Outstanding Dramatic Series

TRIVIA TIDBITS

- As with all Quinn Martin series, the sonorous tones of each episode's narrator belong to resonant actor William Conrad.
- Kimble's wife, Helen, was portrayed in the pilot and in flashbacks by Diane Brewster.
- The murder of Helen Kimble took place on September 19, 1961. The one-armed man's capture occurred on the date of the final episode's broadcast, August 29, 1967, making Richard Kimble's ordeal two years longer than the actual run of the show.
- *The Fugitive*'s format allowed for many guest appearances. Some of the most notable (with the video volume number in parentheses) include: William Shatner (18), Robert Duvall (2, 9), Ron(ny) Howard (4), Kurt Russell (5, 16), Charles Bronson (14), and Ed Asner (13).
- The theme music for the show was written by Pete Rugolo.
- David Janssen died in 1980.

THE GREEN HORNET

ABC, 1966–67, 26 episodes

CAST

Britt Reid/The Green Hornet	Van Williams
Kato	Bruce Lee
Lenore "Casey" Case	Wende Wagner
DA Frank Scanlon	Walter Brooke
Mike Axford	Lloyd Gough

CREATOR: George Trendle
EXECUTIVE PRODUCER: William Dozier
PRODUCER: Richard Bluel

"Faster, Kato!"

The series, set in Washington, D.C., follows the exploits of Britt Reid, crusading editor of the *Daily Sentinel* and secretly the Green Hornet who, with his chauffeur and Oriental assistant, sidekicking Kato, fights crime in his spare time. Considered criminals and wanted by the law, the two masked crime-busters take on the bad guys vigilante-style, generally incapacitate them with a nonlethal gas gun, and then conveniently disappear before the proper law authorities come onto the scene. Not quite as kitsch as that other masked crime-fighter of the time, Batman (also produced by William Dozier and Richard Bluel), the Green Hornet and Kato wore no superhero outfits or flowing capes—they simply put on small black masks with eyeholes, hoping the townsfolk wouldn't recognize Reid in his wide-lapelled suit and wide-brimmed hat and Kato in his chauffeur's uniform.

Britt Reid's mask reminded one of the Lone Ranger—and why not? In fact, he was the grandnephew of the Old West's famed masked man (also created by George Trendle).

The identities of the pair, who tooled around town after villains in the souped-up Black Beauty (a greatly modified 1966 Chrysler Imperial), were not even known to Reid's admiring secretary, Casey, Mike Axford (his hard-nosed ex-cop reporter), or Frank Scanlon (the district attorney).

While stalwart, rather stiff Van Williams (earlier one of the stars of *Bourbon Street Beat* and *SurfSide 6*), played the title role, it would be Bruce Lee, as Kato, who would capture the spotlight with his dazzling martial arts movements and would subsequently go on to become a screen icon. The Green Hornet and Kato were not above giving a helping hand to fellow crime-fighters Batman and Robin on at least one two-part *Batman* adventure, starring with the Dynamic Duo in the episodes "A Piece of the Action"/"Batman's Satisfaction."

VIDEO AVAILABILITY

At time of publication this title had been withdrawn from availability.

TRIVIA TIDBITS

- *The Green Hornet* was created in the mid-1930s and first appeared on radio in 1936 with Al Hodge along with Raymond Hayashi as Kato. The series continued with other actors, uninterrupted through 1952.
- In 1940 there were two *Green Hornet* movie serials, one with Gordon Jones, the other with Warren Hull.
- The theme music for the TV series was an adaptation of Rimsky-Korsakov's "Flight of the Bumble Bee," with trumpeter Al Hirt and Billy May's Orchestra.
- Episodes of the series were edited together and released as a feature (titled *Kato* in Lee's native Hong Kong) to cash in on the Bruce Lee mania of the period.

- Williams retired from acting, went into law enforcement, and returned in a cameo appearance as the director of *The Green Hornet* in 1993's *Dragon: The Bruce Lee Story.*
- Hawaiian-born Jason Scott Lee, who portrayed the title role in *Dragon: The Bruce Lee Story,* has been signed to play Kato again in a new big-screen version. George Clooney had been signed to play Reid, but got out of it to play the Caped Crusader in the next Batman film. The role of Reid in *The Green Hornet* remains uncast as of this writing.

GUNSMOKE

CBS, 1955–75, 156 half-hour episodes,
356 one-hour episodes

CAST

Marshal Matt Dillon	James Arness
Kitty Russell (1955–74)	Amanda Blake
Doc Galen Adams	Milburn Stone
Deputy Chester Goode (1955–64)	Dennis Weaver
Deputy Festus Haggen (1964–75)	Ken Curtis
Newly O'Brien (1967–75)	Buck Taylor
Quint Asper (1962–65)	Burt Reynolds
Bartender Sam (1962–74)	Glenn Strange Robert Brubaker
Clayton Thaddeus Greenwood (1965–67)	Roger Ewing
Nathan Burke (1964–75)	Ted Jordan
Mr. Bodkin (1965–75)	Roy Roberts
Mr. Jones (1955–60)	Dabbs Greer

CREATORS: Norman Macdonnell, John Meston

EXECUTIVE PRODUCERS: Charles Marquis Warren, John Mantley, Philip Leacock

PRODUCERS: Norman Macdonnell, Joseph Drackow, Leonard Katzman,

DIRECTORS: Bernard McEveety, Vincent McEveety, Charles Marquis Warren, Philip Leacock, Ted Post, Tay Garnett, Michael O'Herlihy, Christian I. Nyby II, Robert Totten, Mark Rydell, Leo Penn, William Conrad, Andrew V. McLaglen, Arnold Laven, R. G. Springsteen

The longest-running dramatic show in history, *Gunsmoke,* was on the air for twenty years. The cast, from left: James Arness (Marshal Matt Dillon), Milburn Stone (Doc Galen Adams), Amanda Blake (Kitty Russell), Burt Reynolds (Quint Asper), and Ken Curtis (Deputy Festus Hagen). COURTESY OF PERSONALITY PHOTOS, INC.

Law in Dodge

Gunsmoke holds the record as the most successful, longest-running dramatic show in television history.

Probably the ultimate television western, it followed the whitewashed exploits of upstanding Matt Dillon, frontier marshal of Dodge City in the 1880s. A loner and a bachelor (at least in the series), Dillon was a towering man (perfect for six-foot-seven James Arness, who at first was reluctant to sign for the role, fearing it would stunt his budding film career). His family included Dodge City locals such as Miss Kitty, who ran the Long Branch Saloon (in the radio version she was clearly established as a "working girl," but the prostitute angle was toned down for television); Doc Adams, the town's crusty sawbones; twangy, gimpy Chester Goode, Matt's deputy; grizzled Festus Hagen, who replaced Chester as sidekick later in the series; half-breed blacksmith Quint Asper; gunsmith Buck Taylor; and, of course, Bartender Sam.

Imposing Matt maintained a platonic relationship with Miss Kitty, who acted as his confidante ("Be careful, Matt," she was constantly warning him—which was as close to a paean of love as she ever spoke), while he went about making certain the lawless got their comeuppance and order was maintained in Dodge. It was pointed out by Susan Sackett in *Prime-Time Hits* that "Doc dug enough bullets out of Dillon's 'flesh wounds' to open his own lead mine."

Initially, the show opened with Matt Dillon striding down the main street and pulling his gun on some no-good varmint. Later, when the show expanded to an hour, and was being done in color, the opening was slightly changed and became a touch more violent. An uproar forced the producers to tone it down again. Twelve years into the run, the ratings began to sag, but when the programming executives announced a cancelation of the show, CBS chairman William S. Paley stepped in and personally saved it. (Evidently, it was his favorite show.) The program was moved to a new night (it long was a Saturday night staple), the ratings jumped up, and it was a hit again for the next eight years. The show was so popular from 1961 to 1964 that, while *Gunsmoke* was still running on Saturday nights, reruns of the half-hour version—under the title *Marshal Dillon*—were being run by the network in prime time on Tuesdays.

Arness was as much of a loner off camera as Matt Dillon was on. The network grew increasingly frustrated that it couldn't get its biggest star (literally and figuratively) to boost the show or even talk to the press, and ultimately, Arness tired of the nagging. So CBS finally sent *Gunsmoke* to Boot Hill—after twenty extraordinary years that are still unequaled in prime-time drama.

Arness left town for many years to live on his ranch in Montana, but eventually mellowed and returned for a couple of series. In the late 1980s, he was coaxed back into the saddle to play Matt Dillon again in several TV movies. Rough-hewn Matt by now was somewhat over the hill, long retired as a marshal and now a Colorado trapper, but ever-available to give a hand and a gun, if necessary. Miss Kitty was leaving for New Orleans to open a sporting house. In the next TV movie, Matt learns that long ago he had fathered a child, who's now a grown woman involved in his further adventures. Miss Kitty was gone (Amanda Blake had died of AIDS in 1989), and Dillon was the only one left from the original Dodge City gang.

VIDEO AVAILABILITY

Selected volumes of *Gunsmoke* episodes—including the premiere with John Wayne introducing the show and its star—are available at certain video outlets. The premiere show runs about fifty-two minutes; the others, one or two episodes per volume, run about sixty minutes.

EMMY AWARDS

1957	Best Dramatic Series with Continuing Characters
1958–59	**Dennis Weaver,** Best Supporting Actor (Continuing Character) in a Dramatic Series

1967–68 **Milburn Stone,** Outstanding Performance by an Actor in a Supporting Role in a Drama

TRIVIA TIDBITS

- John Wayne was the first choice to play Matt Dillon, but he declined, suggested his tall protégé (and costar in several movies) James Arness, and agreed to do the on-screen introduction to the series on September 10, 1955 when the show was only a half hour and in black and white.
- William Conrad was Matt Dillon in the radio version of *Gunsmoke* that CBS began broadcasting in 1953, and later directed a number of episodes of the James Arness TV series. On radio, Georgia Ellis was Kitty, Parley Baer was Chester, the marshal's deputy, and Howard McNear (later Floyd the Barber of *The Andy Griffith Show*) played Doc Adams.
- Long after *Gunsmoke*'s twenty-year run on the network, James Arness returned to play Matt Dillon in five TV movies (1987, 1990, 1992, 1993, and 1994).
- James Arness's younger brother, actor Peter *(Mission: Impossible)* Graves, hosts a number of documentaries and reality shows, as well as A&E's *Biography.*

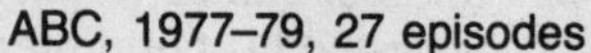

THE HARDY BOYS

ABC, 1977–79, 27 episodes

CAST

Frank Hardy	Parker Stevenson
Joe Hardy	Shaun Cassidy
Fenton Hardy	Edmund Gilbert
Aunt Gertrude Hardy	Edith Atwater
Callie Shaw (1977)	Lisa Eilbacher
Harry Hammond (1978–79)	Jack Kelly
Harry Gibbon (1978–79)	Phillip R. Allen

EXECUTIVE PRODUCER: Glen A. Larson
SUPERVISING PRODUCER: Michael Sloan
PRODUCERS: Joyce Boatman, B. W. Sandefur, Christopher Crowe, Ben Kadish, Joe Boston
DIRECTORS: Glen A. Larson, Stuart Margolin, Fernando Lamas, Ron Satlof, Richard Benedict, Vincent Edwards, Sidney Hayers, Don McDougall, Daniel Haller, Ivan Dixon, Michael Chaffey, Steven H. Stern, Joseph Pevney
WRITERS: Barry Alexander, Robert Pirosh, Michael Sloan, Glen A. Larson, Lee Sheldon, Alan Godfrey

Frank and Joe, teen sleuths

Based on the popular *Hardy Boys* series of books by Franklin W. Dixon (a pseudonym for Edward Stratemeyer, who also wrote the equally popular Nancy Drew mysteries under the name Carolyn Keene), this show followed the exploits of teenage amateur detectives Joe (16) and Frank (18), sons of world-famous investigator Fenton Hardy. These updated tales—the original books were written over the first third of the twentieth century—appealed to contemporary audiences by casting a pair of teen heartthrobs in the leads and involving them in modern-day mysteries.

In one episode, they encountered strange goings-on in Transylvania while attending a rock concert at Dracula's castle—with Lorne Greene as Dracula! Another time they became involved with a trainload of former teen idols, including Edd Byrnes, Troy Donahue, Tommy Sands, Fabian, and Gary Crosby. Helping out, at least for the first season, was daddy Fenton's part-time secretary, Callie Shaw. Later, a CIA operative, Harry Hammond, and a federal agent, Harry Gibbon, were added to help the boys—who really needed no help. Aiding them for a few episodes of the second season was "sister" sleuth Nancy Drew (see separate entry), who had her own series initially alternating weekly with theirs.

VIDEO AVAILABILITY

Eight two-episode sets of *Hardy Boys Mysteries* are available at certain video outlets. Each episode runs about fifty minutes.

TRIVIA TIDBITS

- TV hunk Parker Stevenson later joined the lengthy cast of *Falcon Crest* for the 1984–85 season and became one of the stars of *Baywatch* in its first season.
- Shaun Cassidy, former bubblegum singer and son of Shirley Jones, had a number one hit record with "Da Doo Ron Ron." He began a new career in the mid-1990s as one of the creators and writers of the series *American Gothic.*
- Jack Kelly was TV's onetime Bart Maverick.
- Tim Considine and Tommy Kirk played Frank and Joe in a number of adventures for Disney's *Mickey Mouse Club* TV series in 1956–57, beginning with a twenty-part *Mystery of the Applegate Treasure,* from the very

first Hardy Boys novel in 1927, and followed by the fourteen-part *Mystery of Ghost Farm*.

- An earlier *Hardy Boys* series was animated for Saturday morning TV (1969–71), in which the brothers had a rock band.
- In 1995 *The Hardy Boys* again was resurrected for a syndicated series filmed in France, once again alternating with a new Nancy Drew series. Colin Gray and Paul Popowich are the contemporary Frank and Joe.
- *The Hardy Boys* theme was written by Glen A. Larson and Stu Phillips.

HAVE GUN—WILL TRAVEL

CBS, 1957–63, 156 episodes

CAST

Paladin	Richard Boone
Hey Boy	Kam Tong
Hey Girl	Lisa Lu
McGunnis	Olan Soulé

CREATOR: Sam Rolfe

PRODUCERS: Frank Pierson, Don Ingalls, Robert Sparks, Julian Claman

PRINCIPAL DIRECTORS: Andrew V. McLaglen, Robert Butler, Buzz Kulik, Lewis Milestone, Lamont Johnson, Eliot Silverstein, Gary Nelson, Richard Boone, James Neilson, Ida Lupino, Frank Pierson

PRINCIPAL WRITERS: Gene Roddenberry, Sam Rolfe, Shimon Wincelberg, Harry Julian Fink

"Paladin, Paladin, where do you roam?"

The series, set in San Francisco during the 1870s, depicts the exploits of a man named Paladin, a former army officer turned professional gunman who offers his gun and services to people unable to protect themselves. Paladin—who dressed entirely in black, quoted Keats, Shelley, and Shakespeare, enjoyed haute cuisine and vintage wine, and even read newspapers in Chinese—saw himself as a knight of the Old West. He operated from the Hotel Carlton and was distinguished by his trademark black leather holster that bore a symbol of a paladin (the white chess knight) and a business card that read: "Have Gun—Will Travel. Wire Paladin, San Francisco."

The show, extremely popular and generally in the Top Five during each of its years in first run, owed much to its erudite star, whose ruddy looks and squinty eyes made him an ideal villain in movie westerns during the 1950s. In addition to playing the lead, he directed twenty-seven episodes, had a hand in writing dozens of the scripts, cowrote the show's theme song, and exercised quite a bit of control over casting and the hiring of production personnel. Richard Boone became noted for demanding the very best and getting it, both here and in his subsequent *Richard Boone Show* (1963–64), a dramatic anthology series with an in-house repertory company.

As author Susan Sackett writes in *Prime-Time Hits,* the show "served as a springboard for some of the finest talents in television." Indeed, *Have Gun—Will Travel* brought to the fore such names as Gene Roddenberry, its head writer, who'd go on to create *The Lieutenant* and then the enduring *Star Trek.* And there was Sam Rolfe, one of the show's producers and occasional writers, who later would create *The Man From U.N.C.L.E.* Among its directors were big-screen names like Lewis Milestone (veteran of *All Quiet on the Western Front*), Eliot Silverstein (who would do *Cat Ballou*), John Wayne's protégé Andrew V. McLaglen (he'd direct 88 shows in the series), Frank Pierson (who'd later direct Streisand's *A Star is Born*), and noted actress Ida Lupino (who might just be TV's first woman director).

VIDEO AVAILABILITY

Have Gun—Will Travel is available through Columbia House on a series of cassettes, each containing four half-hour episodes.

TRIVIA TIDBITS

- The show's theme was written by Richard Boone and Sam H. Rolfe, with lyrics by Johnny Western, who sang the song over the opening credits.

- "The Ballad of Paladin" was recorded by Duane Eddy for RCA in 1962.
- Richard Boone, a seventh-generation nephew of Daniel Boone, the famed frontiersman, was a distant cousin of singer Pat—who played three roles in "Genesis," the sixth-season premiere episode.
- Among the show's guest stars: Jack Lord, Robert Blake, George Kennedy, William Conrad, Martin Balsam, Charles Bronson, Victor McLaglen (directed by son Andrew), Lon Chaney, Vincent Price, and Peter Falk.

I, CLAUDIUS

PBS, 1977–78 (first American broadcast), 13 episodes

CAST

Claudius	Derek Jacobi
Livia	Sian Phillips
Caligula	John Hurt
Tiberius	George Baker
Augustus	Brian Blessed
Antonia	Margaret Tyzack
Sejanus	Patrick Stewart
Agrippina	Fiona Walker
Messalina	Sheila White
Livilla	Patricia Quinn
Drusus	Ian Ogilvy
Piso	Stratford Johns
Germanicus	David Ross
Herod	James Faulkner

PRODUCER: Martin Lisemore
DIRECTOR: Herbert Wise
WRITER: Jack Pulman

When in Rome

Over its first seven seasons, PBS developed an impeccable reputation for handsomely produced adaptations of literary classics. Many of these offerings, such as *Vanity Fair,* were British imports broadcast Stateside under its acclaimed *Masterpiece Theatre* banner. The tale of the Roman Emperor Claudius, as dramatized in the sumptuous 1976 BBC production *I, Claudius,* both stunned and mesmerized American audiences—despite an occasional murder or illicit affair figuring into a narrative about the goings-on in Ancient Rome.

I, Claudius was faithfully scripted by Jack Pulman from two novels by Robert Graves (*I,Claudius* and *Claudius, the God*) and related, as viewers were told, "the unvarnished, absolutely true" history of the reigns of the first four rulers of the Roman Empire: Augustus, Tiberius, Caligula, and Claudius. Each of the thirteen episodes (running fifty minutes) opened with the stuttering, clubfooted Emperor Claudius, in old age, frantically recording his family's saga before being poisoned by his scheming wife Agrippina and her son Nero. As Claudius inscribed, his story unfolded before the contemporary viewer—and what a story it became! Countless depictions of poisoning, debauchery, incest, patricide, fratricide, suicide, and an orgy or two tumbled from the television set as dozens of potential heirs and pretenders to the throne were dispatched in what was ultimately a trenchant study of insane ambition and ruthless power.

A helping of humor

This bloodbath could have been rather depressing entertainment, but for a handful of brilliant choices. First, the characters spoke and behaved as contemporary Britishers. Initially, it took a bit of getting used to, but the anachronistic dialogue brought a universal quality to the saga and humanized the assorted participants. Second, there was an unerringly tasteful infusion of humor, often when least expected. The monstrous Livia, wife of Augustus who murdered most of her husband's offspring so that her own son may rule, was given a cool, charming exterior which made her scheming all the more fascinating. After finally poisoning Augustus in episode five, Livia brought her son to view the body, dryly telling him, "By the way, don't touch the figs."

Later, on her deathbed, she pathetically begged her demented grandson, Caligula, to pronounce her a goddess so that she might escape the torments of hell. His reply: "And what makes you think a smelly old woman like you could become a goddess?"

Powerful performances

Ultimately, however, it was the uniformly fine cast that gave *I, Claudius* much of its resonance. Derek Jacobi most likely will always be identified as the intellectually brilliant Claudius, pretending to be a fool to survive his relatives' reigns of terror. His characterization deepened with each episode, even as he fell victim to the corruptions of power. Sian Phillips as Livia, John Hurt as Caligula, and Sheila White as Claudius's treacherous wife Messalina created full-bodied, three-dimensional portraits of evil. At the same time, George Baker managed to humanize his despotic Tiberius until the audience almost pitied him. Shining in supporting roles were Margaret Tyzeck as Claudius' noble mother, Antonia, and Patrick Stewart (long before establishing himself as the Starship *Enterprise*'s chrome-domed Captain Picard) as the brutal Sejanus.

Parental warning

Viewers of *I, Claudius* should be forewarned that there are instances of graphic violence and nudity, which, by television standards, are shocking. It is definitely not for family audiences, but as a stellar example of British drama at its best, it merits repeat viewings.

VIDEO AVAILABILITY

I, Claudius is available, totally uncut, on video and can be found in certain rental outlets. The thirteen episodes are packaged in seven cassettes; the first six contain two episodes each.

TRIVIA TIDBITS

- *I, Claudius* was nominated for an Emmy as Outstanding Limited Series, but lost to *Holocaust.* Herbert Wise also received an Emmy nomination for Outstanding Direction in a Drama Series.
- A film of Robert Graves's book, *I, Claudius,* was begun by Alexander Korda in Britain in 1936, but only two reels were completed. Charles Laughton was cast in the title role, Emlyn Williams was Caligula, and Korda's wife, Merle Oberon, was Messalina. Footage from that aborted production is included in a fascinating documentary, *The Epic That Never Was,* available on videocassette.
- Four minutes of footage were deleted from the BBC *I, Claudius* prior to its American premiere in 1977. The cuts included a bare-breasted African tribal dance and shots of Caligula eating his wife/sister's aborted child.
- The music for the memorable title sequence, featuring a snake slithering across a Roman tile mosaic, was by Wilfred Josephs.

INSPECTOR MORSE

PBS "Mystery!", 1988–96 (first American broadcasts), 28 two-part episodes

CAST

Chief Inspector Morse	John Thaw
Detective Sergeant Lewis	Kevin Whately

CREATOR: Colin Dexter
EXECUTIVE PRODUCER: Ted Childs
PRODUCERS: David Lascelles, Chris Burt, Kenny McBain
DIRECTORS: Roy Battersby, John Madden, Alastair Read, Brian Parker, Peter Duffell, Jim Goddard, Anthony Simmons, Stephen Whittaker
WRITERS: Julian Mitchell, Michael Wilcox, Peter Hammond, Alma Cullen, Anthony Minghella, Denice Doyle

Fie on a policeman's lot

There are detectives all over television—and then there are *detectives*. In the last fifteen years of the twentieth century, the most distinctive one, arguably, might well be Britain's dour, idiosyncratic, opera-loving Inspector Morse (first name a closely guarded secret). According to *Mystery!* host Diana Rigg in the introduction to one of the shows that had a religion-oriented plot, "Stretching out on a sofa and listening to Mozart is Morse's idea of Holy Communion." The grumpy, introspective, bachelor sleuth working out of Oxford, England, became all the rage over there when first introduced in 1987 in *The Silent World of Nicholas Worth,* and by the time he solved his last case in 1993 in *Twilight of the Gods* (shown in the

US in 1996), he had what was thought to be the largest viewing audience in British television.

Prickly Inspector Morse is a true original. A cop who can't stand the sight of blood, he has a passion for his spiffy red Jaguar and good crossword puzzles, is hardly ever given to a smile or a compliment, possesses an expertise on English ale, and has an inbred rudeness—even to his superiors and women. He may appear to be a dunderhead letting his sidekick, Detective Sergeant Lewis, seem to be uncovering all the clues and discarding the many red herrings thrown into the plots of the series, but his innate shrewdness ultimately wins the day and solves the case. "I stumble around," Morse says in the style of Columbo's "one other thing, ma'am" humbleness. "Sometimes I stumble in the right direction."

Occasionally haughty Morse and flunky Lewis find themselves away from the Chief Inspector's home base of Oxford—say in Ireland or Australia (as in *The Promised Land*)—but that only has Morse delightfully crankier than normal, a leisurely pint notwithstanding. Also there is even an occasional touch of romance in Morse's middle-aged life, as with Zoe Wanamaker in *Fat Chance,* where he delves into the death of a female divinity student who wants to become an Anglican priest.

The final image (in *Twilight of the Gods*) of Inspector Morse—unless he can be bribed or blackmailed into embarking on another case—is him driving through a sun-baked Oxford in his Jag for a refreshing sabbatical.

VIDEO AVAILABILITY

Nearly a dozen volumes of *Inspector Morse* mysteries are available at certain video outlets. Each whodunit, originally shown in two parts, runs about 100 minutes.

TRIVIA TIDBITS

- John Thaw, who was honored in 1992 by Queen Elizabeth with a CBE (Commander of the British Empire) for his Inspector Morse, starred as Alfred Doolittle in Peter O'Toole's 1984 West End revival of *My Fair Lady.*

- The definitive book on the series, *The Making of Inspector Morse,* was written by Mark Sanderson.
- Thaw began his career as Laurence Olivier's understudy in London's West End and played many Shakespearean roles with the Royal Shakespeare Company. His wife, Sheila Hancock, starred as the duchess of Trevenick on PBS Masterpiece Theatre's *The Buccaneers,* among others.
- Thaw's previous cop role on British television was as rough-and-tough Jack Regan in the popular *The Sweeney* in fifty-two TV episodes and two feature films.

I SPY

NBC, 1965–68, 82 episodes

CAST

Kelly Robinson	Robert Culp
Alexander Scott	Bill Cosby

EXECUTIVE PRODUCER: Sheldon Leonard
PRODUCERS: David Friedkin, Mort Fine
PRINCIPAL DIRECTORS: Sheldon Leonard, Paul Wendkos, Mark Rydell, Robert Culp, Allen Reisner, Richard Benedict, Richard Sarafian, Alf Kjellin, Earl Bellamy, David Friedkin
PRINCIPAL WRITERS: David Friedkin, Mort Fine, Robert Culp, Garry Marshall, Marion Hargrove, Stephen Kandel, Eric Bercovici

Culp and the Cos

I Spy, following the exploits of and casual relationship between a pair of undercover agents, was a television landmark in its day as the first dramatic series to costar a black actor—a then relatively unknown stand-up comic named Bill Cosby. The often witty interplay between him and colleague Robert Culp set the show apart from the slew of spy series that became popular in the wake of the James Bond phenomenon. Culp, as a Princeton-educated secret agent masquerading as a gregarious tennis pro with an eye for the ladies, and Cosby, as a multilingual Rhodes scholar and explosives expert working undercover as his trainer, hopscotched the world on various assignments for the U.S. government. The two guys weren't supermen.

Costars Robert Culp (left) and Bill Cosby shoot it out with the bad guys in this scene from *I Spy.* Cosby beat out Culp for Best Actor Emmy the first two years of the show; Cosby won again for the third year, but this time Culp wasn't even nominated. COURTESY OF PERSONALITY PHOTOS, INC.

They were wounded, tricked, and lied to by their superiors, and they didn't always best the villains exactly as planned. But somehow they got the job done, belying their carefree manner and friendly banter.

Besides the chemistry between the two leads and the obvious affection their characters had for one another, the series benefited from the location photography. In the three years the show was on the air, the cast and crew traveled around the world for filming, and the name Fouad Said, the director of photography, became as prominent in the credits as Cosby and Culp. Weekly guest stars included the likes of Gene Hackman, Martin Landau, Eartha Kitt, Ivan Dixon, Vera Miles, Lew Ayres, Godfrey Cambridge, Rory Calhoun, Carroll O'Connor, Cicely Tyson, Ronny Howard, Dorothy Lamour, Leslie Uggams, Peter Lawford, and Boris Karloff.

Bill Cosby's breakthrough in a starring role in *I Spy* (as the first African-American in the lead in a regularly scheduled TV drama series) presaged Diahann Carroll's subsequent casting in 1968 in the lead in *Julia*. He and Culp found themselves competing against one another at Emmy time as Best Actor in a Drama Series during the first two years, and the third season had Cosby in the Best Actor category and Culp in the Best Writing one. Inevitably, Cosby won the Emmy for each of the show's three years.

Through the course of the run of *I Spy,* Robert Culp became increasingly involved with writing. In fact, he wrote the premiere episode dealing with a black Olympic star who defected to Red China with his African fiancée). He also directed on occasion, as he had done on his earlier series, *Trackdown*. He and Bill Crosby later teamed up for the feature film, *Hickey & Boggs* (they played seedy private eyes). In 1994 their Kelly and Scotty were called back to service in a TV reunion movie, *I Spy Returns,* now with the leads as grumpy old(er) men looking after their offspring (male and female) who've followed in their dads' footsteps as secret agents.

VIDEO AVAILABILITY

Several *I Spy* collections are available at certain video outlets. Each runs about 100 minutes and contains two episodes: among them, "Happy Birthday Everyone," with Gene Hackman and Jim Backus; "It's All Done With Mirrors," with Carroll O'Connor as a Soviet scientist; and "Plains," with Boris Karloff as an elderly research doctor.

EMMY AWARDS

1965–66 **Bill Cosby,** Outstanding Continued Performance by an Actor in a Leading Role in a Dramatic Series

1966–67 **Bill Cosby,** Outstanding Continued Performance by an Actor in a Leading Role in a Dramatic Series

1967–68 **Bill Cosby,** Outstanding Continued Performance by an Actor in a Leading Role in a Dramatic Series

TRIVIA TIDBITS

- *I Spy* spawned a comic book series for Gold Key Comics, a series of paperback novelizations for Popular Library, a *Mad* magazine satire called "Why Spy?" and a spoof on *Get Smart* entitled "Die, Spy" (with Robert Culp doing a gag appearance as a waiter).
- Bill Cosby later won an Emmy for Outstanding Children's Programming in 1980–81 as a performer on his *New Fat Albert Show.* His *Cosby Show* was named Outstanding Comedy Series during the 1984–85 season.
- Kelly Robinson's gun was a Walther P-38, while Alexander Scott packed a Smith and Wesson.
- The *I Spy* theme was written by Earle Hagen.

THE JEWEL IN THE CROWN

PBS Masterpiece Theatre, 1984–85 (first American broadcast), 14 episodes

CAST

Barbie Batchelor	Dame Peggy Ashcroft
Ahmed	Derrick Branche
Guy Perron	Charles Dance
Sarah Layton	Geraldine James
Lady Manners	Rachel Kempson
Hari Kumar	Art Malik
Susan Layton	Wendy Morgan
Mildred Layton	Judy Parfitt
Ronald Merrick	Tim Piggott-Smith
Count Boronsky	Eric Porter
Daphne Manners	Susan Wooldridge
Lady Chatterjee	Zohra Segal

EXECUTIVE PRODUCER: Dennis Forman
PRODUCER: Christopher Morahan
DIRECTORS: Christopher Morahan, Jim O'Brien
WRITER: Ken Taylor

Glittering jewel

Granada Television's epic production was adapted from Paul Scott's four-volume saga *The Raj Quartet* and made it a best-seller almost twenty-five years after its initial publication. The intricate plot, elegantly realized, dramatized the uneasy, sometimes violent relations between Great Britain and India, the jewel in Queen Victoria's crown, during the 1940s over the last five years before the latter's independence. The story's protagonists are

A scene from the PBS Masterpiece Theatre production of *The Jewel in the Crown.* Charles Dance (right) portrayed Sgt. Guy Perron in the 14-episode series, which won an Emmy for Outstanding Limited Series 1984–85. COURTESY OF PERSONALITY PHOTOS, INC.

caught between the dying British Empire and the birth of a new nation, eager to set its own standards and live by its own rules.

The show was a fascinating portrait of a multitiered culture seething with tensions of class and race, revolving around the star-crossed romance between highbred Englishwoman Daphne Manners and Hari Kumar, a young Indian educated in Great Britain. And between them is Ronald Merrick, a suspicious and bigoted police lieutenant. This visually stunning, emotionally stirring drama of love, betrayal, honor, and deception (shown in England in early 1983) starred the venerable British actress Dame Peggy Ashcroft, who would go to play a similar role in *A Passage to India*—and win an Oscar. On its American premiere, media critic John Leonard wrote in *New York* magazine: "*The Jewel in the Crown* is the best sustained television I've seen in more than 30 years of watching."

VIDEO AVAILABILITY

The complete filmed saga is available at certain video outlets, most recently in a deluxe eight-tape collector's edition, running about 750 minutes.

EMMY AWARD

1984–85 Outstanding Limited Series

TRIVIA TIDBITS

- In addition to Outstanding Limited Series, *The Jewel in the Crown* won Emmy nominations for Peggy Ashcroft as outstanding Lead Actress in a Limited Series or a Special; directors Christopher Morahan and Jim O'Brien; writer Ken Taylor; and production designers Vic Symonds and Alan Pickford.
- Author Paul Scott, who had never been to India, died in 1978, several years before his massive work was put on film.
- Rachel Kempson is the mother of actresses Vanessa and Lynn Redgrave and grandmother of actress Natasha Richardson.

JUDGE ROY BEAN

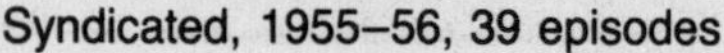

Syndicated, 1955–56, 39 episodes

CAST

Judge Roy Bean	Edgar Buchanan
Letty Bean	Jackie Loughery
Deputy Jeff Taggard	Jack Beutel
Texas Ranger Steve	Russell Hayden

PRODUCER: Russell Hayden

Law west of the Pecos

This syndicated half-hour western, based rather loosely on the exploits of Roy Bean—the storekeeper and self-appointed judge who administered the law west of the Pecos during the 1870s—was a perfect example of the credo often attributed to veteran director John Ford: "When fact becomes legend, print the legend." In effect, facts be damned. The real-life Bean was reportedly a vicious, sleazy varmint who owned the Texas town of Langtry, which he named after the famed actress of the day, Lily Langtry, over whom Bean had become obsessed.

In this series, as played by longtime character actor Edgar Buchanan (in a rare leading role), he'd become a grizzled, though lovable, old codger living with his pretty niece and upholding law and order with his stalwart deputy. This was a far cry from the Judge Roy Bean portrayed innumerable times in Hollywood westerns, most notably by Walter Brennan (who won an Oscar for his performance) in *The Westerner* in 1940; Paul Newman in *The Life and Times of Judge Roy Bean* in 1972; and Ned

Beatty in the TV miniseries, *The Streets of Laredo,* in 1995.

TV's *Judge Roy Bean,* which ran for a single season, was produced by 1930s and 1940s cowboy star Russell Hayden who also played in it as Steve, the Texas Ranger. The cast also included Jackie Loughery (a beauty contestant turned starlet who was Mrs. Jack Webb) and Jack Beutel, best remembered for starring opposite Jane Russell in *The Outlaw,* playing Billy the Kid.

VIDEO AVAILABILITY

Nearly all of the episodes of *Judge Roy Bean* are available at certain video outlets. Each cassette contains two stories and runs about fifty minutes.

TRIVIA TIDBITS

- Edgar Buchanan, who specialized in playing old coots and wily rascals, was a dentist before becoming an actor in the late 1930s.
- Buchanan started his prodigious TV career as Hopalong Cassidy's pal Red Connors (1951–52), but his lasting fame in the medium would be as querulous Uncle Joe on *Petticoat Junction* (1963–69).
- Russell Hayden began his career as Hopalong Cassidy's young sidekick Lucky Jenkins between 1937 and 1941.

LITTLE HOUSE ON THE PRAIRIE

NBC, 1974–82 (plus one-season continuation as *Little House: A New Beginning*), 201 episodes total

CAST

Charles Ingalls	Michael Landon
Caroline Ingalls	Karen Grassle
Laura Ingalls Wilder	Melissa Gilbert
Mary Ingalls Kendall (1974–81)	Melissa Sue Anderson
Carrie Ingalls (1974–82)	Lindsay Green Bush or Sidney Green Bush
Isaiah Edwards (1974–77, 1982–83)	Victor French
Lars Hanson (1974–78)	Karl Swenson
Nels Oleson	Richard Bull
Harriet Oleson	Katherine MacGregor
Nellie Oleson Dalton (1974–81)	Alison Arngrim
Willie Oleson	Jonathan Gilbert
Dr. Baker (1974–78)	Kevin Hagen
Rev. Robert Alden (1974–78)	Dabbs Greer
Eva Beadle Sims (1974–78)	Charlotte Stewart
Ebenezer Sprague (1975–76)	Ted Gehring
Grace Edwards (1976–77)	Bonnie Bartlett
Alie Garvey (1977–80)	Hersha Parady
Jonathan Garvey (1977–81)	Merlin Olsen
Andy Garvey (1977–81)	Patrick Laborteaux
Albert Ingalls (1978–82)	Matthew Laborteaux
Adam Kendall (1978–81)	Linwood Boomer
Eliza Jane Wilder (1979–83)	Lucy Lee Flippin
Almanzo Wilder (1979–83)	Dean Butler
Jenny Wilder (1982–83)	Shannen Doherty

CREATORS: Ed Friendly, Blanche Hanalis, Michael Landon
EXECUTIVE PRODUCER: Michael Landon
PRODUCERS: John Hawkins, Winston Miller, Kent McCray
PRINCIPAL DIRECTORS: Michael Landon, Maury Dexter, William F. Claxton, Victor French, Leo Penn, Alf Kjellin, Lewis Allen
PRINCIPAL WRITERS: Michael Landon, Chris Abbott, John Hawkins, Juanita Bartlett, Dale Eunson, B. W. Sandefur, Arthur Heinneman, Scott Swanton, Robert Vincent Wright

The little house of Landon

After fourteen successful seasons playing Little Joe Cartwright on *Bonanza,* Michael Landon took his idea for a brand new western family drama series from Laura Ingalls Wilder's eight books (written in the 1930s and 1940s) of reminiscences of her youth. The difference was that he added his own closely supervised dimensions of story and character that were not present in the original. He also fathered the show, nurtured the cast and crew, directed and wrote most of the stories, and entirely supervised every minute detail. The show espoused his strong family values: the Ingalls family never lost their spirit while pulling together—weathering hardships such as crop losses on the prairie, dire financial straits, fire, floods, blizzards, and the onset of blindness in daughter Mary. They were, in Michael Landon's vision, a strong, honest pioneer clan whose love and devotion overcame all physical harshness and affairs of the heart—even along the way learning racial understanding when a black family moves to Walnut Grove and when the neighboring Oleson family's daughter married a Jewish accountant—and the episodes invariably taught a moral in their usually simple fifty-two-minute plots. (Occasionally there was a ninety-minute episode and periodically a two-hour one.)

Set in the 1870s in and around the fictional town of Walnut Grove in Plum Creek, Minnesota, *Little House*

Michael Landon, the star of *Little House on the Prairie.* The beloved family western was adapted from Laura Ingalls Wilder's eight books written during the 1930s and 1940s. COURTESY OF PERSONALITY PHOTOS, INC.

on the Prairie was essentially a weekly soap opera in the preautomobile prairie, appealing to the same audience as *The Waltons,* which was on during the same time span. The Ingalls's experiences as frontier homesteaders were viewed through the sentimental eyes of young Laura, the second-born daughter, as *The Waltons* was (in a different time frame) through aspiring writer/son John Boy.

Michael Landon's vision of Charles Ingalls differed somewhat from the one in the original books, in which Pa sported a long beard and the kids were dressed in tattered clothes and went barefoot. This vision clashed with that of purist Ed Friendly, who had obtained the rights to the Laura Ingalls Wilder novels and marketed them to NBC. Ultimately, Friendly departed the show, leaving Landon in charge. Landon's players and stock crew comprised an exceptionally loyal bunch who did not go unrewarded through the years. Landon himself, with his espousal of family values, earned a spot as a much-admired and beloved figure in the entertainment industry to the end.

VIDEO AVAILABILITY

Selected episodes of *Little House,* each running about forty-five minutes, are available at certain video outlets. Also available are two feature-length cassettes—the two-hour pilot and a two-part inspirational episode featuring Ernest Borgnine as a reclusive mountain man who finds young Laura after she runs away, blaming herself for the death of her infant brother.

TRIVIA TIDBITS

- Three *Little House* reunion movies were made—one in 1983 and two in 1984—following the lives of Laura Ingalls and husband Almanzo Wilder into the twentieth century. In the final one, the town of Walnut Grove was blown to smithereens and leveled—to fulfill an agreement with the land's owners to return it to its original state.
- Michael Landon continued his "family values" vision in one more hit series, *Highway to Heaven* (1984–89), as producer, director, writer, and star with *Little House* pal Victor French. Landon's celebrity had become such that his death from pancreatic cancer at fifty-four in 1991 prompted significant media coverage. French died two years earlier.
- Landon created and oversaw (but did not act in) another similar show, *Father Murphy* (1981–84), also set in a prairie town. It starred former football star Merlin Olsen, who had been proud father Jonathan Garvey in *Little House.*
- Cinematographer Ted Voightlander, one of Landon's inner circle among the crew, won two consecutive Emmys for his *Little House* work in 1977–78 and 1978–79.

- After *Little House*, Karen Grassle did little television and seems to have left show business. Melissa Sue Anderson appears occasionally in television movies but has not done another series. Melissa Gilbert, on the other hand, blossomed into adulthood as a star in many TV movies and a couple of short-lived series. She is now married to actor Bruce Boxleitner. Her sister Sara has grown up on TV as the younger daughter on Roseanne.
- David Rose wrote the music for *Little House,* as he had done all of Michael Landon's TV work (*Bonanza, Highway to Heaven,* the three *Little House* TV movies, etc.).

LONESOME DOVE

CBS, 1989, 4 two-hour episodes

CAST

Capt. Gus McCrae	Robert Duvall
Capt. Woodrow F. Call	Tommy Lee Jones
Joshua Deets	Danny Glover
Lorna Wood	Diane Lane
Jake Spoon	Robert Urich
Blue Duck	Frederic Forrest
Dish Boggett	D. B. Sweeney
Newt Dobbs	Rick Schroder
Clara Allen	Anjelica Huston
Sheriff July Johnson	Chris Cooper
Pea Eye Parker	Tim Scott
Elmira Johnson	Glenne Headly
Deputy Roscoe Brown	Barry Corbin
Lippy Jones	William Sanderson
Jasper Fant	Barry Tubb
Dan Suggs	Gavin O'Herlihy
Luke	Steve Buscemi
Big Zwey	Frederic Coffin
Allen O'Brien	Travis Swords

CREATED BY: Larry McMurtry

EXECUTIVE PRODUCERS: Suzanne de Passe, Bill Wittliff, Robert Halmi Jr.

SUPERVISING PRODUCER: Michael Wiesbarth

PRODUCER: Dyson Lovell

DIRECTOR: Simon Wincer

WRITER: Bill Wittliff

Robert Duvall (left) and Tommy Lee Jones briefly brought the TV western back to life in 1989 with their superb portrayals of Captains Gus McCrae and Woodrow F. Call in *Lonesome Dove*. COURTESY OF PERSONALITY PHOTOS, INC.

Trail-busters

The TV western genre, somewhat dormant after the mid-1970s, came roaring back to life in early 1989 with this sprawling production of Larry McMurtry's 1986 Pulitzer Prize-winning novel about friendships, relationships, coming of age, and an epic cattle drive. First telecast over four nights, this eight-hour drama of the Old West told the tale of two longtime pals and former Texas Rangers, garrulous Gus McCrae and taciturn Woodrow Call, who leave the south Texas town of Lonesome Dove with a group of ranch hands called the Outfit (both experienced and at least one greenhorn) to push their herd to the lush ranch country of Montana. The saga was divided into four distinct parts and titled "Leaving," "On the Trail," "The Plains" (which contained a harrowing stampede), and "Return."

The three women's roles in the story are enacted by Diane Lane, as Lorna Wood, the town whore, who persuades Jake Spoon—a charming ex-Ranger who'd had run-ins with Call over the years—to join the Outfit and the hazardous journey, despite Call's and McCrae's misgivings; Anjelica Huston, as Clara Allen, McCrae's old flame who now lives with her husband on a Nebraska farm that happens to be along the trail the Outfit is following; and Glenne Headly, as Elmira, the bored, scheming, pregnant wife of Sheriff July Johnson, who bullies him into following Spoon and is eager to escape her lot.

Multifaceted *Lonesome Dove* belongs in the pantheon of great television epics, alongside *Centennial, Roots,* and *The Winds of War/War and Remembrance*—endlessly exciting, beautifully photographed, superbly cast, and wonderfully realized.

VIDEO AVAILABILITY

The complete *Lonesome Dove* is available at certain video outlets.

TRIVIA TIDBITS

- The 1993 *Return to Lonesome Dove,* a follow-up miniseries, really was not a sequel, having been concocted by CBS but having nothing to do with Larry McMurtry. Nor was the syndicated *Lonesome Dove* series. The official sequel, from another McMurtry book, was *Streets of Laredo* in 1995. A prequel to the original saga, called *Dead Man's Walk,* premiered in 1996.
- Woodrow Call was played in *Return to Lonesome Dove* by Jon Voight; in *Streets of Laredo* by James Garner; and in *Dead Man's Walk* by Jonny Lee Miller.
- In addition to an Emmy nomination for Outstanding Miniseries, *Lonesome Dove* earned seventeen others, including acting ones for Robert Duvall, Tommy Lee Jones, Diane Lane, Danny Glover, and Anjelica Huston. Also nominated were Australian director Simon Wincer, writer Bill Wittliff, photographer Douglas Milsome, composer Basil Poledouris, editor Corky Ehl-

ers, and production designer Cary White. It won seven Emmys in minor categories. *War and Remembrance* beat it out in most of the major categories.

- In May 1996, Larry McMurtry's *Dead Man's Walk,* a prequel miniseries to *Lonesome Dove* starring Jonny Lee Miller as Woodrow and David Arquette as Gus, was aired on ABC-TV.

LOVE FOR LYDIA

PBS Masterpiece Theatre, 1979 (first American broadcast), 12 episodes

CAST

Lydia Aspen	Mel Martin
Edward Richardson	Christopher Blake
Alex Sanderson	Jeremy Irons
Rollo Aspen	Michael Aldridge
Blackie Johnson	Ralph Arliss
Tom Holland	Peter Davison
Aunt Juliana	Rachel Kempson
Aunt Bertie	Beatrix Lehmann
Nancy Holland	Sherrie Hewson
Mr. Bretherton	David Ryall

PRODUCER: Tony Wharmby
DIRECTORS: John Glenister, Piers Haggard, Christopher Hodson, Simon Langton, Michael Simpson, Tony Wharmby
WRITER: Julian Bond

Jazz-age love for "Love"

A sumptuous, elegantly filmed multipart romantic drama, based on Herbert Ernest Bates's novel about Britain's prosperous, "Careless Twenties," *Love for Lydia* revolved around a middle-class young woman who inherited a small-town factory and had love affairs with four suitors. Mel Martin starred as, in the words of one critic, "a British flapper, a stunning spoiled brunette with a thirst for living, an eye for men, and questionable morality." Initially shy as she goes to live with her two maiden aunts, she blossoms, with the help of adoring newspaperman Edward Richardson, into a social butterfly.

Filmed in the Northamptonshire north country, this visual romp proved to be as carefree and leisurely as the period itself.

VIDEO AVAILABILITY

Love for Lydia is available on seven cassettes at certain video outlets. The total running time is about eleven hours.

TRIVIA TIDBITS

- American actress Mel Martin later would play British actress Vivien Leigh to Anthony Higgins's Laurence Olivier in the TV adaptation of *Darling of the Gods,* about the later years of the Oliviers' marriage.
- Jeremy Irons moved on to become a major international movie idol, first opposite Meryl Streep in *The French Lieutenant's Woman* and then an Oscar winner in 1990 as Claus Von Bulow in *Reversal of Fortune.* Most recently he did a particularly vicious turn as the blond, German-accented villain who made Bruce Willis's life hell in *Die Hard With a Vengeance.*

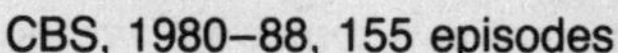

MAGNUM, P.I.

CBS, 1980–88, 155 episodes

CAST

Thomas Sullivan Magnum	Tom Selleck
Jonathan Quayle Higgins	John Hillerman
TC	Roger E. Mosley
Orville "Rick" Wright	Larry Manetti

EXECUTIVE PRODUCERS/CREATORS: Donald P. Bellisario, Glen A. Larson, Tom Selleck, Chas Floyd Johnson
SUPERVISING PRODUCER: Joel Rogosin, Chris Abbott-Fish
PRODUCERS: J. Rickley Dumm, Rich Weaver, Andrew Schenider, Reuben Leder, Steve Miller, Jeri Taylor, Doug Green
DIRECTORS: Roger Young, Donald P. Bellisario, Bruce Green, Lawrence Doheny, Robert Loggia, Rick Kolbe, Ron Satlof, Ray Austin, Rod Daniels, Michael Vejar, Sidney Hayers, Alan J. Levi, Robert Thompson, Gilbert Shilton, James Frawley, Jackie Cooper, Ivan Dixon, Stuart Margolin, Virgil Vogel
WRITERS: Donald P. Bellisario, Glen A. Larson, Babs Greyhosky, Frank Lupo, Chris Bunch, Ken Pettus, Robert Hamilton, Diane Frolov, Caroline Elias, Reuben Leder, Robert Van Scoyk, Rob Gilmer, Andrew Schneider

Hawaii after "Five-O"

Tom Selleck became one of the charismatic television stars of the 1980s as the fun-loving private detective with a penchant for fast cars and beautiful women, living on a luxurious Hawaiian estate in return for providing security for its never seen owner, Robin Masters. Thomas Magnum was an ex-naval intelligence officer who pursued the good life (in his trademark floral shirt, Detroit Tigers baseball cap, and borrowed Ferrari) and took nickel-and-dime sleuthing jobs—at least that was the way they seemed to start out—as a somewhat irresponsible private eye who usually ended up hip-deep in trouble. He parried with Jonathan Higgins (John Hillerman), the haughty majordomo for Robin Masters, and tackled assorted cases with a couple of resourceful 'Nam buddies: TC, who ran a helicopter charter service; and Rick, who owned a Honolulu bar/restaurant/disco called Cafe American (after, of course, Bogart's place in *Casablanca*).

Among the other recurring characters were Kathleen Lloyd as Carol Baldwin, Magnum's assistant DA friend; Elisha Cook as Ice Pick, Rick's gangster acquaintance; Gillian Dobb as Agatha Chumley, an Englishwoman who had a thing for Higgins; and Eugene Roche as Luther Gillis, a hard-nose private eye from St. Louis with whom Magnum would bump heads.

Occasionally guest stars appeared. In one episode, José Ferrer and son Miguel turned up with June Lockhart and daughter Anne. Mercedes McCambridge, Robert Loggia, Scatman Crothers, Darren McGavin, Ernest Borgnine, Vera Miles, Tyne Daly, Leslie Uggams, Sharon Stone as twins (in 1984), and Carol Channing all put in appearances. Ted Danson had a small role in a 1981 episode before becoming Sam Malone on *Cheers*. One who never turned up was Jack Lord, who previously "owned" Hawaii on television as the cop Steve Garrett—frequently referred to on the series as a running gag.

Magnumania on the main island

Most of the episodes had a light touch. In one story, Magnum found himself locked in a bank vault with guest star Carol Burnett, as a starstruck teller; in another, he was saddled on a missing persons case with Frank Sinatra, who played a retired New York police sergeant. A couple of times he did stunt "crossovers," working with Rick and A. J. Simon (Gerald McRaney and Jameson Parker from *Simon and Simon*) and Jessica Fletcher (Angela Lansbury from *Murder, She Wrote*). Other Magnum shows had a somewhat dark undercurrent: one or two featured Vietnam flashback sequences; another had him meeting his long-estranged mother (Gwen Verdon); still another found him seeking his long-lost Eurasian daughter, whose mother was a Vietnamese woman Magnum had married and who later supposedly died. There was one episode in which he time-warped back to the 1930s to solve a case. And another, a complex Dashiel Hammett-type 1940s film noir, was shot in black and white.

The most unusual episode of *Magnum, P.I.* was the one at the end of the 1987 season—called "Limbo"—in which Magnum was seriously wounded in a shootout and hovered between life and death. While a network decision was up in the air about continuing the series, the show suggested that he had been killed and was on his way to heaven. An avalanche of mail made up the minds of the producers and the network, and just before the new season's premiere, the episode was reworked with new footage to allow Magnum to live. The two-hour absolutely final episode, "Resolutions," aired at the end of the 1987–88 season, brought back eighteen cast members reprising roles they had played on-and-off during the eight years of *Magnum, P.I.* Wrapping up the series, Magnum decided to rejoin the navy, and Higgins was revealed to (possibly) be the elusive Robin Masters.

VIDEO AVAILABILITY

More than two dozen *Magnum, P.I.* cassettes are available through Columbia House, with each tape containing two hour-long adventures. Several episodes are also available at certain video outlets.

EMMY AWARDS

1983–84 **Tom Selleck,** Outstanding Lead Actor in a Drama Series
1986–87 **John Hillerman,** Outstanding Supporting Actor in a Drama Series

TRIVIA TIDBITS

- In one 1985 episode, Tom Sellect's real-life father, Robert Selleck Sr., turned up to play Magnum's grandfather.
- Tom Selleck's pursuit of big-screen stardom has been elusive. As a result of his commitment to *Magnum, P.I.,* he had to turn down the role of Indiana Jones. (He was Spielberg's first choice.) After several early film flops (e.g., *High Road to China* in 1983), he had some success in *Three Men and a Baby* (1987) and *Mr. Baseball* (1992). Of Selleck's occasional TV work since *Magnum, P.I.,* his most rewarding seems to be his recurring 1995–96 role on *Friends* as Courteney Cox's much older boyfriend.
- Before becoming Thomas Magnum, Tom Selleck had a recurring role on *The Rockford Files* during the 1979–80 season as playboy detective Lance White.
- Although his Higgins was a British braggadocio, John Hillerman (despite the stuffy Englishman most fans have come to know from his various series) is actually a Texan.
- Following this hit series, Donald Bellisario went on to create *Quantum Leap* and was executive producer along with his actress wife, Deborah Pratt, who occasionally was seen on *Magnum, P.I.* as TC's girlfriend Gloria.
- The show's theme song was written by Mike Post and Pete Carpenter.

THE MAN FROM U.N.C.L.E.

NBC, 1964–68, 105 episodes

CAST

Napoleon Solo	Robert Vaughn
Illya Kuryakin	David McCallum
Alexander Waverly	Leo G. Carroll

CREATOR: Sam H. Rolfe
EXECUTIVE PRODUCER: Norman Felton
PRODUCERS: Sam H. Rolfe, Anthony Spinner, Boris Ingster
DIRECTORS: Leo Penn, Don Medford, Alvin Ganzer, Barry Shear, Sutton Rolley, John Newland, Boris Sagal, Richard Donner, Marc Daniels, Alf Kjellin, Joseph Sargent, John Brahm, Hy Averback
WRITERS: Sam H. Rolfe, Marion Hargrove, Robert E. Thompson, Robert Towne, Boris Ingster, Alvin Sapinsley

Mr. Suave and Mr. Shag, secret agents

The Man From U.N.C.L.E. (an acronym for the fictional, supersecret United Network Command for Law Enforcement) began as an engaging spoof of Ian Fleming's James Bond character, with Fleming himself contributing the original outline and conceiving what would be the pilot episode, "The Vulcan Affair"—later released theatrically as *To Trap a Spy.* Suave Napoleon Solo was teamed with shaggy-haired Russian good guy Illya Kuryakin as U.N.C.L.E. agents to swap witty banter and make the world safe from international baddies working for THRUSH, an organization bent on world domination.

Two men from U.N.C.L.E.—Robert Vaughn (left, as Napoleon Solo) and David McCallum (as Illya Kuryakin). COURTESY OF PERSONALITY PHOTOS, INC.

America's favorite U.N.C.L.E.s

Ultracool Solo and teen heartthrob Kuryakin's assorted, often campy "Affairs" (each episode had the word in the title) pitted them against various dastardly villains using not much more than humorous dialogue and modern spy gadgetry. The bad guys (and women) were sadistic, relishing the roles as evil incarnate. In the first season alone, Solo was flogged by Robert Culp, racked by George Sanders (as the deliciously heinous Squire G. Emory Partridge), drugged by Carroll O'Connor, and vampirized by Martin Landau. Name stars fell over themselves to be nasty to the U.N.C.L.E. guys: Joan Crawford, Jack Palance, Ricardo Montalban, Rip Torn, Eve Arden, Sonny and Cher, Telly Savalas, Nancy Sinatra, et al.

A representative episode, "The Bridge of Lions Affair," guest-starring distinguished actor Maurice Evans, tied a sudden decline in the feline population of London's Soho (archenemy THRUSH was on a catnapping caper) to the theft of a rejuvenation formula, and sent Solo and Kuryakin in opposite directions that both led to the same trap sprung by their nemesis. Another, "The Double Affair," sent the spy twosome to the newly created African nation of Western Natumba to thwart a worldwide crime-for-hire syndicate (WASP, this time, rather than THRUSH) from carrying the assassination of the country's premier at the opening of a major chcmical plant.

Occasionally, David McCallum (as Illya), whose designer turtlenecks created a sweater craze for a time, was assisted by Jill Ireland, then his wife (as Marion Raven), in such episodes as "The Quadripartile Affair" and "The Giuoco Piano Affair." McCallum, who was actually British, became something of a 1960s cult figure, who also wrote and recorded poetry.

U.N.C.L.E. cried "uncle" in 1968 as audience favor turned elsewhere. But in 1983 (the same year Vaughn was the villain in *Superman III*), Solo and Kuryakin, now successful in other enterprises (the former was now in the computer business, the latter the owner of a high fashion boutique), were called back to duty one last time in *The Return of the Man From U.N.C.L.E.: The 15 Years Later Affair,* a made-for-TV movie that the producers felt might prompt a revival of the original series. Leo G. Carroll had passed on and Patrick Macnee (the onetime John Steed of *The Avengers*) was now in charge as Sir John Raleigh. As a gag bit, George Lazenby (007 in *On Her Majesty's Secret Service*) turned up in his guise as James Bond to lend a helping hand. The humorous banter, the winks, and the gadgets were there; unfortunately, the magic wasn't.

VIDEO AVAILABILITY

About two dozen volumes of *The Man From U.N.C.L.E.* are available at certain video outlets. Each runs about 114 minutes and contains two "Affairs," including the 1965 cult episode "The Project Strigas Affair," which guest-starred future *Star Trek* compatriots William Shatner and Leonard Nimoy.

TRIVIA TIDBITS

- During the 1966–67 season, a spin-off show, *The Girl From U.N.C.L.E.*, aired simultaneously with Leo G. Carroll doing double duty as brilliant Alexander Waverly, sending Stefanie Powers as vivacious April Dancer (Mary Ann Mobley played the role in the pilot) and Noel Harrison (Rex's actor son) as hip Mark Slate on assignments.
- David McCallum's original goal in life was to be a famous oboe player, following in the footsteps of his dad, concertmaster of the London Philharmonic Orchestra.
- Archenemy THRUSH was, according to various sources, an acronym for "The Technological Hierarchy for the Removal of Undesirables and the Subjugation of Humanity."
- Jerry Goldsmith composed the theme for the series; Lalo Schifrin handled the week-to-week music.
- Because of the show's tremendous popularity, nine two-part episodes, edited together, and the two-hour pilot were released theatrically as five feature-length movies.
- Robert Vaughn was the *Teenage Caveman* in 1958 and an Oscar nominee for *The Young Philadelphians* in 1959.

MAVERICK

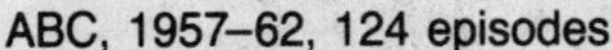

ABC, 1957–62, 124 episodes

CAST

Bret Maverick (1957–60)	James Garner
Bart Maverick	Jack Kelly
Beau Maverick (1960–61)	Roger Moore
Brent Maverick (1961)	Robert Colbert
Samantha Crawford (1958–59)	Diane Brewster
Dandy Jim Buckley	Efrem Zimbalist Jr.
Gentleman Jack Darby	Richard Long
Big Mike McComb	Leo Gordon
Melanie Blake	Kathleen Crowley
Pappy (Beauregard Maverick)	James Garner

CREATED BY: Roy Huggins
EXECUTIVE PRODUCER: William T. Orr
PRODUCERS: Roy Huggins, Coles Trapnell, William L. Stuart
PRINCIPAL DIRECTORS: Budd Boetticher, Leslie H. Martinson, Douglas Heyes, Abner Biberman, Howard W. Koch, Richard L. Bare, Paul Henreid, Montgomery Pittman, Arthur Lubin, George Waggner, Irving J. Moore, Robert Altman
PRINCIPAL WRITERS: James O'Hanlon, Roy Huggins, Marion Hargrove, Gerald Drayson Adams, Gene Levitt, Douglas Heyes, Leonard Praskins

Legend of the West

This classic adult, often tongue-in-cheek western series was an amalgam of drama and humor about a pair of roguish, if rather gun-shy gamblers, brothers Bret and Bart Maverick, who together or separately meet their

Nothing up his sleeve: The crafty Bret Maverick (James Garner, left) and his brother, Bart (Jack Kelly). The show spawned a 1995 movie spin-off, which starred Mel Gibson as Bret and Garner in a surprise role. COURTESY OF PERSONALITY PHOTOS, INC.

share of villains, fellow frontier grifters, and charming damsels while trying to make a decent, semihonest living. Generally, they used their wits rather than their guns to get out of jams. Basically, they were cowards—but they were terrific with cards and dealt their way into viewers' hearts and television legend and brought stardom to a relatively unknown James Garner, the crafty Bret.

There also were other equally larcenous family members who moseyed onto the scene over the life of the series. When James Garner left after three seasons in a dispute with Warner Bros., studio contract player Roger Moore was recruited to play the Mavericks' long-lost

British cousin, Beau, the "white sheep" of the family (a disgrace because he was a war *hero*), and then Brent, another younger brother never previously discussed (Robert Colbert, Warner contract player), stayed around for a season. And on occasion there was Pappy, also played by James Garner, who instilled the clan with what became known as "Pappyisms"—such as "He who fights and runs away lives to run another day" and "Any man who needs to make out a will isn't spending his money properly."

Maverick, most agree, lost most of its hip edge following wry Garner's departure. Thus, it was vital to the producers that in the various incarnations of the show in the late 1970s and early 1980s, Garner's participation in whatever manner was an absolute must.

VIDEO AVAILABILITY

Several episodes of *Maverick,* each running about fifty minutes, are available at certain video outlets. Columbia House also is offering *Maverick: The Collector's Edition* with two episodes to a cassette, and has packaged more than fifteen volumes to date.

TRIVIA TIDBITS

- *Maverick* won the Emmy during the 1958–59 season as Best Western Series, a category used only once before (when the syndicated *Stories of the Century* won in 1954) and never again.
- James Garner left *Maverick* in 1960 in a dispute over money, similar to the Clint Walker situation early on *Cheyenne*. Unlike Walker, Garner never returned to the original series.
- Later *Maverick* incarnations included *The New Maverick* (a 1978 ABC pilot movie) with James Garner and Jack Kelly reprising their roles as Bret and Bart to establish the series for Charles Frank as their Harvard-educated nephew, Ben; *Young Maverick* (CBS 1979–

80) with Frank—it lasted only six episodes, with two more unaired; *Bret Maverick* (NBC 1981–82) with Garner back in the saddle as Bret for seventeen episodes (the last one of which also had Kelly turning up as Bart).

- In 1994 *Maverick* came to the big screen with Mel Gibson as Bret Maverick, Jodie Foster as a conniving grifter, and James Garner as a U.S. marshal who's not all he appears to be.
- The *Maverick* theme was written by David Buttolph and Paul Francis Webster.
- Roy Huggins later created *The Fugitive* and then *The Rockford Files*.

MEDIC

NBC, 1954–56, 59 episodes

CAST

Dr. Konrad Styner	Richard Boone

CREATOR: James E. Moser
PRODUCERS: Frank LaTourette, Worthington Miner
PRINCIPAL DIRECTORS: John Meredyth Lucas, Bernard Girard, John Brahm, Ted Post, Richard Wilson, Worthington Miner
PRINCIPAL WRITERS: John Meredyth Lucas, James E. Moser, Art & Jo Napoleon, John Kneubuhl, Gene L. Coon, Endre Bohem

"Guardian . . . healer . . . comforter."

The granddaddy of TV medical shows, from *Medical Center* and *Ben Casey* (also by creator James E. Moser) to *St. Elsewhere, E.R.* (both of them), and *Chicago Hope,* this anthology series starring Richard Boone as both narrator and actor presented the practice of medicine in a realistic fashion, filmed at real hospitals and clinics with genuine doctors and nurses often used as part of the cast along with a parade of noted and up-and-coming actors. The weekly half-hour drama, broadcast Monday nights at 9:00, was produced in cooperation with the Los Angeles County Medical Association and approached subjects such as cholera, dipsomania, hemophilia, manic depression and postpartum psychosis. *Medic,* in fact, was the first TV drama to show an actual childbirth. A number of performers had their earliest TV roles on the show—Beverly Garland in the show's premiere episode, "White

Is the Color"), John Saxon, Robert Vaughn, and Dennis Hopper. Each drama in this pioneer series opened with Richard Boone, generally dressed in a surgeon's gown, intoning this description of a doctor: ". . . guardian of birth, healer of the sick, and comforter of the aged." The anthology show itself was "dedicated to the profession of medicine, to the men and women who labor in its cause." It fulfilled that aim extremely well for two seasons.

VIDEO AVAILABILITY

More than a half-dozen cassettes are available at certain video outlets, each running about fifty-five minutes and containing two episodes.

TRIVIA TIDBITS

- *Medic* was the first of four series starring Richard Boone. It was followed by *Have Gun—Will Travel, The Richard Boone Show* (a weekly dramatic anthology with a resident cast), and *Hec Ramsey.*
- Among those acting on the series were Richard Crenna, Charles Bronson, Lee J. Cobb, Vera Miles, Hugh ("Ward Cleaver") Beaumont, and Cynthia Stone (then Jack Lemmon's actress wife).
- The *Medic* theme was written by Victor Young. With words added by Edward Heyman, it became known as "Blue Star" and was a hit record for singer Felicia Saunders in 1955. Young and Heyman earlier wrote "When I Fall in Love."

THE MILLIONAIRE

CBS, 1955–60, 205 episodes

CAST

Michael Anthony — Marvin Miller

EXECUTIVE PRODUCER: Fred Henry
PRODUCER: Don Fedderson
DIRECTORS: Robert Altman, James V. Kern, Sobey Martin, Gerald Meyer, James Sheldon

Big bucks from a stranger

Michael Anthony, personal secretary to eccentric multibillionaire John Beresford Tipton (whose face was never seen), had the weekly task of presenting a cashier's check for one million dollars, tax free, to an unsuspecting guest star. The object was to see how this newfound wealth would alter the recipient's life. There was a stipulation, of course, that he or she would forfeit the money if an attempt was made to learn the identity of the mysterious benefactor or if he or she revealed how the fortune was obtained. The extremely popular anthology show—playing on the viewer's fantasy and vicariousness—alternated weekly between drama and comedy.

Mellifluent radio actor Marvin Miller was the munificent Michael Anthony and sonorous voice artist Paul Frees (who over the years did hundreds of cartoon voices) was wealthy, reclusive Mr. Tipton—who indulged in his beneficence from the study of his sixty-thousand-acre estate, Silverstone. Miller once told *TV Guide* that for years after *The Millionaire,* he'd regularly received requests from those wanting their own million-dollar cashier's check, and his customary reply was to dispatch a "check" for "a million dollars' worth of good luck."

The concept was derived from Robert H. Andrews' novel *Windfall,* which initially came to the screen as *If I Had a Million* (a multipart 1932 tale with Gary Cooper, Charles Laughton, W. C. Fields, and dozens of others), and was the basis for assorted movies over the decades. In late 1978 producer Don Fedderson attempted to revive the series in a made-for-TV *Millionaire* movie pilot featuring Robert Quarry as Michael Anthony, and a passel of name guest stars.

VIDEO AVAILABILITY

Several episodes of *The Millionaire* are available at certain video outlets, including one each with Agnes Moorehead and Tuesday Weld. Each volume, running about sixty minutes, traces the story of two recipients.

TRIVIA TIDBITS

- Playing recipients over the show's five seasons were Charles Bronson, John Archer (actress Anne Archer's dad), Carolyn ("Morticia Addams") Jones, Vera Miles, DeForest Kelley, James Daly (Tyne and Tim's dad), Ellen ("Grandma Walton") Corby, Richard Crenna, Vic Morrow, Robert Vaughn, David Janssen, Jack Lord, Rita Moreno, John Carradine, Mary Tyler Moore, and Dennis Hopper.
- The cashier's checks on the series ($205 million worth) were drawn on the Gotham City Trust & Savings Bank. Did Batman know of this?
- *The Millionaire* was syndicated under the title *If I Had a Million.*

MISSION: IMPOSSIBLE

CBS, 1966–73, 172 episodes

CAST

Dan Briggs (1966–67)	Steven Hill
Jim Phelps (1967–73)	Peter Graves
Cinnamon Carter (1966–69)	Barbara Bain
Rollin Hand (1966–69)	Martin Landau
Barney Collier	Greg Morris
Will Armitage	Peter Lupus
Paris (1969–71)	Leonard Nimoy
Dana Lambert (1970–71)	Lesley Ann Warren
Dr. Doug Lang (1970–71)	Sam Elliott
Lisa Casey (1971–73)	Lynda Day George
Mimi Davis (1972–73)	Barbara Anderson

CREATOR AND EXECUTIVE PRODUCER: Bruce Geller
PRODUCERS: Joseph Gantman, Stanley Kallis, William Read Woodfield, Allan Balter, Robert Thompson, John W. Rogers, Robert F. O'Neil, Laurence Heath, Bruce Lansbury
DIRECTORS: Barry Crane, Marvin Chomsky, Richard Benedict, Bruce Kessler, Stuart Hagmann, Robert Butler, Paul Krasny, Virgil W. Vogel, Sutton Roley, Marc Daniels, John Llewellyn Moxey, Alf Kjellin
WRITERS: Bruce Geller, William Read Woodfield, Allan Balter, Robert Thompson

"Your mission, if you decide to accept it . . ."

Mission: Impossible might well have been TV's first pure action series in that it featured little dialogue and even less character development. The stories were complicated, tense plots in which characters had to thwart an enemy operation or even overthrow a dictator in some fictitious country.

When the intrigue-mystery series initially aired, Steven Hill was the I.M.F. (Impossible Missions Force) leader. Devoutly religious, Hill found the production schedule to be prohibitive, and he "resigned" from the agency and in effect left show business for a number of years; today he is the district attorney/sounding board to the team of lawyers on *Law & Order.* Peter Graves stepped into the role, rifling through dossiers at the start of each show and choosing the agents—each a specialist—who would join him on various highly secret, usually international missions that were outlined on the show's trademark self-immolating audio tapes that turned up in the oddest places. The missions included retrieving nuclear warheads, exposing European traitors, framing crime czars, rescuing kidnapped scientists, protecting political defectors, recovering stolen plutonium, and thwarting enemy invasions.

Men, missions—and a woman

A number of the situations in which the leads found themselves—all playing quite seriously—strained credulity. Martin Landau's assorted disguises as the humorless, intense Rollin Hand, master at his craft, always fooled the less-than-clever villains in various generic banana republics and Eastern bloc dictatorships (always English-speaking). Barbara Bain, then his real-life wife (who won three consecutive Emmys in her role of seductive Cinnamon Carter, the sole female member of the team), always distracted bad guy after bad guy, coaxing them to blab their entire scheme, by emotionlessly unbuttoning the top of her blouse.

But all believability was lost when Greg Morris, the handsome African-American member of the I.M.F., an electronics whiz with a genius for splicing wires together and concocting homemade bombs, pretended to be a Nazi officer in full German uniform and strolled through a fictional mittle-European country unchallenged. The left-wing press of the sixties blasted the show for its "glorification" of covert CIA-type operation, but the general public didn't mind.

What the show had going for it—and why its classic status endures—was its sophistication, its film-quality production values, machine-gun editing, emphasis on guile and technology over guts and guns, and memorable staccato theme music, courtesy of Lalo Schifrin, played over the show's distinctive lit match and fuse in the credit sequence.

The show finally played itself out after seven seasons. But before it did, Martin Landau was let go due to his escalating salary demands, and his wife followed him. The two did a television pilot for a young Steven Spielberg that did not sell, and then costarred in *Space: 1999* in England. Landau was replaced by Leonard Nimoy, and Bain by a parade of actresses (Lesley Ann Warren, Lynda Day George, and Barbara Anderson).

Peter Graves remained with I.M.F. until the end, and then years later—now white-haired—was lured back to the role of Jim Phelps, leading an entirely new team of agents in a short-lived ABC revival series (shot in Australia) in the late 1980s. One was Greg Morris's son, Phil, playing original team member Barney Collier's son, Grant. The new series ended in June 1990, but a new generation of fans was introduced to the concept.

In late spring 1996 *Mission: Impossible* came to the big screen, directed by Brian De Palma, with Tom Cruise in the lead. (Peter Graves's Jim Phelps role was played by Jon Voight.) The film was a huge box-office success, despite the fact that only the music bore direct similarity to the original series.

VIDEO AVAILABILITY

Mission: Impossible, unedited and digitally remastered with enhanced sound and image quality, is available through Columbia House in a series of cassettes, each running about 110 minutes and containing two hour-long episodes.

EMMY AWARDS

1966–67	Outstanding Dramatic Series **Barbara Bain,** Outstanding Continued Performance by an Actress in a Leading Role in a Dramatic Series **Bruce Geller,** Outstanding Writing Achievement in Drama
1967–68	Outstanding Dramatic Series
1968–68	**Barbara Bain,** Outstanding Continued Performance by an Actress in a Leading Role in a Dramatic Series

TRIVIA TIDBITS

- Peter Graves—younger brother, as his fans know, of James Arness—is best known to Generation X television viewers as host of assorted reality specials and as cohost of Arts & Entertainment's *Biography.*
- Greg Morris went on to play Robert Urich's cop boss in the latter's series *Vega$* before apparently leaving show business. He died in August 1996.
- Lalo Schifrin's pulsating theme became a record hit, won two 1967 Grammy Awards as Best Instrumental Theme and Best Original Score Written for a Motion Picture or TV Show, and was on *Billboard's* Hot 100 chart for fourteen weeks in 1968. He also had a couple of albums of *Mission: Impossible* music, that also included themes by Jerry Fielding, Kenyon Hopkins, Leith Stevens, Gerald Fried, and other jazz composers who worked on the show.
- The voice of the tape recordings at the start of each show ("Your mission, if you decide to accept it . . .") was that of Bob Johnson.

THE MOD SQUAD

ABC, 1968–73, 124 episodes

CAST

Pete Cochran	Michael Cole
Linc Hayes	Clarence Williams III
Julie Barnes	Peggy Lipton
Capt. Adam Greer	Tige Andrews

CREATOR: Bud Ruskin
EXECUTIVE PRODUCERS: Aaron Spelling, Danny Thomas
PRODUCERS: Harve Bennett, Tony Barrett
PRINCIPAL DIRECTORS: Gary Nelson, Robert Michael Lewis, Don Taylor, Barry Shear, George McCowan, Philip Leacock, Seymour Robbie, Jerry Jameson, Earl Bellamy, Lee H. Katzin, Michael Caffey

Hitting the streets

The Mod Squad has been described in some quarters as the ultimate 1960s series, dealing with three rebellious young dropouts in minor scrapes with the law—the black sheep of a wealthy family, a poor white trash woman with long blond hair, and an angry survivor of the Watts riots with a huge afro and twelve siblings in the ghetto—who are recruited by a special LAPD unit to become undercover cops dealing with the counterculture. Only their immediate superior knew their identities. He had given them a choice: Either work with the police or do time and go back on the streets. Reluctantly, Pete, Julie, and Linc—all played by newcomers—agreed and soon evolved into eager, able undercover cops tooling around

Late 1960s cool—*The Mod Squad* team, from left: Michael Cole (Pete), Peggy Lipton (Julie), and Clarence Williams III (Linc). All three stars were unknowns prior to the series. COURTESY OF PERSONALITY PHOTOS, INC.

town in a 1950 paneled Woody station wagon, fighting drug runners and leather gangs.

The show, created by an ex-cop, Bud Ruskin, and based on his experiences as an undercover narc, evolved from a pilot script he had been marketing around Hollywood for nearly a decade. It ultimately drew the attention of Aaron Spelling; a pilot was made; ABC was sold on it; and *The Mod Squad* quickly captured the youth audience. In a politically incorrect era, the show was hyped as "one white, one black, one blonde."

"The Teeth of the Barracuda," the first episode, explained the show's premise and introduced the three young leads. Among the highlights of the first season were guest appearances by Sammy Davis Jr. as a militant priest and by Robert Duvall as a convicted murderer in "Keep the Faith, Baby." The second season saw dynamic performances by Lee Grant and Richard Dreyfuss in "Mother of Sorrow," about neglect and the vendetta that ensues. *The Mod Squad*'s search for the shooter who seriously wounds their boss in the two-part "The Connection" brought Pete, Linc, and Julie face-to-face with an all-star cast including Richard Pryor, Ed Asner, Robert Reed, Cesar Romero, Stefanie Powers, Bradford Dillman, Barbara McNair, and Cleavon Little.

As the hippie culture faded in the early 1970s, the network decided to disband the Mod Squad after turning it not too successfully into a straight action show driven by an increasing amount of violence. The youthful audience diminished and Pete, Julie, and Linc went to rerun heaven. The four principals were reunited for a final time in 1979 in *The Return of Mod Squad,* a made-for-TV movie.

VIDEO AVAILABILITY

A number of two-episode volumes of *The Mod Squad,* each running about 100 minutes, are available at certain video outlets.

TRIVIA TIDBITS

- Michael Cole did little after *The Mod Squad* was disbanded by the network. Peggy Lipton met and married record producer Quincy Jones and was away from the spotlight (except for the reunion movie) until the late 1980s when she and Jones split and she began taking acting roles again (from *Twin Peaks* as Norma Jennings to the 1996 made-for-TV movie *Justice for Annie*). Clarence Williams III returned to the New York stage and became a respected actor with the Negro Ensemble and other groups, occasionally appearing in films and guest-starring on television (including his own stint on *Twin Peaks*).

- Guests on *The Mod Squad* included Andy Griffith, Milton Berle, Louis Gossett Jr., Ida Lupino, Lesley Ann Warren, David Cassidy and dad Jack Cassidy (separately), executive producer Danny Thomas, Leslie Nielsen, Sugar Ray Robinson, Rocky Graziano, and Martin Sheen. Sammy Davis Jr. appeared three times, while Tyne Daly, Fernando Lamas, and Richard Dreyfuss showed up twice (all in different roles).
- The hip *Mod Squad* theme song was written by Shorty Rogers.

THE NANCY DREW MYSTERIES

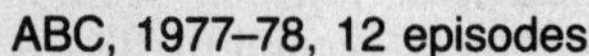

ABC, 1977–78, 12 episodes

CAST

Nancy Drew	Pamela Sue Martin Janet Louise Johnson
Carson Drew	William Schallert
George Fayne (1977)	Jean Rasey
George Fayne (1977–78)	Susan Buckner
Ned Nickerson (1977)	George O'Hanlon Jr.
Ned Nickerson (1978)	Rick Springfield
Bess	Ruth Cox
Sheriff Kane	Robert Karnes

EXECUTIVE PRODUCER: Glen A. Larson
SUPERVISING PRODUCER: B. W. Sandefur
PRODUCERS: Arlene Sidaris, Joe Boston
DIRECTORS: Jack Arnold, E. W. Swackhamer, Christian I. Nyby II, Michael Pataki, Ivan Dixon, Michael Caffey, Joseph Pevney, Keith Atkinson, Richard Benedict, Andy Sidaris
WRITERS: Glen A. Larson, Michael Sloan, Christopher Crowe, James Henerson, Keith Walker, John Ireland Jr., Lee Sheldon

Sleuthing teenager

The Nancy Drew Mysteries, sister show to *The Hardy Boys Mysteries* (see separate entry), was adapted from Carolyn Keene's popular adventure novels of the 1920s and 1930s aimed at youthful readers. Like the Hardys, Nancy was a teenage amateur detective whose dad, a wealthy criminal lawyer, tried discouraging her help but was secretly glad to have it. Nancy's girlfriend and bosom buddy George [sic] Fayne did their sleuthing for a lark ("pubescent peepers" was the term given to them by one TV observer), making things annoying for professional jewel thieves, carnival grifters, kleptomaniacal classmates, fraudulent bankers, and the like.

Since the Hardys and Nancy Drew were actually written by the same person (Edward Stratemeyer) under different pseudonyms, it was only reasonable that both series by prolific TV producer Glen A. Larson (also responsible for *Quincy M.E., The A-Team, The Fall Guy,* and dozens of other lighthearted action series) would be made simultaneously and shown on alternate weeks. *The Hardy Boys Mysteries* became the more popular show, primarily because of Shaun Cassidy's burgeoning stardom as a recording artist, and a decision was made to combine the two, with somewhat flighty Nancy joining Frank and Joe Hardy in the sleuthing department and then playing second fiddle. Pamela Sue Martin decided she didn't like the idea very much and withdrew as Nancy, replaced by Janet Louise Johnson. The Nancy Drew character was dropped after the second (combined) season, and the Hardy Boys continued on for another half season.

VIDEO AVAILABILITY

Eight *Nancy Drew Mysteries* cassettes are available at certain video outlets. Each runs about fifty minutes.

TRIVIA TIDBITS

- Young Bonita Granville—later in life to be TV producer of *Lassie* and *The Lone Ranger*—was Nancy Drew in a series of four movies in the 1930s (with John Litel as her dad).
- *Nancy Drew* returned to television in 1995 in a syndicated series, filmed in France and alternating with new

Hardy Boys adventures. Tracy Ryan is the 1990s Nancy and Joy Tanner plays pal George.

- The theme for the series was written by Glen A. Larson and Stu Phillips.

NORTH AND SOUTH

Book One: ABC, 1985, 6 two-hour episodes
Book Two: ABC, 1986, 6 two-hour episodes

CAST

Virgilia Hazard	Kirstie Alley
Grady (1985)	Georg Stanford Brown
Justin LaMotte	David Carradine
Elkanah Bent	Phillip Casnoff
Isabel Hazard (1986)	Mary Crosby
Madeline Fabray LaMotte	Leslie-Anne Down
Stanley Hazard	Jonathan Frakes
Brett Main Hazard	Genie Francis
Isabel Hazard (1985)	Wendy Fulton
Ashton Main Huntoon	Terry Garber
Constance Flynn Hazard	Wendy Kilbourne
Augusta Barclay (1986)	Kate McNeil
James Huntoon	Jim Metzler
George Hazard	James Reed
Charles Main	Lewis Smith
Billy Hazard (1985)	John Stockwell
Billy Hazard (1986)	Parker Stevenson
Orry Main	Patrick Swayze

Guest stars (1985): Johnny Cash, Olivia Cole, Morgan Fairchild, Robert Guillaume, Hal Holbrook, Gene Kelly, Robert Mitchum, Jean Simmons, David Ogden Stiers, Inga Swenson, Elizabeth Taylor, Forest Whitaker

Guest stars (1986): Lloyd Bridges, Olivia de Havilland, Linda Evans, Morgan Fairchild, Hal Holbrook, Lee Horsley, Nancy Marchand, Wayne Newton, Jean Simmons, James Stewart, David Ogden Stiers, Inga Swenson, Forest Whitaker, Anthony Zerbe

EXECUTIVE PRODUCERS: David Wolper, Chuck McLain
PRODUCERS: Paul Freeman, Robert A. Papazian
DIRECTORS: Richard Heffron, Kevin Connor
WRITERS: Douglas Heyes, Paul F. Edwards, Kathleen A. Shelley, Patricia Green, Richard Fielder, Bill Gordon, B. W. Sandefur, Guerdon S. Trueblood

Epic battles and romances

The sweeping adaptation of John Jakes's Civil War novels (the second based on his *Love and War*), with a stellar cast, was promoted in a massive campaign as television's answer to *Gone With the Wind.* It played out as a sumptuous canvas of epic battles, passionate romance, and fierce friendships that cross the embattled borders of North and South. The saga follows the fortunes (and occasionally misfortunes) of two nineteenth-century families: the Hazards, slave-abhorring ironmasters of Pennsylvania, and the Mains, slave-owning planters of South Carolina. Their lives intertwine when a friendship is formed between one member of each family—Orry Main and George Hazard—who become West Point cadets in 1842, form a business partnership a few years later, marry into each other's families, and then find themselves on opposite sides when war comes. The story follows them from youth to middle age.

Author Jakes's often florid historical fiction covers the twenty years before the war in Book One and the conflagration itself in Book Two. (Book Three belatedly turned up as a six-hour 1994 miniseries covering the start of the Reconstruction.) As in his earlier novels about the Revolutionary War under the encompassing title *The Kent Chronicles*—made into three miniseries in the 1970s—Jakes mixed real-life figures (Hal Holbrook as Abraham Lincoln, Robert Guillaume as Frederick Douglass, Anthony Zerbe as Ulysses S. Grant) with his handsome young protagonists in their spiffy West Point uniforms and his lovely hoop-skirted (and often spitfire) belles. Social issues are broached, war is waged on the battlefield, passions flare on the home front, and familiar guest stars appear (sometimes jarringly and rather incongruously)—all making for lively television a notch or two above the modern-day prime-time dramas such as *Dynasty* or *Falcon Crest.* Many of the attractive lead players would later make names—and faces—for themselves: Kirstie Alley in *Cheers;* Phillip Casnoff as Ol' Blue Eyes in the TV movie *Sinatra;* Patrick Swayze in *Dirty Dancing* and *Ghost;* and Jonathan Frakes in *Star Trek: The Next Generation.*

Reenactors to the fore

The real stars of *North and South,* arguably, were the Civil War reenactors (1,300 of them were on hand to reproduce the conditions of that period in every detail). Their mission—and their passion—was to relive the history of the time, having learned the correct style of giving orders, of marching, of firing muskets of the time—particularly the deadly Sharps rifle, which revolutionized warfare—of performing the era's songs and music, and of general living in mid-nineteenth century America. These admirable and practically indispensable reenactors made the *North and South* saga one of the more convincing costume TV dramas of its era.

VIDEO AVAILABILITY

Both Book One and Book Two of *North and South* are available in sets of six cassettes, each at select video outlets and through Columbia House.

TRIVIA TIDBITS

- John Jakes's first book ran more than 740 pages and sold over 2.8 million copies.
- *North and South* received seven Emmy nominations.

- Between the two miniseries—the equivalent length of twelve feature films—there were thirty principal actors, 100 smaller speaking roles, and more than 5,200 extras.
- Hal Holbrook was actually re-creating his Abraham Lincoln, a role he had done several times earlier on television and on the stage. He won an Emmy for his portrayal in *Sandburg's Lincoln* in 1975–76.

NORTHERN EXPOSURE

CBS, 1990–95, 108 episodes

CAST

Dr. Joel Fleischman	Rob Morrow
Maggie O'Connell	Janine Turner
Maurice Minnifield	Barry Corbin
Chris Stevens	John Corbett
Ed Chigliak	Darren E. Burrows
Holling Vincouer	John Cullum
Shelly Tambo Vincouer	Cynthia Geary
Marilyn Whirlwind	Elaine Miles
Ruth-Anne Miller	Peg Phillips
Rick Pederson (1990–91)	Grant Goodeve
Adam (1991–95)	Adam Arkin
Eve (1991–95)	Valerie Mahaffey
Dave the Cook (1991–95)	William J. White
Sgt. Barbara Semanski (1991–95)	Diane Delano
Leonard Quinhagak (1992–93)	Graham Greene
Bernard Stevens (1991–95)	Richard Cummings Jr.
Mike Monroe (1992–93)	Anthony Edwards
Walt Kupfer (1993–95)	Moultrie Patten
Dr. Phillip Capra (1994–95)	Paul Provenza
Michelle Schowdoski Capra (1994–95)	Teri Polo

CREATORS AND EXECUTIVE PRODUCERS: Joshua Brand, John Falsey

CO-EXECUTIVE PRODUCER: Andrew Schneider

SUPERVISING PRODUCERS: Diane Frolov, Jeff Melvoin, Cheryl Bloch, Robin Green

PRODUCERS: Matthew Nodella, Rob Thompson

DIRECTORS: Joshua Brand, Peter O'Fallon, Dan Lerner, David Carson, Sandy Smolan, Rob Thompson, Bill D'Elia, Michael Fresco, Jack Bender, Nick Marck, Michael Katleman, Dean Parisot, Oz Scott

WRITERS: Joshua Brand, John Falsey, Andrew Schneider, Diane Frolov, Robin Green, Jeff Melvoin, Henry Bromell, Mitchell Burgess, Geoffrey Neigher

Alaska's Riviera

A quirky cult comedy-drama set in the fictional Cicely, Alaska (population 813), *Northern Exposure* begins with a young new doctor coming to town in the person of Manhattan yuppie Joel Fleischman. Fleischman went through medical school at Columbia University on a full grant from the state of Alaska, and now it's payback time—four years, during which time he's the only doctor for hundreds of miles. He's assigned to scenic but remote Cicely, which seems to be owned by hail-fellow-well-met Maurice Minnifield, a swaggering former astronaut. Quite reluctantly, Fleischman sets up shop in a storefront clinic where imperturbable, efficient Marilyn Whirlwind, a chubby Eskimo woman, is his receptionist/assistant.

Entering whiny, self-absorbed Fleischman's life are a host of Cicelians: feisty air-taxi pilot Maggie O'Connell, his pretty landlady who has had a string of boyfriends who've died under mysterious circumstances; Chris Stevens, a poetic ex-con who's a deejay (and seemingly the only employee) at K-BEAR, Minnifield's radio station; Holling Vincoeur, a sixtyish retired adventurer who runs The Brick, the local tavern; Shelly Tambo, Holling's sexy teenage waitress girlfriend whom he later marries; Ed Chigliak, an amiable Eskimo who works for Minnifield, knows everything about pop culture, and dreams about being the next Steven Spielberg; sensible but nosy Ruth-Anne Miller, proprietor of the town's general store, also in property owned by Minnifield; and there's Mort, the scrawny moose who wanders the main street.

Others who turn up include the weird Adam, a grungy backwoodsman but a gourmet chef who sets out a mean meal, and Eve, his hypochondriac New Age girlfriend of twelve years; Bernard Stevens, Chris's erudite African-American brother and soulmate who's the same age (don't ask); Mike Monroe, an ex-lawyer turned environmentalist who lives in a plastic bubble at the edge of town, walks around in a plastic astronaut suit because of toxic chemicals in the air, goes to Fleischman for his allergies, begins a romance with Maggie, and, ultimately cured, takes off for Russia to work for Greenpeace; Leonard Quinhagak, Marilyn's "healer" cousin whom Ed adopts as his shaman; and septuagenarian Walk Kupfer, a doddering handyman with whom Ruth-Anne drifts into a romance.

If he can make it there . . .

Dr. Fleischman is a long way from the Big Apple, and his sanity is sorely tested by the local eccentrics and the laid-back life, but he manages to adjust more or less while never losing sight of the fact that he could be running a lucrative practice on Park Avenue. In one episode, in a medicinal herb-induced dream, he finds himself back in New York with Cicely's folksy regulars transformed into urban sophisticates. Other sometimes gentle, often outrageous episodes (each generally with three distinctive but interwoven plotlines) included the town's annual piano-tossing contest; visits to Fleishman from a wandering rabbi representing Yom Kippurs past, present, and future; Shelly's sudden affliction allowing her not to talk but only to sing uncontrollably; Marilyn being wooed by the Flying Man from a traveling circus; Chris taking his vacation at a monastery; Maggie persuading the town to prepare a Passover seder for its doctor; and the entire town being overcome with fits of madness while awaiting the arrival of spring, marked by the breaking of the ice. The most famous episode, an award winner entitled simply "Cicely," told of the town's founding a century earlier by a lesbian couple, Roslyn, a powerful, robust woman, and Cicely, a vision of grace and beauty. All of the contemporary inhabitants turned up in other roles—with Fleischman as Franz Kafka!

Fleischman not only adjusted but got in touch with the land and went native. (Around this time, actor Rob Morrow had become increasingly disgruntled about his star status and his paycheck, and chose to leave the series for greener pastures on the big screen. The Fleischman character was replaced by a new doctor, Philip Capra, who came to town with his journalist wife Michelle.) The magic of *Northern Exposure*—which kicked off rather tentatively with a handful of episodes in midsummer 1990—had faded by the time of Fleischman's departure, and the series soon disappeared from the CBS schedule by early spring 1995 without really ending.

VIDEO AVAILABILITY

Northern Exposure is available on cassette (two hour-long episodes per tape) through Columbia House and from certain video outlets.

EMMY AWARDS

1991–92 Outstanding Drama Series
Valerie Mahaffey, Outstanding Supporting Actress in a Drama Series
Andrew Schneider and Diane Frolov, Outstanding Writing in a Drama Series
Frank Prinzi, Outstanding Cinematography for a Series

TRIVIA TIDBITS

- Two actors in recurring roles, Adam Arkin and Anthony Edwards, subsequently would go on to become rival doctors on *Chicago Hope* and *E.R.*

- *Northern Exposure,* which received sixteen Emmy Award nominations in each of its first two seasons (more than any other series), was the first television show to feature actors of Eskimo lineage as regulars.

- The eclectic musical underscoring included both mainstream and obscure recordings of the pop, rock, country, and classical fields.

- The show was filmed on location in Bellevue and Roslyn, Washington, not far from the locale of *Twin Peaks.*

- John Cullum, who played Holling, came to the show with credentials from the musical stage. He'd acted in the original *Camelot,* starred in *On a Clear Day You Can See Forever,* toured extensively in *Man of La Mancha,* and won a Tony as star of *Shenandoah.* After leaving Cicely, he returned to Broadway as *Show Boat*'s Cap'n Andy.

- Peg Phillips, who was in her mid-seventies and took up acting only ten years earlier in college after having raised her own children and their children, found a niche in the series after originally coming aboard for a handful of episodes.

PERRY MASON

CBS, 1957–66, 271 one-hour episodes
(plus 24 two-hour NBC movies)

CAST

Perry Mason	Raymond Burr
Della Street	Barbara Hale
Paul Drake	William Hopper
Lt. Arthur Tragg	Ray Collins
Hamilton Burger	William Talman

CREATOR: Erle Stanley Gardner
EXECUTIVE PRODUCERS: Gail Patrick Jackson, Arthur Marks
PRODUCERS: Art Seid, Sam White, Ben Brady
PRINCIPAL DIRECTORS: Earl Bellamy, Jerry Hopper, John Peyser, Christian I. Nyby, Francis D. Lyon, Tony Leader, Ted Post, Richard Donner, James Goldstone, Arthur Hiller, Lewis Allen, Andrew V. McLaglen, Laslo Benedek, Jesse Hibbs, Vincent McEveety, Irving J. Moore, Charles R. Rondeau
PRINCIPAL WRITERS: Stirling Silliphant, Walter Doniger, Al C. Ward, Seleg Lester, Laurence Marks, Malvin Wald, Jonathan Latimer, Jackson Gillis, True Boardman, Sy Salkowitz

For the defense

Attorney turned novelist Erle Stanley Gardner's pluperfect defense lawyer Perry Mason, his fictional alter ego, was created in 1933 and was featured in dozens of books, several films, a radio serial that ran for a dozen years, two television series, and, since 1985, more than two

This woman looks highly suspicious: Perry Mason (Raymond Burr, center) and Paul Drake (William Hopper) crack another case in this scene from *Perry Mason.* COURTESY OF PERSONALITY PHOTOS, INC.

dozen TV movies—twenty-four with Raymond Burr. To those who grew up with television, Raymond Burr is/was Perry Mason (just as he is/was wheelchair-bound police inspector Robert T. Ironside).

For nine seasons, Mason successfully defended his clients on murder charges and solved the whodunits in the courtroom, much to the frustration of his perpetual adversary, beleaguered DA Hamilton Burger, who was determined to convict at least one of Perry's clients. Perry's devoted secretary Della Street and personal investigator Paul Drake were, of course, of invaluable assistance. Often Drake would rush into the courtroom with a deciding clue just as Perry put the eventual guilty party on the stand.

Representative of Perry's challenges are: "The Case of the Fiery Fingers," in which a charming little old lady—who works as a practical nurse—has offered him a five-dollar retainer after telling him she believes her employer intends to murder his invalid wife, and then has to defend the woman who's subsequently charged with the killing; "The Case of the Lame Canary," in which Perry is convinced that a woman on trial for her husband's murder is innocent—and at the climactic trial, has a small, limping canary to prove it; and "The Case of the Caretaker's Cat," in which Perry finds himself hard put to defend the caretaker of a wealthy man's mansion who is charged with murdering the owner and burning the place down.

In his solution of the weekly murder mystery—in which virtually everybody had a reason to commit the crime and thus was suspect—it helped that quite often the witness simply broke down under imposing Perry's merciless cross-examination and confessed to the killing. The last episode of the initial series, *The Case of the Final Fade-Out,* featured Erle Stanley Gardner himself as the presiding judge.

In the final analysis, it was both the presence of hulking actor Raymond Burr, a former screen menace (most memorably as the sinister prosecutor in the 1951 film *A Place in the Sun*), and his chemistry with Barbara Hale—a longtime friend from the days when both were RKO contract players—that made the *Perry Mason* series magical to so many generations of TV watchers.

The three stars of *Perry Mason,* from left: William Hopper (Paul Drake), Barbara Hale (Della Street), and Raymond Burr (Perry Mason). Burr won two Emmys for Best Actor, while Hale garnered one for Best Supporting Actress. COURTESY OF PERSONALITY PHOTOS, INC.

VIDEO AVAILABILITY

A series of Perry Mason cassettes, each with two one-hour episodes, is currently available through Columbia House.

EMMY AWARDS

1958–59	**Raymond Burr,** Best Actor in a Leading Role in a Dramatic Series
	Barbara Hale, Best Supporting Actress in a Dramatic Series
1960–61	**Raymond Burr,** Outstanding Performance by an Actor in a Series

TRIVIA TIDBITS

- Of Perry's 271 original TV cases, the only one he didn't personally win was in January 1963 when Burr was unable to film an episode because of illness, and

Bette Davis was recruited to stand in for him. (Actually, as it turned out, he lost one on a technicality but he promised a swift appeal.)

- Barbara Hale has been Della Street since the beginning of the TV series and came out of semiretirement at Burr's request in 1985 to be Della again on every Perry Mason TV movie, even those in the franchise after Burr's death in 1993.
- In the first several TV Burr/Mason movies, William Katt, Barbara Hale's son, played the part of investigator/legman Paul Drake, Jr.
- Raymond Burr was one of only a few actors (e.g., Carroll O'Connor, Andy Griffith, Buddy Ebsen, and William Conrad) to carry two hugely successful drama series, and jokesters thought it would have been interesting to have Burr as Perry Mason forced to defend Burr as Ironside for some serious crime. (He did manage to star in an *Ironside* reunion TV movie in between his twenty-four *Perry Mason* telefeatures.)
- Guest villains/victims/defendants included: Barbara Eden, Angie Dickinson, Elisha Cook, Robert Redford, Fay Wray, Adam West, James Coburn, Bill Williams (Barbara Hale's husband), Michael Rennie, Walter Pidgeon, Ryan O'Neal, Barbara Bain, and Dick Clark.
- "The Case of the Twice-Told Twist" (from the final season of the original series) was the only episode in color. Burly Victor Buono was the guest star.
- A *Perry Mason* revival starring Monte Markham, with Sharon Acker as Della, played for the 1973–74 TV season, while Raymond Burr was off sleuthing in a wheelchair as Ironside.
- The distinctive, somewhat menacing *Perry Mason* theme was composed by Fred Steiner.

THE PERSUADERS

ABC, 1971–72, 24 episodes

CAST

Danny Wilde	Tony Curtis
Lord Brett Sinclair	Roger Moore
Judge Fulton	Laurence Naismith

CREATOR/PRODUCER: Robert S. Baker

DIRECTORS: Roy Ward Baker, Basil Dearden, Peter H. Hunt, Val Guest, David Greene, Sidney Hayers, Gerald Mayer, Peter Medak, Roger Moore.

Curtis and Moore as Cos and Culp

Two wealthy playboys—self-made Brooklynite Danny Wilde and British aristocrat Brett Sinclair—were brought together at a Riviera party tossed by Judge Fulton, a retired jurist who tricked them into teaming as justice-seeking partners. Although it wasn't exactly love at first sight, Wilde and Sinclair set out on what they considered a lark, hitting all the watering holes on the continent, swapping hip banter, and looking for romance, adventure, and a chance to right wrongs. Their mission: uncovering the facts behind criminal doings on which legal authorities have virtually given up and that Judge Fulton feels warrant investigation. Sort of a poor man's *I Spy,* this British-made series had its two jaunty stars in their devil-may-care element, one-upping one another for a full season.

This was Tony Curtis's first TV series (his only other, *Vega$,* during the 1978–81 seasons) and Roger Moore's fifth (the British *Ivanhoe, The Alaskans, Maverick,* and

The Saint, the last also for *Persuaders* creator/producer Robert S. Baker). Baker, who got media entrepreneur Lew Grade to back the show, explained its genesis: "The original idea sprang from a long line of Hollywood movies which had their basis in a clash of two strong [male] personalities. That kind of relationship had always intrigued me, so when *The Saint* was over, I sat down and worked out *The Persuaders.*"

A good deal of the show's dialogue, it turns out, was ad-libbed. Take, for instance, this bit of raffishness between the pair: On a camping outing, Curtis finds himself with nothing but a blanket for protection, while Moore comes prepared with a deluxe tent, complete with bar and freezer. Although the action was plentiful, the scripts were far-fetched, not overly coherent fantasies, into which trotted such British actors as Joan Collins, Terry-Thomas, Sinead Cusack, Gladys Cooper, Susan George, Denholm Elliott, and Suzy Kendall. *The Persuaders* was not picked up by ABC, but has since thrived in syndication.

VIDEO AVAILABILITY

At least six of the twenty-four episodes in the series are available at certain video outlets. Each episode runs about fifty-two minutes.

TRIVIA TIDBITS

- *The Persuaders* theme was by John Barry, who, like series costar Roger Moore, would find success in the James Bond series.
- Tony Curtis's later TV career would find him playing film producer David O. Selznick on one occasion (and garnering an Emmy nomination), while Roger Moore's would include a turn as Sherlock Holmes.
- Director Roy Ward Baker, who started his career making British documentaries, is best known for his Hammer horror films of the 1960s and as the principal director of TV's *The Avengers.*

PETER GUNN

NBC, 1958–60; ABC, 1960–61; 114 episodes

CAST

Peter Gunn	Craig Stevens
Edie Hart	Lola Albright
Lt. Jacoby	Herschel Bernardi
"Mother" (1958–59)	Hope Emerson
"Mother" (1959–61)	Minerva Urecal
Babby	Billy Barty

CREATOR/PRODUCER: Blake Edwards
EXECUTIVE PRODUCER: Gordon Oliver
PRINCIPAL DIRECTORS: Blake Edwards, Lamont Johnson, Paul Stanley, Boris Sagal, Robert Altman, David Lowell Rich, Walter Grauman, George Stevens Jr., Alan Crosland Jr.
PRINCIPAL WRITERS: Blake Edwards, Tony Barrett, Steffi Barrett, Al C. Ward, Bernard Schoenfeld, Malvin Wald, Robert Blees, Tom Waldman

The Cary Grant of shamuses

With his suave, impeccably groomed but hard-boiled *Peter Gunn*—a private eye with LAPD contacts whose "office" was a jazz spot called Mother's, which happened to be where his sexy girlfriend was a chanteuse—director Blake Edwards created a landmark TV detective show that set the standards for those that followed. Few, though, were punctuated by a score as memorable as the one by Henry Mancini, whose driving title theme remains one of his great legacies. (The prodigious Mancini also found time to score another Blake Edwards detective show, *Mr. Lucky,* almost simultaneously, with an entirely different type of music!) Also setting *Peter Gunn* apart from other private eye shows of the era were the hip dialogue, the innovative camera angles, the underlying sex (simply watch the body language and savor some of the romantic badinage between stars Craig Stevens and Lola Albright), and the clever plots. And there were the wonderfully distinctive supporting players: Herschel Bernardi as the long-suffering police lieutenant pal; imposing, broad-shouldered Hope Emerson as no-nonsense club owner "Mother"; and diminutive Billy Barty as Gunn's snitch. The series relied on very few "name" guests (pre-stardom Diahann Carroll and James Coburn and comic Shelly Berman were three) to distract things. One of the most memorable villains was Ed Wood stock company regular Tor Johnson.

As cool Peter Gunn, urbane lady-killer detective, Craig Stevens—who bore a noticeable resemblance to Cary Grant and demonstrated a great deal of Grant's panache—became an overnight star at age 40, after toiling for years as a somewhat colorless supporting player in films and television in the shadow of his better-known wife, actress Alexis Smith. For Stevens, and for Lola Albright—whose purring voice and sensuous demeanor made her a sex symbol of the day—*Peter Gunn* was a career high point. In 1967 Stevens returned to the character in Blake Edwards's unsuccessful big-screen version, called simply *Gunn,* but the flavor unfortunately could not be recaptured. Albright subsequently went on to do series work, was reunited with Stevens on an episode of his one other series, the short-lived *Mr. Broadway* (1964), and for a time starred in *Peyton Place* as Constance MacKenzie Carson (succeeding Dorothy Malone).

VIDEO AVAILABILITY

Several tape volumes of *Peter Gunn,* each running about fifty-five minutes and containing two episodes, are available at certain video outlets.

TRIVIA TIDBITS

- Craig Stevens later played another notable fictional detective, Nick Charles, to Jo Ann Pflug's Nora, in a 1975 TV pilot called, not surprisingly, *Nick and Nora,* based on Dashiel Hammett's *Thin Man* books. He also starred with David *(U.N.C.L.E.)* McCallum in the brief *Invisible Man* series, derived from the H. G. Wells classic.
- Hope Emerson, the original "Mother," died before the second season began and was replaced by veteran character actress Minerva Urecal.
- Herschel Bernardi, earlier a star in the Yiddish theater, later became Tevye in *Fiddler on the Roof,* following Zero Mostel, and toured in the part for years.
- Henry Mancini, who made a splash with his *Peter Gunn* music, became friendly with B-actor turned writer and director Blake Edwards in the late 1950s and began a collaboration that spanned twenty-nine movies, assorted television work, and even the current Broadway musical, *Victor/Victoria*—in fact, everything that Blake Edwards did from 1959 until Mancini's death in 1994.
- Mancini's two hit albums, *Music From Peter Gunn* and *More Music From Peter Gunn* (and his follow-up two from *Mr. Lucky*), probably made the Blake Edwards series the first TV show with more than one soundtrack recording. *Music From Peter Gunn,* in fact, was the first Grammy winner as Album of the Year.
- The 1989 *Peter Gunn* revival TV movie was television's only reunion show without a single actor from the original cast. It starred Peter Strauss (for Craig Stevens), Barbara Williams (for Lola Albright), Peter Jurasik (for Herschel Bernardi), Pearl Bailey (for Hope Emerson/Minerva Urecal), and David Rappaport (for Billy Barty).

POIROT

London Weekend Television, 1989– ; PBS "Mystery!", 1990– (first American broadcasts)

CAST

Hercule Poirot	David Suchet
Captain Hastings	Hugh Fraser
Chief Inspector Japp	Philip Jackson
Miss Lemon	Pauline Moran

PRODUCER: Brian Eastman, Nick Elliott

PRINCIPAL DIRECTORS: Edward Bennett, Renny Rye, Ross Devenish, Andrew Grieve, Richard Spence, Brian Farnham, Andrew Piddington, Stephen Whittaker, Peter Barber-Fleming, John Bruce, Ken Grieve

PRINCIPAL WRITERS: Clive Exton, Stephen Wakelam, David Reid, Russell Murray, Michael Baker, David Renwick, William Humble

All those little gray cells

Splendidly cast veteran British actor David Suchet first took on the role of Agatha Christie's fastidious Belgian detective, with his neatly trimmed wax mustache, bow tie, and bowler in 1989, and he immediately became the character's definitive interpreter, capturing all the subtle nuances and finicky eccentricities. "A speck of dust," his colleague Captain Hastings noted at one point, "would have caused him more pain than a bullet wound."

Beginning with "The Adventures of the Clapham Cook" (from Agatha Christie's 1951 collection *The Underdog & Other Stories*), the natty narcissist sleuthed his inimitable way through more than forty-five cases on television over the next seven years with the aid of Captain Hastings, with whom he maintains a sort of Watson/Holmes relationship, and loyal, equally meticulous secretary Miss Lemon. A number of the later ones were faux Christie, since Dame Agatha wrote only thirty-odd Poirot mysteries between *The Mysterious Affairs at Styles* (her first book) in 1920 and *Hallowe'en Party* in 1969.

Stylishly set in England in the 1920s and '30s, where, as one critic has observed, "class distinctions were not only accepted but were carefully preserved," the TV series followed the fussy little detective who was accepted in the highest social circles as he snooped around among the upper class and their stately homes. In "Peril at End House" (from Christie's 1932 novel), Poirot, taking the sun in full suit and tie, meets a stunning young woman who, it seems, has nearly been killed three times in the last four days, and soon finds himself gingerly tiptoeing through a landscape filled with odd Australians, scheming hangers-on, hints of cocaine, a will involving an enormous fortune, and a murder. His friend and investigative competitor Chief Inspector Japp is also soon on the case. In "The Adventure of the Cheap Flat" (from Christie's short story collection *Poirot Investigates*), after having attended the cinema with Japp and Hastings and decrying the excessive use of violence in the American gangster film, Poirot gets involved with a young couple who have acquired a flat for a ridiculously low rent and then wonders why an American FBI agent is so interested in the couple's accommodations. Could it be that perhaps stolen blueprints for a new submarine have been secreted in it, as Poirot comes to discover? Or that the couple is being used as a deadly decoy for an assassin? And in *The ABC Murders* (earlier filmed theatrically with an oddly cast Tony Randall as Poirot), the intrepid sleuth works doggedly to learn the secret behind the letters being sent to him by an anonymous killer announcing, in alphabetical order inspired by the ABC Railway Guide, the locations around England at which the next victim will be found.

For nearly fifty years, Christie had a strange relationship with her creation, alternating between exasperation and admiration of obsessive Poirot. It reportedly always irked her that the character that she had so specifically detailed in her books—a tidy little man of about five feet four inches—was so completely ignored by theatrical and film producers through the years. She did not live to see someone play the role who probably would have delighted her. He turned out to be David Suchet. Seven multipart Poirot "series" have made him the shrewd and incomparable center of Public Broadcasting's esteemed *Mystery!* well into the 1990s, but all good things ultimately have to come to an end. "Mon dieu!" as the petite dandy with a compulsion for neatness, symmetry, and a tidy wrap-up to a puzzling case might say.

VIDEO AVAILABILITY

About a dozen volumes of Poirot, each running about fifty minutes, are available at certain video outlets.

TRIVIA TIDBITS

- Best known Poirots: Albert Finney, Peter Ustinov (six times), Tony Randall, Martin Gabel (the first TV Poirot), Austin Trevor (Poirot of the 1930s three times), and Ian Holm.
- David Suchet played Inspector Japp to Ustinov's Poirot in the 1985 TV movie *Thirteen at Dinner.*
- Hercule Poirot's death (Dame Agatha "killed him off" in her novel *Curtain,* published August 1975) made headline news in most of the London papers. Agatha Christie herself died in 1976.

POLDARK

PBS Masterpiece Theatre; Part I: 1977 (first American broadcast), 16 episodes; Part II: 1978 (first American broadcast), 13 episodes

CAST

Ross Poldark	Robin Ellis
Elizabeth	Jill Townsend
George Warleggen	Nicholas Selby
Charles Poldark	Frank Middlemass
Francis Poldark	Clive Francis
Hoblyn	David Garfield
Verity Blamey	Norma Streader
Zachy Martin	Forbes Collins
Jud Payner	Paul Curran
Captain Blamey	Jonathan Newth
Jinny Carter	Gillian Bailey
Mrs. Chynoweth	Ruth Trouncer
Demelza Poldark	Angharad Rees
Dr. Dwight Enys	Richard Morant
George Warleggen	Ralph Bates
Caroline Penvenen	Judy Geeson
Sir John	Clifford Parrish

PRODUCERS: Morris Barry, Tony Coburn, Richard Beynon
DIRECTORS: Paul Annett, Christopher Barry, Kenneth Ives, Philip Dudley, Roger Jenkins
WRITERS: Peter Draper, Jack Pulman, Jack Russell, Paul Wheeler, Alexander Baron, John Wiles, Martin Worth

Swashbuckling in Cornwall

One of the most popular dramas of the 1970s, this BBC serial rivaled *Upstairs, Downstairs* in popularity in Great

Britain. *Poldark,* a tale of adventure and romance in eighteenth-century Cornwall based on the novels of Winston Graham, follows the exploits of a steadfast hero who returns home after British service in the American Revolutionary War. He not only startles his relatives who thought him dead but also finds an estate facing ruin and his sweetheart betrothed to his cousin. It was, as one observer put it, "a three-ring melodramatic circus." When *Poldark* premiered in the United States on *Masterpiece Theatre,* Alistair Cooke introduced it this way: "Now is the time for the party to settle into a spate of loving, dueling, poaching, smuggling, wenching, marrying."

This sweeping romantic epic, magnificently filmed, with Oliver Balydon's sumptuous designs and John Bloomfield's elegant costumes—and a memorable shipwreck—riveted discerning viewers and *Masterpiece Theatre* fanatics for months at a time during the late spring–early summer 1977 and again the following summer. In the title role, Robin Ellis, with his matinee idol appeal, cut a truly dashing figure who captured the hearts of female watchers. His devil-may-care, sometimes tortured Ross Poldark made him a man for, well, two seasons—both highly successful.

VIDEO AVAILABILITY

A six-tape set presenting twelve of the twenty-nine episodes of *Poldark I* and *Poldark II* is available at certain video outlets. The set runs about 720 minutes.

TRIVIA TIDBITS

- Robin Ellis, called in the British press of the seventies "the sexiest man on the telly," was the romantic lead in the BBC's 1979 musical production of *She Loves Me,* broadcast later on PBS's *Great Performances* series. Earlier, he had played the Earl of Essex to Glenda Jackson's Queen Elizabeth I in *Elizabeth R*.

- Judy Geeson, who played Caroline Penvenen, is best remembered by American movie audiences as Sidney Poitier's pretty blond student in *To Sir, With Love*. Contemporary TV viewers will recognize her as Paul Reiser and Helen Hunt's British neighbor in *Mad About You*.
- Music for *Poldark* was written by Kenyon Emrys-Roberts.

PRIDE AND PREJUDICE

Arts & Entertainment, 1996 (first American broadcast),
3 two-hour episodes

CAST

Mr. Darcy	Colin Firth
Elizabeth Bennet	Jennifer Ehle
Mr. Collins	David Bamber
Mr. Bingley	Crispin Bonham-Carter
Caroline Bingley	Anna Chancellor
Jane Bennet	Susannah Harker
Lady Catherine de Bourgh	Barbara Leigh-Hunt
Lt. George Wickham	Adrian Lukis
Lydia Bennet	Julia Sawalha
Mrs. Bennet	Alison Steadman
Mr. Bennet	Benjamin Whitrow
Kitty Bennet	Polly Maberly
Mary Bennet	Lucy Briers
Georgiana Darcy	Emilia Fox
Sir William Lucas	Christopher Benjamin
Lady Lucas	Norma Streader
Charlotte Lucas	Lucy Scott
Miss Anne de Bourgh	Nadia Chambers

EXECUTIVE PRODUCER: Michael Wearing
PRODUCER: Sue Birtwistle
DIRECTOR: Simon Langton
WRITER: Andrew Davies

The mannered gentry

A sumptuous, richly detailed production with a matchless British cast, this wonderful adaptation of Jane Austen's

1813 classic comedy of manners provided six delightful hours of romantic drama in grand style. Generation X somewhat belatedly has discovered Austen. In 1995 alone, three of her works were filmed, ranging from the traditional *Sense and Sensibility* and *Persuasion* to the contemporized *Clueless,* adapted from Austen's *Emma.*

Pride and Prejudice, filmed for the BBC with panache by Simon Langton, photographed by John Kenway, designed by Gerry Scott, and acted with grace and intelligence by a peerless group of players, displays Jane Austen's nineteenth-century charm, humor, and indecisiveness, to say nothing of her durability. Her caustic tale of Georgian manners, vanity, and woeful misunderstanding deals primarily with the vexations of the middle-class Bennet family with many daughters. The second oldest of the girls, independent-minded Elizabeth, has caught the wary eye of brooding Mr. Darcy, a wealthy visitor to the area, who in turn treats her family with disdain. Appalled by his boorish pride, she rejects him out of hand but becomes entangled in an intricate web that involves a romance between Lizzie's sister Jane and Darcy's wealthy friend Bingley. Amidst the romantic doings appear various relatives, pooh-poohing neighbors, scheming friends, and others to flesh out the plot twists. Meanwhile, Mrs. Bennet obsesses over whether her daughters will marry prosperous men. In the vein of early nineteenth-century novels of manners and romantic matters, Austen sees to it that arrogant Darcy, in spite of himself, pursues enchanting Elizabeth until she catches him.

So visually rich and engaging is this adaptation of a nearly 175-year-old classic that it appears as though written only yesterday.

VIDEO AVAILABILITY

Pride and Prejudice is available in a six-cassette boxed set, running somewhat more than 5½ hours, at certain video outlets. A rental version is available on two cassettes.

TRIVIA TIDBITS

- Colin Firth, as the aloof Darcy, has become one of the leading matinee idols of the 1990s in Great Britain. American movie audiences know his work from films such as *Circle of Friends* and *Valmont*.
- Aside from the long-cherished 1940 MGM production of the story with Laurence Olivier and Greer Garson, there have been several other adaptations of the Jane Austen novel, most notably a 1980 British-made television miniseries that aired on PBS in five parts.
- Director Simon Langton's other credits include such PBS fare as *Smiley's People, Jeeves and Wooster,* and episodes of *Upstairs, Downstairs.*

PRIME SUSPECT

PBS "Mystery!", 1992 (first American broadcast);
Episode 1, 112 minutes; Episodes 2 and 3,
56 minutes each

CAST

DCI Jane Tennison	Helen Mirren
Sgt. Bill Otley	Tom Bell
George Marlowe	John Bowe
DCS Kernan	John Benfield
Moyra Henson	Zoe Wanamaker

CREATOR AND WRITER: Lynda La Plante
DIRECTOR: Christopher Menaul

Breaking a case . . .

According to an interview appended to the first broadcast of *Prime Suspect,* series creator/writer Lynda La Plante, while researching an earlier work, telephoned Britain's Scotland Yard to inquire as to how many of the 100-odd detective chief inspectors (DCIs) currently employed in England were female. The response? "Oh, quite a few! Four." At that moment, DCI Jane Tennison and a superior crime drama were born.

As played by distinguished stage and screen actress Helen Mirren, Jane is an intelligent, over-forty veteran of a police force that refuses to accept her role as the inspector in charge of a homicide investigation. When the DCI in charge of solving the murder of a prostitute suddenly dies of a heart attack, Jane seizes the opportunity, pressuring her superior to give her the case. She is instantly caught in a barrage of prejudiced attitudes and

In the *Prime Suspect* series, Detective Jane Tennison (Helen Mirren) not only had to battle serial killers and other riffraff, she had to face extreme sexism among her colleagues in Scotland Yard. *Prime Suspect 2* (1992–93) and *Prime Suspect 3* (1994–95) each won Emmys for Outstanding Miniseries.
COURTESY OF PERSONALITY PHOTOS, INC.

blatant sabotage, spearheaded by her second-in-command, Sgt. Otley (masterfully played by Tom Bell). Not only does Jane have to prove that the team's prime suspect, George Marlowe, is the true murderer, she must prove *herself,* in a way that no male inspector would ever have to. In addition to the pressure she faces from her dour superior officer to make an arrest, she must struggle to resolve a deteriorating relationship with her live-in lover.

. . . breaking a mold

If Jane Tennison represents a breakthrough in the fictional London of the series, she's a groundbreaker as far as television drama goes, as well. Other than charming, eccentric amateur sleuths such as Agatha Christie's Jane Marple or Jessica Fletcher of *Murder, She Wrote,* or tough, but subservient, police officers like Cagney and Lacey, most female television crime fighters are male fantasy figures (*Charlie's Angels, Police Woman, The Bionic Woman, Wonder Woman,* etc.). Jane Tennison is the first official, employed, realistic female police detective on television, which makes *Prime Suspect* historically important.

Just as impressive, however, is how well the show works as a mystery while it plays on the gender angle. Every step Tennison takes to prove Marlowe's guilt—each success, each setback—is inextricably linked to her own situation. As further murders are discovered, one begins to suspect that perhaps Marlowe is innocent—maybe Jane's ambition and her desire to prove herself are clouding her judgment. The final outcome, both surprising and inevitable, is immensely satisfying.

It is an extremely mature, masterful story, impeccably performed, especially by Mirren, Bell, and John Bowe (as Marlowe, the suspect). One is constantly surprised by deft, imaginative touches, such as Marlowe singing "You'll Never Walk Alone" while visiting his mum in a nursing home.

The success of *Prime Suspect* led to two sequels (see separate entries)—as well as an American knockoff (CBS's *Under Suspicion*) in 1994–95. It is gratifying to know that Jane Tennison has unquestionably proven herself, in her world *and* ours.

VIDEO AVAILABILITY

Prime Suspect is available in certain rental outlets on two cassettes, running approximately 225 minutes.

TRIVIA TIDBITS

- Jane Tennison and her first case are slated to hit American movie screens in a Hollywood version of *Prime Suspect,* in development. Ironically, much-honored British actress Helen Mirren, who has become identified with the role, was not considered for the part.
- Ralph Fiennes makes a striking, brief, early appearance as one of the suspects.
- The atmospheric theme music to *Prime Suspect* is by Stephen Worbeck.

PRIME SUSPECT 2

PBS "Mystery!", 1993 (first American broadcast), 4 episodes

CAST

DCI Jane Tennison	Helen Mirren
DI Oswald	Colin Salmon
Jason Reynolds	Matt Burdock
DCS Kernan	John Benfield

CREATOR: Lynda La Plante
DIRECTOR: John Strickland
WRITER: Allan Cubitt, from a storyline by Lynda La Plante

New case, new prejudices

In the original British miniseries, *Prime Suspect* (see separate entry), Detective Chief Inspector Jane Tennison proved herself capable of leading a serial murder investigation in the face of extreme sexism from her fellow officers. In the first sequel, *Prime Suspect 2,* the capable detective finds herself facing several new challenges: quitting her chain-smoking habit, fighting departmental chauvinism, and solving another murder.

When the ten-year-old remains of a young black woman are discovered in the backyard of a London residence, the black community is in an uproar. To assuage racial unrest, Tennison's superior officer, Detective Chief Superintendent Kernan, insists that Jane use a black officer, Detective Inspector Oswald, in her investigation. Unbeknownst to Kernan, Tennison has had a romantic liaison with Oswald, which threatens to undermine her position on the force. When a black suspect commits suicide after a rough interrogation session with Oswald, the original murder is nearly forgotten in a morass of allegations, inquests, and civil unrest.

Like its predecessor, *Prime Suspect 2* is well acted, well written, and holds the attention throughout. However, like most sequels, it lacks the impact of the first series. The racial tensions explored here provide a fine source for drama, but Jane Tennison's role is diminished because, unlike sexism, the issue does not directly relate to her. Both her relationship with her team members and with Oswald take a backseat to the many suspects on hand. Even so, in comparison to other examples of the genre, *Prime Suspect 2* is exciting, worthwhile viewing.

VIDEO AVAILABILITY

Prime Suspect 2 is available in certain rental outlets on two cassettes, running approximately 225 minutes.

EMMY AWARD

1992–93 *Prime Suspect 2,* Outstanding Miniseries

TRIVIA TIDBITS

- Helen Mirren earned an Emmy nomination as Outstanding Lead Actress in a Miniseries or Special, but lost to Holly Hunter (for *The Positively True Adventures of the Alleged Texas Cheerleader-Murdering Mom*).

PRIME SUSPECT 3

PBS "Mystery!", 1994 (first American broadcast), 4 episodes

CAST

DCI Jane Tennison	Helen Mirren
Sgt. Bill Otley	Tom Bell
Colin Jenkins	David Thewlis
Vera Reynolds	Peter Capaldi
Jake	Michael J. Shannon
Inspector Hall	Mark Strong
Superintendent Halliday	Struan Rodger
Commissioner Chiswick	Terrence Hardiman
Edward Parker-Jones	Ciaran Hinds

CREATOR/WRITER: Lynda La Plante
EXECUTIVE PRODUCER: Sarah Head
PRODUCER: Paul Marcus
DIRECTOR: David Drury

On the streets of Soho

In this third series following the progress of bad-tempered, hard-as-granite Jane Tennison, the London police chief detective is newly transferred from homicide to Soho's vice squad, where her team includes Sgt. Bill Otley, her old adversary. Her assignment: to head a massive cleanup of the area's runaways and "rent boys"—teen prostitutes. Her attention is diverted, though, to a possible murder when the scorched body of a fifteen-year-old is found in a burned-out apartment belonging to a transvestite cabaret singer. Further investigation leads to Colin Jenkins, a thug known to lure preteen and teenage boys into working the streets. She and the team soon find themselves dealing with a pedophile ring implicating a number of VIPs and involving high-level cover-ups.

This gritty entry in the saga of Jane Tennison, DCI, was thought by many to be superior to its award-winning predecessor, at least on a par with the exceptional original from two years earlier, in which she also tangled with veteran sergeant Bill Otley, still disgruntled that her job should have been his.

Because of subject matter, parental guidance is recommended.

VIDEO AVAILABILITY

Prime Suspect 3 is available in certain rental outlets on two cassettes, running approximately 225 minutes. Other self-contained two-hour episodes of *Prime Suspect* (filmed 1995–96) are also available.

EMMY AWARD

1994–95 *Prime Suspect 3,* Outstanding Miniseries

TRIVIA TIDBITS

- The show's Emmy was its second in a row, an unprecedented event for a PBS presentation.
- Emmy nominations for *Prime Suspect 3* went to Helen Mirren as Outstanding Lead Actress in a Miniseries (second consecutive year) and Lynda La Plante for Outstanding Writing in a Miniseries or Special.
- In 1994, in addition to her Emmy nomination, Helen Mirren won both an Oscar nomination for Best Supporting Actress in the film *The Madness of King George* and a Tony nomination for Best Actress for Broadway's *A Month in the Country.*

RAWHIDE

CBS, 1959–66, 217 episodes

CAST

Gil Favor (1959–65)	Eric Fleming
Rowdy Yates	Clint Eastwood
Pete Nolan (1959–62, 1964–65)	Sheb Wooley
Wishbone	Paul Brinegar
Jim Quince	Steve Raines
Joe Scarlett (1959–64)	Rocky Shahan
Harkness "Mushy" Musgrove (1959–65)	James Murdock
Hey Soos Patines (1961–64)	Robert Cabal
Clay Forrester (1962–63)	Charles Gray
Ian Cabot (1965–66)	David Watson
Jed Colby (1965–66)	John Ireland
Pee Jay (1965–66)	L. Q. Jones
Simon Blake (1965–66)	Raymond St. Jacques

CREATOR AND EXECUTIVE PRODUCER: Charles Marquis Warren

PRODUCERS: Endre Bohem, Vincent Fennally, Bernard L. Kowalski, Bruce Geller, Ben Brady

DIRECTORS: Richard Whorf, Andrew McLaglen, Ted Post, Charles Marquis Warren, Buzz Kulik, Jesse Hibbs, George Sherman, Jack Arnold, Stuart Heisler, Harmon Jones, Gene Fowler Jr., R. G. Springsteen, Joseph Kane, Allen Reisner, Anton Leader, Justus Addiss, Tay Garnett, Sobey Martin

WRITERS: Fred Friedberger, David Swift, Endre Bohem, Al C. Ward, David Victor, Winston Miller, Samuel A. Peeples, Buckley Angell, Louis Vittes, Clair Huffaker, Charles Larson

Head 'em up! Move 'em out!

The last great television western of the fifties, the all-male *Rawhide* hit the trail for a long run cattle drive with Eric Fleming as trail boss Gil Favor and twenty-seven-year-old Clint Eastwood—in his only TV series—as his trusty ramrod, Rowdy Yates. On the Sedalia Trail from north Texas to Kansas and back, they—along with Sheb Wooley as scout Pete Nolan, crusty Paul Brinegar as Wishbone the cook, and assorted wranglers and drovers—"kept them dogies rollin'" while encountering rustlers and renegades, predators and pioneers, storms and stampedes, and guest stars ranging from Barbara Stanwyck, Barbara Eden, and Elizabeth Montgomery to Troy Donahue, Frankie Avalon, and Mickey Rooney, as well as Ed and Keenan Wynn (separately).

Charles Marquis Warren, one of the creators of *Gunsmoke,* had just directed a Joel McCrea western film called *Cattle Empire* and concocted a similar concept called *Cattle Drive* (which happened to be the title of an earlier McCrea cowboy flick). CBS, which was elated with *Gunsmoke,* to say the least, bought Warren's premise and ordered a pilot—and was not hurt by its similarity to *Wagon Train* and John Wayne's earlier *Red River.* Rather than being a simple drama set in the American West, *Rawhide* would concentrate on the harsher aspect of frontier life. Although the show was not an overnight success, eventually it became the third most popular TV western series after the aforementioned *Gunsmoke* and *Wagon Train* during its eight years in prime time (and remains the fourth longest running western in TV history). When Eric Fleming left, along with Sheb Wooley, after the seventh season, Clint Eastwood's Rowdy Yates became the trail boss and—because of a small western Eastwood made in Italy during the hiatus between seasons in summer 1964 (released in the U.S. three years later as *A Fistful of Dollars*)—Eastwood found enduring stardom.

Rawhide finally came to the end of the trail a couple of days after New Year's 1966, with the herd never having been delivered to market. It left prime time for that great roundup in the sky, but later found great success in syndication. The show's theme song has been spoofed all over TV and film during the three decades that followed—most notably by Frankie Laine in Mel Brooks's *Blazing Saddles* and by Dan Aykroyd and John Belushi in *The Blues Brothers.*

VIDEO AVAILABILITY

The *Rawhide* video collection—two hour-long episodes per cassette—is available through Columbia House. Selected episodes are also available at certain video outlets.

TRIVIA TIDBITS

- The title of every episode during the first five seasons began with the word "Incident."
- Eric Fleming left the show after its seventh season to pursue a film career, but drowned while on location in the Amazon in 1966.
- Clint Eastwood, who played Rowdy Yates through the entire run of *Rawhide* (with the exception of five of the 217 episodes), graduated from television afterward and never came back as an actor. He did, however, return to direct Sondra Locke, his actress companion at the time, in a 1985 episode of Steven Spielberg's *Amazing Stories* series.
- Veteran movie cowboy Sheb Wooley, who had a number one comedy record hit, "The Purple People Eater," just before *Rawhide* premiered, left the series briefly after the fourth season to pursue a record career, but never was able to follow up his earlier smash.
- Comic sidekick Paul Brinegar got the part of Wishbone because creator Charles Marquis Warren liked the way he played the identical part (under a different name) in *Cattle Empire* earlier.

- Joining the series as drover Simon Blake at the start of its final season gave Raymond St. Jacques the distinction of being the first black performer to be a regular in a television western.
- Frankie Laine sang the whip-cracking *Rawhide* theme song, which was written by Dimitri Tiomkin and Ned Washington—the composing team responsible for "High Noon" and "The High and the Mighty." Laine once also appeared on-camera, guest-starring in the episode "Incident on the Road to Yesterday," playing a cowpoke who tries to repent for having stolen money as a youngster and finds himself with a price on his head.

RICH MAN, POOR MAN

ABC, February–March 1976, 12 hours

CAST

Rudy Jordache	Peter Strauss
Tom Jordache	Nick Nolte
Julie Prescott	Susan Blakely
Axel Jordache	Edward Asner
Sue Prescott	Gloria Grahame
Mary Jordache	Dorothy McGuire
Teddy Boylan	Robert Reed
Willie Abbott	Bill Bixby
Virginia Calderwood	Kim Darby
Clothilde	Fionnula Flanagan
Duncan Calderwood	Ray Milland
Teresa Santoro	Talia Shire
Bayard Nichols	Steve Allen
Asher Berg	Craig Stevens
Marsh Goodwin	Van Johnson
Irene Goodwin	Dorothy Malone
Kate Jordache	Kay Lenz
Arthur Falconetti	William Smith

CREATOR: Irwin Shaw
EXECUTIVE PRODUCER: Harve Bennett
PRODUCER: Jon Epstein
DIRECTORS: David Greene, Boris Sagal
WRITER: Dean Reisner

A family in flux

Irwin Shaw's 1970 best-seller was the inspiration for this extremely popular all-star miniseries, which was presented under the *ABC Novel for Television* umbrella and starred "three exciting new performers" (as network publicity releases proclaimed): Peter Strauss and Nick Nolte as the very different Jordache brothers and Susan Blakely as their pal. The sprawling story, broken into one- and two-hour "chapters," examined America's shifting social and moral values from the end of World War II to the early 1960s with a show biz who's who playing lovers, friends, relatives, and foes.

Industrious and ambitious Rudy and tough and independent Tom, a boxer, sons of an abusive immigrant father (Edward Asner) and a compassionate mother (Dorothy McGuire), go off into the world—one to make it big as a captain of industry, the other to become a tormented lost soul—while their friend Julie Prescott, Rudy's great love (a character encompassing several women in Shaw's book) brings triumph and disaster to both.

The success of the audience-grabbing miniseries (later retitled *Rich Man, Poor Man—Book I*) encouraged the network to air a spin-off weekly series, *Rich Man, Poor Man—Book II,* for the 1976–77 season. The twenty-one hour-long episodes continued events in the life of Rudy Jordache—now a U.S. Senator—and Julie Prescott, now his wife after a couple of unpleasant marriages. It threw the spotlight on Julie's son, Billy Abbott (played by James Carroll Jordan), and Wesley (played by Gregg Henry), the son of Tom Jordache who was killed by vicious, eye-patched Arthur Falconetti at the end of the original show. In the final episode, Rudy Jordache, gun in hand, faces down Falconetti to avenge brother Tom's death and they shoot it out, with both lying on a sidewalk apparently bleeding to death.

Rich Man, Poor Man also spawned a two-part 1979 TV movie called *Beggarman, Thief,* focusing on Rudy and Tom's sister, Gretchen (played by Jean Simmons)—who was unmentioned in both of the predecessors but was in Irwin Shaw's book—and Tom's widow, Kate (Lynn Redgrave, taking over the role played in the miniseries by Kay Lenz). A moviemaker, Gretchen strives to pull the family together after the murder of Tom in the miniseries and the disappearance of Rudy in the spin-off series.

VIDEO AVAILABILITY

The complete twelve hours of the original *Rich Man, Poor Man* are available on six two-hour cassettes through Columbia House.

EMMY AWARDS (23 nominations)

1975–76 **Edward Asner,** Outstanding Lead Actor for a Single Appearance in a Drama Series
Fionnula Flanagan, Outstanding Single Performance by a Supporting Actress in a Drama Series
David Greene, Outstanding Directing in a Drama Series
Alex North, Outstanding Achievement in Music Composition for a Series

TRIVIA TIDBITS

- *Rich Man, Poor Man* was not only television's first hit miniseries, but also the second highest rated show of the season, after *All in the Family.*
- *Rich Man, Poor Man* was Emmy-nominated as Outstanding Limited Series but lost to *Upstairs, Downstairs Masterpiece Theatre* on PBS.
- Not especially well known before starring in the miniseries, Nick Nolte moved on to a major big-screen career. Peter Strauss, on the other hand, continued almost exclusively in television and became the so-

called King of the Miniseries (after Richard Chamberlain). Susan Blakely moved back and forth between theatrical movies and television over the subsequent years. All three received Emmy nominations for their performances in the miniseries.

THE ROCKFORD FILES

NBC, 1974–80, 118 episodes

CAST

Jim Rockford	James Garner
Joseph "Rocky" Rockford	Noah Beery Jr.
Det. Dennis Becker	Joe Santos
Angel Martin	Stuart Margolin
Beth Davenport (1974–78)	Gretchen Corbett
Lt. Alex Diehl (1974–76)	Tom Atkins
Lt. Doug Chapman (1976–80)	James Luisi
John Cooper (1978–70)	Bo Hopkins
Lance White (1979–80)	Tom Selleck

CREATORS: Stephen J. Cannell, Roy Huggins
EXECUTIVE PRODUCER: Meta Rosenberg
SUPERVISING PRODUCER: Stephen J. Cannell
PRODUCERS: Chas Floyd Johnson, Juanita Bartlett, David Chase, J. Rickley Dumm
DIRECTORS: Jerry London, Stephen J. Cannell, Alex Grasshoff, Russ Mayberry, Corey Allen, Joseph Pevney, Reza S. Badiyi, Richard T. Heffron, Bernard L. Kowalski, Alexander Singer, Michael Schultz, William Wiard, Vincent McEveety, Christian I. Nyby II,
WRITERS: Stephen J. Cannell, Juanita Bartlett, Robert Hamner, Gloryette Clark, Don Carlos Dunaway, Edward J. Lasko, Howard Berk, Rudolph Borchert, David Chase

Malibu's shamus

James Garner's Jim Rockford ranks up in the top pantheon of legendary TV detectives, not for his sleuthing abilities but for his humanity and his nonchalance. And no one in television played humanity and nonchalance better than James Garner, who continues to make acting look so easy. When introduced in a made-for-TV movie in spring 1974, Jim Rockford had been jailed for five years on a bum rap. He earned his private investigator's license, drove a gold Pontiac Firebird, and worked out of his house: a trailer on the Malibu Beach, which he described as "cheap, tax-deductible, earthquake-proof, and when I get a case out of town, I take it with me." Frequently helping him on his cases was his semiretired father/best friend who lived with him. Also giving Rockford assistance, not always welcome, is so-called friend, Angel, a scrounge and con man who had served time with Rockford and is always looking out for "Numero Uno." At the police station, Rockford has a tenuous friendship with the exasperated Dennis Becker, a sergeant (later lieutenant) who, despite misgivings, bends regulations here and there to help him. Beth Davenport, an assistant DA who had a relationship of sorts with Rockford, was around (for the first four seasons) to bail him out if he ran afoul of the law (or, more likely, was framed).

From the first episode—entitled, appropriately, "The Kickoff Case"—*The Rockford Files* had Jimbo (as Angel regularly called him) mixing legwork with a touch of bribery, cheap disguises, and eavesdropping—but always paying the price by getting beaten up once or twice, drugged, or shot at in each show. All the while, Rockford took it on the chin with a smart-alecky grin, a wisecrack, or a few dirty tricks of his own to foil the bad guys. He might have been easygoing—which made him so endearing to critics and fans through the years—but he could also be petulant. "Two inches to the right and you might be missing that eye," he was told by his dad Rocky after being winged by a bullet. To which Rockford responded, "Look at it this way. Two inches to the left and it would have missed me completely!"

Among the show's guest stars were Joseph Cotten, Jill Clayburgh, Lindsay Wagner, Jackie Cooper, Sharon

Gless, Linda Evans, Rob Reiner, Louis Gossett Jr., Chuck McCann, Rita Moreno, and Lauren Bacall.

As with *Maverick* fifteen years earlier, James Garner became embroiled with the studio, either over money or "creative differences," and walked—or, more accurately, because he was beset by assorted ailments, *limped*—away from the show, calling the final season to an abrupt halt. As with the subsequent *Maverick* series, he renewed his participation on his own terms. In the case of *The Rockford Files,* now exercising creative control as one of the executive producers, Garner returned to the role (a bit heavier, somewhat slower, a touch grumpier) in a series of CBS-TV movies in the mid-1990s, rejoined by Stuart Margolin and Joe Santos. Noah Beery Jr. had died but is fondly recalled in these shows, and his photo is prominently displayed in Rockford's trailer.

VIDEO AVAILABILITY

The complete run of *The Rockford Files* is available on tape (two hour-long episodes to a cassette) through Columbia House. Selected tapes are also available in certain video outlets.

EMMY AWARDS

1976–77	**James Garner,** Outstanding Lead Actor in a Drama Series
1977–78	Outstanding Drama Series
1978–79	**Stuart Margolin,** Outstanding Supporting Actor in a Drama Series
1979–80	**Stuart Margolin,** Outstanding Supporting Actor in a Drama Series

TRIVIA TIDBITS

- In the TV-movie pilot of *The Rockford Files,* Robert Conley played the role of Rocky, which was taken over by Noah Beery Jr.

- Stuart Margolin, Angel of the series, worked with pal James Garner not only in *The Rockford Files* but also earlier in *Nichols* (as Mitch, the blustery town bully) and later in *Bret Maverick* (as comic half-breed Philo Sandine). In addition, he is a prolific director of TV movies and sitcoms.
- The one spin-off from this series was the very short-lived *Richie Brockelman, Private Eye,* with Dennis Dugan (now a TV director) as a youthful, college-educated PI who occasionally turned up to give Jim Rockford a helping hand.
- Tom Selleck had a recurring role in the show's final season as a rival PI who annoyed Rockford because he was better looking and always got results without breaking a sweat.
- James Garner's brother Jack, who finds a part in just about everything Garner does, played the recurring role of police captain McEnroe.
- The show's theme song, written by Mike Post and Pete Carpenter, became a chart record in the mid-1970s.

ROOTS

ABC, 1977, 8 episodes

CAST

Kunta Kinte	LeVar Burton
Kunta Kinte (older)	John Amos
Ninta	Cicely Tyson
Fiddler	Louis Gossett Jr.
Chicken George	Ben Vereen
Nyo Boto	Maya Angelou
Capt. Thomas Davies	Edward Asner
Evan Brent	Lloyd Bridges
Tom	Georg Stanford Brown
Squire James	Macdonald Carey
Mathilda	Olivia Cole
Grill	Gary Collins
Tom Moore	Chuck Connors
Mingo	Scatman Crothers
Ol' George Johnson	Brad Davis
Missy Anne	Sandy Duncan
Mrs. Reynolds	Lynda Day George
John Reynolds	Lorne Greene
Stephen Bennett	George Hamilton
Sen. Arthur Justin	Burl Ives
Noah	Lawrence-Hilton Jacobs
Mrs. Moore	Carolyn Jones
Jemmy Brent	Doug McClure
Irene	Lynne Moody
Ames	Vic Morrow
William Reynolds	Robert Reed
Sam Bennett	Richard Roundtree
Kadi Touray	O. J. Simpson

Bell	Madge Sinclair
Drummer	Raymond St. Jacques
Kizzy	Leslie Uggams
Slater	Ralph Waite

CREATOR: Alex Haley
EXECUTIVE PRODUCER: David L. Wolper
PRODUCER: Stan Margulies
DIRECTORS: David Greene, John Erman, Gilbert Moses, Marvin J. Chomsky
WRITERS: William Blinn, Ernest Kinoy, James Lee, M. Charles Cohen

An American family

Roots remains in television annals as a monumental event—the most watched dramatic series ever. This exceptional twelve-hour saga of an American family—author Alex Haley's own—sweeping through 100 tumultuous years of masters and slaves, victories and defeats: from West Africa in the 1750s through the end of the American Civil War; from the arrival of a young Kunta Kinte (played by then-newcomer LeVar Burton) in chains in 1787 through the family's freedom following the War between the States.

Populating this timeless hundred-year tapestry was an extraordinary all-star cast, who brought together to one project the greatest array of African-American actors to that time on television—from John Amos to Ben Vereen.

The series begins in a village in Gambia, with Omoro Kinte lifting his newborn son to the sky (the symbol for the complete saga) and naming him Kunta Kinte in the ancient tradition. Flash-forward to Kunta coming of age in the Mandinka manhood ritual, his terrifying capture as a teenager by slavers, his voyage in chains across the Atlantic (a voyage punctuated by a bloody shipboard mutiny), his eventual sale to the aristocratic Reynolds family,

Roots remains one of the greatest achievements of TV drama. In eight episodes totaling twelve hours, the saga of Kunta Kinte and his lineage entranced a record number of viewers, featured the greatest African-American stars of the day, and dealt head-on with the sensitive issue of slavery. The show also introduced young LeVar Burton (as young Kunta Kinte) to audiences. COURTESY OF PERSONALITY PHOTOS, INC.

and his meeting with an American-born slave called Fiddler, his first and only friend.

Kunta Kinte's unparalleled tale continued for several generations in the original *Roots* (John Amos took over the role from LeVar Burton in the later segments) and his grandson, named Chicken George (Ben Vereen, highly memorable in the part), eventually becomes the first free man in the family. Chicken George's son, Tom, a blacksmith on the eve of the Civil War, smells the abolition of slavery in the air. After being recruited and cruelly mistreated as an army smithy, Tom ultimately finds himself and his family in the tiny town of Henning, Tennessee, as the miniseries ends, bringing freedom to the descendants of Kunta Kinte.

VIDEO AVAILABILITY

The milestone miniseries, uncut for video, is available at certain tape outlets in six ninety-minute volumes or in a single box set running 570 minutes. Time-Life Video is also offering the complete *Roots* saga (including the miniseries sequel and the later Christmas movie called *Roots: The Gift*) on fourteen tapes.

EMMY AWARDS

1976–77 *Roots,* Outstanding Limited Series
Louis Gossett Jr., Outstanding Lead Actor for a Single Appearance in a Drama or Comedy Series
Edward Asner, Outstanding Single Performance by a Supporting Actor in a Comedy or Drama
Olivia Cole, Outstanding Single Performance by a Supporting Actress in a Comedy or Drama
David Greene, Outstanding Directing in a Drama Series (single episode)
Ernest Kinoy and William Blinn, Outstanding Writing in a Drama Series (single episode)
Gerald Fried and Quincy Jones, Outstanding Music Composition for a Drama Series
Neil Travis, Outstanding Editing for a Drama Series

TRIVIA TIDBITS

- *Roots* and its sequel, *Roots: The Next Generations* (see separate entry), received 145 awards, including twelve Emmy Awards and the George Foster Peabody Award.
- LeVar Burton was a young actor discovered in the drama department of the University of California when chosen to play the central role of Kunta Kinte. Today he's best known for his role as Lt. Geordi La Forge, the blind helmsman of the new Enterprise on *Star Trek: The Next Generation*. Burton was in only parts 1 and 2 of the original *Roots* (John Amos took over the role of Kunta Kinte as he moved toward middle age) but returned for the later TV movie, *Roots: The Gift* (1988), which was concocted as an inspirational

Yuletide incident in the original saga, putting Kunta Kinte and friend Fiddler on the Underground Railroad one Christmas Eve.

- Composers Quincy Jones and Gerald Fried shared music credits for the miniseries, but it was the latter who was responsible for the distinctive theme.
- Author Alex Haley also wrote *The Autobiography of Malcolm X*.
- The series was groundbreaking in its use of nudity and graphic violence. Some critics accused the series of over-simplifications and historical inaccuracies.

ROOTS: THE NEXT GENERATIONS

ABC, 1979, 7 episodes

CAST

Tom Harvey	Georg Stanford Brown
Irene Harvey	Lynne Moody
Queen Haley	Ruby Dee
Dad Jones	Ossie Davis
Simon Haley	Dorian Harewood
Zeona	Diahann Carroll
Alex Haley	James Earl Jones
Malcolm X	Al Freeman Jr.
George Lincoln Rockwell	Marlon Brando
Col. Frederick Warner	Henry Fonda
Mrs. Warner	Olivia de Havilland
Beeman Jones	Greg Morris
Andy Warner	Marc Singer
Jim Warner	Richard Thomas
Elizabeth Harvey	Debbi Morgan
Chicken George	Avon Long
Bob Campbell	Harry Morgan
Lee Garnet	Roger E. Mosley
Harry Owens	Gerald McRaney
Will Palmer	Stan Shaw
Bertha Palmer	Irene Cara
Bubba Haywood	Bernie Casey
Big Slew Johnson	Rosie Grier
Francey	Pam Grier
Lt. Hamilton Ten Eyck	John Rubinstein
Cynthia Palmer	Beah Richards
Lyle Pettijohn	Robert Culp
Ab Decker	Brock Peters

Dr. Horace Huguely	Paul Winfield
Mrs. Hickinger	Dina Merrill
Nan Branch Harvey	Debbie Allen
Lila	Carmen McRae
Cmdr. Robert Munroe	Andy Griffith

CREATOR: Alex Haley
EXECUTIVE PRODUCER: David L. Wolper
PRODUCER: Stan Margulies
DIRECTORS: John Erman, Charles S. Dubin, Georg Stanford Brown, Lloyd Richards
WRITERS: Ernest Kinoy, Sydney A. Glass, Thad Mumford, Daniel Wilcox, John McGreevey

An American family—the next hundred years

The seven-part fourteen-hour $18 million continuation of the epic *Roots* saga, covering the 1880s through 1960, differed from the original miniseries, which was based on two Alex Haley books. *Roots: The Next Generations,* in which the descendants of Kunta Kinte become the leading black family in Henning, Tennessee, was developed by noted writer Ernest Kinoy from an oral history by Haley (played in the final chapter by James Earl Jones). Haley had covered the time between his ancestors' move to Henning, which ended the first *Roots* miniseries, and the present in about thirty pages, just sketching it in. The printed history had been used up, so Haley talked into a tape recorder, retelling the tales of his family he had heard as a child. His spoken family memoir produced some thousand pages of transcript.

This part of the unprecedented saga began with Tom Harvey (Georg Stanford Brown), Kunta Kinte's great-grandson, having established a marginal existence in Henning, and forbidding his elder daughter's (Debbi Morgan) marriage to a light-skinned black. It concluded by having Alex Haley, as himself, making a return pilgrimage to West Africa. There an oral historian, or griot, told him of the disappearance of Kunta Kinte some 200 years earlier. This provided a closure to the extraordinary circle.

VIDEO AVAILABILITY

All seven chapters of *Roots: The Next Generations* are available in a boxed set at certain video outlets. The total running time is about 685 minutes. In addition, the complete Roots saga, including the original 1977 miniseries and the 1988 Christmas story, a TV movie called *Roots: The Gift,* are available, together with *Roots: The Next Generations,* in sixteen volumes from Time Life Video.

EMMY AWARDS

1978–79 *Roots: The Next Generations,* Outstanding Limited Series
Marlon Brando, Outstanding Supporting Actor in a Limited Series or a Special (single or continuing performance)

TRIVIA TIDBITS

- Marlon Brando's ten-minute cameo appearance in the final chapter of this miniseries as neo-Nazi George Lincoln Rockwell, sitting for the real Rockwell's famed 1960 *Playboy* interview by Alex Haley, was erroneously publicized at the time as his television acting debut. That actually took place thirty years earlier in TV's infancy, when he acted in "I'm No Hero," broadcast live on January 9, 1949, as part of an anthology series, *Actors Studio* (featuring Actors Studio members), on ABC—then broadcasting only locally in New York. Brando had requested to the producers that he play a racist villain on the show.
- Al Freeman Jr. (as Malcolm X) and Paul Winfield (as Dr. Horace Huguley, dean of the college where Alex Haley's father landed a teaching job in the 1930s) were

up against Brando for an Emmy as Outstanding Supporting Actor. Ruby Dee (as Queen Haley, Alex's grandmother) received a nomination as Outstanding Supporting Actress, as did writer Ernest Kinoy (for chapter 1) and the makeup artists.

RUMPOLE OF THE BAILEY

PBS "Mystery!", 1980–95 (first American broadcast), six episodes per season

CAST

Horace Rumpole	Leo McKern
Guthrie Featherstone	Peter Bowles
Hilda Rumpole	Peggy Thorpe-Bates Marion Mathie
Judge Bullingham	Bill Fraser
Claude Erskine-Brown	Julian Curry
Liz Probert	Abigail McKern Samantha Bond
Phyllida Erskine-Brown	Patricia Hodge

CREATOR: John Mortimer
EXECUTIVE PRODUCER: John Frankau, Lloyd Shirley
PRODUCERS: Irene Shubik, Jacqueline Davis
DIRECTORS: Herbert Wise, John Glenister, Roger Bamford, Julian Aymes, Mike Vardy, Donald McWhinnie, Stuart Burge, Martyn Friend
WRITERS: John Mortimer, Julian Aymes

Old grump in powdered wig

Leo McKern first appeared in 1978 on British television as Horace Rumpole, the curmudgeonly barrister with a fondness for poetry and claret, as well as the stench of Old Bailey, his shameless courtroom ploys, and his constant tweaking of the establishment. He's also the grumbling husband of She Who Must Be Obeyed, with whom he's constantly sparring. His priorities, as he tells his formidable Hilda: "Steak and kidney pudding, the jury

Peggy Thorpe-Bates as Hilda Rumpole and Leo McKern as barrister Horace Rumpole in the British series *Rumpole of the Bailey.* COURTESY OF PERSONALITY PHOTOS, INC.

system, presumption of innocence, and Wordsworth." Rumpole, created by noted author and playwright John Mortimer, was first seen in America in 1980—with what has come to be known as the Rumpole Repertory Company—and he's been with us on and off through the mid-1990s, grumpily shuttling his way between legal chambers and Pomeroy's pub, where it is always his pleasure to quaff the house wine.

John Mortimer once said: "When I wrote the first Rumpole story in the mid-seventies, I thought Alastair Sim would be excellent in the part, but sadly, Mr. Sim was dead and unable to take it on." Happily Leo McKern could—and no one could see the grumpy Horace as anyone else. McKern's schtick as Rumpole is as much of a delight as Peter Falk's as Columbo—and has become just as much of a television tradition. The rebellious old darling, a defiantly mischievous unmade bed of a man, barrister at law of 3 Equity Court in the Temple, divided his time between battling his wife, solving cases that are rather beneath Scotland Yard, defending petty criminals (a painter accused of forgery, anxious to tease art connoisseurs; a man accused of satanism when his young daughter is found wearing a devil's mask in her school playground; etc.), quoting the Bard, and tilting at the world's windmills of stuffiness and hypocrisy.

VIDEO AVAILABILITY

Eight tape volumes of *Rumpole of the Bailey,* with two of his intriguing cases per cassette, are available at certain video outlets. The first four also are available in a boxed set.

TRIVIA TIDBITS

- Australian-born Leo McKern has been a familiar figure on the big screen, playing conniving Thomas Cromwell in *A Man for All Seasons,* humorously menacing The Beatles in *Help!,* and enacting the role of Ryan in David Lean's *Ryan's Daughter.* On TV he was Gloucester to Olivier's *King Lear,* arms dealer Zaharov in *Reilly: Ace of Spies,* and among "the new Number 2's" in Patrick McGoohan's *The Prisoner.*
- Peggy Thorpe-Bates, years before playing the nagging Hilda Rumpole, was Leo McKern's *mother* in a London stage production of *Uncle Vanya.*
- *Rumpole*'s creator John Mortimer served as a QC (Queen's Counsel) for thirty-six years before hanging up his wig in 1984. He also wrote the TV adaptation of Evelyn Waugh's *Brideshead Revisited* (see separate entry).
- There were thirty-six cases in the *Rumpole* TV series.

SHERLOCK HOLMES

PBS "Mystery!"

The Adventures of Sherlock Holmes: Series 1, 1985 (first American broadcast), 7 episodes; Series 2, 1985 (first American broadcast), 6 episodes

The Return of Sherlock Holmes: Series 3, 1986 (first American broadcast), 7 episodes; Series 4, 1988 (first American broadcast), 6 episodes, including 2 two-hour specials

The Case-Book of Sherlock Holmes: Series 5, 1991 (first American broadcast), 6 episodes

The Memoirs of Sherlock Holmes: Series 6, 1995–96 (first American broadcast), 6 episodes

CAST

Sherlock Holmes	Jeremy Brett
Doctor Watson (series 1–2)	David Burke
Doctor Watson (series 3–6)	Edward Hardwicke
Mrs. Hudson	Rosalie Williams
Irene Adler (series 1)	Gayle Hunnicutt
Inspector Lestrade	Colin Jeavons
Mycroft Holmes	Charles Gray
Professor Moriarty (series 2)	Eric Porter

CREATOR: Arthur Conan Doyle

EXECUTIVE PRODUCER: Michael Cox

PRODUCER: June Wyndham Davies

DIRECTORS: Paul Annett, Alan Grint, John Bruce, David Carson,

WRITERS: Alexander Baron, Anthony Skene, Jeremy Paul, Alan Plates, Alfred Shaughnessy, Paul Finney

Baker Street's master sleuth

The Granada Television series of Sherlock Holmes adventures—initially aired in Great Britain between 1984 and 1994—has established itself as the definitive dramatization of Sir Arthur Conan Doyle's stories featuring Holmes and Watson. To the modern generation, the late Jeremy Brett will always be Holmes, just as Basil Rathbone had put his Hollywood stamp on the character between the late 1930s and the mid-1950s on radio, in films, on stage, and on television. In forty-three TV productions, including five that were feature-length, Brett sleuthed his way through the great Arthur Conan Doyle tales. Brett and the producers took meticulous care to be faithful Doyle in style, atmosphere, and respect for the revered characters.

As David Stuart Davies wrote in the mystery/horror quarterly *Scarlet Street,* a magazine devoted in part to Holmesiana, "Producer Michael Cox's vision of the series was clear and central to its success: to put the Sherlock Holmes of Arthur Conan Doyle's imagination on the screen. There would be no Rathbone-like updating, no playing around with the hero's sexuality, no preposterous new plots." Jeremy Brett shared that vision and admitted going over the details of the Holmes character time and again with Dame Jean Conan Doyle. In one of several lengthy interviews with *Scarlet Street* not long before his death, Brett said—about Holmes's supposed great love, Irene Adler, for instance: "There is this great shock to Holmes in "A Scandal in Bohemia," when, dressed as an old clergyman, he is ministered to by Irene. Now Holmes has never been so close to a female breast before, She's close to him, this beautiful woman with all the sweet essences of her sex. What is going on in his mind? Confusion? Uncertainty? Is this onslaught of femininity the reason he refers to her as 'the woman'? I learned to question these things when playing Holmes."

To Brett's Holmes there were two Watsons: early on,

there was David Burke; subsequently Edward Hardwicke. And there was just one Mrs. Hudson, Rosalie Williams—from the first case, "A Scandal in Bohemia," to the last, "The Mazarin Stone." Originally only thirteen episodes were planned with Brett and Burke, concluding with "The Final Problem," in which Holmes and archenemy Professor James Moriarty tumbled over the Reichenbach Falls in Switzerland (actually filmed there).

Following is a complete list of the Brett/Holmes adventures. Unless noted, each is one hour long.

"The Abbey Grange"
"The Blue Carbuncle" (Burke as Watson)
"The Boscombe Valley Mystery"
"The Bruce-Partington Plans"
"The Cardboard Box"
"The Copper Beeches" (Burke as Watson)
"The Creeping Man"
"The Crooked Man" (Burke as Watson)
"The Dancing Men" (Burke as Watson)
"The Devil's Foot"
"The Disappearance of Lady Frances Carfax"
"The Dying Detective"
"The Eligible Bachelor" (two hours)
"The Empty House"
"The Final Problem" (Burke as Watson)
"The Golden Pince-Nez"
"The Greek Interpreter" (Burke as Watson)
"The Hound of the Baskervilles" (two hours)
"The Illustrious Client"
"The Last Vampyre" (two hours)
"The Man With the Twisted Lip"
"The Master Blackmailer" (two hours)
"The Mazarin Stone"
"The Musgrave Ritual"
"The Naval Treaty" (Burke as Watson)
"The Norwood Builder" (Burke as Watson)
"The Priory School"
"The Problem of Thor Bridge"
"The Red Circle"
"The Red-Headed League" (Burke as Watson)
"The Resident Patient" (Burke as Watson)
"A Scandal in Bohemia" (Burke as Watson)

"The Second Stain"
"Shoscombe Old Place"
"The Sign of Four" (two hours)
"Silver Blaze"
"The Six Napoleons"
"The Solitary Cyclist" (Burke as Watson)
"The Speckled Band" (Burke as Watson)
"The Three Gables"
"Wisteria Lodge"

VIDEO AVAILABILITY

All of the Brett Holmeses are available at certain video outlets. Each cassette runs about fifty minutes. The five features (*The Sign of the Four, The Hound of the Baskervilles, The Master Blackmailer, The Last Vampyre,* and *The Eligible Bachelor*) run 120 minutes each.

TRIVIA TIDBITS

- A young Jeremy Brett played Nikolas Rostov in the 1956 film version of *War and Peace* starring Audrey Hepburn. A slightly older Jeremy Brett played Freddie Eynsford-Hill and sang "On the Street Where You Live" in the 1964 film of *My Fair Lady,* also starring Audrey Hepburn.
- In a Los Angeles stage production in late 1980, Jeremy Brett was Watson to Charlton Heston's Holmes in a version of Paul Giovanni's *The Crucifer of Blood.*
- Jeremy Brett and Edward Hardwicke played Holmes and Watson on the London stage in a yearlong run of *The Secret of Sherlock Holmes* (1988–89).
- Edward Hardwicke is the son of veteran actor Sir Cedric Hardwicke.
- Jeremy Brett died in September 1995, two months to the day before Robert Stephens, who portrayed the Great Detective in Billy Wilder's *The Private Life of Sherlock Holmes,* passed away.
- The 1993 production of *The Golden Pince-Nez* was the only one without Doctor Watson (Edward Hardwicke was occupied elsewhere) so Sherlock's brother Mycroft was brought in as a substitute.

- Jeremy Brett's failing health limited his appearance in "The Mazarin Stone" (the final Holmes shown in America), so Charles Gray as Mycroft took the major footage after the script was quickly rewritten. The last one Brett completed was *The Cardboard Box,* which thus became the final one in the series.
- Notable television Holmeses through the years include: Ronald Howard (who starred in the early 1950s series), Basil Rathbone (Holmes in fourteen theatrical films and on TV in 1953 on *Suspense*), Peter Cushing, Christopher Lee, Edward Fox, Christopher Plummer, Edward Woodward, Roger Moore, Charlton Heston, and Peter O'Toole (who supplied the voice in a series of Australian-made animated cartoons).
- According to *The Guinness Book of Records 1996,* Sherlock Holmes is the most portrayed character ever appearing in films: 211 total.

THE SIX WIVES OF HENRY VIII

CBS, 1971 (first American broadcast), 6 episodes, 90 minutes each

CAST

Henry VIII, King of England	Keith Michell
Catherine of Aragon	Annette Crosbie
Anne Boleyn	Dorothy Tutin
Jane Seymour	Anne Stallybrass
Anne of Cleves	Elvi Hale
Catherine Howard	Angela Pleasence
Catherine Parr	Rosalie Crutchley

PRODUCERS: Mark Shivas, Ronald Travers
DIRECTORS: John Glenister, Naomi Capon
WRITERS: Rosemary Anne Sisson, Nick McCarty, Ian Thorne, Jean Morris, Beverley Cross, John Prebble

Historical drama, at its best

"Divorced, beheaded, died. Divorced, beheaded, survived." For generations, this is how schoolchildren memorized the fate of King Henry VIII's six spouses. However, anyone who watches the marvelous BBC period production, *The Six Wives of Henry VIII,* will no longer need that old rhyme, for each woman's remarkable story is beautifully written, performed, and decidedly memorable.

First shown on in Great Britain in 1970, the series had its U.S. premiere on CBS in August 1971 and was rebroadcast by PBS the following January as part of its *Masterpiece Theatre* series.

In *The Six Wives,* each queen is given her own episode,

Keith Michell as the title character in the British series *The Six Wives of Henry VIII.* Michell also starred in a 1973 feature film adaptation of the series. COURTESY OF PERSONALITY PHOTOS, INC.

written by a different playwright, allowing each of six actresses a tour-de-force, scenery-chewing opportunity (in disciplined British fashion, of course). One is hard put to pick a favorite among Annette Crosbie's defiant Catherine of Aragon, Dorothy Tutin's fiery Anne Boleyn, Anne Stallybrass's docile Jane Seymour, Elvi Hale's comic Anne of Cleves, Angela Pleasence's headstrong Catherine Howard, or Rosalie Crutchley's devout Catherine Parr.

The stories are told independently of one another, yet the entire series is unified by Keith Michell's stunning portrayal of the gifted, egomaniacal monarch whose marital problems and quest for an heir led to his country's break from Papal Catholicism and ultimately the establishment of the Church of England. We watch him age from a slender, love-struck young man wooing Princess Catherine of Aragon to an obese, gout-ridden, wheezing old man smitten by teenage Catherine Howard, who would betray him. Complex issues of church and state are intertwined with the personal conflicts of each episode in such a way that the series becomes a marvelous teaching device for anyone interested in English history.

VIDEO AVAILABILITY

The entire series is available in a deluxe six-tape set, running nine and a half hours, at certain video outlets.

EMMY AWARD

1971–72 **Keith Michell,** Best Single Performance by an Actor in a Leading Role for "Catherine Howard."

TRIVIA TIDBITS

- Keith Michell repeated his role as Henry VIII in a 1973 feature film adaptation of the series, entitled *Henry VIII and His Six Wives.* Unfortunately, the wives were recast and the film was not successful.
- For several seasons, Michell had a recurring role on *Murder, She Wrote* as Jessica Fletcher's raffish British colleague Dennis Stanton, reformed jewel thief. Musical comedy aficionados remember him from the 1961 Broadway version of *Irma La Douce.*

THE STREETS OF SAN FRANCISCO

ABC, 1972–77, 119 episodes

CAST

Lt. Mike Stone	Karl Malden
Inspector Steve Keller (1972–76)	Michael Douglas
Inspector Dan Robbins (1976–77)	Richard Hatch
Jean Stone	Darlene Carr
Lt. Lessing	Lee Harris
Officer Haseejian	Vic Tayback

CREATOR: Edward Hume
EXECUTIVE PRODUCER: Quinn Martin
SUPERVISING PRODUCER: Russell Stoneman
PRODUCERS: John Wilder, Cliff Gould, William Robert Yates, Adrian Samish, Arthur Fellows
PRINCIPAL DIRECTORS: Virgil W. Vogel, Walter Grauman, William Wiard, Barry Crane, Robert Day, John Badham, Harry Falk, George McCowan, William Hale, Michael Preece, Michael O'Herlihy
PRINCIPAL WRITERS: Edward Hume, Del Reisman, Mort Fine, Paul Savage, Jim Byrnes, Dorothy C. Fontana, Robert Malcolm Young, Guerdon Trueblood, Jack B. Sowards, Albert Ruben, Rick Husky

Law in the city by the bay

The strong chemistry between Karl Malden as a hard-nosed veteran cop up from the ranks and Michael Douglas (his only TV series) as his younger, college-educated criminologist partner drove *The Streets of San Francisco* to the top ranks of TV's memorable police shows. *Streets* was based on characters from the Carolyn Weston novel

Police investigators Stone (Karl Malden, left) and Keller (Michael Douglas) track down a killer in this scene from *The Streets of San Francisco.* Michael's father, Kirk, was an old pal of Karl's from back in the late 1930s. COURTESY OF PERSONALITY PHOTOS, INC.

Poor, Poor Ophelia, and was introduced to TV audiences as a made-for-TV movie pilot. The source novel involved a pair of Santa Monica detectives—old pro Al Krugg and young colleague Casey Kellog—who took on the sticky case of a murdered girl. The movie (and series) changed the location and the names of the cops, but everything else was there—and clicked. Prolific producer Quinn Martin (whose trademark besides action dramas was having William Conrad as his perennial off-screen narrator) mixed all the right ingredients to make his show a hit: terrific leads, good scripts, solid direction, nice atmosphere, and all on-location filming.

As Mike Stone and Steve Keller, Karl Malden and Michael Douglas tracked down criminals in the Bay Area using modern police methods, sometimes arguing over how things should be done, but always admiring one another. Stone, a gruff but compassionate widower with a college-age daughter (Darleen Carr, who had a recurring role for the first few seasons), inevitably thought of Keller as his son. After the fourth season, Michael Douglas became eager to move on, and he finally left to pursue a movie career as both actor and producer. His character, Steve Keller, was written out of the show (he was off pursing a career as a college professor), but returned for the initial two episodes of the 1976–77 season to be officially taken off the force and, later, in a 1992 TV reunion movie of sorts, *Back to the Streets of San Francisco,* to be officially killed (off camera). Douglas was there only through flashback footage. Stone inherited a new partner, a more athletic, less cerebral Inspector Dan Robbins (Richard Hatch), but the formula had changed and *The Streets of San Francisco* were closed at season's end.

VIDEO AVAILABILITY

Several episodes of *The Streets of San Francisco* are available at certain video outlets, including the two, edited together, in which Michael Douglas is bumped off and Richard Hatch is introduced.

TRIVIA TIDBITS

- An in-joke on *Streets* had Karl Malden as Stone invariably opening his office door and barking to an underling: "Sekulovich, bring me coffee!" Sekulovich, Malden's real name, was used here in virtually every episode and in everything he did on television and in films after becoming a name of sorts.
- Malden and Douglas's dad, Kirk, had been acting pals since the late 1930s when Karl was still Mladen Sekulovich and Kirk was Isidore Demsky. It was their acting coach (later to be Mrs. Karl Malden) who convinced them to change their professional names.
- Although Malden has done a great deal of television since *Streets,* his only other series was the short-lived

Skag (six episodes in early 1980). His latter-day job: telling one and all not to leave home without it—an American Express credit card, that is. He also served a term as president of the Motion Picture Arts and Sciences.

- Among the guest bad guys: Rick Nelson, Robert Wagner, Brenda Vaccaro, Leslie Nielsen, Martin Sheen, Ida Lupino, Peter Strauss, Joseph Cotten, Stefanie Powers, Maurice Evans, Meredith Baxter-Birney and David Birney (separately), and Don Johnson.
- Paul Sorvino's short-lived 1976 series, *Bert D'Angelo, Superstar,* was a *Streets* spin-off.
- *The Streets of San Francisco* theme was written by Patrick Williams.

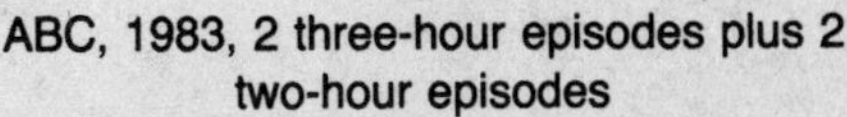

THE THORN BIRDS

ABC, 1983, 2 three-hour episodes plus 2 two-hour episodes

CAST

Ralph de Bricassart	Richard Chamberlain
Meggie Cleary	Rachel Ward
Fiona "Fee" Cleary	Jean Simmons
Rainer Hartheim	Ken Howard
Justine O'Neill	Mare Winningham
Anne Mueller	Piper Laurie
Paddy Cleary	Richard Kiley
Luddie Mueller	Earl Holliman
Luke O'Neill	Bryan Brown
Dane O'Neill	Philip Anglim
Mary Carson	Barbara Stanwyck
Vittorio Contini-Verchese	Christopher Plummer
Frank Cleary	John Friedrich
Mrs. Smith	Allyn Ann McLerie
Harry Gough	Richard Venture
Judy	Stephanie Faracy
Pete	Barry Corbin
Young Meggie	Sydney Penny

EXECUTIVE PRODUCERS: David L. Wolper, Edward Lewis
PRODUCER: Stan Margulies
DIRECTOR: Daryl Duke
TELEPLAY: Carmen Culver

Life and lust in the outback

This ten-hour dramatization of Carson McCullough's sprawling novel of forbidden love—after *Roots*, the most

A prime-time soap packaged as a miniseries, *The Thorn Birds* featured an all-star cast headlined by Richard Chamberlain (as Ralph de Bricassart) and Barbara Stanwyck (as Mary Carson). The miniseries was outdone only by *Roots* as the most-watched miniseries of all time. COURTESY OF PERSONALITY PHOTOS, INC.

watched television miniseries in history—followed the fortunes of one Australian family over a forty-two-year period beginning in 1915, as well as a charismatic country priest, the women in his life, and an illicit fling he had as a young prelate.

The Thorn Birds, played on a vast canvas by a stellar cast, begins with a handsome parish priest (Richard Chamberlain) being lusted after by the wealthy, manipulative mistress (Barbara Stanwyck, in her final role) of the largest and richest sheep station in Australia's outback with the promise of leaving her vast financial empire to the church. When her attentions are rejected, she brings her impoverished brother and his family from New Zealand and entrusts them to manage her empire and possibly inherit it upon her death. The ambitious priest is charmed by their young daughter, and over the years a deep rapport develops between them that eventually turns to passion. The secret romance can only lead to disaster, especially since he is being groomed for an important position at the Vatican.

Several notches above prime-time soap operas ranging from *Dallas* to *Knots Landing* and today's *Melrose Place,* this rich, multitextured, magnificently photographed continuing drama riveted the attention of 110 million viewers over its week-long premiere and became a worldwide favorite in the succeeding months. In 1996, CBS aired a follow-up miniseries that brought back only Richard Chamberlain (now fourteen years older), whose character grew old and died in the initial saga.

VIDEO AVAILABILITY

The Thorn Birds is available as an eight-hour four-tape set at certain video outlets and from Reader's Digest Video.

EMMY AWARDS

1982–83 **Barbara Stanwyck,** Outstanding Actress in a Limited Series or a Special
Richard Kiley, Outstanding Supporting Actor in a Limited Series or Special
Jean Simmons, Outstanding Supporting Actress in a Limited Series or Special

TRIVIA TIDBITS

◆ In addition to three Emmy acting awards, there were thirteen other nominations including production as Outstanding Limited Series (*Nicholas Nickleby* won) and others for acting by Richard Chamberlain, Bryan Brown, Christopher Plummer, and Piper Laurie, as well as for director, photography, music, costume design, and editing.

- Although set in Australia, the entire production was filmed in California's Simi Valley and on the Hawaiian island of Kauai.
- British model-turned-actress Rachel Ward (as the older Meggie) and rugged Australian actor Bryan Brown (as the brutish Luke O'Neill, who wooed, wed, and deserted her in the story) married in real life during the production.
- Richard Chamberlain, in his mid-forties at the time, played the central role aging from his twenties to his sixties. In the follow-up, at age sixty, he portrayed the priest in his forties.
- Henry Mancini wrote the score to *The Thorn Birds.*

TWIN PEAKS

ABC, 1990–91, 29 episodes

CAST

Agent Dale Cooper	Kyle MacLachlan
Sheriff Harry S Truman	Michael Ontkean
Jocelyn (Josie) Packard	Joan Chen
Catherine Martell	Piper Laurie
Pete Martell	Jack Nance
Leland Palmer	Ray Wise
Sarah Palmer	Grace Zabriskie
Laura Palmer/Madeleine Ferguson	Sheryl Lee
Maj. Garland Briggs	Don Davis
Bobby Briggs	Dana Ashbrook
Big Ed Hurley	Everett McGill
Nadine Hurley	Wendy Robie
James Hurley	James Marshall
Benjamin Horne	Richard Beymer
Audrey Horne	Sherilyn Fenn
Jerry Horne	David Patrick Kelly
Donna Hayward	Lara Boyle Flynn
Dr. William Hayward	Warren Frost
Eileen Hayward	Mary Jo Deschanel
Shelly Johnson	Madchen Amick
Leo Johnson	Eric Da Re
Hank Jennings	Chris Mulkey
Norma Jennings	Peggy Lipton
Dr. Lawrence Jacoby	Russ Tamblyn
Deputy Tommy "Hawk" Hill	Michael Horse
Albert Rosenfield	Miguel Ferrer

CREATORS/EXECUTIVE PRODUCERS: David Lynch, Mark Frost
DIRECTOR: David Lynch (at least three episodes, including the premiere).

Agent Dale Cooper (Kyle MacLachlan) developed a taste for the coffee and cherry pie in the Twin Peaks diner, but it took him 29 episodes to solve the murder of Laura Palmer. *Twin Peaks,* a very strange mystery/allegory from film director David Lynch, also featured Sherilyn Fenn as Audrey Horne. COURTESY OF PERSONALITY PHOTOS, INC.

Peak-*ing interest obtusely*

"Who killed Laura Palmer?" was the bizarre mystery that became the springboard for offbeat writer/director David Lynch's first foray into television amidst a great deal of media hype in the spring of 1990. Lynch, the man behind such cult feature films as *Eraserhead, Dune,* and *Blue Velvet,* concocted—with Mark Frost—this surrealistic, nonlinear continuing drama about the murder of a local high school prom queen in the fictional northwest logging town of Twin Peaks (her body was found in a plastic bag in the opening scenes) and of a mystical FBI agent, Dale Cooper, who teams up with the local sheriff (named Harry S. Truman) to unravel the increasingly baffling case. Kyle MacLachlan (who starred in Lynch's *Dune* and *Blue Velvet*) played the clairvoyant agent, who became partial to the local diner's cherry pie and "damn fine coffee," which he swigged ceaselessly while pursuing his investigation, finding the town had more than its share of secrets and suspects, and dictating his thoughts into a microcassette recorder to his never-seen secretary.

As the series progressed and became more convoluted and bizarre, Agent Cooper encountered dancing midgets, towering giants muttering epigrams, an evil spirit known as Bob, the strange Log Lady, his hard-of-hearing bureau chief (played by David Lynch), and a weirdo shrink with Q-Tips sticking out of his ears. Audiences slowly dropped away until only the hard-core fans were left, not enough to warrant the network to continue airing the show.

Cooper did manage to solve the initial mystery (although the killer's identity in the series is not the same as the one in the feature version shown in Europe, where the show had a fanatical following) and then was faced with another one even stranger. The cast was then reassembled for a less-than-successful theatrical movie, which was actually a prequel to the series, called *Twin Peaks: Fire Walk With Me.*

VIDEO AVAILABILITY

The entire *Twin Peaks* series is available at certain video outlets on six cassettes, each containing five episodes and running 240 minutes. In addition, there exists a *Twin Peaks* Six Pack, a boxed set containing all the episodes; a special *Twin Peaks* tape containing an all-new solution to the Laura Palmer murder, running 113 minutes; and David Lynch's 1992 feature *Twin Peaks: Fire Walk With Me,* running 134 minutes.

TRIVIA TIDBITS

- *Twin Peaks* reunited two of the stars of *West Side Story:* Richard Beymer and Russ Tamblyn.
- The show returned *The Mod Squad*'s Peggy Lipton to series television after a seventeen-year hiatus. Michael Ontkean, costar of *The Rookies*, another vintage police show from the 1960s, also was a *Twin Peaks* regular—playing a cop.
- Miguel Ferrer is the actor son of José Ferrer and Rosemary Clooney (and therefore related to George Clooney).
- Michael Horse, who played the deputy, costarred as Tonto in the 1981 film *The Legend of the Lone Ranger.*
- Angelo Badalamenti wrote the show's distinctive, if rather morose, score.

THE UNTOUCHABLES

ABC, 1959–63, 114 episodes

CAST

Eliot Ness	Robert Stack
Agent Martin Flaherty	Jerry Paris
Agent William Longfellow	Abel Fernandez
Agent Jack Rossman	Steve London
Agent Enrico Rossi	Nicholas Georgiade
Agent Cam Allison	Anthony George
Agent Lee Hobson	Paul Picerni

EXECUTIVE PRODUCERS: Quinn Martin, Jerry Thorpe, Leonard Freeman

PRODUCERS: Howard Hoffman, Alan A. Armer, Alvin Cooperman, Lloyd Richards, Charles Russell, Fred Freiberger

PRINCIPAL DIRECTORS: John Peyser, Stuart Rosenberg, Robert Butler, Walter Grauman, Ida Lupino, Paul Wendkos, Laslo Benedek, Robert Florey, Tay Garnett, Jerry Hopper, Howard W. Koch, Richard Whorf, Abner Biberman, Robert Gist, Leonard J. Horn, Alex March

PRINCIPAL WRITERS: W. R. Burnett, Louis Pelletier, Sy Salkowitz, David Karp, William Spier, Alvin Sapinsley, Ernest Kinoy, John Mantley, Ben Maddox, George Eckstein, Richard Collins. John D. F. Black, Max Ehrlich

Don't mess with Ness

The real-life exploits of G-man Eliot Ness and his elite group of Treasury Department agents were the influence

The violent shoot-outs in *The Untouchables* thrilled action fans, but some saw it as a bad influence. Robert Stack (Eliot Ness) won the Emmy for Outstanding Performance by an Actor in a Series, 1959–60. COURTESY OF PERSONALITY PHOTOS, INC.

for this vintage cop show. Based on Ness's memoirs, written with Oscar Fraley, *The Untouchables* began life as a two-part pilot on *Desilu Playhouse* in spring 1959, and later released theatrically as *The Scarface Mob.* The show, narrated in a distinctive staccato speech pattern by Walter Winchell, traced the team's attempt to put Al Capone and confederates behind bars in 1930s Chicago. (The real Ness actually did help send Capone up the river.) Some call the bullet-riddled show the flip side of *Dragnet,* where nobody ever pulled a gun and not a shot was fired.

Tight-lipped and stone-faced Robert Stack, attired traditionally in wide-brimmed fedora and a three-piece suit, with his badge as a Fed pinned to his vest, went gunning—almost emotionlessly—with his boys for scarfaced Al Capone (played snarlingly by Neville Brand). Sometimes the Untouchables, as they were known for their incorruptible status and their dedication as lawmen, got to tangle with the Kansas City mob or the Purple Gang from Detroit. Audiences lapped it up and producer Quinn Martin sold ABC on a weekly series where the Feds, led by righteous, steely-eyed Ness, could take on Baby Face Nelson, Ma Barker, Mad Dog Coll, Dutch Schultz, Bugs Moran, and other gangsters of the day. Bathtub gin flowed, vintage black sedans squealed around corners, machine gun bullets flew—never before or since to such an extreme on a one-hour television drama. *The Untouchables* became a rip-roaring TV staple for four seasons.

Besides watching Robert Stack barking orders, busting up speakeasies, fanning the scene with his tommy gun—despite the fact that the real Ness reportedly never fired a weapon—and facing down his frequent nemesis, Capone enforcer Frank Nitti (Bruce Gordon), it was a blast seeing name stars chewing the scenery as lawbreakers. Van Johnson was initially offered the role of Eliot Ness, and, to his admitted everlasting regret, he turned it down.

Who can forget Elizabeth Montgomery as a hard-boiled, gun-toting moll in "The Rusty Heller Story"? Or Peter Falk as mobster Nate Selko, the mastermind in a major heist in "The Underground Bank"? Or Barbara Stanwyck throwing her weight around in "Search for a

Dead Man"? Or Charles Bronson in a vicious mode in "The Death Tree"? Or Robert Redford as a Prohibition era hoodlum in "Snowball"?

Along the way, *The Untouchables* became the target of protests from various corners. At one end there were growing concerns about its unrelenting violence; on the other, Italian-American groups began bombarding the network with complaints about giving all the fictitious hoodlums (aside from the giants of 1930s gangsterdom) names ending in vowels. This problem was adjudicated later in the series by naming the villains Smith, Jones, Grant, and the like.

Ness and his incorruptible associates fired their last volley in the spring of 1963, but he came out of TV retirement briefly in 1991 to clear the name of a murdered colleague (and possibly kick off a revival series) in the TV movie *The Return of Eliot Ness*, set in 1947. (Stack appeared not to have aged a day in the twenty-eight-year interval.) Meanwhile, Kevin Costner co-opted the role of Eliot Ness in Brian De Palma's popular big-screen production of *The Untouchables* in 1987. "For better or worse," wrote Richard Meyers in *TV Detectives*, "Robert Stack and *The Untouchables* have carved a niche for themselves in TV detective history. It remains the best gangbuster series ever."

VIDEO AVAILABILITY

The Untouchables is available in a series of cassettes, each featuring two hour-long episodes, from Columbia House. The 1959 feature-length pilot, *The Scarface Mob*, is available at certain video outlets.

EMMY AWARD

1959–60 **Robert Stack,** Outstanding Performance by an Actor in a Series

TRIVIA TIDBITS

- Quinn Martin and Robert Stack again joined forces as producer and star for the 1976–77 series *Most Wanted.* Subsequently, Stack went became familiar to a whole new generation as host/narrator of the hit nonfiction series *Unsolved Mysteries,* which began its long run in September 1988.
- Jerry Paris, who initially played Agent Martin Flaherty, left the series to join *The Dick Van Dyke Show* as neighbor Jerry Helper. He then moved on to become a top-flight TV series writer and director, most notably of *Mork and Mindy* and *Happy Days,* until his death in 1986.
- Lawrence Dobkin, who had a recurring role as hoodlum Dutch Schultz, also left acting to become an in-demand director on drama series.
- Nelson Riddle not only wrote the theme to *The Untouchables* but also had a hit album of music he composed for the series.
- *The Untouchables* returned to television as a first-run syndication series in the 1992–93 season, starring Tom Amandes as Ness and William Forsythe as Capone.

THE WALTONS

CBS, 1972–81, 178 episodes

CAST

John Walton	Ralph Waite
Olivia Walton (1972–80)	Michael Learned
John-Boy Walton (1972–77)	Richard Thomas
John-Boy Walton (1979–81)	Robert Wightman
Zeb "Grandpa" Walton (1972–78)	Will Geer
Esther "Grandma" Walton (1972–79)	Ellen Corby
Mary Ellen Walton	Judy Norton-Taylor
Jason Walton	Jon Walmsley
Erin Walton	Mary Elizabeth McDonough
Ben Walton	Eric Scott
Elizabeth Walton	Kami Cotler
Jim-Bob Walton	David S. Harper
Ike Godsey	Joe Conley
Corabeth Godsey (1974–81)	Ronnie Clare Edwards
Mamie Baldwin	Helen Kleeb
Emily Baldwin	Mary Jackson
Rev. Matthew Fordwick (1972–77)	John Ritter
Rosemary Forwick (1973–77)	Mariclare Costello
Sheriff Ep Bridges	John Crawford

CREATOR/NARRATOR: Earl Hamner Jr.

EXECUTIVE PRODUCERS: Lee Rich, Earl Hamner Jr.

PRODUCERS: Robert L. Jacks, Andy White, Rod Peterson

PRINCIPAL DIRECTORS: Ralph Senensky, Lawrence Dobkin, Harry Harris, Philip Leacock, Bernard McEveety, Alf Kjellin, Ivan Dixon, Robert Butler, Harvey S. Laidman,

Lee Phillips, Jack Shea, Gabrielle Beaumont, Stan Lathan,

PRINCIPAL WRITERS: Earl Hamner Jr., John McGreevey, John Furia Jr., Claire Whittaker, Nancy Greenwald, Nigel McKeand, Carol Evan McKeand, Colby Chester, William Bast, Robert Malcom Young, Calvin Clements Jr., Joanna Lee, Robert Pirosh

Family values from John-Boy and kin

The Waltons, one of the most popular family drama series in all of television, followed the lives of a close-knit clan as the various members worked their way through Depression era America and World War II, as seen through the sentimental eyes of the eldest son, John-Boy, an aspiring writer. Earl Hamner Jr. used his own reminiscences to create this longtime favorite, which extolled the simple virtues of chastity, honesty, thrift, family virtue, and love.

This heartwarming continuing saga found the loving Walton family headed by John and Olivia developing and maturing through the years. John-Boy, who wanted to be a novelist for as long as he could remember, went through high school and then college before starting up his own local newspaper and ultimately left for New York when his novel was accepted by a publisher. Eldest sister Mary Ellen decided she wanted to become a nurse and eventually met and married a doctor, only to lose him in the attack on Pearl Harbor. Olivia, the matriarch, developed tuberculosis toward the end of the series and was sent off to a sanitarium for treatment. (Actually, Michael Learned, who played the role, decided she wanted to leave to pursue other acting opportunities, and the show's writers accommodated her with this plot thread explaining her absence.)

Adjustments were also made along the way following the death of Grandpa Walton (Will Geer) before the 1978–79 season began and the stroke suffered by Grandma Walton (Ellen Corby) in the fall of 1976, incor-

Real family values: *The Waltons* were in a sense the American family of *Little House on the Prairie* transplanted to the Depression era. Top row, from left: Ralph Waite (John), Michael Learned (Olivia), Jon Walmsley (Jason), Judy Norton-Taylor (Mary Ellen), and Richard Thomas (John-Boy). Bottom row, from left: Mary Elizabeth McDonough (Erin), Kami Cotler (Elizabeth), Will Geer (Zeb, aka "Grandpa"), Ellen Corby (Esther, aka "Grandma"), Eric Scott (Ben), and David Harper (Jim-Bob). COURTESY OF PERSONALITY PHOTOS, INC.

porating into the script the afflictions of actors who played the roles. Richard Thomas, as John-Boy (the alter ego of creator Earl Hamner), moved on in 1977, but returned briefly on several occasions.

The genesis for the series was the 1963 theatrical movie, *Spencer's Mountain,* with Henry Fonda and Maureen O'Hara, based on Hamner's semiautobiographical 1960 novel about his youth in the Blue Ridge Mountains of Virginia. The film moved the setting to the Grand Tetons in Wyoming, but Hamner was disheartened by the results. Ultimately, the project came back to him and the subsequent TV pilot and series returned the location to his family's Appalachia.

The Waltons, as expected, was a bigger hit in middle and rural America than in metropolitan areas, but it found a particular homespun niche and enjoyed a long and prosperous run—not unnoticed by other producers and networks who, during the era, mounted similar shows espousing family values, such as *Little House on the Prairie.*

VIDEO AVAILABILITY

Episodes of *The Waltons* are available through Columbia House. Each video contains two one-hour episodes. Also available individually at certain video outlets are: *The Homecoming* (1971), the pilot movie that began it all; *A Thanksgiving Story* (1975); *The Children's Carol* (1978); *A Day for Thanks on Walton's Mountain* (1982)—all running about 100 minutes each—and a special hour-long Waltons salute, hosted by Earl Hamner Jr., running about sixty minutes.

EMMY AWARDS

1972–73 *The Waltons,* Outstanding Drama Series
Richard Thomas, Outstanding Continued Performance by an Actor in a Leading Role, Drama
Michael Learned, Outstanding Continued Performance by an Actress in a Leading Role, Drama
Ellen Corby, Outstanding Continued Performance by an Actress in a Supporting Role, Drama
John McGreevey, Outstanding Writing Achievement in Drama, Series

1973–74 **Michael Learned,** Outstanding Continued Performance by an Actress in a Leading Role, Drama
Joanna Lee, Outstanding Writing Achievement in Drama, Series

1974–75 **Will Geer,** Outstanding Continued Performance by an Actor in a Supporting Role, Drama

	Ellen Corby, Outstanding Continued Performance by an Actress in a Supporting Role, Drama
1975–76	**Michael Learned,** Outstanding Continued Performance by an Actress in a Leading Role, Drama
	Ellen Corby, Outstanding Continued Performance by an Actress in a Supporting Role, Drama
1976–77	**Beulah Bondi,** Outstanding Lead Actress in a Single Appearance in a Drama

TRIVIA TIDBITS

- The two-hour movie pilot, *The Homecoming,* starred Andrew Duggan, Patricia Neal, and Edgar Bergen, as father, mother, and grandfather, along with the series younger actors playing the same roles. It remains a Christmas TV perennial.
- There were several two-hour reunion episodes over the years since the series ended: in 1982, *Wedding on Walton's Mountain* (dealing with daughter Erin's marriage), *Mother's Day on Walton's Mountain,* and *A Day for Thanks on Walton's Mountain;* in 1993, *A Walton Thanksgiving Reunion;* and in 1995, *A Walton Wedding* (John-Boy's).
- Each show ended with a night shot of the Walton home and the voices of each family member wishing the other goodnight as the bedroom lights went out one after another.
- *The Waltons* theme was written by Jerry Goldsmith.
- Before *The Waltons,* Hamner's writing for television included some of the last *Twilight Zone* episodes.

WAR AND REMEMBRANCE

ABC, November 1988, 7 episodes (18 hours)

WAR AND REMEMBRANCE: THE FINAL CHAPTER

ABC, May 1989, 5 episodes (11¼ hours)

CAST

Victor "Pug" Henry	Robert Mitchum
Natalie Henry	Jane Seymour
Byron Henry	Hart Bochner
Pamela Tudsbury	Victoria Tennant
Rhoda Henry	Polly Bergen
Leslie Slote	David Dukes
Aaron Jastrow	John Gielgud
Warren Henry	Michael Woods
Janice Henry	Sharon Stone
Alistair Tudsbury	Robert Morley
Carter "Lady" Aster	Barry Bostwick
Hack Peters	Mike Connors
Avram Rabinovitz	Sami Frey
Berel Jastrow	Topol
Palmer Kirby	Peter Graves
Sammy Mutterperl	John Rhys-Davies
Philip Rule	Ian McShane

Harry Hopkins	William Schallert
Werner Beck	Bill Wallis
Brig. Gen. Armin von Roon	Jeremy Kemp
Gen. Dwight D. Eisenhower	E. G. Marshall
Adolf Hitler	Steven Berkoff
Winston Churchill	Robert Hardy
Franklin Delano Roosevelt	Ralph Bellamy
Harry Truman	Richard Dysart

CREATOR: Herman Wouk
EXECUTIVE PRODUCER/DIRECTOR: Dan Curtis
PRODUCER: Barbara Steele
WRITERS: Earl W. Wallace, Dan Curtis, Herman Wouk

The world in mid-century turmoil

The continuation of Herman Wouk's epochal two-volume saga that started with *The Winds of War* (see separate entry) begins one week after Pearl Harbor and dramatizes the historic milestones of World War II. The hugely expensive *War and Remembrance* was so long (at nearly thirty hours), it was scheduled as two miniseries aired by ABC over seven evenings during the November 1988 ratings sweeps, and another five evenings during the May 1989 sweeps. Like its predecessor, *War and Remembrance* follows fictional career naval officer Pug Henry and his family all over the globe. Most of the cast repeated their roles, with the exception of Jane Seymour (who took over for Ali MacGraw), Hart Bochner (for Jan-Michael Vincent), Michael Woods (for Ben Murphy), Leslie Hope (for Lisa Eilbacher), John Gielgud (for John Houseman), and Robert Hardy as Churchill (for Howard Lang). Soon to be a star, Sharon Stone took over the part from Deborah Winters as Janice, one of Pug and Rhoda Henry's daughters-in-law.

At the core of this expansive production was an exceptionally moving segment involving the Holocaust, with Jane Seymour and a memorable John Gielgud as Pug

Henry's Jewish daughter-in-law and her elderly uncle trapped in Europe and sent to the concentration camps. This quite graphic portion of the saga prompted the network to add a cautionary warning on the particular night of its showing.

VIDEO AVAILABILITY

A seven-tape set of the first part of *War and Remembrance* and a five-tape set of the second part are available at certain video outlets, as is a seven-tape set of the original, *The Winds of War.*

EMMY AWARD

1988–89 *War and Remembrance,* Outstanding Miniseries

TRIVIA TIDBITS

- Barbara Steele, the producer, is remembered by cult film fans as the raven-haired heroine of numerous British, Italian, and American horror movies of the 1960s. She also had a small acting role in *The Winds of War* and was in the short-lived 1990 prime-time revival of *Dark Shadows.*
- *War and Remembrance* earned fifteen Emmy nominations, including Jane Seymour as Outstanding Actress in a Miniseries, John Gielgud as Outstanding Actor in a Miniseries, and Polly Bergen as Outstanding Supporting Actress in a Miniseries. Director Dan Curtis and cinematographer Dietrich Lohmann (for part 11, dealing with the Holocaust) were also nominated.
- This miniseries had an unprecedented eighteen-month production schedule, which began in February 1986.

THE WILD WILD WEST

CBS, 1965–69, 104 episodes

CAST

James T. West	Robert Conrad
Artemus Gordon	Ross Martin
Jeremy Pike	Charles Aidman
Pres. Ulysses S. Grant	James Gregory

CREATOR: Michael Garrison
EXECUTIVE PRODUCERS: Philip Leacock, Michael Garrison
PRODUCERS: Leonard Katzman, Fred Freiberger, Collier Young, John Mantley, Gene L. Coon, Bruce Lansbury
PRINCIPAL DIRECTORS: Richard Sarafian, William Whitney, Bernard Kowalski, Don Taylor, Irving J. Moore, Harvey Hart, Lee H. Katzin, Mark Rydell, Richard Donner, Ralph Senesky, Robert T. Sparr, Marvin J. Chomsky, Alan Crosland Jr.
PRINCIPAL WRITERS: Gilbert Ralston, John Kneubuhl, Oliver Crawford, Henry Sharp, Richard Landau, Stephen J. Kandel, Stanford Whitmore, Calvin Clements, Jackson Gillis, Gene L. Coon, Ken Kolb

The excellent adventures of Jim and Art

This fanciful series set in the Old West chronicled the exploits of two resourceful Secret Service agents under the administration of Ulysses S. Grant, using prototypes of twentieth-century gadgetry to catch their nineteenth-century adversaries—radicals, revolutionaries, mad scientists, and other diabolical criminals intent on taking over all or part of the United States. James T. West, the dapper one with an eye for the ladies, and sidekick Ar-

James T. West (Robert Conrad) in a bit of a jam in this episode from *The Wild Wild West.* Rory Calhoun had actually been the first choice for the role of West. COURTESY OF PERSONALITY PHOTOS, INC.

temus Gordon, a master of disguises and dialects, traveled the West in a customized railroad car with an arsenal of anachronistic weapons. The two swapped humorous banter with devious opponents who soon found themselves no match for our heroes. *The Wild Wild West* was a hip sci-fi/spy/cowboy series—TV's first. The premise was basically James Bond stuff of a century earlier—something on the order of *Maverick* combined with *The Man From U.N.C.L.E.*

Each of their weekly adventures was titled "The Night of . . ." and had them crossing swords—as well as derringers, primitive lasers, and other weapons—with imaginatively named villains such as Count Carlos Manzeppi (an evil magician played by rotund Victor Buono with a young Richard Pryor as a henchman), deranged geologist Orkney Cadwallader (Burgess Meredith), Ecstacy La Joie (Yvonne Craig), Fabian Lavendor (Carroll O'Connor), Asmodeus the Great (Don Rickles), Maharajah Singh (Boris Karloff), Baron Hinterstoisser (Harvey Korman), Doctor Faustina (Ida Lupino), Brutus the Bonebreaker (Percy Rodrigues), and Dr. Horace "The Falcon" Humphries (Robert Duvall).

West and Gordon's perennial adversary was the megalomaniacal dwarf, Dr. Miguelito Loveless (played by Michael Dunn, the Oscar-nominated character actor who committed suicide in 1973), who was usually accompanied by hulking, seven-foot-tall Voltaire (Richard Kiel, later famous as James Bond villain Jaws). They first tangled in "The Night the Wizard Shook the Earth," in which the demented little fellow whose family once owned much of California threatened to detonate some sort of superexplosive device to get the land back. When next they met, in "The Night of the Whirring Death," Loveless—still bent on taking over California—used such weapons as exploding toy soldiers, trains, and phonographs against a cabal of millionaire bondholders.

Another meeting between Jim and Miguelito ("The Night of the Murderous Spring") had the latter trying to destroy West's—and America's—sanity with hallucinogenic drugs that turn users into killers. Miguelito Loveless knew no bounds in his deviousness, but Jim West was also up to him—or perhaps down to him. Particularly with colleague Artemus Gordon lurking nearby in some disguise—who invariably stepped in with assistance whenever James West found himself outnumbered by at least five to one.

The series left the airwaves after a weak fourth season, but Jim and Artemus were called out of retirement by their new boss (played by Harry Morgan) in two self-spoofing reunion movies, *The Wild Wild West Revisited*

(1979) and *More Wild Wild West* (1980), both directed by Burt Kennedy and written by William Bowers. In the first, they go after Miguelito Loveless Jr. (Paul Williams), in the second their quarry is mad Secretary of State Henry Messenger (Victor Buono), who is out to wipe out the entire family of the prominent Paradises—all five of whom are played by Jonathan Winters. CBS aired some *Wild Wild West* reruns during the summer of 1970, with some violence cut to please the standards of the period.

VIDEO AVAILABILITY

Several episodes of the series, including the pilot, are available at certain video outlets. Each runs about sixty minutes. Both of the reunion TV movies are also available. In addition, Columbia House is offering the entire series in two one-hour episodes per cassette.

TRIVIA TIDBITS

- Rory Calhoun was the original choice for the role of James T. West.
- Dimitri Tiomkin and Ned Washington were initially contracted by CBS to write the theme for the show, but creator Michael Garrison found it to be too staid and formal for his concept. The theme music to *The Wild Wild West* was ultimately written by Richard Markowitz.
- Garrison originally had acquired the rights in the mid-1950s to a book called *Casino Royale,* by a little-known author named Ian Fleming, but couldn't interest anyone in developing it into a viable project. Instead, he ended up concocting an Old West James Bond, but died on the eve of the premiere of *The Wild Wild West.*
- Ross Martin, who won an Emmy nomination for playing Artemus Gordon, died shortly after the second of the two reunion movies—precluding a resumption of the series. He was absent much of the final season, when he was replaced by Charles Aidman and other

Ross Martin (left, as Artemus Gordon) and Robert Conrad (as James T. West), the stars of *The Wild Wild West.* Anachronistic weaponry was this duo's secret for success in the Old West. COURTESY OF PERSONALITY PHOTOS, INC.

substitute sidekicks. Robert Conrad has gone on to star in eight other series, most of the later ones for his own production outfit, A. Shane Company, named after one of his two sons.

- Guest star Agnes Moorehead won an Emmy during the 1966–67 season for Outstanding Performance by an Actress in a Supporting Role in a Drama ("The Night of the Vicious Valentine" episode).
- In addition to the "Night of . . ." titles, the show's other trademark was the ingenious gimmick geared to the one-hour format—each commercial break would end on a cliff-hanger freeze-frame, inserted clockwise around the opening credit graphic.

THE WINDS OF WAR

ABC, 1983, 4 three-hour episodes plus 3 two-hour episodes

CAST

Victor "Pug" Henry	Robert Mitchum
Natalie Jastrow	Ali MacGraw
Byron Henry	Jan-Michael Vincent
Aaron Jastrow	John Houseman
Rhoda Henry	Polly Bergen
Madeline Henry	Lisa Eilbacher
Leslie Slote	David Dukes
Berel Jastrow	Topol
Warren Henry	Ben Murphy
Fred "Palmer" Kirby	Peter Graves
Brig. Gen. Armin von Roon	Jeremy Kemp
Franklin Delano Roosevelt	Ralph Bellamy
Pamela Tudbury	Victoria Tennant
Eleanor Roosevelt	Elizabeth Hoffman
Adolf Hitler	Gunter Meisner
Hermann Goering	Rene Kolldehoff
Winston Churchill	Howard Lang
Josef Stalin	Anatoly Shaginyan
Benito Mussolini	Enzo Castellari
Luigi Gianelli	Edmund Purdom
Bunky Thurston	Lawrence Pressman
Wolf Stoller	Barry Morse
Mrs. Stoller	Barbara Steele

CREATOR/WRITER: Herman Wouk
PRODUCER/DIRECTOR: Dan Curtis

Wouk and war

Herman Wouk's massive best-seller, published in 1971 and following the fortunes of an American naval officer

Eighteen hours of American history, adapted from Herman Wouk's best-selling novel. The cast of *The Winds of War,* from left: Ben Murphy (as Warren Henry), Victoria Tennant (as Pamela Tudbury), Robert Mitchum (as Victor Henry), Polly Bergen (as Rhoda Henry), Lisa Eilbacher (top, as Madeline Henry), Ali McGraw (bottom, as Natalie Jastrow), and Jan-Michael Vincent (as Byron Henry). COURTESY OF PERSONALITY PHOTOS, INC.

and his family from the onset of World War II through Pearl Harbor, became an eighteen-hour television event spread over seven nights. Anchored by veteran actor Robert Mitchum, heading a stellar cast, it related the story of a fictional navy captain who was an eyewitness to history, hobnobbing with the great world figures of the time while juggling a personal life with a frosty wife, a beautiful mistress, and several adult children.

The story continued in the dramatization of Wouk's even lengthier sequel, *War and Remembrance* (see separate entry), which came to television in two sprawling parts in fall 1988 and late spring 1989 (29¼ hours), making the entire production longer than many regular series.

VIDEO AVAILABILITY

The Winds of War is available in a seven-tape set at certain video outlets, as is a seven-tape set of the first part of *War and Remembrance,* and a five-tape set of the second part.

TRIVIA TIDBITS

- *The Winds of War* received thirteen Emmy nominations, including Outstanding Limited Series (it lost to the TV production of Broadway's *Nicholas Nickleby*), as well as Supporting Actor and Actress (Ralph Bellamy and Polly Bergen). It did win for Charles Correll and Stevan Larner's photography and Tommy Welsh's costume supervision.
- Ralph Bellamy, whose portrayal of FDR in the 1958 Broadway production and the 1960 film of *Sunrise at Campobello* remains definitive, was back as Roosevelt in *The Winds of War* and *War and Remembrance.* In effect, he was playing the part for thirty years and was eighty-four at the time of the latter TV production—although FDR was just sixty-three when he died.
- The dramatization of the Wouk novel technically marked Robert Mitchum's TV acting debut, although a television movie he made following the production aired first.
- The epic miniseries had initially been announced by ABC as a 1979 production running twelve hours (six less than what finally was shown four years later).
- *The Winds of War* was filmed over a span of fourteen months (267 locations in six countries) at a cost in excess of $40 million—the most ever for a television production to that time.
- The music was composed by Bob Cobert (who does most of producer/director Dan Curtis's shows) and the soundtrack is available on CD and cassette.

SCIENCE FICTION / FANTASY / HORROR SERIES

"To boldly go where no one has gone before." Anyone even remotely familiar with the *Star Trek* phenomenon will recognize these nine words as part of the introduction to that series. But it applies equally as well to the science fiction genre in general. For over four decades, television science fiction/fantasy series have taken us to strange, exotic worlds in both mind and space, where a writer's imagination knows no bounds and an audience is transported with him or her into exhilarating flights of fancy.

These are not limited merely to the fields of space shows and sci-fi. The various *Star Trek* series, *Space Patrol, Battlestar Galactica, Buck Rogers, The Starlost, Rocky Jones—Space Ranger, Tom Corbett: Space Cadet,* and even *Superman*, all feature aliens and futuristic occurrences, but many of these programs overlap with cop shows, adventure cliff-hangers, war movies, and other genres. Science fiction/fantasy also deals with the occult, the unexplainable, and the bizarre: Rod Serling with *The Twilight Zone;* Dan Curtis with *Dark Shadows* and *Kolchak: The Night Stalker;* Steven Spielberg with *Amazing Stories;* and even the Cryptkeeper with *Tales From the Crypt.* Whether in series form with regular characters or as anthologies in which assorted writers create new stories each week with new characters, these programs have thrilled and chilled audiences through irony, black humor, special effects, and, occasionally, gore. Through it all, however, the best science fiction strives to reflect life on earth and show where changes need to be made in society.

Above and beyond

Science fiction on television, which began in the days of the medium's "innocence"—shows like *Captain Video and His Video Rangers, Out There, Space Patrol, Rod Brown of the Rocket Rangers,* and *Tom Corbett: Space Cadet* were among the early shows—effectively came of age with *The Twilight Zone* in 1959, despite the fact that all of the stories on that series were not necessarily limited to the sci-fi genre. The sixties brought to television, in consecutive years, *Voyage to the Bottom of the Sea* (1964) and *Lost in Space* (1965), both from Irwin Allen, and then *Star Trek* (1966)—bringing the genre to full bloom. Although the explosive impact of *Star Trek* would take a number of years, it would change not only television in the sci-fi arena but also the entire entertainment world, with increasingly sophisticated special effects and refined production values.

Fantastic journeys

Star Trek and many of the other space and intergalactic adventures that followed incorporated themes of comradeship, sacrifice, self-sufficiency, race relations, and social values, while not forgetting to mix in a modium of tension-relieving humor and impressive high-tech gadgetry. Many view these as futuristic westerns, adapting the old formula (right down to the basic good guy/bad guy themes) and transferring it to the new millennium. What the likes of Rod Serling and Gene Roddenberry had refined, others twisted to their own visions. Aside from the benchmark *Star Trek* and its progeny, TV has, most notably, given us *UFO* and *Space: 1999* by Gerry and Sylvia Anderson, Great Britain's answer to Roddenberry as space movie pioneers, and *Blake's 7*, by Britisher Terry Nation (who also concocted *Doctor Who*). There also were the home-grown *Buck Rogers in the 25th Century* and *Battlestar Galactica/Galactica 1980*, both from Glen A. Larson, and the two other Irwin Allen series, *Land of the Giants* and *Time Tunnel*. And lest we forget, there were lighthearted space shows like Hanna-Barbera's animated *The Jetsons*.

Earthbound tales

Besides the planet-hopping outer space shows, there have been those earthbound fantasy dramas transfixing viewers dealing with the occult, the psychological, the paranormal, the downright creepy, and those from the don't-look-under-the-bed school. The likes of *Suspense* and *Danger* in TV's early days to the contemporary *X-Files* have captured the imaginations of television audiences, bringing them close encounters with the unknown. Thrillers in this mold—with UFO sightings, possible aliens among us, or a pod person or two—have over the TV decades probed the seams of reality, both stimulated and frightened rabid viewers regularly, challenged their collective minds, and held them enthralled.

Horrors!

As audiences have always delighted in a good scare, horror show creators have been telling their tales in one form or another, usually infusing them with both humor and irony, for as long as one can remember. These are, in effect, campfire ghost stories that, since television came along, have permeated the medium and increasingly—since viewers are eating them up—are being augmented with more blood and gore. Contemporary shows like *Monsters, Tales From the Darkside,* and most notably *Tales From the Crypt,* with its cackling, skeletal, animatronic host, continue to lightheartedly frighten viewers who simply come back again and again for more shocks and goose bumps.

Superheroes

Mythological as well as comic book heroes—from the indomitable Superman to the immensely popular Hercules and Xena: Warrior Princess—in their battles for good over evil, have been television staples through the decades and vicarious alter egos for viewers of all ages. Their adventures, extraordinary as they might be, have attracted avid TV watchers and have created far-reaching fan clubs, making the fantastic accessible and, to many young viewers, giving the illusion of being in the realm of possibility.

Spotlighted in these pages are more than two dozen television series that represent these sometimes parallel, sometimes intersecting and interlocking genres—the line has become blurred over the years—that are available on video to continue to delight fans of all ages. There's something out there or down there—and it might well be fun.

THE ADVENTURES OF SUPERMAN

Syndicated, 1952–57, 104 episodes
(first 52 in black and white)

CAST

Clark Kent/Superman	George Reeves
Lois Lane (1951)	Phyllis Coates
Lois Lane (1953–57)	Noel Neill
Jimmy Olsen	Jack Larson
Perry White	John Hamilton
Inspector Bill Henderson	Robert Shayne
Jor-El, Superman's Krypton father	Robert Rockwell
Lara, Superman's Krypton mother	Aline Towne
Eban Kent	Tom Fadden
Martha Kent	Dani Nolan

CREATORS: Jerry Siegel, Joe Shuster

PRODUCERS: Whitney Ellsworth, Robert Maxwell, Bernard Luber

DIRECTORS: Thomas Carr, Lee Sholem, George Blair, Harry Gerstad, Lew Landers, George Reeves, Howard Bretherton

WRITERS: Whitney Ellsworth, Robert Maxwell, Dennis Cooper, Ben Peter Freeman, Lee Backman, Monroe Manning, David Chantler, Eugene Solow, Jackson Gillis, Leroy H. Zehren

Krypton's gift to pop culture

Of all the comic book superheroes, none has surpassed *Superman,* whose never-ending battle for truth, justice, and the American way is legendary—from newspapers and comics to radio, movies, television, and even the

Superman (George Reeves) and his first Lois Lane (Phyllis Coates).
COURTESY OF PERSONALITY PHOTOS, INC.

Broadway musical stage. Few are unfamiliar with the *Superman* story, beginning with his arrival on Earth from the doomed planet Krypton and continuing with his upbringing by the kindly Kents of Smallville, USA, who found him as an infant where his space ship had crash-landed on their farm. Only they were aware of the young Clark's superpowers, and at twenty-five he decided to use his great abilities to benefit mankind. To this end, Clark went to the big city of Metropolis, and, to keep his true identity of Superman a secret, acquired a job as a mild-mannered, bespectacled reporter for the crusading *Daily Planet*. The Man of Steel's crime-battling adventures—and his/Clark's hot-and-cold relationship with rival reporter Lois Lane, cub reporter/photographer Jimmy Olsen, and blustery editor Perry White—made up the basics of this enduring saga as each week he saved one or the other of them from harm while confronting assorted villains, mad scientists, and other evildoers.

The production values on this low-budget—almost campy—series were incredibly poor, with the actors wearing virtually the same outfits to allow for footage from different episodes to be recycled. But the show was a hit and remains a favorite in reruns four decades later, perpetuated as a crusade by Jack Larson, who has become a latter-day keeper of the Superman flame.

Video Availability

Selected episodes of the George Reeves series, two to a cassette, each accompanied by a *Superman* cartoon of the early 1940s, are available at certain video outlets. Columbia House has begun issuing cassettes of all the *Superman* shows in thc 1950s series.

TRIVIA TIDBITS

- George Reeves directed the final three episodes in 1957.
- The series was launched with a one-hour 1951 feature *Superman and the Mole Men,* later re-edited as a two-part broadcast episode.
- Noel Neill played Lois Lane on-and-off for ten years, including two fifteen-chapter movie series with Kirk Alyn as the Man of Steel: *Superman* (1948) and *Atom Man vs. Superman* (1950). She maintained that she never made more than $225 a week playing the part.
- Noel Neill and Kirk Alyn did cameos in the big-screen *Superman* (1978) as Lois Lane's mom and dad. Neill also turned up with Jack (Jimmy Olsen) Larson in an episode of *The Adventures of Superboy* in 1992.
- George Reeves's death in on June 16, 1959 remains a provocative mystery. Was it suicide (he was despondent by being permanently typecast as Superman) or was it murder (a jealous lover was thought to be involved)?
- Reeves appeared uncredited in *From Here to Eternity* in order to avoid recognition as Superman.
- Producer Whitney Ellsworth put together two *Superman* spin-offs in the early 1960s: a *Superpup* pilot with

little person Billy Curtis in a canine caped costume and the street clothes of one Bark Bent, and the 1962 *Adventures of Superboy* with a young George Reeves look-alike, John Rockwell. Neither aired.

- *Superman* was created in the 1930s by teenage pals Jerry Siegel and Joe Shuster, who sold off all the rights for a mere $200 and ended up living most of their lives on the edge after losing several lawsuits over the years for residuals. Ultimately, with the success of the Christopher Reeve *Superman* movies, Warner Bros. gave them a lifetime pension. Shuster died in 1993, Siegel in early 1996.
- Playing Superman seems to a carry with it a curse. First, Kirk Alyn never was able to find a role of significance after playing Superman. Then, George Reeves came to an unfortunate end. Recently, there was the tragedy of Christopher Reeve, Superman #3, who broke his neck in a horse-riding accident. Dean Cain, who plays the role on TV in the hugely popular *Lois & Clark*, must secretly be wondering about life after being the Man of Steel.
- Although telecast in black and white, some episodes were filmed in color in anticipation of the future of color TV.

AMAZING STORIES

NBC, 1985–87, 45 episodes

Anthology series with no recurring cast members

EXECUTIVE PRODUCER: Steven Spielberg
PRODUCER: David E. Vogel
DIRECTORS: Steven Spielberg, Martin Scorsese, Clint Eastwood, Robert Zemeckis, Tim Burton, Burt Reynolds, Paul Bartel, Danny DeVito, Tobe Hooper, Tom Holland, Lesli Linka Glatter, Matthew Robbins
WRITERS: Steven Spielberg, Richard Matheson, Stu Krieger, Michael McDowell, Mick Garris

Steven's noble ambitions

Steven Spielberg, who began his fabled career directing episodic television in 1969, was lured back to the medium in the mid-1980s with a fantastic offer from NBC—a firm two-season commitment—to produce and occasionally direct a series of "little" half-hour-long stories, sometimes scary, sometimes ironical, sometimes whimsical (on the style of the old *Alfred Hitchcock Presents* series), along with full creative control. With the Spielberg name attached, the anthology series attracted Hollywood names, both behind the camera and in front of it—people who don't normally do television.

Spielberg himself directed the first episode, "Ghost Train," a *Poltergeist*-themed tale starring Drew Barrymore and Roberts Blossom, and "The Mission," with Kevin Costner as a B-17 pilot leading a World War II bombing run. One of the most unusual tales in the series was a dark-humored cartoon by director Tim Burton called "Family Dog," an animated view of life through the eyes of a family's put-upon pet pooch. Others included: Burt Reynolds directing former wife Loni Anderson in "Guilt Trip"; Clint Eastwood directing girlfriend Sondra Locke and Harvey Keitel in "Vanessa in the Garden"; and Danny DeVito directing wife Rhea Perlman and costarring with her in "The Wedding Ring." Another World War II theme show, "No Day at the Beach," starring Charlie Sheen, was filmed in grainy black and white.

During its first season, *Amazing Stories* was paired on Sunday nights with the new *Alfred Hitchcock Presents,* a similar anthology series, but the network—while honoring its commitment to two full seasons—then seemingly lost interest in the ambitious show and played the "see if you can find it" game so that it lost whatever audience it had cultivated. Subsequently, the episodes were combined into feature-length movies for TV syndication.

VIDEO AVAILABILITY

A half-dozen *Amazing Stories* collections—two and three episodes each—are available at certain video outlets. Submitted for MPAA ratings (rarely used for TV programming), some episodes were given "G," "PG," and "PG-13" designations.

TRIVIA TIDBITS

- Among the stars acting out the various, often quite innovative, stories were Kevin Costner, Danny DeVito and Rhea Perlman, Milton Berle, Sid Caesar, Drew Barrymore, Charlie Sheen, Loni Anderson, Gregory Hines, and Patrick Swayze.
- John Williams, Spielberg's favorite composer—from *Jaws* and the *Indiana Jones* movies to *ET, the Extra-terrestrial* and *Schindler's List*—wrote the *Amazing Stories* theme.
- CBS obtained the rights to a *Family Dog* spin-off series. Delayed several years, it surfaced for a brief run in the summer of 1993.

BATTLESTAR GALACTICA

ABC, 1978–79, 18 episodes

GALACTICA 1980

ABC, 1980, 9 episodes

CAST

Commander Adama	Lorne Greene
Captain Apollo (1978–79)	Richard Hatch
Lieutenant Starbuck (1978–79)	Dirk Benedict
Lieutenant Boomer (1978–79); *Colonel Boomer* (1980)	Herb Jefferson Jr.
Lieutenant Athena (1978–79)	Maren Jensen
Cassiopea (1978–79)	Laurette Spang
Flight Sergeant Jolly (1978–79)	Tony Swartz
Boxey (1978–79)	Noah Hathaway
Colonel Tigh (1978–79)	Terry Carter
Count Baltar (1978–79)	John Colicos
Voice of Imperious Leader (1979)	Patrick Macnee
Voice of Lucifer (1979)	Jonathan Harris
Sheba (1979)	Anne Lockhart
Captain Troy (1980)	Kent McCord
Lieutenant Dillon (1980)	Barry Van Dyke
Jamie Hamilton (1980)	Robyn Douglass
Xavier (1980)	Richard Lynch
Dr. Zee (1980)	Robbie Rist

CREATOR/EXECUTIVE PRODUCER: Glen A. Larson
SUPERVISING PRODUCERS: Leslie Stevens, Michael Sloan
PRODUCER: John Dykstra
DIRECTORS: Glen A. Larson, Richard A. Colla, Chris Nyby Jr., Daniel Haller, Rod Holcomb
WRITERS: Glen A. Larson, Don Bellisario, Michael Sloan, Leslie Stevens, Frank Lupo

Seeking Earth

Television's answer to *Star Wars* was the very expensive *Battlestar Galactica,* launched in the fall of 1978 as an epic journey into the seventh millennium of time, in which twelve tribes of humans are engaged in a terrifying thousand-year war with the robot Cylon race. The heavily promoted series, which cost a staggering $1 million an episode, kicked off with a three-hour premiere under the guidance of producer John Dykstra, the noted visual effects supervisor for *Star Wars* and other sci-fi movies.

The only battlestar left after a surprise attack by the evil Cylons, the mile-wide Galactica was commanded by silver-haired Adama, the last surviving member of the Council of Twelve, the colonial ruling body. His mission: lead the 220 starships of the fleet out of harm's way toward Earth with his daredevil son Apollo, who commands the Galactica's elite Blue Squadron—a fleet of one-man Viper fighters—and Starbuck, Apollo's fast-talking wingman in the squadron. The weekly Cylon encounters and the show's spectacular hardware and computerized gizmos—plus guest stars like Jane Seymour, Ray Milland, Lloyd Bridges, Roy Thinnes, Ray Bolger, Kirk (Superman) Alyn, and Barry Nelson—turned the series into a somewhat cult phenomenon during its rather brief life. The novelty wore off as the show began to recycle old plots and clichés—which is why it got tagged *Battlestar Ponderosa* by some pundits.

Midseason tinkering to counter slipping ratings accounted for a number of cast changes, and then a complete overhaul at the start of season two—with a somewhat lower budget. For starters, the series title was changed to *Galactica 1980* (taking place 30 years later). Adama, now with a full white beard, had new officers under his command: Troy, his adopted grandson, and Dillon, Troy's lifelong friend. And there was earthling Jamie Hamilton, a TV newswoman. The other holdover aside from Adama was Blue Squadron officer Boomer, promoted here from lieutenant to colonel. The battles with the Cylons continued, but most of the action took place on Earth. The pizzazz was gone—and so was the show after nine episodes.

VIDEO AVAILABILITY

About a dozen episodes of *Battlestar Galactica* and its reworked sequel *Galactia 1980* are available at certain video outlets. Each runs about fifty minutes, other than the edited theatrical version.

TRIVIA TIDBITS

- An edited version of the three-hour premiere episode was also released theatrically in "Sensurround."
- Fred Astaire made a rare TV acting appearance, as an aging con man who may be Starbuck's long-lost father. Astaire did this as a favor to his grandson, who was a fan of the show.
- Muffit the Daggitt, Galactica's robot pet, was played by Evie the Chimp.
- Series creator Glen A. Larson has insisted that the show was in the works long before *Star Wars*.
- The stirring *Battlestar Galactica* theme music was composed by Larson and Stu Phillips and performed by the Los Angeles Philharmonic Orchestra.

BEAUTY AND THE BEAST

CBS, 1987–90, 57 episodes

CAST

Asst. DA Catherine Chandler (1987–89)	Linda Hamilton
Vincent	Ron Perlman
Father (Jacob Wells)	Roy Dotrice
Deputy DA Joe Maxwell	Jay Acavone
Diana Bennett (1989–90)	Jo Anderson
Gabriel (1989–90)	Stephen McHattie

CREATOR: Ron Koslow
EXECUTIVE PRODUCERS: Paul Junger Witt, Tony Thomas
PRODUCERS: Ron Koslow, Lynn H. Guthrie, Ken Koch, George R. R. Martin
DIRECTORS: Richard Franklin, Alan Cooke, Paul Lynch, Thomas J. Wright, Victor Lobl, Christopher Leitch, Gus Trikonis
WRITERS: Ron Koslow, David Peckinpah, George R. R. Martin, Andrew Laskos, Virginia Aldridge

Between two worlds

Decidedly offbeat, and quick to become a worldwide cult favorite, *Beauty and the Beast*—derived from the famed fairy tale—was a contemporary fable mixing romance and action. The main characters were beautiful crime-fighting attorney Catherine Chandler and the powerful and grotesque, but intelligent and compassionate Man/Beast who loved and protected her, though he lived in a labyrinth world beneath Manhattan. Their special love story, the poetic dialogue, the handsome sets, and the diffuse photography made this a surprise hit when it pre-

True love and romance: crime-fighting attorney Catherine Chandler (Linda Hamilton) and Vincent, the Beast (Ron Perlman). When Hamilton's character was killed off, *Beauty and the Beast*'s magic was lost. COURTESY OF PERSONALITY PHOTOS, INC.

miered in late 1987 and even turned Vincent, the beast (heavily made-up, unknown, mellifluous-voiced Ron Perlman), into a quite unlikely matinee idol. Vincent, born frighteningly grotesque and abandoned as an infant, was reared and educated by his adoptive father (played by distinguished British actor, Roy Dotrice), himself a learned recluse living in a vast complex of tunnels and chambers below the city. Throughout the unorthodox relationship between Catherine and Vincent—which did not result in even a kiss until well into the series and ultimately ended up with an interspecies child being born—the chemistry between Hamilton and Perlman was quite palpable.

When Linda Hamilton decided after the second season to leave the series to pursue a film career, a decision was made by the producers to have the baby stolen by a ruthless, well-connected criminal and her character killed when she tried to reclaim the child. A new leading lady—as an investigator for the NYPD—was introduced, but the magic was gone (she was never quite prepared for a relationship with the furry one) and the show limped to a midseason demise—although three extra first-run episodes turned up in the nearly viewerless dog days of summer.

VIDEO AVAILABILITY

Eight fifty-minute cassettes and three 100-minute feature-length ones are available at certain video outlets, as well as a gift set including the pilot, "Once Upon a Time in New York," the feature-length "Above, Below and Beyond," and "Though Lovers Be Lost."

TRIVIA TIDBITS

- *Beauty and the Beast* received an Emmy nomination in its first and second seasons as Best Drama Series but lost to *thirtysomething* and *L.A. Law*, respectively. Ron Perlman was nominated as Lead Actor in a Drama Series for both seasons. Linda Hamilton was nominated as Best Actress for the second season.
- For the pilot episode, Ron Koslow earned a nomination for writing; Judy Evans for costume design.
- Roy H. Wagner received an Emmy for his photography of the pilot, Lee Holdridge for his theme music, and

John Mansbridge and Chuck Korian for the art direction and set decoration. For the second season, Holdridge again won an Emmy, this time for writing the music (and songwriter Melanie for the words) to the song "The First Time I Love Forever."

BLAKE'S 7

Syndicated, 1985–89 (first American broadcast), four 13-part series

CAST

Roj Blake	Gareth Thomas
Jenna Stannis	Sally Knyvette
Kerr Avon	Paul Darrow
Calley	Jan Chappell
Dayna Mellanby	Josette Simon
Vila Restal	Michael Keating
Olag Gan	David Jackson
Del Tarrant	Steven Pacey
Soolin	Glynis Barber
Servalan	Jacqueline Pearce
Commander Travis	Stephen Greif Brian Croucher
Zen/Orec	Peter Tuddenham
Servalan's aide	Peter Craze

CREATOR: Terry Nation
PRODUCERS: David Maloney, Vere Lorrimer
DIRECTORS: Michael E. Briant, Pennant Roberts, Vere Lorrimer, David Maloney, Fiona Cumming, Jonathan Miller, Douglas Camfield, Gerald Blake
WRITERS: Terry Nation (most episodes), Chris Boucher, Roland Holmes, Roger Parkes, Allan Prior, James Follet, Ben Steed, Trevor Hoyle

Against the Federation

Blake's 7, a British cult sci-fi favorite (1978–81), is set in the future when Earth's surface has been transformed into a radioactive wasteland following a holocaust. The inhabitants are now forced to live in domed cities controlled by the Federation and are kept in line by suppressant drugs that are blended into their entire food supply.

The show was really a one-hour space adventure series featuring many interconnected episodes. Its initial protagonist, Roj Blake, is an Alpha-grade dissident determined to free humanity from the Federation, a ruthless futuristic dictatorship whose power extends to various colonies in the galaxy. His loyal, if ragtag, crew of "interstellar terrorists" on the Liberator: Jenna Stannis, one of the best smuggler pilots in the galaxy when she turned to crime; Kerr Avon, self-reliant computer and electronics genius; Cally, an alien whose humanoid race has allowed her to excel in mind reading and telekinesis; Vila Restal, an avowed coward whose ability to open locks and bypass security systems borders on genius; Olag Gan, a gentle giant; and Zen, the Liberator's computer with the annoying habit of withholding information from the crew.

The show maintained the overall *Blake's 7* title, although Blake and Jenna were killed off at the end of the second series. (Gan had been dispatched in episode five.)

Dyna Mellanby, skilled weapons expert and huntress, and Del Tarrant, overconfident smuggler and reckless mercenary were later added in the third series, and Cally and Zen never made it beyond the beginning of the fourth series.

VIDEO AVAILABILITY

Blake's 7 is available in twenty-six two-episode volumes, each running about 100 minutes, at certain video outlets.

TRIVIA TIDBITS

- Creator Terry Nation, who wrote all thirteen episodes of the show's first series and a number of them in the succeeding three, is the man credited for creating the Daleks, *Doctor Who's* most famous enemy.

◆ Gareth Thomas earlier had roles in two other memorable British series, *Z Cars* and *Coronation Street,* as well as the BBC's multipart adaptation of *How Green Was My Valley,* shown in the US on *Masterpiece Theatre* in late 1976.

BUCK ROGERS IN THE 25TH CENTURY

NBC, 1979–81, 33 episodes

CAST

Capt. William "Buck" Rogers	Gil Gerard
Col. Wilma Deering	Erin Gray
Dr. Elias Huer (1979–80)	Tim O'Connor
Twiki	Felix Silla
Voice of Twiki	Mel Blanc, Bob Elyea
Princess Ardala (1979–80)	Pamela Hensley
Hawk (1981)	Thom Christopher
Admiral Asimov (1981)	Jay Garner
Dr. Goodfellow (1981)	Wilfrid Hyde-White
Ensign Moore (1981)	Alex Hyde-White
Lieutenant Devlin (1981)	Paul Carr

DEVELOPED FOR TELEVISION: Glen A. Larson, Leslie Stevens
EXECUTIVE PRODUCERS: Glen A. Larson, John Mantley
SUPERVISING PRODUCERS: Bruce Lansbury, Calvin Clements
PRODUCERS: David O. Connell, Richard Caffey, Jock Gaynor, John Stephens
DIRECTORS: Daniel Haller, Michael Caffey, Sig Neufeld Jr., Dick Lowry, Philip Leacock, Leslie Martinson, David Moessinger, Larry Stewart, Jack Arnold, Vincent McEveety, Bernard McEveety, Barry Crane, Victor French, John Patterson

Swashbuckling in deep space

The hero of the popular 1930s comic strip—which inspired a couple of theatrical cliff-hanging serials in the early days of World War II—Buck Rogers was a dashing, happy-go-lucky adventurer. For this television series, he is resurrected as a swaggering astronaut from the twentieth century on a deep space probe, caught in a time warp and returned to Earth five hundred years later where he becomes an unofficial agent for the Earth Defense Directorate, led by Dr. Elias Huer. Buck is sent on intergalactic missions with teammate Wilma Deering, commander of Earth's defense squadron, and robot sidekick Twiki to ensure the safety of the universe.

Among the guest stars whom Buck and companions would meet either at his home base in New Chicago or in outer space were Jamie Lee Curtis, Peter Graves, Cesar Romero, Frank Gorshin, Gary Coleman, Jerry Orbach, Julie Newmar, Roddy McDowall, and Jack Palance. In the episode with the last two, set on the planet Vistula, Buck and Wilma trace the plot of a man named Kaleel (Palance), who has been selling slaves to the planet's governor and secretly building an attack fleet, which Buck must destroy before they can reach Earth. In another, Buck is forced to save Wilma from the dreaded "Space Vampire," a demon who drains the living soul from people. And then there's always the threat from Buck's perennial nemesis, seductive Ardala, a Draconian princess (played by Pamela Hensley), who has a thing for him and is determined to snare him at any cost.

In the second season, the format was changed and Buck, Wilma, and Twiki—joined by a birdman named Hawk—were aboard the spaceship *Searcher,* attempting to find the "lost tribes" of Earth who had fled the planet after a nuclear war.

The futuristic series was Glen A. Larson's second attempt at a hit weekly sci-fi adventure, following *Battlestar Galactia* (see separate entry), whose expensive sets and gadgets were recycled here. This updated *Buck Rogers* was light-years away from the version aired on ABC almost thirty years earlier. Initially, it was a feature-length movie that premiered theatrically six months before the TV series.

VIDEO AVAILABILITY

Nine episodes of the series, each running about fifty minutes, as well as the 1979 feature film (later edited down to serve as the series pilot), are available at certain video outlets.

TRIVIA TIDBITS

- *Buck Rogers* was based on the 1929 comic strip conceived by John F. Dille, which evolved into a fanciful radio series spanning the 1930s (starring, alternately, Matt Crowley, Curtis Arnall, Carl Frank, and John Larkin).
- Buster Crabbe (who had previously played Tarzan and Flash Gordon) was the screen's first Buck Rogers in the 1939 Universal twelve-episode cliff-hanger serial.
- In the 1950–51 TV series, Buck Rogers was played first by Kem Dibbs and then by Robert Pastene, Wilma Deering by Lou Prentis, and Dr. Huer by Harry Southern.
- William Conrad was the series narrator during its first season.
- Composer Bruce Broughton won an Emmy for scoring the 1981 episode, "The Satyr." Nominations that season also went to cinematographer Ben Coleman ("Hawk" episode) and costume designer Alfred E. Lehman ("The Dorian Secret" episode).
- The robot Twiki was first voiced in the TV series by Mel Blanc. A monetary dispute with the producers caused him to leave after the initial season, but fans of the show forced his return after the first five episodes of season two.
- Ill-fated *Playboy* Playmate of the Year and subject of the film *Star 80* Dorothy Stratten guest-starred on an episode of the show as "the most beautiful woman in the universe."

DARK SHADOWS

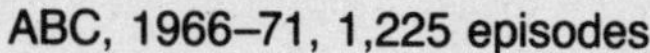

ABC, 1966–71, 1,225 episodes

CAST

Quentin Collins	David Selby
Elizabeth Collins Stoddard	Joan Bennett
Dr. Julia Hoffman/Magda	Grayson Hall
Barnabas Collins	Jonathan Frid
Victoria Winters	Alexandra Moltke
David Collins	David Hennessy
Carolyn Stoddard/Charity	Nancy Barrett
Roger Collins/Edward Collins	Louis Edmonds
Maggie Evans/Rachel Drummond	Kathryn Leigh Scott
Angelique/Cassadra	Lara Parker
Willie Loomis/Desmond Collins	John Karlen
Peter Bradford/Jeff Clark	Roger Davis
Daphne Harridge	Kate Jackson
Laura Collins	Diana Millay
Prof. Elliot Stokes/Count Petofi	Thayer David

CREATOR/EXECUTIVE PRODUCER/PRINCIPAL DIRECTOR: Dan Curtis

PRODUCERS: Robert Costello, Peter Miner

DIRECTORS: Leila Swift, Penberry Jones, Henry Kaplan, John Sewick, Jack Sullivan, Dennis Kane, Sean Sullivan

PRINCIPAL WRITERS: Ron Sproat, Sam Hall, Gordon Russell, Malcolm Marmorstein, Joe Caldwell

Echoing footsteps and sinister doings

This cult, almost campy, half-hour soap opera ran in the late afternoons for five years and offered vampires,

Jonathan Frid as vampire Barnabas Collins on *Dark Shadows.* Frid became an unlikely cult hero and sex symbol, at one time receiving as many as 6,000 fan letters per week.
COURTESY OF PERSONALITY PHOTOS, INC.

ghosts, haunted houses, werewolves, black magic, and other Gothic trappings. Created by Dan Curtis—the man behind such diverse TV entertainment as *Dracula, Dr. Jekyll and Mr. Hyde,* and *The Winds of War—Dark Shadows* found a particularly avid audience among teenagers. It was part *The Haunting of Hill House* (by Shirley Jackson) and part *The Turn of the Screw* (by Henry James).

Television's first occult, and often otherworldly, soap, set in and around brooding Collinwood near the small fishing village of Collinsport, Maine, *Dark Shadows* told the continuing story of Victoria Winters, a young woman hired as governess for ten-year-old David Collins. There she discovered herself involved in the supernatural existences of his extended family—including the 175-year-old vampire, Barnabas (played by Jonathan Frid, who became an unlikely, fanged matinee idol). Collinwood held within the dark shadows of its silent corridors the unspoken secrets of the Collins family: brooding Quentin, David's werewolf uncle; Roger, David's creepy father; aristocratic Elizabeth Stoddard, Quentin and Roger's married sister and the family matriarch; and the long-lost, bloodlusting cousin Barnabas, who returned from the dead and gave the series—creaking along in its first season—an infusion that soon made *Dark Shadows* American TV's hottest daytime attraction. There also were Willie Loomis, the looney groundskeeper; Julia Hoffman, the psychiatrist who tried to "cure" vampire Barnabas and ended up lusting after him; and assorted other characters.

Over the course of the show—which was rife with wonderful bloopers, silly dialogue, collapsing sets, etc.—the increasingly thickly plotted proceedings moved back and forth through the centuries, with the actors all playing several roles. In *USA Today* in December 1990, on the eve of his *Dark Shadows* revival show, Dan Curtis said that the original "brings back the memories of my youth—I was brash—we broke every rule in daytime because we had no experience," and then went on to note that though others tried to copy *Dark Shadows* over the years, "they'd always failed because no one ever really seemed to understand what made the original series unique—it was not a horror show but a Gothic romance."

Dark Shadows proved to be the rare daytime show to find a lucrative afterlife in syndication and a perennial following in a number of fan clubs.

VIDEO AVAILABILITY

More than fifty cassettes, each with four episodes, are available at certain video outlets. There are also a number of tape compilations: *Scariest Moments from Dark Shadows; The Best of Barnabas; Dark Shadows: 1849 Flashback; Dark Shadows: Behind the Scenes; Dark Shadows Music Videos; Dark Shadow Bloopers;* and the 1991 *Dark Shadows: 25th Anniversary.*

TRIVIA TIDBITS

- Two theatrical movies—with much higher production values than the TV series—were made by MGM reuniting many players from the original series and directed by Dan Curtis: *House of Dark Shadows* (1970) and *Night of Dark Shadows* (1971).

- Dan Curtis's gorier, sexier, hour-long prime-time resurrection of *Dark Shadows* on NBC in early 1991—starring Ben Cross, Joanna Going, Jean Simmons, Roy Thinnes, and Barbara Steele—never made much of an impression and had a stake put through its heart by the network after only thirteen episodes (all are available on video).
- Nice-guy vampire Jonathan Frid found himself a cult hero, receiving around 6,000 letters a week.
- Robert Cobert wrote the music to *Dark Shadows,* as he did for every Dan Curtis show. His haunting "Quentin's Theme" became a Top twenty chart hit in summer 1969 and earned a Grammy nomination as Best Instrumental Theme. (It lost to John Barry's "Midnight Cowboy.")
- The Canadian-made knockoff series, *Strange Paradise,* with its 195 episodes syndicated beginning in 1969, attempted to cash in on the success of *Dark Shadows.*
- Alexandra Moltke, the original Victoria Winters, later gained notoriety as Claus Von Bulow's mistress, surfacing during the sensational trial of the early 1980s.

DOCTOR WHO

Syndiated, 1963–89 (premiered on PBS in 1975)

CAST

The Doctor (1963–66, 29 stories/ 134 episodes)	William Hartnell
The Doctor (1966–69, 21 stories/ 113 episodes)	Patrick Troughton
The Doctor (1970–74, 24 stories/ 128 episodes)	Jon Pertwee
The Doctor (1974–81, 43 stories/ 172 episodes)	Tom Baker
The Doctor (1981–84, 20 stories/ 68 episodes)	Peter Davison
The Doctor (1984–86, 11 stories/ 41 episodes)	Colin Baker
The Doctor (1987–89, 12 stories/ 42 episodes)	Sylvester McCoy

CREATORS: Sidney Newman, Donald Wilson

PRODUCERS: Verity Lambert, Mervyn Pinfield, John Wiles, Innes Lloyd, Peter Bryant, Derrick Sherwin, Barry Letts, Dave Martin, Philip Hinchcliffe, Graham Williams, John Nathan-Turner

DIRECTORS: Waris Hussein, Christopher Barry, Richard Martin, John Crockett, Mervyn Pinfield, Douglas Camfield, Derek Martinus, Chris Clough, Peter Moffatt, Alan Wareing

WRITERS: Anthony Coburn, Terry Nation, David Whitaker, Dennis Spooner, Ian Stuart Black, Innes Lloyd, Gerry Davis

Tom Baker as rogue Time Lord Dr. Who. Many U.S. fans regard him as the favorite of the series of actors who played the role. This British science fiction classic has been syndicated since 1963. COURTESY OF PERSONALITY PHOTOS, INC.

Who's who?

One of the most durable series in television history, the low-budget British-made science fiction favorite followed the exploits of a mysterious time traveler—a rogue renegade Time Lord (known as Doctor Who) from the planet Gallifrey. The 750-year-old wizard uses futuristic technology to accomplish his ends, and usually was accompanied on his cosmic journeys by an attractive female. Though not actually human, the doctor finds it convenient to use human form. As originally conceived by the BBC, *Doctor Who* was "an irascible, absentminded, unpredictable old man, running away from his own planet in a time machine [the TARDIS, for Time and Relative Dimensions in Space], which looked like a police box on the outside, but was in fact a large space station inside."

Since actors playing the title role came and went over time, the doctor, in his various incarnations (he has thirteen lives), became an ambiguous character whose looks and personality change. Every few years he experienced a "regeneration"—either as a feisty old man, a dandy with elegant clothes and an ultra high-tech auto, a frump with a twenty-foot long scarf, a middle-aged salt, etc.—all doing battle with a host of weird creatures (and not so high-tech special effects).

The doctor's most famous enemies were the Daleks, a race of robotlike warriors whose sole purpose in life is conquest. The Daleks, introduced in the six-part fourth story and returning to do battle over the years, were from the fertile mind of writer Terry Nation, subsequently famous for *Blake's 7,* another cult sci-fi series.

The brainchild of Sidney Newman, who several years earlier had created *The Avengers,* and Donald Wilson, who several years later would create *The Forsyte Saga* for television, *Doctor Who* was an immediate sensation in Great Britain (even though it had the unfortunate luck to premiere on November 23, 1963, the day after JFK's assassination, limiting its audience) and became a national passion in the U.S. on PBS for the past two decades. In mid-1990s, a new series was begun in Great Britain with Paul McGann as the latest doctor, whose time machine malfunctions and is forced to land in San Francisco on December 30, 1999. A two-hour pilot movie of this latest adventure premiered on Fox in spring 1996.

VIDEO AVAILABILITY

More than fifty volumes of *Doctor Who,* in various configurations and compilations, are available on cassette at certain video outlets.

TRIVIA TIDBITS

- *Dr. Who* is the longest-running dramatic show in world TV history.
- Two feature-length films starring Peter Cushing as the doctor, both released in the mid-1960s, had him and his freedom-fighting companions doing battle with the grasping Daleks: *Doctor Who and the Daleks* (1965)

and *Daleks: Invasion Earth 2150 A.D.* (1966). Both are available on tape.

- Tom Baker, the most popular of the doctors in America, starred as Rasputin in the 1972 movie *Nicholas and Alexandra* and the villain Koura in the 1974 film *Golden Voyage of Sinbad.*
- Sylvester McCoy, the seventh doctor, returned for the opening of the mid-1990s reincarnation of the show to provide continuity before "morphing" into Paul McGann.
- The music for *Doctor Who* was composed by Ron Grainer.

FREDDY'S NIGHTMARES

Syndicated, 1988–90, 44 episodes

CAST

Freddy Krueger	Robert Englund

In your dreams

Spawned by Wes Craven's imaginative, low-budget 1984 smash *A Nightmare on Elm Street* and its three sequels (a fourth came later as did a belated fifth), *Freddy's Nightmares* was a one-hour horror/suspense anthology series. As in the features, the fearsome, dream-haunting fiend, Freddy Kreuger—with his natty chapeau, terribly disfigured face, and razor blade claw-glove—was the demonic host. Freddy would introduce the inhabitants of the town of Springwood, where the locals are plagued by nightmares in which they died horrible and/or bizarre deaths. Most of tales were structured in two parts, with one of the survivors of the first becoming one of the victims in the second. The syndicated series, recycled like *Friday the 13th* and other slasher movies that became pop culture phenomenons of the 1970s and 1980s, generally played around the country as date shows on late Friday or Saturday nights.

Robert Englund, whose portrayal of Freddy (originally a vengeful child-killer) on the big screen turned him into, arguably, the most famous horror icon since Peter Cushing and Christopher Lee, gloated shamelessly as he took the terrified viewer through the self-contained chillers. On one, a frustrated housewife dreams of winning big money—and losing her husband—on a game show, although Freddy puts in his bid for his share of the loot; on another, a medical student (played by Jayne Mansfield's actress daughter Mariska Hargitay) is obsessed with her frightful nightmares—which feature Freddy and his "cut-up" ways, a twisted fellow student, and her abusive grandmother; and a third in which a lightning-fast hot rod may or may not be a teenager's ticket out of Springwood.

Freddy, with his warped sense of humor, and the fictional all-American town of Springwood were the only recurring elements of the unusually violent anthology series as derived from Wes Craven's original concept. To reassure viewers, this sardonic disclaimer greeted them: "No one under the age of eighteen will be murdered in this show."

VIDEO AVAILABILITY

A number of *Nightmares* are available at certain video outlets—each cassette running about 50 minutes.

TRIVIA TIDBITS

- Robert Englund made his directing debut in 1988 with the satanic horror film *976-Evil,* and played the title role in the 1989 screen version of *The Phantom of the Opera.*
- Genre director Wes Craven, who "created" Freddy Krueger, has a master's degree in philosophy, was a humanities instructor at Johns Hopkins, and found his niche in films with movies such as *Last House on the Left* (which he wrote, directed, and edited), *The Hills Have Eyes,* and *Swamp Thing.*

THE HITCHHIKER

HBO, 1983–88, 39 episodes; USA, 1989–90, 46 episodes

CAST

The Hitchhiker (1983–84)	Nicholas Campbell
The Hitchhiker (1984–90)	Page Fletcher

EXECUTIVE PRODUCERS: Jean Chalopin, Lewis Chesler, Andy Heyward, Riff Markowitz, Richard Rothstein
SUPERVISING PRODUCER: David Latt
PRODUCER: Gil Adler
DIRECTORS: Ivan Nagy, Christopher Leitch, David Wickes, John Laing, Thomas Baum, Colin Bucksey
WRITERS: Jeremy Lipp, Christopher Leitch, Thomas Baum, William Gray, John Kent Harrison

Thumbing rides to hell

Moody and often graphic, this Canadian-made suspense anthology mixed greed, lust, murder—and mysterious strangers. Each episode was hosted by an enigmatic drifter in tight jeans who introduced each story, interacted a bit, and then went unseen until the fade-out. In one of the macabre *Hitchhiker* thrillers, "In the Name of Love," a hit woman falls in love with the man she is supposed to kill; in another, "Made for Each Other," two killers become friends, with bizarre consequences; in a third, "Best Show," Ken *(thirtysomething)* Olin is a crass yuppie lawyer who attempts to hide an accidental death and is exposed in a chilling sequence of events.

Assorted TV faces appeared in this series, usually with a noted American actor in the lead. Among them: Robert Vaughn, Geraldine Page, Susan Blakely, David Dukes,

Kirstie Alley, Darren McGavin, Edward Albert, Elizabeth Ashley, Stephen Collins, Tom Skerritt, and Sandra Bernhard, and international actors such as Klaus Kinski and Franco Nero. The HBO programs, like similar series of the day (such as *Red Shoes Diaries*), featured female nudity, adult situations, and adult language, and were in effect R-rated. Subsequently, USA Cable acquired *The Hitchhiker* series with new, toned-down PG-rated episodes.

VIDEO AVAILABILITY

A continuing number of volumes of *The Hitchhiker,* each running about ninety minutes and containing three episodes from the anthology series, are available at certain video outlets.

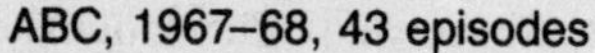

THE INVADERS

ABC, 1967–68, 43 episodes

CAST

David Vincent	Roy Thinnes
Edgar Scoville (second season)	Kent Smith

CREATOR: Larry Cohen
PRODUCERS: Quinn Martin, Alan A. Armer
DIRECTORS: Joseph Sargent, Paul Wendkos, Sutton Roley, John Meredith Lucas, Robert Butler, Jesse Hibbs, William Hale, Don Medford, Lewis Allen
WRITERS: Anthony Spinner, George Eckstein, Dan Ullman, John W. Bloch, Don Brinkley, Alan A. Armer, Robert Sherman, Laurence Heath, Earl Hamner Jr., Barry Oringer, David W. Rintels, William Blinn

Are they here?

Architect David Vincent, while driving on a lonely country road, witnesses the landing of a craft from another galaxy in the dead of night and spends the rest of the cult series in a desperate attempt to convince the disbelieving world that "the nightmare has already begun." *The Invaders* is somewhat like Quinn Martin's *The Fugitive,* reworked as a sci-fi show with the protagonist always on the run from those who feel he should be locked up or even done away with. The 1960s alien paranoia drove this popular series which, in its underlying theme of basic mistrust, drew a thin *Invasion of the Body Snatchers* line between who are the extraterrestrials (in human form) and who aren't. Weekly are-they-or-are-they-not aliens included such names as Roddy McDowall, Suzanne Pleshette, Jack *(Hawaii Five-O)* Lord, Michael Rennie, Gene Hackman, Burgess Meredith, Sally Kellerman, and Edward Asner. Kevin McCarthy and Dana Wynter, the stars of *Invasion of the Body Snatchers*, turned up in separate episodes—"Watchers" and "The Captive," respectively.

But it would be David Vincent, played by Roy Thinnes in his most famous TV role, running around from week to week sounding the alarm. The invaders, as he soon discovered, had no pulse or heartbeat because they had no hearts, but they did have slightly mutated hands (watch for that crooked fourth finger). For Vincent, it was a lonely crusade until he found at least one person who believed him. Then, of course, that person could have been one of *them* . . .

The imaginative series ran for a season and a half, but a frustrated and increasingly paranoic Vincent never managed to quell his own doubts and fears or even convince the populace of the dangers. On the other hand, the otherworldlies and mutants never succeed in destroying the one man who could expose them. Indeed, when an updated version of *The Invaders* aired as a two-part, four-hour TV movie in November 1995, Roy Thinnes was still racing around the countryside obsessively tracking the alien invasion three decades later.

VIDEO AVAILABILITY

More than a dozen cassettes of *The Invaders*, each running about fifty-three minutes, are available at certain video outlets. The two-part TV movie is also available on video as a two-tape set.

TRIVIA TIDBITS

- The music for *The Invaders* was by Dominic Frontiere of *Outer Limits* fame.
- Actor William Conrad was the durable show's unseen narrator, at least over the opening credits—as he was on most Quinn Martin series.

- Although this was an anthology-type show with no regulars save Roy Thinnes, many of the actors turned up again and again but as different characters. In one episode, rare for its time, "The Vise," the entire cast was black (except for Thinnes).
- The show has a strong following in Europe, especially France and Germany.
- The true form of the aliens was glimpsed only once, in the final season.

KOLCHAK: THE NIGHT STALKER

ABC, 1974–75, 22 episodes

CAST

Carl Kolchak	Darren McGavin
Tony Vincenzo	Simon Oakland
Ron Updyke	Jack Grinnage
Monique Marmelstein	Carol Ann Susi
Gordon Spangler	John Fiedler
Emily Cowles	Ruth McDevitt

CREATOR: Jeff Rice
EXECUTIVE PRODUCER: Darren McGavin, Cy Chermak
PRODUCER: Paul Playdon
DIRECTORS: Gene Levitt, Don Weis, Allen Baron, Alex Grashoff, Don McDougall, Michael Caffey, Vincent McEveety, Gordon Hessler, Seymour Robbie
WRITERS: Jimmy Sangster, David Chase, Michael Kozoll, Paul Playdon, Stephen Lord, Paul Mastrogeorge, Larry Markes

Newshound with a cross to bear

Darren McGavin's wonderfully bemused and then terrified performance as wisecracking Carl Kolchak—a seedy, straw-hatted reporter on the trail of vampires in modern day Las Vegas in two ninety-minute made-for-TV movies pilots written by Richard Matheson (*The Night Stalker* in 1971 and *The Night Strangler* in 1972)—provided the basis for this series which was quick to find cultdom but limited to a single season. In it, the intrepid newshound with the snappy patter found himself transplanted to Chicago with his apoplectic editor, Tony Vincenzo, and soon up against all kinds of demons and bloodsuckers and devils while probing mysterious Windy City goings on. From Chicago the two moved on to Los Angeles and then to Portland. (Vincenzo prayed he'd left Kolchak behind at every move.) While chasing down stories, Kolchak would invariably encounter zombies, werewolves, Aztec mummies, and men who sold their souls to the devil. His biggest challenge was to convince Vincenzo to run his incredible stories.

Based on the *Kolchak* novels by Jeff Rice, the series offered often wry but creepy tales and surrounded its incredulous crime reporter with a gallery of oddball colleagues and associates: squeamish, prissy fellow newsman Ron Updyke; Miss Emily, the eccentric advice columnist; ditsy, overeager coworker Monique Marmelstein; mordant morgue attendant Gordy the Ghoul, among others. Show titles like "The Ripper," "Zombie," "Vampire," "Werewolf," "Primal Scream," and "The Energy Eater" whetted weekly audience appetites, which were mainly sated by the show's black humor.

It was creative differences—and money—that prevented the show from having a second season.

VIDEO AVAILABILITY

Several cassettes of the show—two episodes to a tape—are available at certain video outlets.

TRIVIA TIDBITS

- *Kolchak: The Night Stalker* premiered on Friday, September 13, 1974. That same night, another show, Clint Walker's *Kodiak,* also debuted, confusing matters. Meanwhile, Kolchak and Kodiak had to contend with Telly Savalas's *Kojak,* which was then beginning its second season.
- Prolific Darren McGavin's first TV series was *Crime Photographer* (1951–52), followed by *Mike Hammer*

(1958), *Riverboat* (1959–61), and *The Outsider* (1968–69).

- Guests on the show included Tom Skerritt, William Daniels, Keenan Wynn, Dick Van Patten, Dick Gautier, Richard Kiel, Dwayne Hickman, Tom Bosley, Phil Silvers, Carolyn Jones, and Kathie Browne (who was Mrs. Darren McGavin).
- Gil Melle composed the *Kolchak: The Night Stalker* theme.

LOST IN SPACE

CBS, 1965–68, 83 episodes

CAST

Prof. John Robinson	Guy Williams
Maureen Robinson	June Lockhart
Maj. Donald West	Mark Goddard
Judy Robinson	Marta Kristen
Will Robinson	Billy Mumy
Penny Robinson	Angela Cartwright
Dr. Zachary Smith	Jonathan Harris
Robot	Bob May

CREATOR/PRODUCER: Irwin Allen
DIRECTORS: Tony Leader, Sobey Martin, Paul Stanley, Nathan Juran, Don Richardson, Ezra Stone, Harry Harris, Justus Addis, Sutton Roley, Irving J. Moore, Alvin Ganzer, Alexander Singer, Paul Stanley
WRITERS: Peter Packer, Jackson Gillis, Barney Slater, Norman Lessing, Shimon Wincelberg, William Welch, Carey Wilbur

Outerworld family adventures

Science-fiction king Irwin Allen built this series, one of the earliest in the space genre of the 1960s, around the concept of a family of space travelers in far-off 1997. Inspired by *Swiss Family Robinson,* by way of Gold Key Comics' *Space Family Robinson,* it initially was at a serious level but soon moved into lighthearted campy fantasy—with intergalactic hippies, cowboys, pirates, dragons (a delightful episode with Hans Conried entitled "The Questing Beast") and even talking six-foot carrots

The Robinsons, America's favorite space family, from left: Marta Kristen (Judy), Jonathan Harris (Dr. Smith), June Lockhart (Maureen), Angela Cartwright (Penny), Guy Williams (John), and Mark Goddard (Major Donald West). COURTESY OF PERSONALITY PHOTOS, INC.

(in "The Great Vegetable Rebellion"). There was even an episode in which Robby the Robot (from the classic theatrical movie *Forbidden Planet*) was the guest star, playing a robotoid with a will of its own, helping the Robinsons with their chores, while secretly planning to kidnap them for its master on an alien planet.

One of America's best-loved nuclear families of the day, the Robinsons—Dad's an astrophysicist, Mom's a biochemist—were part of Earth's first test-colonization mission to far off Alpha Centauri in their spaceship *Jupiter 2*, when it fell victim to sabotage by villainous stowaway Zachary Smith. All were hopelessly lost in space when the ship crash-landed on an unknown planet—although not obscure enough to prevent a parade of weekly guest stars from finding it. The comically ruthless, rather bumbling Dr. Smith—who somehow managed to endear himself to the other passengers (he was supposed to have disabled the ship on the launch pad, not in outer space)—continued to get the crew into various misadventures, usually with antagonism from resourceful young Will Robinson and the all-purpose Robot. As the now-grown Billy Mumy likes to recall, when comparisons are made between *Lost in Space* and the other sixties space adventure, *Star Trek:* "Their Spock was our Robot. Their Bones was our Smith, only Smith was more of a parody than Bones."

Of the series' eighty-three episodes—the first twenty-nine in black and white—the most famous one was a two-parter entitled "The Keeper," guest-starring Michael *(The Day the Earth Stood Still)* Rennie as an intergalactic zookeeper who seems to view the Robinsons more as specimens than as humans.

Seven seasons after *Lost in Space* left prime-time television (with the Robinsons et al. still lost in the far-flung reaches of the galaxy), Irwin Allen went on to produce a version of the source material, *Swiss Family Robinson.* It lasted only twenty-six episodes.

VIDEO AVAILABILITY

Tapes of *Lost in Space* are available through Columbia House, two one-hour episodes per cassette. The first one includes not only the premiere episode, "The Reluctant Stowaway," but also the rarely seen pilot to the series, "No Place to Hide."

TRIVIA TIDBITS

- The theme music was written by Johnny Williams. (He had not yet become the more dignified John, who would compose the scores to *Star Wars, Superman,* and *Close Encounters of the Third Kind,* among others.)
- A Hanna-Barbera animated cartoon version of *Lost in Space* was shown in 1973 as an ABC pilot. Jonathan

Harris returned to provide the unmistakable voice of sinister Zachary Smith.

- The *Lost in Space* phenomenon was such that it could attract 30,000 fans at a cast reunion party in Boston 25 years after its premiere. Only Guy Williams (born Armando Catalano), who also was famed as Zorro in the Disney TV series, was not there—he had died in 1989.
- Mark Goddard left show business a few years after *Lost in Space* and became a high-school teacher in western Massachusetts.
- Bill Mumy, in the mid-1980s, collaborated with actor Miguel Ferrer (of *Twin Peaks*) on Marvel Comics' *Comet Man* series of books.
- Among the familiar TV faces encountered in outer space by the Robinsons were John Carradine, Daniel J. Travanti, Warren Oates, Michael Ansara, Kurt Russell, Wally Cox, Werner Klemperer, Al (Grandpa Munster) Lewis, and Ted ("Lurch") Cassidy.

MONSTERS

Syndicated, 1988–90, 52 episodes

Horror anthology series with no recurring characters

CREATORS: Richard P. Rubinstein, Mitchell Galin
EXECUTIVE PRODUCER: Richard P. Rubinstein
PRODUCERS: Anthony Santa Croce, Erica Fox

The creepy-crawlies

Monsters, a blend of realism and mysticism, suspense and dry humor, was produced by the same people who had previously created *Tales From the Darkside* (see separate entry) to which it bore a strong resemblance. The thirty-minute show was filmed on an accelerated schedule on both coasts: fifteen episodes of the first season in New York at the Astoria Studios and nine at the Hollywood Stages Studios in Los Angeles.

Most of the well-produced and frequently irreverent shows in this anthology series provided a good scare, like those old midnight terror tales on radio. The monsters were wonderfully gross and delightfully gruesome, thanks mainly to noted special effects makeup consultant, Dick Smith. The often gory stories themselves, with actors such as David McCallum, Adrienne Barbeau, Linda Blair, Robert Lansing, Tempestt Bledsoe, and Meatloaf, crawled with ghouls, zombies, aliens, witches, werewolves, vampires, prehistoric creatures, and assorted weirdos and eccentrics.

In the episode called "All in a Day's Work," Adrienne Barbeau plays a white magic witch—divorced and living with a young son—making a reasonable go of it tossing together love potions and other "small magic" stuff. The big time comes when, at the behest of a visitor who's being trailed by his own double, she conjures up a demon from the lower depths to help banish the Doppelganger, and then finds she doesn't know how to get rid of the creature. "One Wolf's Family" revolves around a young woman who brings her boyfriend home to meet her werewolf folks (played by Jerry Stiller and Anne Meara).

Wry tales like these and other visual equivalents of those in which radio specialized in the 1930s and 1940s made *Monsters* a particular favorite among horror aficionados.

VIDEO AVAILABILITY

Several two-episode *Monsters* cassettes, each running about forty-five minutes, are available at certain video outlets.

TRIVIA TIDBITS

- The series was initially promoted with a wry campaign, as with a comic ad that noted: "Discover *Monsters* . . . because there's more than just dust bunnies under your bed."
- The show's music was composed by Barry Ennis.

ONE STEP BEYOND

ABC, 1959–61, 94 episodes

HOST AND DIRECTOR: John Newland
CREATOR: Merwin Girard
EXECUTIVE PRODUCER: Larry Marcus
WRITERS: Merwin Gerard, Larry Marcus, Collier Young, Francis Cockrell, Don M. Mankiewicz, Catherine Turney, Charles Beaumont, Gabrielle Upton, Paul David, Martin Benson

Assorted bumps in the night

One of the premier occult shows of its time—it initially aired as *Alcoa Presents* but will always be remembered under its syndication title of *One Step Beyond*—this series of dramatizations was based on strange or unexplainable true events. Host and director John Newland was the one thread woven through all ninety-four episodes of supposed case histories of supernatural phenomena, which included confrontations with ghosts and various aspects of ESP, both frequent themes. The black-and-white photography added to the moody texture of the whole affair, which ran initially from the beginning of January 1959 through the Fourth of July 1961.

Many of the top names in episodic television acted in the Tuesday night ten-o'clock staple. Pernell Roberts and Bruce Gordon (before becoming Adam Cartwright on *Bonanza* and Frank Nitti on *The Untouchables*, respectively) co-starred in the particularly eerie tale called "The Vision": Elizabeth Montgomery was the star of "The Death Waltz"; and Joan Fontaine, "The Visitor." Others featured Christopher Lee as an officer acquitted of a murder he insisted he committed in "The Sorcerer"; Charles Bronson is a spectral boxing story, "The Last Round"; and Albert Salmi in the notable two-part "Peter Hurkos Story," about a man with ESP who uses his gift to help the police.

More than fifteen years after the series left the air, John Newland, in his dual capacity as on-camera host and director, teamed again with producer Merwin Gerard and writer Collier Young to revive the show in syndication, this time in color. It was called *The Next Step Beyond,* but it was unable to recapture its old audience or attract enough of a new one, and disappeared after only a few months of the 1978 season.

VIDEO AVAILABILITY

At the time of this writing, this title had been withdrawn from availability.

TRIVIA TIDBITS

- John Newland, one of the significant figures from network television's earliest days, was among the regulars in the medium's first soap opera, *One Man's Family,* and was part of the repertory company and director of both *The Loretta Young Theater* (1954–61) and *Thriller* (see separate entry).
- As director of every episode of *One Step Beyond* and its later companion *The Next Step Beyond,* Newland, now nearly eighty, remains a unique craftsman in television.

THE OUTER LIMITS

ABC, 1963–65, 49 episodes

CAST

Control voice	Vic Perrin

CREATOR/EXECUTIVE PRODUCER: Leslie Stevens
PRODUCER: Joseph Stefano, Ben Brady
DIRECTORS: Leslie Stevens, Byron Haskin, Laslo Benedek, James Goldstone, Leonard Horn, Gerd Oswald, Paul Stanley, Abner Biberman, John Erman, John Brahm, Alan Crosland, Charles Haas, Felix Feist
WRITERS: Leslie Stevens, Meyer Dolinsky, Allan Balter, Joseph Stefano, Dean Riesner, Anthony Lawrence, William Bast, Robert Specht, Harlan Ellison, Dan Ullman, John Mantley, Seeleg Lester

"We are controlling transmission . . ."

One of the most memorable sci-fi anthology series of all time, *The Outer Limits* had no recurring characters—except for unseen narrator Vic Perrin. Each week the show presented one new monster and/or alien being and, within the limits of its early 1960s budget, some rather incredible special effects and makeup work. Like *The Twilight Zone* and others of that ilk, *The Outer Limits* offered some fascinating weekly excursions in science fiction and the otherwise bizarre with an ensemble of top acting talent, exceptional writing (by such science fiction masters as Harlan Ellison), and black-and-white film noir–style camerawork.

In the premiere episode, "The Galaxy Being," written and directed by creator Leslie Stevens, Cliff Robertson

A creature from "The Chameleon" episode of *The Outer Limits*. Robert Duvall (not pictured) was featured as an intelligence agent in the episode. COURTESY OF PERSONALITY PHOTOS, INC.

is a radio engineer experimenting with a 3-D television receiver when he tunes in a being from another planet. In "The Chameleon," Robert Duvall turns up as an intelligence agent who disguises himself to infiltrate a gaggle of intergalactic creatures. In one famous episode, "I Robot"—a reworking of the Frankenstein premise—a humanoid is put on trial for murdering its creator.

In "The Inheritors," the show's only two-parter, four men wounded in Vietnam by bullets made from the ore of a meteorite have each developed a kind of "second brain" that boosted their IQs to genius level and linked their consciousness together to form a "group mind." Starring were Robert Duvall, James Shigeta, Ivan Dixon, and Steve Ihnat. Other stars appearing during the show's run were Martin Sheen, William Shatner, Leonard Nimoy (twice), Robert Culp (three times), Martin Landau, and Shirley Knight.

The initial season of the show offered some of television's eeriest, most creative moments. The quality dropped in the second season with the mass departure of the original innovative team. The network made the suicidal decision to reposition the series from Mondays to Saturdays opposite the powerhouse *Jackie Gleason Show,* and the Gothic ambiance gave way to more conventional science fiction fare. The ratings fell and *The Outer Limits* was out only halfway through season two. There was a resurrection, however, three decades later, with a Canadian-produced, somewhat gory new version on Showtime, which was then edited for syndication.

With its distinctive opening warning from a disembodied voice, "There is nothing wrong with your television set. Do not attempt to adjust the picture. We are controlling transmission," *The Outer Limits* continues casting a spell on Generation X audiences as it did on their parents in the 1960s.

VIDEO AVAILABILITY

All episodes, including a two-parter, and "The Sand Kings," pilot to the new series, are available at certain video outlets. They run about fifty-one minutes each. (The two-parter and "The Sand Kings" are approximately 100 minutes each.)

TRIVIA TIDBITS

- Leslie Stevens wrote and produced the pilot episode and submitted the idea to ABC under the title *Please Stand By.* He later produced such shows as *McCloud, Buck Rogers in the 25th Century,* and *Battlestar Galactica.* He also wrote the occult-theme *Incubus* (1966), which has the distinction of being the only film spoken entirely in Esperanto.
- Joseph Stefano, the initial series producer and a frequent writer, was the screenwriter of Hitchcock's *Psycho.*
- Dominic Frontiere composed the eerie, futuristic music to *The Outer Limits.*

THE PRISONER

ATV, 1967–68 (Great Britain); CBS, 1968–69
(first American broadcast); 17 episodes

CAST

Number 6	Patrick McGoohan
Number 2	Guy Doleman, Eric Portman, Peter Wyngarde, Mary Morris, Leo McKern, Anton Rodgers, Derren Nesbit, John Sharpe, Colin Gordon, Patrick Cargill, Clifford Evans

CREATOR/EXECUTIVE PRODUCER: Patrick McGoohan
PRODUER: David Tomblin
DIRECTORS: Don Chaffey, Pat Jackson, Peter Graham Scott, Joseph Serf (a pseudonym Patrick McGoohan sometimes used in the credits), Robert Asher, David Tomblin, Patrick McGoohan
WRITERS: George Markstein, David Tomblin, Vincent Tilsley, Anthony Skene, Paddy Fritz, Terrence Feely, Joshua Adam, Michael Cramoy, Gerald Kelsey, Roger Parkes, Roger Woodis, Patrick McGoohan

Crème de la spy genre crème

The Prisoner, the enigmatic, thought-provoking British-made series, centers on a fiercely independent onetime intelligence agent, who finds himself kidnapped and trapped for unknown reasons in the Village—an idyllic, mysterious Kafkaesque community where people are referred to only by number. All attempts to escape are thwarted by a giant malevolent sphere called Rover.

It's a mad mad mad mad world: Patrick McGoohan as Number Six on *The Prisoner.* This Kafkaesque British series has cult followings on both sides of the Atlantic. COURTESY OF PERSONALITY PHOTOS, INC.

Number 6, as the Prisoner's come to be known (believed by many to be John Drake, the character star Patrick McGoohan played previously on *Danger Man/Secret Agent*), spent much of his time trying to flee the village or at least discover the identity of Number 1, the person believed to run the Village. In one episode, "Free for All," Number 2 suggests that the Prisoner run in the Village elections, but, forced to undergo "The Test" by an electronic machine, the Prisoner emerges brainwashed, and, though he finally wins the election, he finds himself totally impotent. In another, "Once Upon a Time" (written and directed by McGoohan), the Prisoner is challenged by Number 2 to a grueling week-long interrogation that only one of them can survive.

Originally, *The Prisoner* was to have been a seven-part miniseries. However, while it was being produced, TV mogul Lord Lew Grade asked McGoohan to expand it to a full twenty-six-episode series—the better to sell it to the U.S. market. But the original production crew had other commitments and left after the thirteenth episode. McGoohan cobbled together a replacement crew and managed to turn out four more shows, however.

As the series ended, in the episode "Fall Out," Number 6 finally earned the right not to be called by a number—and in effect found out that *he* was Number 1.

The symbolic show, born during the cinematic spy boom of the 1960s, remains a powerful if paranoid vision of modern society, attacking conformity, technology, and the power of government.

The great 17:

1. "The Arrival"
2. "The Chimes of Big Ben"
3. "A, B & C"
4. "Free for All"
5. "The Schizoid Man"
6. "The General"
7. "Many Happy Returns"
8. "Dance of the Dead"
9. "Do Not Forsake Me, Oh My Darling"
10. "It's Your Funeral"
11. "Checkmate"
12. "Living in Harmony" (not shown in U.S. first run, but in syndication)
13. "A Change of Mind"
14. "Hammer Into Anvil"
15. "The Girl Who Was Death"
16. "Once Upon a Time" (written and directed by McGoohan)
17. "Fall Out" (written and directed by McGoohan)

Patrick McGoohan has never been able to move away from *The Prisoner,* despite his acting and directing on other shows through the years. In 1996, McGoohan was persuaded to become part of a big-screen version of the series in some capacity other than star.

VIDEO AVAILABILITY

The entire series is available on individual tapes, each running about fifty minutes, at certain video outlets. In addition, there is the original, never-aired version of the second episode (see above) with different dialogue, re-shot scenes, a new musical score, and alternate closing credits. Also available is *The Prisoner Video Companion,* a behind-the-scenes look at the making of the show, featuring interviews with McGoohan.

TRIVIA TIDBITS

- *The Prisoner* was filmed in the Welsh village of Portmeirion, which has become a mecca for the show's army of fans.
- Colin Gordon played the milk-drinking Number 2 twice and Leo McKern three times.
- The only female Number 2 was Mary Morris (in "Dance of the Dead"). Actor Trevor Howard was scheduled to play the part, but illness forced a rewrite of the script and a replacement.
- The music for *The Prisoner* was composed by Ron Grainer.

QUANTUM LEAP

NBC, 1989–93, 95 episodes

CAST

Dr. Samuel Beckett	Scott Bakula
Albert Calavicci ("The Observer")	Dean Stockwell

CREATOR: Donald Bellisario

EXECUTIVE PRODUCERS: Donald Bellisario, Deborah Pratt, Michael Zinberg

DIRECTORS: James Whitmore Jr., David Hemmings, Gilbert Shilton, Aaron Lipstadt, Virgil Vogel, Joe Napolitano, Mike Vejar, Ivan Dixon, Alan J. Levi, Harvey Laidman, Michael Switzer, Chris Hibler, Michael Zinberg, John Cullum, Michael Watkins, Debbie Allen

WRITERS: Donald Bellisario, Deborah Pratt, Tommy Thompson, Scott Shepherd, Chris Ruppenthal, Richard C. Oakie

A small leap for mankind, a big leap for Sam Beckett

Quantum Leap remains one of the most innovative latter-day time travel shows, chronicling the adventures—sometimes dramatic, sometimes lighthearted—of physicist Sam Beckett, a victim of an experiment gone awry. With his one recurring pal, Al, a wry former astronaut who appears to him only as a hologram, Sam jumps backward and forward through time and "leaps" into bodies (young and old, male and female) of people—even animals—in need of help. His part in a particular situation was determined by a sarcastic computer named Ziggy, who communicated through Al. Al, however, never

Various "leaps" of Dr. Samuel Beckett (Scott Bakula) on *Quantum Leap.* Beckett didn't simply enter other time periods, he entered the bodies of various individuals in order to help them resolve situations. While the audience saw the same actor, the other characters saw him as the individuals whose bodies he entered. COURTESY OF PERSONALITY PHOTOS, INC.

seemed able to give Sam all the information he needed other than sketchy details of his new identities, and Sam was forced to improvise his way through each one.

Sam leaped only within his own life span and could change events only to a degree. Ordinary people's lives could be altered, but history couldn't; to the viewer, Sam appeared as himself no matter whose body he was occupying—even if he was a teenage girl or a dog—but to those around him he was that person. In one episode, Scott Bakula/Sam Beckett finds himself as a bouncer in a Texas strip joint, helping one of the dancers (Julie Brown, one of the show's rare "name" guests) kidnap her baby. In another, he's leaped in as the third singer in a 1960s black girl group. And in a third, he tries to prevent Marilyn Monroe from killing herself. Other "leaps" include: into the star of *Man of La Mancha* on tour, at which point he realizes he doesn't know a single line, let alone the score; into the body of a high-heeled beauty contest hopeful; into the body of a male stripper in a skimpy Zorro outfit; into the body of a female rape victim; into the body of Dr. Ruth Westheimer, the diminutive sex therapist; into the body of a black medical student involved with a white woman; and into the body of a man trapped on a deserted island with Brooke Shields.

There were two other "leaps" that count among the most intriguing: Sam becoming Lee Harvey Oswald on November 22, 1963, with his finger on the trigger at the Dallas Book Depository; and, in a multipart show, aired months apart, trying to change his own family history by going to Vietnam in a frantic attempt to save his older brother one day before the latter is killed by the Viet Cong.

At the end of each show, Sam would learn from bemused Al the outcome of his leap and he would prepare for what the show's producers described as his next "kiss with history."

VIDEO AVAILABILITY

Many episodes of *Quantum Leap* are available on cassette at certain video outlets. The pilot episode runs about ninety-three minutes; the others, about forty-eight minutes.

EMMY AWARDS

1989–90 **Michael Watkins,** Outstanding Cinematography: "Pool Hall Blues" episode

1990–91 **Michael Watkins,** Outstanding Cinematography: "The Leap Home—Part 2, Vietnam, April 7, 1979" episode

TRIVIA TIDBITS

- Donald Bellisario previously created *Airwolf* and *Magnum, P.I.*
- *Quantum Leap* was Emmy nominated as Outstanding Drama Series for the first three of its four seasons.
- Scott Bakula and Dean Stockwell were nominated for an Emmy as Outstanding Actor in a Drama Series and Outstanding Supporting Actor in a Drama Series, respectively, for each of the series' four years.

ROCKY JONES, SPACE RANGER

Syndicated, 1954–55, 39 episodes

CAST

Rocky Jones	Richard Crane
Verna Ray	Sally Mansfield
Winky	Scotty Beckett
	Bill Lechner
Biffen Cardoza	James Lydon
Bobby	Robert Lyden
Yarra	Dian Fauntelle
Professor Newton	Maurice Cass
Professor Mayberry	Reginald Sheffield
Secretary Drake	Charles Meredith
Juliandra	Ann Robinson

CREATOR AND PRODUCER: Roland Reed
DIRECTOR: Hollingsworth Morse, William Beaudine

Good guy in space

The thirty-minute Saturday morning exploits of Rocky Jones, a twenty-first century space ranger who commanded a spaceship called *The Orbit Jet* and vied with interplanetary evil and interstellar pirates to protect the planets of a united solar system, differed from most of the early 1950s sci-fi shows in that it was produced on film rather than live. In addition, they were generally done in the form of movie serials, telescoped to three parts (later edited into individual features).

Richard Crane, a handsome, cleft-jawed B-actor who had some movie leads in the 1940s, played Rocky Jones in the image of a space-age scout leader in a T-shirt and baseball cap. Rocky's flight pals: Verna Ray, his navigator; Winky, his copilot; and Bobby, a ranger in training. The crew was under the command of Secretary Drake, head of the Space Rangers who worked for United Worlds, and had the services of Professor Newton, a scientist with a knack for designing lifesaving inventions to order.

Although aimed at young audiences, the series incorporated as subtext some strong antiwar sentiments, camouflaged pleas for disarmament during an era of atomic weapons buildups, and warnings about the hazards of nuclear contamination. The last is in evidence in the episode "The Forbidden Moon," when Rock and friends endeavor to save the queen of Medina, who has become a radiation victim.

Like *Rod Brown of the Rocket Rangers,* a live 1953 network show to which it always has been compared (the CBS series produced by William Dozier featured soon-to-be-stars Cliff Robertson and sidekick Jack Weston and such creative talent as young John Frankenheimer), and, like *Tom Corbett: Space Cadet*—another series of the same general time period (it ran at one time or another on ABC, NBC, CBS, and Dumont)—*Rocky Jones, Space Ranger* had a stalwart hero zipping around the galaxy with his steadfast crew in a craft that for its time seemed rather sophisticated. By later standards, it looks like a crude, patchwork affair with blinking lights and assorted dials on the control panels, and none too sturdy sets. What Rocky Jones had over its competition: It was filmed and could be preserved. It also exploited a merchandising boom, which included a popular 45 rpm record on Columbia called "Rocky Jones and the Space Pirates," sung by "Rocky Jones," as well as comic books, clothes, toys, novelties, and Rocky Jones pins resembling presidential campaign buttons. These today are collectors' treasures, recalling a nostalgic series from America's early romance with space.

VIDEO AVAILABILITY

Neary a dozen tapes of the show, each with three episode making a complete story running about seventy-nine minutes, are available at certain video outlets.

TRIVIA TIDBITS

- Although the series didn't premiere until January 20, 1954, it actually was made two years earlier.
- James Lydon, who played a ranger from the planet Herculon, will always be remembered as Henry Aldrich in the 1940s films.
- The *Rocky Jones* comic book was on the stands two years before the show's first airdate, and nearly two dozen other manufacturers were marketing products as it went into production in early 1952.

SPACE: 1999

Syndicated, 1975–77 (first American broadcast), 48 episodes

CAST

Cmdr. John Koenig	Martin Landau
Dr. Helena Russell	Barbara Bain
Maya (second season)	Catherine Schell
Prof. Victor Bergman (first season)	Barry Morse
Tony Verdeschi (second season)	Tony Anholt
Capt. Alan Carter	Nick Tate
David Kano (first season)	Clifton James
Sandra Benes	Zienia Merton
Yasko	Yasuko Megazumi
Paul Morrow (first season)	Prentis Hancock
Dr. Bob Mathias	Anton Phillips
Dr. Ben Vincent	Jeffrey Kisson
Commissioner Simmonds	Roy Dotrice

CREATORS: Gerry & Sylvia Anderson
EXECUTIVE PRODUCER: Gerry Anderson
PRODUCERS: Sylvia Anderson, F. Sherwin Greene, Fred Freiberger
DIRECTORS: Val Guest, Kevin Connor, Charles Crichton, Peter Medak, Ray Austin, Lee H. Katzin, Robert Lynn, Tom Clegg, David Tomblin
WRITERS: George Bellak, Christopher Penfold, Anthony Terpoloff, Tony Barwick, Edward Di Lorenzo, Johnny Byrne, Charles Woodgrove

To the galaxy! To the ramparts!

Space: 1999 reworked Gerry & Sylvia Anderson's *UFO* (see separate entry) with a massive budget—at around

$300,000 per episode, it was one of television's most expensive shows of its time. This hour-long British-made intergalactic fantasy, costarring the formerly married American actors Martin Landau and Barbara Bain, was set primarily on Moonbase Alpha, a lunar research colony on the moon, the dark side of which man has been using as a nuclear waste dump. Stolid John Koenig was in command of a mission to oversee the launch of a deep-space probe, with Helena Russell (who also narrated) serving as the base's chief medical officer and Professor Bergman as the scientific officer. Koenig's ship was, in effect, the moon itself, and, when a massive nuclear explosion causes it to be sent out of its orbit and careening into space, Koenig and the 310 colonists find themselves shooting between galaxies.

The marooned earthlings, considered invaders by the inhabitants of other planets, struggled to combat the life-forms of distant worlds—ranging from blobs of living foam and gigantic carnivorous squids to sexy robots (as in *Star Trek*) developed by advanced civilizations and all manner of futuristic hardware, both animate and inanimate. The popularity of the series in Great Britain was such that guests of the caliber of Christopher Lee, Peter Cushing, Margaret Leighton, Joan Collins, Leo McKern, and Ian McShane wanted to be part of it. In "Collision Course," Leighton was the fearsome queen of the huge planet Astheria; in "The Missing Link," Cushing played his incomparable mad scientist in space.

The series itself became a visual, if painfully slow-paced, showcase, but many of the plots were criticized for their scientific inaccuracy. Isaac Asimov, for one, reportedly admonished the show for being scientifically preposterous. He noted that neither the moon nor Earth could survive an explosion of the magnitude required to send Earth's only satellite on a wild junket into space, and even if the moon were to survive this first catastrophe, it would take lifetimes for it to run into another inhabited planet. Since the Alphans are on an accidental course, it would take even longer. *Space: 1999* simply had abandoned science—although, of course, this was supposed to be simple entertainment. As one writer put it succinctly: *Space: 1999* became Cancelled: 1977.

VIDEO AVAILABILITY

A number of volumes of this cult sci-fi series, each running about sixty minutes, are available at certain tape outlets as well as through Columbia House.

TRIVIA TIDBITS

- The special effects were created by Brian Johnson, one of the designers for Kubrick's *2001: A Space Odyssey.*
- Martin Landau and Barbara Bain worked together previously on *Mission: Impossible* as well as on a *Gilligan's Island* TV movie.
- Barry Morse was the erstwhile Lieutenant Gerard pursuing David Janssen in *The Fugitive;* Roy Dotrice would later play Father on TV's *Beauty and the Beast* series.
- Barry Gray, Vic Elms, and Derek Wadsworth shared duties providing the music for the show.

SPACE PATROL

ABC, 1950–54 (15 minutes daily), 900+ episodes;
1950–55 (30 minutes weekly), 210 episodes

CAST

Commander Buzz Corry	Ed Kemmer
Cadet Happy	Lyn Osborn
Carol Karlyle	Virginia Hewitt
Mr. Karlyle	Norman Jolley
Colonel Henderson	Paul Cavanaugh
Tonga	Nina Bara
Dr. Von Meter	Rudolph Anders
Maj. Robbie Robertson	Ken Mayer
Kitt Corry	Glen Denning
Evil Prince Bacarrati	Bela Kovacs

CREATOR: Mike Moser
PRODUCER AND DIRECTOR: Dick Darley
ASSOCIATE PRODUCER: Bela Kovacs
WRITERS: Lou Spence, Norman Jolley, Lou Houston, Mike Moser

"High adventure in the wild reaches of space . . ."

This durable, pioneering TV space show (more than 1,100 episodes in fifteen- and thirty-minute form combined) followed the exploits of Commander Buzz Corry and his colleagues in the *Space Patrol* in the city of Terra, a twenty-first century Earth-based organization responsible for the safety of the United Planets: Earth, Mars, Venus, Jupiter, and Merury. *Space Patrol* is believed to be television's first Saturday morning West Coast production broadcast live across the country.

The program itself was from the acting-from-the-seat-of-your-pants school, with performers reading their lines scrawled on the walls of the set. The show had in its star Ed Kemmer a real-life air hero playing the fictional space jockey. Kemmer had been a pilot who was shot down over Germany during World War II and used his time in a POW camp to study acting.

Buzz Corry went on missions tracking aliens, intergalactic bad guys, even shrinking cities, with his sidekick Cadet Happy, who was fond of exclaiming "Smokin' Rockets, Buzz!" Corry's love interest was blond Carol Karlyle, who happened to be the daughter of the Secretary General of the United Planets.

When *Space Patrol* was trimmed to one program a week by 1955, the budget skyrocketed—to $25,000. That went to pay for a cast of five to fifteen actors, two directors, five electricians, seven prop men, nine carpenters, a full technical crew, and the crack special-effects team of Oscar, Paul, and Franz Dallons. Ed Kemmer, the show's star, later admitted: "You can't believe the sponsors (Ralston Purina, Wheat and Rice Chex, and Nestle). They wanted us [Kemmer and costar Lyn Osborn] to eat their cereal and make Nestle's Quik right after a fight scene. We could be up in the rafters of the studio catwalk and have to rush down, sometimes with real blood on our faces from a hit that connected."

Space Patrol made its last trip on February 26, 1955.

VIDEO AVAILABILITY

Three volumes of *Space Patrol*, each running ninety minutes and containing three episodes, are available at certain video outlets, along with a feature-length episode running about seventy-eight minutes.

TRIVIA TIDBITS

- Corey's first spaceship was *Battle Cruiser 100*. His second starcruiser: *Terra IV*. His third: *Terra V*.

- *Space Patrol* was the first television series to present an episode in 3-D.
- Initially, the show was a live local one in Los Angeles in early 1950. At the time, Kitt Corry was the original leader of the Space Patrol.
- Ed Kemmer went on to a long career in television soap operas, such as *The Edge of Night* and *As the World Turns.*

STAR TREK

NBC, 1966–69, 79 episodes

CAST

Capt. James T. Kirk	William Shatner
Mr. Spock	Leonard Nimoy
Dr. Leonard "Bones" McCoy	DeForest Kelley
Lt. Uhura	Nichelle Nichols
Lt. Sulu	George Takei
Engineer Montgomery "Scotty" Scott	James Doohan
Nurse Christine Chapel	Majel Barrett
Ensign Pavel Chekov (1967–69)	Walter Koenig
Yeoman Janice Rand (1966–67)	Grace Lee Whitney

CREATOR AND EXECUTIVE PRODUCER: Gene Roddenberry

PRODUCERS: Gene Roddenberry, Gene L. Coon, John Meredyth Lucas, Fred Freiberger, Robert H. Justman

DIRECTORS: Marc Daniels, Lawrence Dobkin, James Goldstone, Leo Penn, Harvey Hart, Vincent McEveety, Gerd Oswald, Marvin Chomsky, John Erman, Joseph Pevney, Ralph Senensky, John Newland

WRITERS: D. C. Fontana, Robert Bloch, Richard Matheson, Gene Roddenberry, Adrian Spies, John Meredyth Lucas, Shimon Wincelberg, Gene L. Coon, Paul Schneider, Theodore Sturgeon, Harlan Ellison

Beam me up, Scotty

The most significant "space show" in television history, *Star Trek* was not an overwhelming success during its initial three-season run on NBC, reaching a peak rating of only 52. This was hardly a sign of what would develop over the next three decades, as the show would spawn

Star Trek: The legendary crew of the starship *Enterprise.* Seventy-nine episodes, four TV spin-offs (including a cartoon version), and seven feature films make this show the most successful of all shows to cross over from TV to film. From left: James Doohan (Scotty), Walter Koenig (Chekov), DeForest Kelley (Dr. McCoy), Majel Barrett (Nurse Chapel), William Shatner (Captain Kirk), Nichelle Nichols (Uhura), George Takei (Sulu), and Leonard Nimoy (bottom, Mr. Spock). COURTESY OF PERSONALITY PHOTOS, INC.

seven hugely successful theatrical films and four belated spin-off series (including an animated cartoon version), all of which would have longer runs than the original. In later syndication, however, *Star Trek* and its late 1980s successor *Star Trek: The Next Generation* (see separate entry) have become two of the most popular and lucrative properties in all of entertainment, according to *Variety.*

Although the first episode of the series, called "The Cage," was filmed in late 1964 (with Jeffrey Hunter as Captain Christopher Pike), it did not originally air. Later it was retooled and incorporated into the two-part "The Menagerie" (episode #11–12). It would not be until September 8, 1966 Earth time when the crew, now with William Shatner as James T. Kirk in command, would—in the episode "The Man Trap"—first go boldly where no man (in the films, "one") has gone before. (Actually, "Where No Man Has Gone Before" was the title of episode #3, filmed in early summer 1965.) The series itself and the crew we have come to know did not take shape until then.

The *Enterprise*'s crew has become etched in the minds and hearts of millions of "Trekkies" internationally: the soldier/warrior Captain Kirk; the pointy-eared Mr. Spock, the ship's half-Vulcan science officer, obsessed with logic and disdainful of human emotion; sarcastic (and often plain crabby) Bones McCoy, the chief medical officer; Scotty, the worrywart chief engineer; Uhura, the beautiful communications officer; Sulu, the Japanese navigator who dreams of being a swashbuckler; Pavel Chekov, the Rusian helmsman who came aboard during the second season; lovesick for Mr. Spock Nurse Christine Chapel; and, in the first season, Yeoman Rand. These able officers and their Spaceship *Enterprise* ("the finest vessel in the fleet") cruised at warp speed in all manner of intergalactic adventures in the name of the Federation Council and Starfleet Command. Along the way, they confronted several entities and alien races—bloodthirsty Klingons, telepathic Talosians, furry Tribbles, warring Romulans, an ancient space probe called Nomad, and even a serpentlike humanoid called a Gorn.

Star Trek dealt with a number of subjects. "Let Me Be Your Last Battlefield" (#70), for instance, focused on racial prejudice, with guest star Frank Gorshin as a half black/half white alien; a "Pattern of Force" (#50) concerned the resurrection of Nazi Germany. On the other hand, "The Trouble With Tribbles" (#44) was one of the more comically offbeat episodes, in which some furry little creatures multiply all over the *Enterprise*. The trouble with Tribbles, as the crew learns, is that they are born pregnant; all they do is eat and reproduce, and the more they eat, the faster they multiply—and the starship happens to be on a mission to transport a rare wheat grain, a Tribbles delicacy.

The show also featured a host of guest stars. In one classic episode (written by famed science fiction writer Harlan Ellison), "The City on the Edge of Forever" (#28), Kirk and Spock find themselves chasing McCoy through a time vortex back to Earth during the Roaring Twenties where they meet Joan Collins, as a self-appointed social reformer in a storefront mission. In another, "Space Seed" (episode #22), the show introduced Ricardo Montalban as Khan, a tyrannical leader of a rebel crew in suspended animation aboard a derelict spaceship when encountered by the *Enterprise.* Years later Montalban would reprise the role in *Star Trek II: The Wrath of Khan.* "Assignment: Earth" (#55), guest-starring Robert Lansing and Teri Garr, was an unsold pilot for a projected spin-off.

Wagon train to the stars

Gene Roddenberry, who had sold his concept to skeptical NBC as a "*Wagon Train* to the stars," strove to make *Star Trek*'s message hopeful, portraying man as frail and flawed but, most often, motivated by a vision of morality and nobility. He wanted Kirk and colleagues to seek not coercion but cooperation among races—not domination but equality. Although the show never won an Emmy, it did receive nine nominations during its relatively brief network stay, including Outstanding Dramatic Series (1966–67 and 1967–68), losing both times to *Mission: Impossible.* Leonard Nimoy was nominated three times for Outstanding Supporting Actor in a Drama (1966–67, 1967–68, and 1968–69).

Star Trek has established a permanent place in our pop culture. Not only is a model of the *Enterprise* on display at the Smithsonian Institution in Washington, but there is also a permanent *Star Trek* exhibit at the National Air and Space Museum. How many other television series have been so honored?

VIDEO AVAILABILITY

The original tape voyages of the Starship Enterprise, 79 in all, are available at certain video outlets (each running about fifty minutes) and through Columbia House (two episodes per cassette). Also available: the never-aired original *Star Trek* pilot, running about seventy-three minutes, and the 1991 *Star Trek 25th Anniversary Special,* featuring interviews and reminiscences with all the original members and creator Gene Roddenberry. It runs about 100 minutes.

TRIVIA TIDBITS

- The show's creator Gene Roddenberry, labeled by *Variety* "American mythmaker," died in October 1991, shortly before the *Star Trek 25th Anniversary Special* aired. His ashes were shot into outer space by NASA.
- The popularity of the show had grown to such a point that in 1976, the first U.S. space shuttle was renamed the *Enterprise* after NASA reportedly received nearly 400,000 requests.
- Majel Barrett, who played Nurse Christine Chapel in the original series and appeared as a different character on *Star Trek: The Next Generation,* was Mrs. Gene Roddenberry in real life. She also supplied the voice of the ship's computer.
- William Shatner, James Doohan, and Walter Koenig were the only *Enterprise* crew members to appear in all seven feature films. Shatner directed *Star Trek V: The Final Frontier* (1989) and shares story writing credit. Leonard Nimoy directed both *Star Trek III: The Search for Spock* (1984) and *Star Trek IV: The Voyage Home* (1986).
- The animated cartoon version of *Star Trek,* with all of the original stars doing the voices of their characters,

Captain James T. Kirk (William Shatner, left) and First Officer Mr. Spock (Leonard Nimoy) in a characteristic pose in front of the shuttlecraft. Despite *Star Trek*'s incredible later popularity, it never earned an Emmy or surpassed a rating of 52 during its initial run. COURTESY OF PERSONALITY PHOTOS, INC.

aired on NBC on Saturday mornings from 1974 to 1975 (twenty-two episodes).

- As with many other TV personalities of the time, Leonard Nimoy and William Shatner attempted recording careers. Among others, Nimoy cut a version of "Proud Mary" and Shatner did "Lucy in the Sky With Diamonds." Rhino Records' *Golden Throats* CD series has made some of their tracks available again.
- William Shatner, author, has had a number of best-selling sci-fi books under the overall title *Tek War.* Sev-

eral of these have been turned into syndicated made-for-TV movies and a series (eighteen episodes) in the mid-1990s, with Shatner as executive producer and occasional performer. He recently published a *Star Trek* novel bringing Kirk back to life.

- Alexander Courage wrote the *Star Trek*'s famous identifying theme music. Other film/TV composers who did individual episodes: Fred Steiner, Sol Kaplan, Gerald Fried, George Duning, and Jerry Fielding.
- Mark Lenard, who has become identified in the role of Sarek, Spock's father, played a Romulan in an earlier episode of the show.

STAR TREK: THE NEXT GENERATION

Syndicated, 1987–94, 178 episodes

CAST

Capt. Jean-Luc Picard	Patrick Stewart
Cmdr. William Riker	Jonathan Frakes
Lt. Geordi La Forge	LeVar Burton
Lt. Tasha Yar (1987–88)	Denise Crosby
Lt. Worf	Michael Dorn
Dr. Beverly Crusher	Gates McFadden
Counselor Deanna Troi	Marina Sirtis
Lt. Cmdr. Data	Brent Spiner
Ensign Wesley "Wes" Crusher (1987–93)	Wil Wheaton
Transorter Chief Miles O'Brien (1988–89)	Colm Meaney
Dr. Katherine "Kate" Pulaski (1988–89)	Diana Muldaur
Guinan (1988–93)	Whoopi Goldberg
Keiko O'Brien (1991–93)	Rosalind Chao
Alexander Roshenko (1992–94)	Brian Bonsell

CREATOR AND EXECUTIVE PRODUCER: Gene Roddenberry
CO-EXECUTIVE PRODUCERS: Maurice Hurley, Rick Berman, Michael Piller
PRODUCERS: Robert H. Justman, Burton Armus, Herbert Wright, Robert Lewin, John Mason, Mike Gray
DIRECTORS: Corey Allen, Rob Bowman, Cliff Bole
WRITERS: Gene Roddenberry, D. C. Fontana, Michael Piller, Maurice Hurley

Another voyage beyond the stars

Moving boldly back to television eighteen years after the original *Star Trek* (see separate entry) had left prime-

Captain Picard (Patrick Stewart, right) guides young prodigy Wesley Crusher (Wil Wheaton) in his training as Ensign. Crusher's mom (Gates McFadden), Dr. Beverly Crusher, looks on. When the show first began, Captain Picard had some difficulty adjusting to children on board the *Enterprise.* COURTESY OF PERSONALITY PHOTOS, INC.

time television, *Star Trek: The Next Generation,* set near the beginning of the twenty-fourth century, sent a revamped *Enterprise* with a fresh young crew on a mission to explore all-new worlds and new civilizations. This *Enterprise* not only boasted a holodeck room and an ability to split in half but also had children on board.

The show moves forward approximately eighty-five years after the journeys of Kirk, Spock, and the original Starfleet crew. Erudite, bald-pated Captain Jean-Luc Picard is now in charge; woman-chasing William Riker is the *Enterprise*'s new first officer; sightless Geordi La Forge, who "sees" by the use of a magical VISOR (Visual Input Sensory Optical Reflector) over his eyes, is engineer; Worf, the only Klingon aboard, was raised by Russian parents and is weapons officer; Data is a yellow-eyed android possessing superior strength and a phenomenal memory, but longs to be human; Wes Crusher is a brilliant teenage ensign, whose mom is the ship's chief medical officer; Deanna Troi, the half-human, half-Betazoid Starfleet counselor with a special form of telepathic ability; and Tasha Yar is the ship's security chief, who dies while on a mission. Occasionally turning up is Guinan (Whoopi Goldberg in a recurring role), the alien humanoid hostess of "Ten Forward," the *Enterprise*'s lounge. On hand for several episodes was an alien godlike being named Q—played to smug perfection by John de Lancie—who pops on and off the *Enterprise* at whim to judge Captain Picard and all of humankind while deciding whether the human race is fit to explore the galaxy.

The adventuresome, quite imaginative shows—complete with xenophobia-inspired monster aliens, interspecies beings, and the encyclopedic house android—along with dazzling special effects (light-years ahead of the original series), had the crew constantly endeavoring to make the universe safe. Their adventures were frequently harrowing experiences for the characters and tested their strength, courage, and morality. In one episode, Picard was abducted by the Borg, a hivelike race of zombie crusaders who share all their thoughts as one mind and seek to take over the universe. Picard is actually turned into one of the Borgs, and his knowledge is nearly used to completely destroy the Federation's fleet of ships.

And there was romance aboard the *Enterprise,* to say nothing of about 2,000 passengers. Dr. Crusher apparently had a soft spot for Picard and somewhere along the way married (and divorced) him—according to the final chapter in the saga.

Guest stars have included: Joe Piscopo, who came aboard the *Enterprise* in the episode "The Outrageous Okona" to teach poker-faced Data the art of being funny; John Tesh, as a Klingon warrior in "The Icarus Factor"; and legendary rocker and longtime "Trekkie" Mick Fleetwood, as an alien in "Manhunt." Majel Barrett (Mrs. Gene Roddenberry), who was Nurse Chapel in the original *Star Trek,* made several appearances as the flaky mother of Deanna Troi and continued to supply the ship's computer voice.

In 1993, *Star Trek: The Next Generation* subsequently begot the series *Star Trek: Deep Space Nine.* Two years later, *Star Trek: Voyager* was spawned—finally with a woman, actress Kate Mulgrew, at the helm. For a while the first two series overlapped on television, and currently the last two overlap.

VIDEO AVAILABILITY

Nearly fifty volumes of *Star Trek: The Next Generation,* each running about fifty minutes, along with the feature-length pilot, running about ninety-six minutes, are available at certain video outlets. The series is also available through Columbia House, with two one-hour episodes per tape.

EMMY AWARDS

1987–88 **William Ware Theiss,** Costume Design for a Series ("The Big Goodbye" episode)

Werner Keppler, Michael Westmore, and **Gerald Quist,** Achievement in Makeup for a Series ("Conspiracy" episode)

TRIVIA TIDBITS

- In addition to its several Emmy Awards, the series was awarded the George Foster Peabody Award, one of television's most prestigious, "for excellent, thought-provoking entertainment programming," for its first season. During its season, it received eight Emmy nominations in technical categories.
- DeForest Kelley put in a cameo appearance in the debut show, as the 137-year-old Dr. McCoy. Leonard Nimoy and James Doohan also made separate visits in their guises of Spock and Scotty. Mark Lenard, who played Sarek (Spock's father) in the original series, also appeared in *The Next Generation*. Kirk (William Shatner) and Picard starred together in the "crossover" film, *Star Trek Generations* (1994), with Scotty and Chekov (Walter Koenig) also turning up.
- Golden-tongued Patrick Stewart, from England's Royal Shakespeare Company, is known to American theatergoers for his one-man *A Christmas Carol,* with which he tours every holiday season and plays all the roles, and for *The Tempest* from 1996.
- Jonathan Frakes, who had directed several episodes of the show as well as *Deep Space Nine,* makes his big-screen directing debut with *Star Trek: First Contact,* the second of the "Next Generation" movies, which went into production in spring 1996.
- LeVar Burton first came to television right out of college to star as Kunta Kinte in *Roots* (see separate entry).
- This was the last series in which Gene Roddenberry had a direct hand. He died in October 1991. He had been selling scripts to countless television shows (such as *Dragnet, Naked City, Dr. Kildare,* etc.) since the 1950s, was head writer on *Have Gun—Will Travel* (see

separate entry), and creator of *The Lieutenant* with Gary Lockwood and Robert Vaughn in 1963.

- Between *Star Trek* and *Star Trek: The Next Generation* there have been more than 100 *Star Trek* novels published.

TALES FROM THE CRYPT

HBO, 1989– ; FOX, 1994–

Voice of Crypt Keeper John Kassir

EXECUTIVE PRODUCERS: Richard Donner, David Giller, Walter Hill, Joel Silver, Robert Zemeckis
PRODUCERS: William Teitler, Joel Silver, Richard Donner
DIRECTORS: Richard Donner, Walter Hill, Robert Zemeckis, Tom Holland, Howard Deutch, Randa Haines, Tobe Hooper, Arnold Schwarzenegger, Tom Hanks, Michael J. Fox, William Friedkin, John Frankenheimer, Joel Silver
WRITERS: Terry Black, Robert Reneau, Fred Dekker, Frank Darabont, Andy Wolk, Richard Matheson, Gilbert Adler, A. L. Katz, Harry Anderson

Voices and vices from the dead

Based on the William M. Gaines classic *Tales From the Crypt* comics of the 1940s and 1950s, this garish, ghoulish horror-humor anthology series attracted some of Hollywood's top talent, both in front of the camera and behind it. The cult thirty-minute show, filled with gore and gratuitous sex (at least in the HBO version), has as its host a talking skeleton with a frightful cackle, a gleeful sense of the macabre, and terrible puns. The Crypt Keeper (created by Kevin Yagher) generally offers a campy, fang-in-cheek introduction to each episode, which begins with a comic book page that comes to life.

The show was created by a passel of major big-screen producer-directors who indulged in short-form films of about 20–25 minutes. Richard Donner (of the *Superman* and *Lethal Weapon* films) directed the debut show called "Dig That Cat . . . He's Really Gone!"—about a mad scientist who implants the "nine lives" portion of a cat's brain into a seedy street bum. (The story was originally published in the *Crypt* comic books as "The Haunt of Fear.") A later show, "Korman's Kalamity," starred Harry Anderson (of *Night Court* and *Dave's World*) as a henpecked cartoonist who works for *Tales From the Crypt* comics and discovers he has a very special gift: His most macabre creature illustrations have a fiendish habit of coming to life and killing people. In "The Reluctant Vampire," a mild-mannered vampire (Malcolm McDowell) thinks he's found the perfect job, as a night security guard at a local blood bank, until a shortage of blood forces him to revert to old habits.

Today's top stars such as Tom Hanks, Kyle MacLachlan, Michael J. Fox, and Arnold Schwarzenegger cut their teeth as directors on the series. Schwarzenegger, for instance, directed "The Switch," in which a wealthy old man (William Hickey), in love with a beautiful young woman (Kelly Preston), switches his body with a hunk (Rick Rossovich), only to discover after spending all his money on surgery that the lady is out for the loot, not the looks.

Among those who clamored to act in these short films were Christopher Reeve, Demi Moore, Donald O'Connor, Priscilla Presley, Don Rickles, Adam West, Brooke Shields, Joe Pesci, and Bruce Boxleitner. Kirk Douglas even made a rare excursion into television acting, starring in Zemeckis's "Yellow" as a World War I martinet who is forced to court-martial his cowardly lieutenant son, played by his real son, Eric Douglas.

Generally blood flows freely, heads fall off, limbs are severed, and at least one female on each show takes off her shirt, but these lurid scenes were toned down when *Crypt* went into syndication. All of this is riotous to the Crypt Keeper in his weekly wrap-up of the deliciously grisly proceedings.

The HBO films of *Tales From the Crypt* changed their home base in 1996 to England, with primarily British actors and directors. Bob Hoskins directed and starred in the first of the new series, and others such as Natasha Richardson, Emma Samms, and Anthony Andrews appearing in the first few episodes.

An animated Saturday morning version of the show, *Tales From the Crypt Keeper,* aired on ABC beginning in late 1993, and the feature-length *Tales From the Crypt Presents Demon Knight,* based on the HBO *Crypt* series, turned up on the big screen in 1995. A second *Crypt* movie, *Bordello of Blood,* followed in summer 1996.

VIDEO AVAILABILITY

A number of *Tales From the Crypt* collections, three stories per tape, running about ninety minutes, are available at certain video outlets. In addition, there are several collections of the animated version, *Tales From the Crypt Keeper,* running forty-four minutes with two episodes on each tape.

TRIVIA TIDBITS

- The theme to the series was written by Danny Elfman, who scored such films as *Batman, Beetlejuice,* and *The Nightmare Before Christmas.*
- The 1972 feature *Tales From the Crypt,* with Ralph Richardson as the Crypt Keeper, was also inspired by E. C. Comics but was done as a straight horror anthology. Stephen King and George A. Romero paid tribute to E. C. Comics' grisly titles with their 1982 anthology movie *Creepshow.*

TALES FROM THE DARKSIDE

Syndicated, 1984–88, 92 episodes

Horror anthology series with no recurring actors

CREATED BY: George A. Romero
EXECUTIVE PRODUCERS: George A. Romero, Richard P. Rubinstein, Jerry Golod

Sojourns in the unexpected

George A. Romero, who had made his name with the 1968 low-budget classic *Night of the Living Dead,* was the mastermind of this stylish half-hour anthology of horror stories, many with endings of humor in irony—in the O. Henry manner. A feature film, consisting of four gruesome stories, was released in 1990, with a cast headed by Deborah Harry and Christian Slater. In its own way, creepy *Tales From the Darkside* (with several stories by Stephen King) resembled the more macabre episodes of *The Twilight Zone,* and, like the one (and newer) Rod Serling creation, it was cast with veteran actors (such as Darren McGavin, Peggy Cass, Eddie Bracken, Keenan Wynn, Danny Aiello, and Phyllis Diller, as well as contemporary TV stars such as Harry Anderson (of *Night Court* and later *Dave's World*) and Justine Bateman (of *Family Ties*).

Episodes using Romero's patented mix of slapstick and Grand Guignol include "If the Shoe Fits . . ." starring Dick Shawn as Beau Gumbs, a shameless, crafty politician and leading contender for the governor's mansion. "Politics is a game," he says. "It's got nothing to do with the issues. People want a good time, and I'm just the man to give it to 'em." And so he does, the politician-as-showman gradually but inevitably transforms into the circus clown he's always been—right down to the baggy pants, oversized shoes, and big red nose.

Another was "Grandma's Wish," in which a typical suburban family—Dad, Mom, mall-shopping daughter—decide it would be better for forgetful Grandma to be placed in a nursing home. They assure her she can have anything she wants during her final days with them, and she makes a silent wish. Suddenly, calamities befall her kin who become prisoners to their injuries; they learn what it's like to become forgetful and hard of hearing and what it means to grow old in a culture of the young.

Spooky *Tales From the Darkside* and its forays into fear and fright later begot a similar show, *Monsters* (see separate entry), concocted by the same creative team.

VIDEO AVAILABILITY

Six volumes of *Tales From the Darkside,* each running about 100 minutes and containing five varied episodes, are available at certain video outlets.

TRIVIA TIDBITS

◆ Creator Romero also coproduced the feature-length *Tales From the Darkside: The Movie* (1990), revolving around three fright-inducing stories (one by Romero, adapted from Stephen King) a teenage boy tells to Deborah Harry, who plays a suburban cannibal holding him captive and preparing to cook him.

THRILLER

NBC, 1960–62, 67 episodes

HOST: Boris Karloff
EXECUTIVE PRODUCER: Hubbell Robinson
PRODUCERS: Fletcher Markle, William Frye, Maxwell Shane
DIRECTORS: Fletcher Markle, Arthur Hiller, John Brahm, Laslo Benedek, Maxwell Shane, John Newland, Ray Milland, Ida Lupino, Paul Henreid, William Claxton, Ted Post, Richard Carlson
WRITERS: Robert Bloch, Barre Lyndon, Alan Caillou, Richard Matheson, Evelyn Beckman, Philip MacDonald, John Kneubuhl, Maxwell Shane

Tingling of the spine

Thriller lived up to its title. A black-and-white mystery/suspense anthology, hosted by the venerable Boris Karloff (who even starred in five or six shows in the series), *Thriller* told of people suddenly trapped in unexpected, sometimes terrifying, situations fostered through emotion, greed, or the threat of crime. This show developed into a class act—based on the pedigrees of the series' behind-the-camera talents.

The show, which mixed horror tales set in Gothic mansions laced with cobwebs and more ghoulish ones dealing with creatures from the dead, was packed with familiar names such as Elizabeth Montgomery, Richard Chamberlain, William Shatner, Marlo Thomas, an up-and-coming Mary Tyler Moore (twice), George Kennedy, Warren Oates, Beverly Garland, Leslie Nielsen, Mort Sahl, and Rip Torn. Karloff himself joined Patricia Medina and Sidney Blackmer in a version of Edgar Allan Poe's "The

Premature Burial," one of the most frightening episodes in the series. He also gave a tour-de-force performance in "The Last of the Summervilles," about a young couple trying to do away with their dotty and very rich old aunt.

Initially, the guiding lights behind *Thriller* were Hubbell Robinson, one of the great producing figures in television's formative years; Fletcher Markle, the innovative producer/director best remembered heretofore for *Suspense* on radio and TV; and story editor James P. Cavanaugh. When creative differences split the team, the production company brought in Maxwell Shane and William Frye to alternate as producers of the crime shows and horror ones, respectively. It was Frye who recruited short-story writer Robert Bloch, a Hitchcock regular (and author of *Psycho*), to help evoke the proper atmosphere, and he turned out a number of stories for the series—notably "Yours Truly, Jack the Ripper." Directed by actor Ray Milland and starring John Williams (the stiff upper lip British actor, not the American film composer or the classical guitarist), it told of a gentleman who believes a string of contemporary murders to have been committed by the original Ripper, who has maintained his youth by taking the lives of others.

With the demise of *Thriller,* this ilk of dark-sided anthology shows would fall exclusively into the hands of Rod Serling, whose *Twilight Zone,* in fact, was running concurrently with it.

VIDEO AVAILABILITY

A number of *Thriller* episodes, each running about fifty minutes, are available at certain video outlets.

TRIVIA TIDBITS

- Pete Rugolo wrote the original, somewhat incongruous jazz-tinged music to *Thriller.* Jerry Goldsmith then came up with the more subtle mood-enhancing theme and Morton Stevens the spine-chilling underscoring.

- The creative makeup on the shows was done primarily by Jack Barron, a veteran of Universal Pictures' monster makeup department.
- Several of the stories originated in the long-cherished *Weird Tales* magazine, which was a popular item in the 1930s and 1940s.

THE TWILIGHT ZONE

CBS, 1959–64, 156 episodes

HOST/NARRATOR: Rod Serling
CREATOR/EXECUTIVE PRODUCER: Rod Serling
PRODUCERS: Buck Houghton, William Froug, Herbert Hirschman
PRINCIPAL DIRECTORS: Robert Stevens, John Brahm, Lamont Johnson, Montgomery Pittman, Allen Reisner, Mitchell Leisen, Ida Lupino, Buzz Kulik, Boris Sagal, John Rich, Jack Smight, Douglas Heyes, Richard Donner
PRINCIPAL WRITERS: Rod Serling, Charles Beaumont, Richard Matheson, E. Jack Neuman, George Clayton Johnson, Earl Hamner Jr., Anthony Wilson

Many dimensions

"You're traveling through another dimension, a dimension not only of sight and sound but of mind . . ." So intones Rod Serling as an introduction to the classic sci-fi series *The Twilight Zone,* but, more than any other opener, these words epitomize the unique appeal of this influential program.

When Rod Serling began toying with the idea of a science fiction/fantasy anthology series, he had already established himself as a power to contend with in the television industry. Those who identify Serling solely with *Zone* may be surprised to learn that by 1959 he was already one of the most respected and well-known writers in the medium, with such widely praised original dramas as *Requiem for a Heavyweight* and *Patterns* to his credit. The premiere of a new Serling drama for such live anthology showcases as *Playhouse 90* was an event, and his

Cliff Robertson and Edy Williams star with a wooden pal in *The Twilight Zone* episode "The Dummy." COURTESY OF PERSONALITY PHOTOS, INC.

work was often compared to that of Arthur Miller and Tennessee Williams.

When Serling chose to abandon live special-event television to devote his time and energy to a half-hour filmed fantasy program, his network and most critics were confused. Interviewing Serling prior to *Zone*'s premiere, Mike Wallace asked, "Does this mean you've given up on writing anything important for television?" Like most pioneers, Serling had to drag both his audience and his network into his vision.

Several things about *The Twilight Zone*'s format appealed to Serling. Unlike live television, *Zone*'s filmed format would allow for multiple reruns, a consideration that was relegating series like *Playhouse 90* to TV history. The fantasy aspect of *Zone* would allow Serling to make social and political points relatively free of censorship, since the "parable" nature of the genre often masked the underlying message. Most important, *Zone*'s anthology format would allow him free rein to explore many different locales and character types.

Ironic justice

At first, CBS didn't know what to make of its star writer's pet project. The network finally allowed him to make a pilot, which resulted in "Where Is Everybody?" Rod Serling wrote the episode, which eventually launched the series on October 2, 1959. It told the simple story of a man wandering through a deserted town; ultimately, he is revealed to be an astronaut suffering from isolation-induced hallucinations. The episode set the tone, style, and essential elements of the series.

The Twilight Zone, unlike its sci-fi descendant, *The Outer Limits,* was not limited to the genre expectations, per se. Relatively few of the stories were set in alien worlds or have aliens in them. Many of the show's settings were mundane, making the unusual plot turns all the more terrifying. While most episodes have some supernatural elements, some do not. Not all of the episodes have the famed "twist endings" either. What then is the common bond among these 156 "journeys into a wondrous land"? Two qualifies: justice and irony.

Whether set in the Old West or modern-day Manhattan, a *Zone* episode's protagonist would usually not get what he or she expects, but rather what he or she truly deserves. Fate and otherworldly forces play tricks on these people, but eventually justice is done; if the outcome is unpleasant, its source is usually an inherent flaw in the protagonist's character. In the classic "Time

One of the all-time greatest half hours in television history: Burgess Meredith in the *Twilight Zone* episode known as "Time Enough at Last," in which he plays a myopic bank teller who reads in a bank vault, thereby surviving a nuclear holocaust. COURTESY OF PERSONALITY PHOTOS, INC.

Enough at Last," a myopic bank teller named Henry Bemis (Burgess Meredith) wishes to live in a world where he can read to his heart's content, unhindered by human interference. While Bemis reads in a bank vault, a nuclear holocaust occurs and leaves him as the world's sole survivor. Rejoicing that now, finally, he can exclusively commune with literature, his glasses fall and smash, leaving him virtually blind—and alone. As much as we may like and even sympathize with Bemis, the ending is a just one, implying that, as one of Bemis's books would have it, "no man is an island." Yet, since we've grown to like and pity this man, the ending is a heartbreaking one, not easily forgotten.

The surprise twists that conclude many *Zone* stories are an obvious result of the ironic style that pervades the show. It isn't enough that a silent, isolated woman destroy two ray-gun toting creatures in "The Invaders." The revelation that *they* are the earthlings and *she* is the alien gives the tale extra depth and alternative meanings. One of the strongest proofs of *Zone*'s artistry is that even after knowing the "twist," one is still mesmerized by the episode during repeated viewings.

Serling himself wrote more than half of the scripts for the series, which also ensured a consistency of tone and style. Many were based on short stories published in fantasy magazines, perfect for the show's half-hour format.

After the series concluded its third season, CBS executives, in a misguided attempt to increase ratings (which were never more than average), insisted that the show's running time be doubled. There were eighteen hour-long episodes produced, with mixed results. The one-two punch of the finest *Zone*s was lost, although several of these longer shows were still effective.

High quality

Returning to a half-hour format for its final season, the show's quality level remained remarkably high. Unlike many series that fizzle during their last months, the program produced some of its most famous entries in its fifth year. "Living Doll" features Telly Savalas as a man terrorized by a children's toy, "Talky Tina," which smilingly tells him "I'm Talky Tina and I don't like you!" The moving "In Praise of Pip" deals with the Vietnam War (perhaps the first television drama to do so) as a father exchanges his life for his wounded-in-action son. For sheer terror and bravura acting one must view the classic "Nightmare at 20,000 Feet," in which a disturbed man

Richard Deacon (later, bald Mel Cooley on *The Dick Van Dyke Show*) and Robby the Robot in the *Twilight Zone* episode "The Brain Center at Whipple's." COURTESY OF PERSONALITY PHOTOS, INC.

(played by future *Star Trek* star William Shatner) in a plane during a storm sees a strange creature through the window on the aircraft's wing. This memorable episode was redone—with John Lithgow—as part of *Twilight Zone—The Movie* in 1983 and has been spoofed on *The Simpsons* and in *Ace Ventura—When Nature Calls.*

These are just a handful of the great episodes that retain their narrative power more than thirty years after their premiere. There are literally dozens of superb *Zones*, waiting to be discovered by a video renter. And

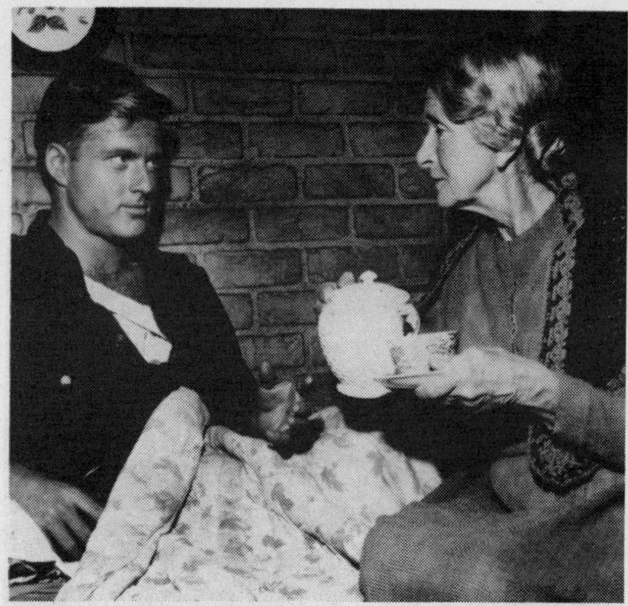

Star gazers love spotting actors who were unknown when they appeared on *The Twilight Zone.* Here Robert Redford stars opposite Gladys Cooper in an episode titled "Nothing in the Dark." COURTESY OF PERSONALITY PHOTOS, INC.

for those who might think that they've "seen them all," remember, the video versions are uncut. So if you're under thirty-five and think you've seen all of "The Eye of the Beholder," think again. Yet somehow, perhaps you have seen them, but in another dimension: *The Twilight Zone.*

VIDEO AVAILABILITY

There are numerous volumes of *The Twilight Zone* available for rental and/or purchase from certain video outlets and in a series of four-episode videos from Columbia House. Each volume from video outlets, running roughly fifty-two minutes, contains two episodes. There are also two "special" collections available. A detailed listing follows.

VOL.	EPISODE TITLES
1	"Nothing in the Dark," "The Invaders"
2	"Time Enough at Last," "The Monsters Are Due on Maple Street"
3	"Nightmare at 20,000 Feet,"* "The Odyssey of Flight 33"
4	"Steel," "A Game of Pool"
5	"Walking Distance," "Kick the Can"*
6	"Mr. Dingle the Strong," "Two"
7	"A Passage for Trumpet," "The Four of Us Are Dying"
8	"Long Distance Call," "I Sing the Body Electric"
9	"The Lonely," "Probe 7—Over and Out"
10	"The Obsolete Man," "Death's-Head Revisited"
11	"Perchance to Dream," "Shadow Play"
12	"The Prime Mover," "The Fever"
13	"The Hitch-hiker," "The Sixteen-Millimeter Shrine"
14	"The Grave," "The Last Rites of Jeff Myrtlebank"
15	"The Purple Testament," "A Quality of Mercy"
16	"The Last Flight," "*King Nine* Will Not Return"
17	"To Serve Man," "Judgment Night"
18	"Mr. Denton on Doomsday," "The Shelter"
19	"The Trade-Ins," "Third From the Sun"
20	"Once Upon a Time," "The Fugitive"
21	"Nick of Time," "Static"
22	"The Dummy," "The Lateness of the Hour"

*Episode remade in the 1983 big-screen version, along with "It's a Good Life" and one new story.

Special video volumes

"Night of the Meek" The *Zone*'s only Christmas show, starring Art Carney, is available on a twenty-five minute special cassette.

"Treasures of *The Twilight Zone*" A double cassette celebration of the series features a 1959 "trailer" for the show, an interview with Rod Serling, and six episodes: the classic "Eye of the Beholder," "The Howling Man," the pilot episode ("Where Is Everybody?"), "The Masks," the rarely seen "The Encounter," and the French, Oscar-winning short film, *An Occurrence at Owl Creek Bridge* (shown as an episode during the *Zone*'s network run). The package runs 190 minutes.

EMMY AWARDS

1959–60 **Rod Serling,** Outstanding Writing Achievement in Drama

1960–61 **Rod Serling,** Outstanding Writing Achievement in Drama

George Clemens, Outstanding Achievement in Cinematography for Television

TRIVIA TIDBITS

- Two actors hold the record for the most *Zone* appearances: Jack Klugman and Burgess Meredith (four each).
- The "Kanamits," those mysterious aliens with the book *To Serve Man,* were nine feet tall and weighed 350 pounds.
- A French-made short film, *An Occurrence at Owl Creek Bridge,* was acquired by the *Zone* producers and broadcast as the final episode of the last season, to save money. The film went on to win an Oscar for Best Short Subject.
- Bernard Herrmann, famed composer of film scores for many Hitchcock classics (*Psycho, Vertigo, North by Northwest,* etc.), wrote the original theme music for

the *Zone,* replaced near the end of the first season by the now-famous theme by Marius Constant. Herrmann did, however, continue to contribute music for many *Zone* episodes, including "The Lonely," "The Eye of the Beholder," and "Living Doll."

- Six episodes from the second season were videotaped, rather than filmed—part experiment, part cost-cutting measure. They are instantly identifiable, looking and sounding more theatrical than the rest of the *Zone* (and with rough-looking edits). Three are presently available on video: "The Lateness of the Hour," "Long Distance Call," and "Night of the Meek."
- Two comic episodes were intended as pilots for other series: "Mr. Bevis" and "Cavender Is Coming." Both featured guardian angels; neither made it to the network's schedule (although "Cavender" featured an early appearance by CBS star-to-be Carol Burnett).
- A new color hour-long version of *The Twilight Zone,* aired on CBS for two seasons (1985–87). Each episode contained three stories of varying length. Sci-fi writer Harlan Ellison was creative consultant and Charles Aidman had the narrator role (Rod Serling had passed away). Subsequently, these episodes were pared down to thirty minutes each for syndication in 1988, and thirty more first-run episodes were added.
- After *The Twilight Zone* series ended, Rod Serling co-scripted the first *Planet of the Apes* movie (1968) and returned to television as host of *Night Gallery* (1970–73).

UFO

Syndicated, 1972–73 (first American broadcast),
26 episodes

CAST

Cmdr. Edward Straker	Ed Bishop
Col. Alec Freeman	George Sewell
Capt. Peter Karlin	Peter Gordeno
Lt. Gay Ellis	Gabrielle Drake
Col. Paul Foster	Michael Billington
Gen. James Henderson	Grant Taylor
Miss Ealand	Norma Ronald
Miss Holland	Lois Maxwell
Lt. Mark Bradley	Harry Baird
Lt. Lew Waterman	Gary Meyers
Lt. Joan Harrington	Antonia Ellis
Lt. Nina Barry	Dolores Mantez
Dr. Douglas Jackson	Vladek Sheybal

CREATORS: Gerry & Sylvia Anderson
EXECUTIVE PRODUCER: Gerry Anderson
PRODUCER: Reg Hill
DIRECTORS: Gerry Anderson, David Lane, Ken Turner, Alan Perry, Ron Appleton, David Tomblin, Jeremy Summers
WRITERS: Gerry & Sylvia Anderson, Tony Barwick, Ian Scott Stewart, Ruric Powell, Alan Pattillo, Alan Fennell, David Tomblin

Watch the skies!

This popular British-made aliens-might-be-coming space series (filmed in 1969), much admired for its sophisticated special effects, was the first live-action adventure show from Gerry & Sylvia Anderson, noted for the earlier innovative puppet series, *Captain Scarlet* and *The Thunderbirds.* In *UFO*—set in the "futuristic" world of the 1980s—they tackled, with great imagination and glossy special effects, the U.S. government's supposed cover-up of a spate of Unidentified Flying Object sightings and landings, and had stalwart Edward Straker leading a team to investigate for a private agency called SHADO (Supreme Headquarters, Alien Defense Organization). Their mission: to prevent mass hysteria and panic that might result if citizens discovered they were being invaded by extraterrestrials.

Straker and colleagues operated beneath a film studio, where strange comings and goings would not seem out of place, and had at their disposal a fleet of submarines with surface-to-air missiles, aircraft, land vehicles, space modules, satellites, and a secret moon base constructed by SHADO. There even were an underwater airplane launcher and a Space Intruder Detector (SID), ever-alert to track oncoming UFOs. The stories themselves were filled with violence, green-faced otherworldlies, and a number of very sexy females.

Despite a successful first season (more so in Great Britain) and requests for an additional twenty-four episodes, a decision was made to revamp the entire series, and eventually it was transformed into *Space 1999* (see separate entry).

VIDEO AVAILABILITY

Four volumes of the series, each containing two episodes and running about 120 minutes, are available at certain video outlets.

TRIVIA TIDBITS

- Creator Gerry Anderson later produced a similar series called *Space Precinct.* It starred Ted Shackleford (from *Knots Landing*) and ran in syndication in the

United States for twenty-two episodes during the 1994–95 season.

- Sylvia Anderson was also credited with creating the show's Century 21 fashions.
- The imaginative special effects were under the supervision of Derek Meddings, who designed a set of cars and futuristic jeeps to jazz up the live-action exteriors.
- Lois Maxwell moonlighted on this series as Miss Holland, Straker's secretary. Her more familiar characterization was that of Miss Moneypenny in the James Bond films.

VOYAGE TO THE BOTTOM OF THE SEA

ABC, 1964–68, 110 episodes

CAST

Adm. Harriman Nelson	Richard Basehart
Cmdr. Lee Crane	David Hedison
CPO Curley Jones (1964–65)	Henry Kulky
Chief Francis Sharkey (1965–68)	Terry Becker
Lt. Cmdr. Chip Morton	Bob Dowdell
Crewman Sonar (1964–65)	Nigel McKeand
Crewman "Ski" Kowalski	Del Moore
Crewman Sparks	Arch Whiting
Crewman Patterson	Paul Trinka
Crewman Stu Riley (1964–66)	Allan Hunt
Crewman Malone (1964–65)	Mark Slade
Doc	Richard Bull
	Wright King
	Wayne Heffley

CREATOR AND EXECUTIVE PRODUCER: Irwin Allen

PRINCIPAL DIRECTORS: Irwin Allen, John Brahm, Leonard Horn, James Goldstone, Alan Crosland, Felix Feist, Sobey Martin, Gerd Oswald, Josef Leytes, Laslo Benedek, Harry Harris, Leo Penn, Jerry Hopper, Alex March, Sutton Roley, Gerald Meyer, Justus Addiss, Abner Biberman, Tom Gries, Charles Rondeau, Robert Sparr

PRINCIPAL WRITERS: Irwin Allen, Richard Landau, Harlan Ellison, John McGreevey, Berne Giler, Alan Caillou, William Tunberg, Robert Hamner, William Read Woodfield, Albert Gail, Shimon Wincelberg, Allen Balter, William Welch, Rik Vollaerts, Robert Vincent Wright, Sidney Marshall

Diving to the unknown

With its lavish special effects and a format flexible enough to allow the writers to concoct any kind of story from monsters to espionage, the hour-long *Voyage to the Bottom of the Sea*—sort of an undersea *Star Trek*—was probably the most successful of Irwin Allen's four network series of the 1960s (the others: *Lost in Space, The Time Tunnel,* and *Land of the Giants*). Originally a well-received 1961 feature film for Allen, the show recycled the expensive sets and some of the footage, reworked the premise—the crew of the atomic-powered glass-nosed research submarine *Seaview* encounter monsters from the deep, aliens from space, mad scientists, underwater civilizations, international spies, and unexpected time warps. Allen sold it to ABC based on the color pilot.

In the film, Walter Pidgeon starred as Admiral Nelson, the craft's designer and builder and the man in charge of scientific research, and Robert Sterling played Captain Crane, the overall commander of the ship. On television, these roles went to sonorous Richard Basehart and David Hedison (who previously had starred in *Five Fingers* on TV and *The Fly* in the movies).

John Cassavetes made a memorable appearance in the episode "The Peacemaker" as a turncoat scientist who realizes too late that a super bomb of his creation threatens the world's balance of power. Carroll O'Connor turned up (literally) in the episode "Long Live the King" as a stranger on a rowboat picked up by the *Seaview* in the middle of the ocean. And in "The Wax Men," Michael Dunn portrayed a devious clown who inveigled his way abroad the submarine and began replacing crew members with wax dummies. Other guest villains the crew encountered included Vincent Price, Edgar Bergen, George Sanders, Edward Asner, Victor Buono, Leslie Nielsen, and, in an early role, Robert Duvall as a hairless alien "sleeper"—revived by the crew—who secretly plans an invasion.

The rare female touch

Although *Voyage* had no women regulars, some (such as Linda Cristal, Gia Scala, Jill Ireland, Yvonne Craig, and Karen Steele) did find their way aboard as guest stars. And although the pilot episode ("Eleven Days to Zero" with Eddie Albert) was shot—but not shown—in color, the thirty-one shows that followed during the season were filmed in black and white. Under L. B. Abbott, one of the leading special effects geniuses of the era at 20th Century Fox, footage from various Fox movies such as Allen's own *The Lost World* and *The Enemy Below*—as well as the theatrical predecessor to the series—was expertly incorporated into various episodes.

Voyage to the Bottom of the Sea had a memorable four-year run encountering the unknown below. When the network decided at the end of the 1967–68 season that the show had run its course, it put the *Seaview* (and its later companion craft, the *Flying Fish,* a mini-sub that could fly the air at fantastic speeds) into dry dock, filling the Sunday night time slot with Irwin Allen's next sci-fi show, *Land of the Giants.*

VIDEO AVAILABILITY

A series of episodes of *Voyage to the Bottom of the Sea,* including the pilot shown for the first time in color, are available through Columbia House—two one-hour shows per cassette.

TRIVIA TIDBITS

- In addition to the theme by Paul Sawtell, *Voyage to the Bottom of the Sea* had among its regular composers John Williams, Nelson Riddle, Jerry Goldsmith, Leith Stevens, and Harry Geller.
- Esteemed science fiction writer Harlan Ellison wrote at least one episode under the nom de plume Cordwainer Bird.

- L. B. Abbott won an Emmy for Special Photographic Effects during the show's first season and shared another with Howard Lydecker during the second; Winton C. Hoch won an Emmy for cinematography during the second.
- Following *Voyage* and his other three sci-fi adventure series, Irwin Allen returned to the big screen and earned his appellation as "The Master of Disaster" with such all-star hits as *The Poseidon Adventure* and *The Towering Inferno.*

THE X-FILES

Fox, 1993–

CAST

Fox Mulder	David Duchovny
Dana Scully	Gillian Anderson

CREATOR/EXECUTIVE PRODUCER: Chris Carter
CO-EXECUTIVE PRODUCERS: James Wong, Glen Morgan, R. W. Goodwin
PRODUCERS: Joseph Patrick Finn, David Nutter, Rob Bowman, Kim Manners
SUPERVISING PRODUCER: Howard Gordon, Charlie Craig
DIRECTORS: Robert Mandel, Daniel Sackheim, Harry Longstreet, Joe Napolitano, Jerrold Freeman, William Graham, David Nutter, Larry Shaw, Rob Bowman, R. W. Goodwin, Kim Manners, Michael Vejar
WRITERS: Chris Carter, Glen Morgan, James Wong, Chris Ruppenthal, Howard Gordon

The truth is out there

Becoming *the* cult series of the 1990s virtually from its premiere, the cool, eerie *X-Files* tracks its two unconventional FBI agents Mulder and Scully as they chase around the country on cases the government is loath to investigate: UFO kidnappings, psychic transference, a liver-eating humanoid, an "escalating fetishist" (necrophile, to the uninitiated), cannibalism in Atlantic City, killer computers, "flukeworms" (or human-size parasites), monster sightings, murderous cockroaches, a dude who can switch genders at will, and assorted paranormal activities and unexplained phenomena. Truth-seeking Fox "Spooky" Mulder is a believer of sorts (it's hinted that his sister might have been abducted by aliens); his no-nonsense, initially skeptical female partner, Dana Scully—a doctor with a degree in forensic pathology—skulks around keeping a wary eye on him, apparently on "orders from above." However, in one episode, "Beyond the Sea," with Brad Dourif as a nutcake prisoner, the show's concept was temporarily reversed, with Scully becoming the believer and Mulder the skeptic.

In a different episode, they snoop around a military base that may be using alien technology in its aircraft; in another, they pursue a serial killer who might just have been doing his deeds for more than 100 years; in a fourth, they stumble upon encrypted files revealing that the government has been aware of extraterrestrial life for a half century and that Mulder's father might have been involved in a related project.

X-cellent adventures of Mulder and Scully

Generally sober-faced Mulder and Scully are the show's only regulars, and, as the series progresses, a sexual tension between the two has begun to develop. The two are supported by a few recurring characters: bureaucratic FBI Assistant Director Walter S. Skinner (Mitch Pileggi); a mysterious Washington informant known rather predictably as Deep Throat (Jerry Hardin); a slimy mutant toothpaste tube named Eugene Tooms (Doug Hutchison) who morphs into assorted gross figures; the enigmatic Cigarette-Smoking Man (William B. Davis); and Conundrum, played by someone billed only as The Enigma. On rare occasions there would be a name guest star. Peter Boyle, for one, materialized as an odd duck, an insurance salesman whose psychic abilities lead Mulder and Scully to the victim of a serial killer who mutilates his prey; Carrie Snodgress, for another, played a woman who swears to a UFO sighting but is nabbed by government agents and "classified" (government lingo for keeping a subject away from the press).

The success of *The X-Files* brought on a rush of similar shows about the paranormal, but none has matched it either in popularity of in the fervor of its army of fans.

VIDEO AVAILABILITY

An increasing number of episodes of *The X-Files* are available at certain video outlets, starting with Volume One: "Pilot Episode" and "Deep Throat."

TRIVIA TIDBITS

- *The X-Files* won a Golden Globe Award as Best Dramatic Series on Television during the 1994–95 season, the first regular science fiction series so honored. It also has spawned a top-selling Topps comic; Issue #1, dated January 1995, sold out in one day.
- The show received seven Emmy nominations for the 1994–95 season, including Outstanding Drama Series, writing, cinematography, and editing.
- Avid *X-Files* fans are known as X-philes.
- During the initial season, the FBI must have been watching, because the agency complained that Mulder carried the wrong kind of gun—a Glock 19, which is a DEA gun. Theirs, the FBI told the producers, is a Sig Sauer Model 226, which is now what Mulder packs.
- Before his *X-Files* role, Yale graduate David Duchovny was best known for playing the transvestite detective Dennis/Denise on *Twin Peaks* and as host/narrator of Showtime's erotic *Red Shoes Diaries* series. Before hers, Gillian Anderson was a virtual TV un-

known, with only some Off-Broadway credits to her name.

- The series' inspirations include *Kolchak: The Night Stalker* (an acknowledged favorite of *X-Files* creator Chris Carter) and Robert Heinlein's novel *The Puppet Masters.*

VARIETY SERIES

Variety's the spice

"Something familiar, something peculiar . . . something appealing, something appalling." To paraphrase Stephen Sondheim by way of rascally Roman slave Pseudolous and cohorts in the musical *A Funny Thing Happened on the Way to the Forum,* this is what variety is all about. At least as it was initially defined by Ed Sullivan's *Toast of the Town* in the early days of television, and for his next twenty-three amazing years on the tube with variations on the same theme.

Toast of the Town—and *The Ed Sullivan Show,* as it later would be renamed—defined the variety show on television, just as *Admiral Broadway Revue* (with Sid Caesar and Imogene Coca, the forerunner to *Your Show of Shows*), *Cavalcade of Stars* (first with Jack Carter, then Jerry Lester, then Jackie Gleason), *Arthur Godfrey and His Friends, Broadway Open House,* Milton Berle's *Texaco Star Theater,* and the *Colgate Comedy Hour* later. Even *Rowan and Martin's Laugh-In, Monty Python's Flying Circus,* and *Saturday Night Live,* in their own way, owe a great debt to those pioneering programs in the medium's history.

Send in the clowns

Variety often means just what it seems: a program that features a wide cross-section of entertainment, including comedy sketches, musical numbers, magicians, illusionists, dancers, comics, jugglers, pop and classical recording artists, and other show business "eccentrics." This mix of talents would be one of the backbones of television throughout its commercial history. Virtually all the variety shows were hosted by a star performer—either a comedian or a singer—who frequently participated in sketches as well as with the talent. Ed Sullivan, and, to a lesser extent, Howard Cosell, were among the rare exceptions. Though it can be said Sullivan was a "personality" with specific mannerisms and speech patterns, he wasn't a comedian, singer, dancer, or even actor. His main gift was his extraordinary eye for talent.

Variety show became the standard through the 1950s and 1960s, with hit weekly programs starring Red Skelton, Jackie Gleason, Perry Como, Bob Hope, Dinah Shore, Garry Moore, Judy Garland, and Danny Kaye, all of whom had the ability to appeal to different age groups. The changing social climate of the sixties divided the generations and only a handful of regularly scheduled weekly variety shows remained—*The Hollywood Palace, Hee Haw,* and *The Carol Burnett Show.* As Burnett's show wound down, sketch comedy moved to late-night TV, with *Saturday Night Live* attracting hip young viewers with its unique brand of outrageous humor. It went on to become the longest running regularly scheduled entertainment program in television history, other than perhaps *The Tonight Show* under Johnny Carson's stewardship.

An entertainment potpourri

Except for the extraordinarily long-lived *SNL,* the variety series has evolved into an occasional, though extremely popular ice-skating extravaganza, a pop or country music special, a once-in-a-while magic show with the likes of David Copperfield, or a glittering Siegfried and Roy spectacular from Las Vegas. Another form of variety show that has appeared in the 1980s and 1990s, begun on cable television, features one or more stand-up comics in a comedy club setting. Numerous cable TV specials have spotlighted the talents of Robin Williams, Whoopi Goldberg, Jerry Seinfeld, Jay Leno, Martin Lawrence, Paul Reiser, Richard Belzer, Roseanne, Ellen DeGeneres, Paula Poundstone, Louie Anderson, Sinbad, and Sandra Bernhard, to name a few. With significantly "cleaned up" material, variations on this variety genre have found their way into syndicated television.

The assorted areas of pop culture and the arts—basically American, but also from abroad (the Beatles and the Rolling Stones, Marcel Marceau and the Ballet Russe, Señor Wences and the Ballet Folklorico of Mexico, Pablo Casals, Antonio Carlos Jobim, the Kirov Ballet, etc.) found themselves on the same stages through the glory years of the television variety show. Many of their performances, captured for posterity on tape, can be savored by viewers who were "there"—i.e., in front of the tube when these artists were on—and by younger ones who weren't yet born. Nearly a dozen variety shows, culled from a number of classic series of the genre and available on cassette from selected video stores and rental outlets, are spotlighted on the succeeding pages. They are prime examples of a glittering time in television history that offer delightful viewing and a matchless visit in the arts.

BENNY HILL

Syndicated, 1969–89, 111 episodes

HOST: Benny Hill
CREATOR: Benny Hill
EXECUTIVE PRODUCER: Denis Spencer
PRODUCERS/DIRECTORS: John Street, Keith Beckett, Mark Stuart, David Bell, John Robins, Peter Frazer-Jones, Dennis Kirkland
WRITERS: Benny Hill, Dave Freeman

The Hill is alive

Pudgy Benny Hill, a longtime London music hall knockabout comic who became a media darling on TV, hosted and starred in this often bawdy British variety show that ran nearly continuously in England for three decades beginning in the mid-1950s. The U.S. version, edited down to thirty minutes, made zany Hill—often referred to as the bad boy of British comedy—a cult figure on this side of the Atlantic. For America, the show was a mixture of sketches and segments taken from various hour programs over the years, almost haphazardly, so that the unbridled Hill would literally age or become youthful in back-to-back bits. Filled with outrageous puns, double entendres, and loads of buxom beauties in skimpy outfits, *The Benny Hill Show* was a blend of comedy routines, slapstick, silly songs, inventive silent film sequences, and quick takes. It can be said to be the forerunner of *Rowan and Martin's Laugh-In* and its various imitators.

As a writer, singer, comedian, and actor, Hill became one of Britain's highest-paid performers. The impish, often lecherous star, with a company of regulars playing

Benny Hill (center), the lovable burlesque imp, and his lovely entourage. COURTESY OF PERSONALITY PHOTOS, INC.

assorted roles and no name guests, regularly bulldozed his way through one outrageous comedy routine or leeringly "blue" song after another—quite often in drag—convulsing audiences with his brand of naughty humor. On his shows, he rarely appeared in less than a dozen guises, and in one hour special, he played twenty-six different parts in thirty-seven minutes—from impious minister to nagging housewife to lusty surgeon to sexy pop singer. The show also features a parade of his outlandish alter egos: saucy Madge the Manicurist, irrepressible Tommy Tupper, the Halitosis Kid (a western hero with lethal bad breath!), meek Morris Dribble, and many others.

Great Britain's beloved Benny Hill has been described as a somewhat vulgar version of America's Red Skelton in style and Jackie Gleason in shape. His celebrity was such that at his death in 1992 at age sixty-five, the British entertainment industry went into a week-long period of mourning. His best gag-filled work, happily, has been preserved on tape.

VIDEO AVAILABILITY

A number of hour-long cassette samplers of Benny Hill's loony brand of comedy and wacky hijinks are available at certain video outlets.

TRIVIA TIDBITS

- Before becoming a household name on American television, Benny Hill was familiar to U.S. audiences in comic roles in films such as *Chitty Chitty Bang Bang* and *Those Magnificent Men in Their Flying Machines.* In later years, he was also featured in the "Su-Su-Sudio" music video with Phil Collins.
- In addition to creating the show and writing virtually all the material, Benny Hill wrote most of the music and original songs and riotous limericks.
- Boots Randolph wrote the show's recurring theme, "Yakkety Sax."

CANDID CAMERA

ABC, 1948; NBC, summer 1949; CBS, 1949–50;
ABC, 1951–52; NBC, summer 1953; CBS, 1960–67;
Syndicated, 1974–80; CBS, summer 1990

HOST: Allen Funt
CREATOR AND EXECUTIVE PRODUCER: Allen Funt
PRODUCER: Bob Banner, Richard Birglia
DIRECTORS: Herb Gardner, Bob Schwartz

Smile! You're on . . .

Candid Camera, one of the most durable programs of its type, was in fact the granddaddy of today's somewhat more serious reality shows. After a several years on radio (as *Candid Microphone*), Allen Funt's creation came to television in 1948 and has remained on the air, in one form or another, into the 1990s. The simplest of ideas, it featured real people being caught in embarrassing situations (usually carefully set up by Funt and his staff) by a hidden camera—and, before that, a hidden microphone. The people, of course, later were asked to sign a release to allow their filmed or taped foolishness to be shown on national television (and reportedly most were good sports and permitted it).

Among the classics from the hundreds of segments was the one featuring a car being pushed into a service station with a member of Funt's staff (often it would be erstwhile *Your Hit Parade* singer Dorothy Collins or funny lady Fannie Flagg) playing a confused driver wondering why the motor would not turn over and to have the unsuspecting mechanic lift the hood to find no engine. Another memorable one was about the "Talking Mailbox" in

Candid Camera host Allen Funt (right) and occasional cohost Durwood Kirby COURTESY OF PERSONALITY PHOTOS, INC.

which a disembodied voice coming from inside the receptacle asks passersby for help or directions. A third had Funt's staff putting up a tollbooth between Pennsylvania and Delaware, stopping drivers, and telling them that Delaware was "closed" for the day. And still another had a comely young lady standing on a sidewalk looking for assistance with her two suitcases. Each helpful male who happened along found that the suitcase he went to pick up (hers was empty) contained 500 pounds of cement.

The original idea came to Funt while, in the service during World War II, he surreptitiously recorded his fellow soldier's gripes and then aired them on Armed Forces Radio. He took this idea to ABC Radio in 1947, kicking off an amazing career in broadcasting. Not being entirely comfortable in front of the TV camera, Funt used a long parade of cohosts, including Jerry Lester, Arthur Godfrey, Durwood Kirby, Bess Myerson (Miss America), John Bartholomew Tucker, Phyllis George (Miss America), Jo Ann Pflug, Betsy Palmer, and finally, his son, Peter Funt. Guest pranksters on the show ranged from Jayne Mansfield to Woody Allen to Dolly Parton.

After decades of staging his classic gags of people caught in the act of being themselves and of interviewing youngsters (a delightful offshoot of the original concept), Allen Funt retired in 1990, staying on only as a consultant, and son Peter took the reins. In 1991, a syndicated version of the show, *The New Candid Camera,* starred Dom DeLuise but failed to attract enough of an audience to continue for more than one season. The original show also spawned such shows as *People Do the Craziest Things, Totally Hidden Video,* and the most successful one, *America's Funniest Home Videos.*

VIDEO AVAILABILITY

A number of *Candid Camera* tape collections, running either thirty or sixty minutes, are available at certain video outlets. *What Do You Say to a Naked Lady?* (see below) is also available on tape.

TRIVIA TIDBITS

- Funt produced and directed an adult theatrical version of *Candid Camera* in 1970, *What Do You Say to a Naked Lady?,* and an obscure 1971 follow-up, *Money Talks.*
- There were several hour-long *Candid Camera* NBC specials through the years, including *The Candid Camera Special* (1981), with Loni Anderson and Valerie Harper as Allen Funt's cohosts, and *Candid Camera Looks at the Difference Between Men and Women* (1983), with Stephanie Zimbalist hosting with Funt.

- The show was so popular that it was copied in home-grown versions in Great Britain, Italy, France, Japan, Germany, and Russia.
- Sid Ramin wrote the jaunty theme song, "Smile, You're on Candid Camera!"

THE ED SULLIVAN SHOW
(aka TOAST OF THE TOWN)

CBS, 1948–71

HOST: Ed Sullivan
PRODUCERS: Jack Meegan, Ed Sullivan, Robert Precht, Marlo Lewis, Stu Erwin Jr., Ken Campbell
DIRECTORS: John Wray, Jacques Andre, Tim Kiley

The REALLY big shew!

A true institution, *The Ed Sullivan Show* had the longest continuous run of any prime-time entertainment program in television history. It was a Sunday night staple for twenty-three years, mixing pop music stars, grand opera divas, jugglers, animal acts, stand-up comics, magicians, sword-swallowers, mentalists, movie stars promoting their films, baton twirlers, ballet artistes, and vaudeville skits in a weekly potpourri of pure family entertainment. Overseeing it all was the rather awkward Ed Sullivan, a former newspaper columnist whose beat was New York show business, with a stumbling delivery (making him fodder for impressionists and impersonators for years) but a hand on the pulse of the viewing public and an uncanny eye for talent.

The show inconspicuously began its extraordinary run as *Toast of the Town* on the night of June 20, 1948 on a meager budget of $1,375. Two young stars introduced on that show were Dean Martin and Jerry Lewis, who split $200, the lion's share of the show's talent budget of $375. Also on that debut telecast were Richard Rodgers and Oscar Hammerstein II, concert pianist Eugene List, and the original June Taylor Dancers (later to become staples

The Fab Four and the man who presented them in front of a record number of American TV viewers. From left: Ringo Starr, George Harrison, Ed Sullivan, John Lennon, and Paul McCartney. The Beatles were the first British Invasion act to appear on *The Ed Sullivan Show,* blazing the path for other groups such as the Rolling Stones and the Dave Clark 5. COURTESY OF PERSONALITY PHOTOS, INC.

on Jackie Gleason's program). From there it became a grand parade of talent ranging from the Bolshoi Ballet to bouncing brown bears to Crosby and Hope to the Beatles, whom Ed introduced to America in one landmark, fan-shrieking event—the most watched of its time. (The week before the Fab Four's appearance in 1964, Ed announced at the end of his show: "Next week, the Beatles and the Pietà.") There also was the hip-swiveling young performer from Memphis named Elvis Presley who also brought down the house in three engagements with Ed Sullivan in 1956 and 1957. Elvis was shown performing only from the waist up because of CBS's censors.

Through the years, everybody who was anybody in show business did the Ed Sullivan Show—including the likes of Clark Gable, Humphrey Bogart, and Spencer Tracy—who *never* appeared on television. And those celebrities who weren't onstage were introduced from the audience. Favorites were asked back again and again, like the delightful mechanical Italian mouse called Topo Gigio, who invariably requested "Kees me, Eddie!" and to tuck him into his tiny bed; assorted Sullivan impersonators such as John Byner, Frank Gorshin, Rich Little, and Jackie Mason; and the thickly accented ventriloquist, Señor Wences and his talking box ("'S all right?" "'S all right!").

Acerbic comic Fred Allen made the memorable comment that "Ed Sullivan will be around as long as someone else has talent," and once tried to categorize Sullivan. "He doesn't sing, he doesn't dance, he doesn't tell jokes," Allen observed, "and he does them all equally well." But he certainly was enthusiastic, his pained expression bursting into a smile as he became an unabashed cheerleader for every act and every performer. Who can forget the night he urged the audience after Sergio Franchi sang on the 1965 Christmas show, "Let's REALLY hear it for 'The Lord's Prayer'!"?

Among those making their debuts on Ed's stage were a ten-year-old, polio-stricken violinist named Itzhak Perlman; Judy Garland's talented teenaged daughter, Liza Minnelli; a Borscht Belt performer, Myron Cohen, who went on to make forty more appearances on the show; Canadian comics Wayne and Shuster, who headlined a record fifty-three times; a young New York comic in a three-piece suit and a foot-long cigar, Alan King; rock 'n roll artists such as the Dave Clark 5, the Jackson 5, the Doors, and the Rolling Stones; and Jim Henson's Muppets.

Ed Sullivan, a towering figure in the pantheon of television, was truly one of a kind, as was his show. It ended on June 6, 1971, but several specials followed. Although Ed died in 1974, the show's amazing popularity continued, as witness several high-rated CBS prime-time retrospective "Best of" specials in the 1990s.

VIDEO AVAILABILITY

About a dozen volumes of *The Ed Sullivan Show,* including special salutes to Lucille Ball, Walt Disney, and MGM, are available at certain video outlets. Most run about sixty minutes. There are also several "Very Best" collections, running about 100 minutes.

EMMY AWARDS

1955	Best Variety Series
1971	Special Emmy to Ed Sullivan

TRIVIA TIDBITS

- Robert Precht, one of the longtime producers, was Ed's son-in-law and remains the keeper of the Sullivan flame, carefully guarding all rights to the show.
- Among the Ed Sullivan firsts (according to *TV Guide*): first to stage an ice show on television; first to present ballet and opera stars on TV; first to incorporate dramatic skits and musical numbers from Broadway productions (featuring the current performers) into a TV variety show; first to take his TV show on the road; and first to present politically and racially unpopular performers, thus defying blacklists.
- Ray Bloch was the musical conductor for the show during its entire run.

THE ERNIE KOVACS SHOW

NBC, 1955–56 (including a daily mid-morning program and prime-time summer replacement for *Caesar's Hour*)

CAST

Ernie Kovacs, Edith Adams, Henry Lascoe, Matt Dennis, Barbara Loden, Bill Wendell, Peter Hanley, Bob Hamilton Trio

CREATOR: Ernie Kovacs
PRODUCERS: Perry Cross, Jack Hein
DIRECTORS: Barry Shear, Jack Hein
WRITERS: Ernie Kovacs, Rex Lardner, Deke Heyward, Alan Robin

Television genius

Ernie Kovacs was a true original, a pioneer in television with a show (actually a series of shows) that was unstructured, totally innovative, and wildly imaginative. As ABC News analyst and syndicate columnist Jeff Greenfield has written, "He was, by conventional standards, an itinerant performer, now a local hit in Philadelphia, now a morning host on CBS, now a part-time 'Tonight Show' host, now a summer replacement for Sid Caesar in 1956. His entire career spanned little more than a decade. . . . Yet no one who is old enough to have watched the first years of television will ever forget his presence, and few who perform comedy today on the small screen fail to reflect his influence."

Ernie Kovacs was *The Ernie Kovacs Show.* A stocky man with a large black mustache and an ever-present cigar, he marched through his potpourri of satire and

Ernie Kovacs (shown here as poetry lover Percy Dovetonsils) was a pioneer in absurd comedy. His antics on TV would later inspire David Letterman and many other outrageous comics. COURTESY OF PERSONALITY PHOTOS, INC.

video chicanery with a parade of distinctive characters—from Bavarian disc jockey Wolfgang von Sauerbraten and perennially sloshed kiddie TV show host Miklosh Maklosh, to mincing poet Percy Dovetonsils and the wordless lost soul he called Eugene, who on occasion would do the entire show without a sound. In addition, there was the idiosyncratic Nairobi Trio, three musicians in ape suits and derbies who played only one song endlessly. And Kovacs displayed an endless genius for blackout sketches and sight gags in which he created his own virtual reality, generally accompanied by tinny-sounding classical recordings (frequently Kurt Weill's "Mack the Knife").

He consistently broke through the so-called fourth wall of the television set, literally putting his mouth to the lens of the camera to confide in the viewer up close. Kovacs regularly skewered other television shows (*You Asked for It* became his *You Asked to See It*) and devastatingly caricatured Edward R. Murrow's famous Marilyn Monroe interview—with Kovacs as Murrow and Edie Adams as Monroe.

Edie Adams (she was still Edith at the time) began as Ernie's singer in Philadelphia, became his chief foil and coconspirator, and then his wife. She later became a star on Broadway (in *Wonderful Town* and *Li'l Abner*), went into films, starred in assorted TV musical specials and several sixties series, and will always be remembered for her sexy commercial for Muriel Cigars and her famous Mae West-style line: "Why don't you pick one up . . . and smoke it sometime."

The man and his cheroot

Kovacs had so many unforgettable, extraordinarily ingenious routines, it is difficult to single one out. Some of his most outrageous gags include: pouring water from a pitcher and having it go up rather than down; creating a room tilted at a thirty-degree angle so that objects defied gravity by dropping straight down; staging a poker game to Beethoven's Ninth; synchronizing autonomously moving office furnishings to a popular song medley; trapping himself in a six-foot-tall bottle rapidly filling with water; lobbing pies against a sheet of glass placed between himself and the camera; walking into a photographer's darkroom and exiting in negative; and having a submarine periscope slowly rise from the tub where a pretty lady is luxuriating in a bubble bath.

What made Kovacs's show so memorable was not what he said, but the visual aspect of the assorted routines and sketches. Much of what he did he accomplished literally by the seat of his pants. He reportedly seldom rehearsed (except probably for the more complicated gimmicks) and did the entire show live, making the flubs seem to be part of the routine.

From his last show in 1962 (broadcast after his death) to 1977, Kovacs went largely unseen, until some of the best of his programs were packaged and rereleased, first on college TV stations and then on public television, to a whole new audience.

The Ernie Kovacs Show, in effect, was the precursor to *Rowan and Martin's Laugh-In, Beyond the Fringe, Monty Python's Flying Circus, Saturday Night Live,* and much of what the Second City troupe later did. But Ernie was the pioneer, and even today his wild imagination and antics inspire young comedians and devastate fans.

VIDEO AVAILABILITY

Selections from Kovacs's TV shows are available in the five-volume video series *The Best of Ernie Kovacs* at certain tape outlets.

TRIVIA TIDBITS

- Ernie Kovacs effectively began his career with two daily fifteen-minute shows in Philadelphia in 1950, a wake-up program called *3 to Get Ready* and, later the same morning, a cooking show, *Deadline for Dinner* (he slyly pronounced it "Dead Lion for Dinner"). These, and his later *Ernie in Kovacsland* and *Kovacs on the Corner,* on the local NBC station, earned him a ticket to New York.
- Prior to starring in *The Ernie Kovacs Show* for NBC, he did *Kovacs Unlimited,* a forty-five minute weekday afternoon show for CBS (1952–54).
- Edie Adams has reported that when Ernie was writing, a sign outside his den would flash NOT NOW! She also said that behind his desk was mounted a stuffed rhinoceros from whose mouth flowed a waterfall.

- Kovacs received an Emmy nomination for Best Comedian in a Series (1956–57) but lost to Sid Caesar. He finally did win an Emmy (posthumously) for Outstanding Achievement in Electronic Camera Work (1961–62).
- Kovacs was also a dramatic actor, starring in an adaptation of Marcel Pagnol's *Topaze* on *Playhouse 90,* working on a number of other TV dramas during the medium's Golden Age, and appearing in ten feature movies.
- Kovacs's final work was an ABC special, taped one week before his death in a January 1962 auto accident while returning from a Hollywood party. (Edie Adams happened to be in another car following him.) The show was aired without commercials a few days later on what would have been his forty-third birthday.
- Lanky actor Jeff Goldblum portrayed chunky Ernie Kovacs in *Ernie Kovacs: Between the Laughter,* a dramatic 1984 TV movie about the famed comedian's little-known custody battle for his young daughters following a bitter divorce from his first wife. Edie Adams not only was credited as technical adviser on the film but also turned up in a cameo as Mae West.

THE JUDY GARLAND SHOW

CBS, 1963–64, 26 programs

EXECUTIVE PRODUCER: Norman Jewison
PRODUCERS: Gary Smith, William Colleran, George Schlatter, Bill Hobin, John Bradford
DIRECTORS: Bill Hobin, Dean Whitmore
WRITERS: Arne Sultan, Marvin Worth, John Bradford
MUSICAL DIRECTOR: Mort Lindsey
SPECIAL MUSICAL MATERIAL: Mel Tormé

Another rainbow for Judy

This was legendary entertainer Judy Garland's only television series. Unfortunately, CBS threw her up against the Sunday night powerhouse *Bonanza,* which—as it turned out and was expanded on in singer Mel Tormé's later book on his own experiences with the show, *The Far Side of the Rainbow*—was just another disheartening event in Garland's later career.

CBS, in hindsight, didn't know what to do with the treasure it had in magnetic Judy, other than to try molding her into was has been described as "the superstar next door." *The Judy Garland Show* tried different things each week in its search for the proper format. One week it would be Garland alone in a concert setting; the next it would have her working gamely with comedian Soupy Sales. The producers tried her in two-women shows, having her perched on a tall stool doing medleys with a young Barbra Streisand (in her first significant TV work) on one unforgettable program and veteran Ethel Merman on another. Then they tested the waters by having her pouring tea for, reminiscing with, and performing alongside her old movie pal Mickey Rooney; or dancing with Ray Bolger, with whom she had done *The Wizard of Oz* in 1939 and *The Harvey Girls* in 1946; or doing skits and musical numbers with Martha Raye, Peter Lawford, and Rich Little; or singing with the Count Basie Band; or working with daughter Liza Minnelli, then just 17. The producers even gave her a sidekick of sorts in talented Jerry Van Dyke—Dick's younger brother, who would go on to TV's infamous *My Mother, the Car* and since 1989 has co-starred as Luther Van Dam on *Coach*.

While this quite expensive show seeking a format proceeded through the season, Judy Garland did what Judy Garland has always done best—she sang her heart out, and much of the time there was magic. Of the several hundred songs she performed over the twenty-six weeks, there were some truly memorable performances, and from the show came one of Garland's most inspired albums, a "soundtrack" recording (actually a compilation from several of her concert shows) entitled *Just for Openers*. It included her stirring "Battle Hymn of the Republic," which she performed to great response several times during the course of the series, and, of course, "Over the Rainbow," which she performed memorably in a clown/tramp outfit on one of the shows in this musical series.

The Judy Garland Show was a noble attempt to bring the star's incandescence into the living room week in and week out. Under other circumstances that did not have to deal with creative disputes and Judy's well-publicized personal problems, it could have been one of television's all-time great variety series.

VIDEO AVAILABILITY

Two collector's treasuries from *The Judy Garland Show*, each running about fifty minutes, are available at certain video outlets. One is the 1963 Christmas show with her children, Liza Minnelli and Lorna and Joey Luft, along with Jack Jones and Mel Tormé. The other is a compilation from shows with Streisand, Merman, and young Liza.

TRIVIA TIDBITS

- The show's opening theme, naturally was "Over the Rainbow." The closing one, written especially for Garland by Charles L. Cooke and Howard C. Jeffrey, was "Maybe I'll Come Back."
- The famous set for the show—the word "JUDY" fifteen feet high in lights, together with a lighted double runway in the form of a cross—was copied, more or less, several years later for one of Elvis Presley's television specials, although Elvis turned the runway into a circle.
- Executive producer Norman Jewison went on to become one of the film's premier producer-directors, with such movies as *Fiddler on the Roof, The Russians Are Coming! The Russians Are Coming!, In the Heat of the Night,* and *Moonstruck.*

THE MONKEES

NBC, 1966–68, 50 episodes

CAST

Davy (guitar)	Davy Jones
Mike (guitar)	Mike Nesmith
Peter (guitar)	Peter Tork
Mickey (drums)	Mickey Dolenz
Mrs. Purdy (neighbor)	Jesslyn Fax
Mr. Babbitt (landlord)	Henry Corden

CREATORS AND EXECUTIVE PRODUCERS: Bob Rafelson, Bert Schneider

PRODUCER: Ward Sylvester

DIRECTORS: Bob Rafelson, Bruce Kessler, James Frawley, Alex Singer, Peter H. Torkelson, David Winters

American mop-tops

The Monkees, a mod, freewheeling musical group tripping to cultdom through zany misadventures and a batch of hit records, were inspired, of course, by the Beatles and their films, *A Hard Day's Night* and *Help!* Created by Bob Rafelson and Bert Schneider, who would go on to produce movies such as *Head* (starring the Monkees), *Easy Rider,* and *Five Easy Pieces,* among others, the Monkees were initially four unknowns who were chosen for their acting abilities, not their musical skills. Although they ultimately played on their records and gained some respect in the music industry (the Beatles admitted to being fans), they were jokingly referred to as the "Pre-Fab Four." But they had the last laugh, fondly remembered for their music and comedy three decades later.

The "Pre-Fab Four," from left: Davy Jones, Mickey Dolenz, Peter Tork, and Michael Nesmith. *The Monkees* TV show received much criticism for its synthetic origins, but even the Beatles claimed to be among their fans. COURTESY OF PERSONALITY PHOTOS, INC.

When the idea for a half-hour TV variety/sitcom was first concocted, the show's producers placed an ad in *Variety* under the headline "Madness" that called for "four insane boys." Among the unknowns who showed up for auditions were Stephen Stills (who later joined the rock group Buffalo Springfield and then Crosby, Stills, and Nash), Danny Hutton (who later became part of the rock group Three Dog Night), Harry Nilsson, diminutive Paul Williams, and even a would-be performer named Charles Manson. Thought was given to perhaps hiring real rock groups, such as the Lovin' Spoonful, but Rafelson and Schneider concluded that amateurs would be better for what they had in mind. "If you hired professionals, you wouldn't get the primitiveness we were looking for," Rafelson told the press at the time.

Hey, hey, we're the Monkees

Ultimately, four young men were brought together—Mike Nesmith, Mickey Dolenz, Peter Tork, and Britisher Davy Jones—and put into the hands of savvy record producer Don Kirshner, who was to mold them into a rock sensation in a six-week comedy improvisation course. Nesmith and Tork were real musicians and songwriters, while Dolenz first picked up the guitar and later turned to drums. All four contributed vocals to the Monkees' tracks. The marketing of the Monkees was under way. Under Kirshner's guidance, the foursome came out with a single, "Last Train to Clarksville," which sold 400,000 copies before the TV show even debuted. Ultimately, it became a number one chart smash, as did the follow-up, "I'm a Believer," which became the number one record of 1967. (Both were recorded with the group singing over tracks performed by real musicians.)

Between the release of the two records, *The Monkees* premiered on NBC on September 12, 1966, and TV's first rock 'n roll sitcom was born. The boys romped, rather than acted, through episodes and frantically paced routines built around music and gimmicky photography—a precursor to today's music videos. In addition to performing their hit records, which had been written by top songwriters like Boyce & Hart, Neil Diamond and Carole King (e.g., "A Little Bit Me, A Little Bit You" and "Pleasant Valley Sunday"), the Monkees melded wild pun-punctuated humor and outrageous sight gags with satirical sketches that also included incongruous guest appearances ranging from Frank Zappa to Liberace. In one episode, "Monkees Get Out More Dirt," their monkeyshines abounded as the boys competed for the affections of Julie Newmar (Catwoman on *Batman*); in another, "The Monsterous Monkee Mash," they encountered the Wolfman, the Mummy, and Frankenstein's monster at Count Dracula's castle. The quartet's songs regularly would be worked into the hokey plot. "Forget That Girl" accompanied one sketch in which Peter fell in love with a debutante who was way out of his league. There was at least one frenetic chase in every episode of the show, and often the four were found running in every direction—forward, backward, up, down, even upside down—being pursued by spies, mad scientists, angry landlords, etc.

Classic rock or camp TV?

Unfortunately, despite being extremely popular among younger audiences, *The Monkees* found tough TV competition in its second season in *Gunsmoke.* NBC dropped the show rather than moving it to a different timeslot. The group returned to television one final time for a spring 1969 NBC special, *33⅓ Revolutions per Monkee.* After that, Peter Tork left and the others continued performing together for a while in concert and on records. By the early 1970s, they all went their separate in ways various areas of show business, and sometimes one or two of them popped up as guests on various contemporary sitcoms. But *The Monkees,* as a show, lived on. CBS snapped up the original series and put it into Saturday morning reruns for several years. And when CBS was through with it, ABC picked it up and did the same thing. *The New Monkees,* with a totally new group of unknowns, premiered in syndication in September 1987 but was gone after thirteen episodes.

VIDEO AVAILABILITY

Various Monkees cassettes, each running about fifty minutes and containing two zany shows, are available at certain tape outlets. Rhino Records, which has acquired *The Monkees* series, has released all the episodes in a limited edition box set, with individual two-episode tapes to follow. Also available is *The Monkees: Heart and Soul,* their first music video reuniting Mickey Dolenz, Davy Jones, and Peter Tork, with song from their album *Pool It,* interviews, and doses of classic Monkees madness. It runs forty minutes.

EMMY AWARDS

1966–67 Outstanding Comedy Series
James Frawley, Outstanding Directorial Achievement in Comedy

TRIVIA TIDBITS

- The Monkees' only feature movie, the far-out *Head* (1968), which also featured such diverse personalities as Annette Funicello, Victor Mature, and Frank Zappa, was cowritten by Bob Rafelson and his pal, up-and-coming actor Jack Nicholson. *Head* is also available on home video from Rhino.
- Combined, the Monkees' first four albums on Colgems (*The Monkees, More of the Monkees, HEADquarters,* and *Pisces, Aquarius, Capricorn & Jones, Ltd.*) were number one on the *Billboard* chart for thirty-one consecutive weeks. From 1966 to 1968, they had six million-selling singles and eleven Top Forty songs.
- The Monkees received Grammy nominations in 1966 for "Last Train to Clarksville" as Best Contemporary Recording (it lost to "Winchester Cathedral") and for Best Contemporary Group Performance (losing to The Mamas & The Papas' "Monday, Monday"). In 1967 they were nominated for "I'm a Believer" for Best Performance by a Vocal Group and Best Contemporary Group Performance, but lost both times to the Fifth Dimension for "Up, Up and Away."
- Because of Davy Jones's burgeoning celebrity as one of the Monkees, another young British rock singer with the same name who was trying to break into the business had to change his—to David Bowie.
- Long before becoming a Monkee, Mickey Dolenz starred as twelve-year-old orphan Corky in the children's adventure series *Circus Boy* (1956–58). Dolenz,

the son of veteran character actor George Dolenz, was then using the name Mickey Braddock. Mickey's daughter Ami continues the family acting tradition.

- When the Monkees did a concert tour in the summer of 1967, Jimi Hendrix was the opening act. Reportedly, the kids didn't dig him and he quit the tour.
- Mike Nesmith, the Monkee with the wool hat, was the only one from the group to break into the Top Forty on his own, as a writer ("Different Drum") and as a performer ("Joanne"). Today a TV, video, and movie producer (for one, *Repo Man*, starring Emilio Estevez), he also won the first video Grammy for his hour-long *Elephant Parts*. He is also credited with creating what is now MTV—or at least the concept of video TV. Nesmith's mom invented and patented Liquid Paper.
- Davy Jones, Peter Tork, and Mickey Dolenz made cameo appearances in 1995's nostalgia fest, *The Brady Bunch Movie*.

MONTY PYTHON'S FLYING CIRCUS

PBS, 1969–74 in U.K., 1974–80 in U.S., 45 programs

CAST

The Python Troupe	Graham Chapman John Cleese Terry Gilliam Eric Idle Terry Jones Michael Palin

PRODUCERS: John Howard Davies
DIRECTORS: Ian MacNaughton, Terry Gilliam
WRITERS: John Cleese, Graham Chapman, Eric Idle, Terry Jones, Michael Palin, Terry Gilliam

Something completely different

This zany cult series—wild half hours of off-the-wall, free-form British comedy featuring skits, blackouts, satires, and animation—brought to television one of the most innovative comedy troupes ever. The five English comics who appeared on camera in various guises and doing outrageous things were abetted by a sixth member, Terry Gilliam, the only American-born Monty Python member. The ingenious, somewhat eclectic Gilliam created Python's distinctive animation.

Michael Palin and Terry Jones (who'd performed together since Oxford), John Cleese and Graham Chapman (who'd toured together in Cambridge University's comedy revue), and Eric Idle, a younger Cambridge student, first worked together when hired by David Frost in the mid-1960s as writers for his satirical series *The Frost Re-*

Brother, can you spare a dime? Four members of *Monty Python's Flying Circus* beg the public broadcasting audience for some cash. Clockwise, from top: Michael Palin, Terry Gilliam, Terry Jones, and Graham Chapman. Gilliam, the only American in the British troupe, was primarily the show's animator; today, he is a noted filmmaker, with credits such as *Time Bandits, Brazil,* and *12 Monkeys.* COURTESY OF PERSONALITY PHOTOS, INC.

ports (the follow-up to his irreverent *That Was the Week That Was*). The five went their separate ways when Frost's show ended, but occasionally met to discuss doing a program together. Terry Gilliam, an acquaintance of Cleese's from New York, then found himself in England and Cleese got him a job with the BBC. He became part of the group-in-search-of-a-comedy-concept—in the style of British radio's *The Goon Show* (Peter Sellers and Spike Milligan were part of that wacky troupe) and *Beyond the Fringe,* the early 1960s comedy revue with Dudley Moore and Peter Cook. In 1969,the BBC tried to team Palin and Cleese for their own show, but they refused unless all six of them were hired—and Monty Python was born.

Primarily Monty Python, along with a stock company of players, satirized history, hypocrisy, bureaucracy, and even television itself: boring talk shows, pretentious documentaries, and rumors that the Queen might be tuning in (after watching *The Virginian*). There were shows about a giant hedgehog terrorizing London, small-town ladies restaging historic events by beating each other up with umbrellas, serious meetings by the Society for Putting Things on Top of Things, a "Summarize Proust" contest, and lectures by the Minister of Silly Walks (John Cleese's devilish creation).

The troupe's fondness for the absurd might be exemplified by assembling Mao, Che, Lenin, and Marx on a quiz show competing to answer questions about English football teams; by staging a mock court-martial for a soldier accused of "trivializing the war" by snapping wet towels at the enemy; or by the dead parrot sketch, which explores the problems of returning a defective product to the point of purchase—in this case, taking the bird back to a pet shop because not only won't it talk, it's dead.

And Now for Something Completely Different (1972), Monty Python's first movie, was a collection of many of the troupe's sketches and animated bits from the series. Among them: "Upper-Class Twit of the Year," "The World's Deadliest Joke," and "The Lumberjack Song."

British comedy at its outrageous best: Five members of Monty Python in Nazi garb. From left: Terry Jones, Michael Palin, Terry Gilliam, Eric Idle, and Graham Chapman. COURTESY OF PERSONALITY PHOTOS, INC.

Monty Python remains a unique program in the annals of television. Probably the closest American TV would come to it: *Saturday Night Live* (see separate entry)—in its early years.

VIDEO AVAILABILITY

More than two dozen Python collections are available on tape at certain video outlets. Each runs about sixty minutes.

TRIVIA TIDBITS

- According to *TV Guide,* before settling on the name *Monty Python's Flying Circus,* the troupe toyed with calling the show either "Owl Stretching Time," "Toad Elevating Moment," "Sex and Violence," "A Horse, a Spoon, and a Basin," "Unlike a Bloody Stumbling Boot," or "Gwen Dibley's Flying Circus."

- After the series, the troupe reunited to make three internationally successful films: *Monty Python and the Holy Grail* (1975) (codirected by Terry Gilliam and Terry Jones); and *Life of Brian* (1979) and *Monty Python's Meaning of Life* (1983) (both directed by Terry Jones). There also was a 1982 performance film, *Monty Python Live at the Hollywood Bowl.*
- John Cleese went on to star with Connie Booth, then his wife, in the hit series *Fawlty Towers* (see separate entry) and appear in such movies as *The Great Muppet Caper, Yellowbeard* (along with Eric Idle and Graham Chapman), *Silverado,* and *A Fish Called Wanda* (for which he received an Oscar nomination for Best Screenplay).
- Eric Idle later acted in Gilliam's *Adventures of Baron Munchausen* (1989), among other films, and became associated with Beatle George Harrison in the movie business. Idle also teamed with Neil Innes, the resident Python musician, to create a Beatles parody called the Rutles, which was turned into the feature-length TV movie *All You Need Is Cash.*
- Director Terry Gilliam has developed a cult following for films outside his Python work, including *Brazil* (1985), *The Fisher King* (1991), *Adventures of Baron Munchausen* (1989), and *12 Monkeys* (1995).
- Terry Jones followed Terry Gilliam into film writing and directing, and made *Erik the Viking* (1989) with the odd team of Tim Robbins and Mickey Rooney.
- Michael Palin cowrote and acted in Gilliam's *Time Bandits* (1981); played a hapless clergyman in *The Missionary* (1982); and was the stuttering lackey in *A Fish Called Wanda.* He also has done several lighthearted BBC documentaries, including *Around the World in 80 Days with Michael Palin.*
- Graham Chapman, who originally had planned to become a physician (after college he interned by day and performed comedy at night), put his life story into his

book *The Liar's Autobiography.* According to obituaries, he died of complications due to cancer in 1989.

- Producer John Howard Davies began his career as a talented British child actor best known for his starring role in David Lean's memorable 1948 film *Oliver Twist.*

THE RED SKELTON SHOW

NBC, 1951–53; CBS, 1953–70; NBC, 1970–71

HOST: Red Skelton
PRODUCERS: Nat Perrin, Seymour Berns, Cecil Barker, Freeman Keyes, Gerald Garner, Bill Hobin, Ben Brady
WRITERS: Red Skelton, Dave O'Brien, Nat Perrin, Seymour Berns, Sherwood Schwartz, Al Schwartz, Martin Ragaway, Arthur Phillips, Hal Goodman

Seeing Red

Essentially a visual comedian from whom virtually all stand-up comics were descended (Red had been doing it since the 1930s and is still at it), Red Skelton established himself as a beloved American clown—in the true sense of the word—who was a TV superstar for twenty years. He's the "other" TV redhead, in company with Arthur Godfrey and Lucille Ball (with whom he made a number of films and frequently traded TV appearances).

The son of a circus clown, Red Skelton became one of the brightest stars in radio during the 1940s and made the transition to television with ease. In addition to doing consistently hilarious skits with assorted big-name guests and a mime sketch which he called "The Silent Spot," he brought along with him from radio his music director David Rose and a memorable stable of humorous characters: Cauliflower McPugg, the punch-drunk boxer; Willie Lump-Lump, the drunk; San Fernando Red, the con man; Clem Kididdlehopper, the befuddled rustic; Sheriff Deadeye, the scourge of the West; nasty Bolivar Shagnasty; Gertrude and Heathcliffe, the goofy seagulls; and the obnoxious Mean Widdle Kid with his favorite expres-

Red Skelton (right), America's perennial TV clown for twenty years.
COURTESY OF PERSONALITY PHOTOS, INC.

sion, "I dood it!" Red became each of the characters simply by twisting his ever-present hat into a new shape on his head. For television he created his most famous alter ego, the mute hobo Freddie the Freeloader (whose character, of course, would have been completely lost on radio).

Clowning around

Virtually all of his shows opened with Skelton standing in front of a stage curtain for a laugh-filled monologue—Red himself seemed always to be enjoying himself as much as the audience did, frequently getting a kick out of his own jokes—and ended by having him, hat in hand, humbly thanking his adoring audience and wishing them a fond "God bless." Then—to prevent him from overstaying his welcome—a pair of hands would reach out from under the curtain, grab Red's ankles, and force him to fall flat on his face and be dragged off. Few show business comics were said to have taken as many pratfalls—or to have done them better. It was a talent he perfected in tent shows, vaudeville and live presentations on the Loew's and RKO circuits in the 1930s, in which he'd invariably walk out on stage after being introduced, step up to the microphone, miss his mark, and tumble into the orchestra pit. (This part of his act seriously injured him a number of times throughout his career.)

Two of Skelton's most memorable routines, which he did in the various media, were "The Donut Dunker," in which he demonstrates the assorted techniques for dunking donuts in coffee, and his "Guzzler's Gin" bit, as a pitchman who gets sloshed while pushing his product. This latter sketch was the inspiration for Lucille Ball's later "Vitameatavegamin" health tonic routine, which became one of her classics.

Although revered, Red Skelton was treated shabbily by the medium. Despite his show being in the Top Ten for its entire twenty-one-year run, he was summarily canceled, and then effectively disappeared from TV. In retaliation, and somewhat embittered, he consistently refused to allow clips of his hundreds of shows to be included in any retrospectives of comedy television on the networks. In the late 1980s, Red reemerged on television after years of trouping around the country doing everything from county fairs (where he sold his greatly admired clown paintings) to Vegas clubs to Carnegie Hall. He did a number of specials for HBO, and his adoring audience of old fans and new generation cheered his wholesome humor, his timeless comic characters, and his newly added, wistful patriotic tribute as an elderly veteran waving a small flag.

Though Red Skelton appears today on TV only infrequently, he's still trouping after sixty-odd years, and he remains a beloved figure to those who grew up laughing at and with him on the stage, in films, on radio, and for twenty-one years on network television.

VIDEO AVAILABILITY

Ten hour-long cassettes culled from Red Skelton's half-hour weekly shows are available at certain video outlets. In addition, there is a special hour-long all-pantomime show that he did with the other famous mime, Marcel Marceau.

EMMY AWARDS

1951	Best Comedy Show
1960–61	**Sherwood Schwartz, Al Schwartz, Dave O'Brien, Red Skelton,** Outstanding Writing Achievement in Comedy
1985–86	**Red Skelton,** Ninth Annual Governor's Award (for his long career)

TRIVIA TIDBITS

- Many of Skelton's routines through the years were written by his friend Dave O'Brien, whom film buffs remember as the creator and hero/victim of dozens of "So You Want to Be a . . ." MGM comedy shorts of the 1940s.
- Jerry Lewis has always credited Red Skelton as his idol and prime inspiration.
- Brothers Sherwood and Al Schwartz, who wrote for Skelton, went on to create *Gilligan's Island* and *The Brady Bunch.*
- Skelton appeared in many MGM films in the 1940s, including *Whistling in the Dark* (1941), *Ziegfeld Follies* (1946), and *Merton of the Movies* (1947).

SATURDAY NIGHT LIVE

NBC, 1975– , 400 programs through February 24, 1996

THE REGULARS (alphabetically)

Dan Aykroyd (1975–79)
Jim Belushi (1983–85)
John Belushi (1975–79)
Dana Carvey (1986–92)
Chevy Chase (1975–76)
Ellen Cleghorne (1991–94)
Billy Crystal (1984–85)
Jane Curtin (1975–1980)
Joan Cusack (1985–86)
Denny Dillon (1980–82)
Robert Downey Jr. (1985–86)
Brian Doyle-Murray (1980–82)
Robin Duke (1981–84)
Nora Dunn (1985–91)
Christine Ebersole (1981–82)
Chris Farley (1990–94)
Gilbert Gottfried (1980–81)
Mary Gross (1981–1985)
Christopher Guest (1984–85)
Anthony Michael Hall (1985–86)
Brad Hall (1982–84)
Rich Hall (1984–85)
Phil Hartman (1986–94)
Jan Hooks (1986–91)
Melanie Hutsell (1991–94)
Victoria Jackson (1986–92)
Tim Kazurinsky (1981–84)
Gary Kroeger (1982–85)
Julia Louis-Dreyfus (1982–85)
Jon Lovitz (1985–91)
Gail Matthius (1980–81)
Michael McKean (1994)
Tim Meadows (1991–94)
Dennis Miller (1986–91)
Garrett Morris (1975–80)
Eddie Murphy (1980–84)
Bill Murray (1977–80)
Mike Myers (1989–1994)
Kevin Nealon (1986–94)
Laraine Newman (1975–80)
Joe Piscopo (1980–84)
Randy Quaid (1985–86)
Gilda Radner (1975–80)
Ann Risley (1980–81)
Chris Rock (1991–92)
Charles Rocket (1980–81)
Tony Rosato (1981–82)
Adam Sandler (1991–94)
Rob Schneider (1990–94)
Harry Shearer (1979–80, 1984–85)
Martin Short (1984–85)

David Spade (1990–94)
Pamela Stephenson (1984–85)
Julia Sweeney (1990–94)
Terry Sweeney (1985–86)
Danitra Vance (1985–86)

CREATOR: Lorne Michaels
EXECUTIVE PRODUCER: Dick Ebersol
PRODUCERS: Lorne Michaels, Jean Doumanian, Dick Ebersol, Michael O'Donoghue, Bob Tischler
DIRECTOR: Dave Wilson
PRINCIPAL WRITERS: Dan Aykroyd, Peter Aykroyd, Anne Beats, Jim Belushi, John Belushi, John Bowman, Andy Breckman, Chevy Chase, Larry David, Tom Davis, Brian Doyle-Murray, Ellen L. Fogle, Al Franken, Phil Hartmann, Judy Jacklin, Tim Kazurinsky, Andrew Kurtzman, Lorne Michaels, Eddie Murphy, Bill Murray, Michael Meyers, Kevin Nealon, Michael O'Donoghue, Sarah Paley, Joe Piscopo, Tony Rosato, Adam Sandler, Herb Sargent, Rob Schneider, Harry Shearer, Martin Short, Terry Southern, Tracy Tormé, Fred Wolf, Allan Zweibel

Not ready for prime time

An irreverent, consistently hip, often daring live show that became the darling of critics and an entire generation of baby boomers who were the show's loyal core audience, *Saturday Night Live* was a late-night television phenomenon right from its premiere on October 11, 1975. Most who are knowledgeable about television agree that the show's first five years—with comics Chevy Chase, Gilda Radner, John Belushi, Dan Aykroyd, Bill Murray, Jane Curtin, Laraine Newman, and Garrett Morris, who formed "The Not Ready for Prime Time Players"—produced some of the highest-quality, most topical comedy in all of television. Almost all of these stars, and others who followed, like Eddie Murphy, Billy Crystal, Jon Lovitz, Martin Short, Julia Louis-Dreyfus, Dana Carvey, et al., would go on to continuing fame in film or on other TV shows.

One of the earlier incarnations of *Saturday Night Live,* from left: Bill Murray, Jane Curtin, Gilda Radner, Garrett Morris, Laraine Newman.
COURTESY OF PERSONALITY PHOTOS, INC.

The premise for the *Saturday Night Live,* that Lorne Michaels and Dick Ebersol initially pitched to NBC was for a ninety-minute weekly topical variety show featuring rock 'n roll satire, political parody, changing hosts, and a cast of improvisational unknowns who'd done almost no TV, but had honed their craft at such comedy hotbeds as Second City and National Lampoon. Since the network had nothing else going for it after the late local news on Saturdays, the brass bought the idea and added a new dimension to television history. For the first two seasons, the show was called "NBC's Saturday Night." The word *Live* was added officially in May 1977. Short films by comedian Albert Brooks and by Gary Weiss and a special puppet segment created by Jim Henson were among the show's early elements.

Cutting-edge greatness

The brilliant creative team of producers and writers (many of whom were also performers) and the fresh, almost crazed, on-air talent offered an extraordinary array of outlandish sketches in a program that had a different guest host each week: an entertainment figure—a comedian such as Robin Williams; a musician such as Paul Simon; an actor such as John Travolta; or even a politician in the news, such as White House baby boomer George Stephanopoulos, consumer advocate Ralph Nader, New York mayors Ed Koch (several times) and Rudoph Giuliani, New York governor George Pataki, and the Reverend Jesse Jackson. Some of the leading musical artists also appeared on the show: the Rolling Stones, The Kinks, Santana, Devo, George Harrison, Paul McCartney, Ringo Starr, Rickie Lee Jones, Queen, Bon Jovi, Sting, La Toya Jackson, and Nirvana.

Resident zanies

In the early days, Chevy Chase (his catchphrase: "I'm Chevy Chase . . . and you're not") would pratfall his way through assorted routines and do faux newscasts. Gilda Radner played a lisping Barbara Walters clone named "Baba Wawa" and a smarmy loudmouth, Roseanne Rosanadana (after a Manhattan newsperson, Roseanna Scotto). As confused commentator Emily Litella, she did rambling editorials on the "Weekend Update" news segment and invariably mixed up her topic (she talked about "sax and violins" while intending to discuss "sex and violence"). Dan Aykroyd and Jane Curtin would turn up in pointy silly headgear as the outerspace Coneheads who try to adapt to American suburban culture. John Belushi was outrageous as a samurai warrior, a disgruntled bee, and an arm-flailing Joe Cocker. Belushi and Aykroyd put together a musical duo, The Blues Brothers, which began as a joke but became a real hit act that led to a hit movie.

The early 1980s *SNL* players. From left, back row: Jim Belushi, Christopher Guest, Mary Gross, Rich Hall; front row: Gary Kroeger, Julia Louis-Dreyfus, Harry Shearer, Pamela Stephenson, Billy Crystal, Martin Short. COURTESY OF PERSONALITY PHOTOS, INC.

Bill Murray made his presence known as slimy Nick the Lounge Lizard. One other future star appearing frequently on the show was Steve Martin, who began as a comedian sporting novelty acts as balloon animal-making and using props such as an arrow through his head.

Through the years, as the original performers—several alumni of the famed Second City troupe in either Toronto or Chicago—moved on to pursue burgeoning careers, they were replaced by the likes of Denny Dillon (later to costar on HBO's *Dream On*), Gilbert Gottfried, Joe Piscopo, Charles Rocket, Tim Kazurinsky, Laurie Metcalf (multiple Emmy winner later on *Roseanne*), Brian Doyle-Murray (Bill Murray's brother), Jim Belushi (John's brother), Martin Short, Billy Crystal, Julia Louis-

The short-lived team from the 1985–86 season of *Saturday Night Live*, from left: Nora Dunn, Danitra Vance, Randy Quaid, Robert Downey Jr., Anthony Michael Hall, Terry Sweeney, Joan Cusack, Jon Lovitz. COURTESY OF PERSONALITY PHOTOS, INC.

Dreyfus and Brad Hall (they later married; she became a star on *Seinfeld*, while he became a major TV writer/producer, creating shows like *The Single Guy*), Harry Shearer (later of Spinal Tap), Jon Lovitz (star of the animated *The Critic*), Dana Carvey and Mike Myers (who created party dudes Garth and Wayne), Ben Stiller (now film actor and director), Phil Hartman, Jan Hooks, Norm MacDonald, Chris Farley, Adam Sandler, and on and on. Of the second wave of stars Eddie Murphy and Billy Crystal were the first to make the crossover to the big time in films.

Masters of the middle years

Eddie Murphy became a sensation with his uproarious adult takeoffs on personable Mr. Rogers, the children's television host with his gentle homilies and ever-present cardigan sweater (Murphy called his satire "Mr. Robinson's Neighborhood"); Buckwheat, the onetime Little Rascal who, to Eddie, is no longer so little and has an adult career as a pop singer; and Play-Doh commercials figure Gumby ("I'm a Gumby, dammit . . . an entertainer, an actor, and an eraser"). Murphy also created memorable figures like Velvet Jones, the dynamic infomercial pitchman, and Dion, the fey hairdresser, and did a devastating Ed Norton to Joe Piscopo's Ralph Kramden. Billy Crystal came to *SNL* from *Soap* (see separate entry) and brought with him on-target impressions of Sammy Davis Jr., Muhammad Ali (starring in, for one, the parody "Kate and Ali" with Martin Short as Katharine Hepburn), and, most famous of all, slick show business gossiper Fernando (after Fernando Lamas), insincerely telling each of the celebrity guests at his Fernando's Hideaway, "You look marvelous!" Martin Short, from this period, was best known for his Ed Grimley Jr., a nerdish, excitable figure with a pained expression and greased hair was combed to a point that stuck about six inches straight up. Jon Lovitz brought to *SNL* his Tommy Flanagan, president of Pathological Liars Anonymous, who confidently boasted about everything. Dana Carvey not only was the smug, self-satisfied Enid Strict, the Church Lady, but also George Bush; one half of the Austrian weight-lifting team of Hans and Franz (Kevin Nealon was the other half), two pumped-up guys; and bespectacled, shaggy-haired, babe-watching Garth, who, with buddy Wayne Campbell (Mike Meyers), hosted an access cable TV show from their basement. Like Eddie Murphy and Billy Crystal, Martin Short and Dana Carvey moved on to films. (Carvey also had a couple of controversial and rather short-lived TV comedy series in the mid-1990s.)

Through the *SNL* years there also have been the outrageous commercial parodies that have become enshrined in the minds of the shows army of fans: "Super Bas-o-Matic" (a juice blender for turning an entire bass into a drink); "Swill" (bottled water dredged from Lake Erie);

The not-ready-for prime-time team of the late 1980s, from left, back row: Phil Hartman, Jan Hooks, Mike Myers; front row: Dennis Miller, Dana Carvey, Victoria Jackson, Kevin Nealon. COURTESY OF PERSONALITY PHOTOS, INC.

"Dysfunctional Family Christmas" (a record album of songs for families who have a tough time with the holidays); "The Love Toilet" (for those who never want to be apart); and "Norman Bates School for Motel Management."

About ten years into the show, turmoil started to reign with constant changes in the producing and writing staff, and at one point there were forty-two regulars on the show and a noticeable dip in creativity. Lorne Michaels, who had left in 1980 for other opportunities, was recruited to return in 1985 and tighten up the ship, which, by its twentieth year, had regained a good portion of its original luster. Some of those who had gone on to greater fame came back for periodic visits (John Belushi, of course, had died in 1982 and Gilda Radner in 1989) and, in the late 1990s, all is still alive and well on *Saturday Night Live,* its hipness still pretty much intact for Generation X as it had been early for the Baby Boomer generation.

Hour-long "Best of Saturday Night Live" compilations continue to run in syndication, and many edited down to thirty minutes air on Comedy Central.

VIDEO AVAILABILITY

Nearly fifty *Saturday Night Live* tape collections, most running about ninety-two minutes, are available at certain video outlets.

EMMY AWARDS

1975–76	Outstanding Comedy-Variety or Music Series
	Chevy Chase, Outstanding Continuing or Single Performance by a Supporting Actor on Variety or Music
	Dave Wilson, Outstanding Directing in a Comedy-Variety or Music Series
	Outstanding Writing in a Comedy-Variety or Music Series
1976–77	Outstanding Writing in a Comedy-Variety or Music Series
1977–78	**Gilda Radner,** Outstanding Continuing or Single Performance by a Supporting Actress in Variety or Music

TRIVIA TIDBITS

- A number of popular skits that were developed on *SNL* were expanded into feature-length movies: *The Blues Brothers* (1980), with John Belushi and Dan Aykroyd; *Wayne's World* (1992), with Dana Carvey and

Mike Myers; *The Coneheads* (1993), with Aykroyd and Jane Curtin, plus other *SNL* players past and present; *CB-4* (1993), with Chris Rock and Phil Hartman; *It's Pat! The Movie* (1994), with Julia Sweeney; and *Stuart Saves the Family* (1995), with Al Franken.

- Of all the original players who went on to other things, primarily a search for big-screen success, Jane Curtin alone found the stardom on television (and a number of Emmys) in her own hit 1980s series, *Kate & Allie,* and in the 1996 series *3rd Rock From the Sun,* ironically, like the Coneheads, dealing with an alien family (although she's an uptight earthling here). She also did drama, including a television remake of Alfred Hitchcock's *Suspicion.*
- A prolonged film and television writers' strike in 1981 severely limited the number of *SNL* original shows that season, with a great many reruns put into its time slot.
- *Saturday Night Live* celebrated its fifteenth anniversary with a much-heralded prime-time retrospective in September 1989. Somebody at the network forgot to count, however, since the special ran a year early, 1989 being only *SNL*'s fourteenth year.
- In the 1990s, Dan Aykroyd and Jim Belushi (in his late brother's place) have resurrected the Blues Brothers as a successful touring act and now have several House of Blues clubs across the country.

YOUR SHOW OF SHOWS

NBC, 1950–54, 160 programs

REGULARS

Sid Caesar
Imogene Coca
Carl Reiner
Howard Morris (1951–54)
Robert Merrill (1950–51)
Marguerite Piazza (1950–53)
Bill Hayes (1950–53)
Jerry Ross & Nellie Fisher (1950–52)
Mata & Hari (1950–53)
Jack Russell
Billy Williams Quartet
Judy Johnson (1950–53)
James Starbuck
Bambi Lynn & Rod Alexander
Show of Shows Ballet Company

CREATOR AND PRODUCER: Max Liebman
DIRECTORS: Max Liebman, Nat Hiken
WRITERS: Mel Brooks, Larry Gelbart, Mel Tolkin, Neil Simon, Woody Allen, Bill Persky, Sam Denoff, Danny Simon

The golden age of variety

Your Show of Shows, an ambitious ninety-minute weekly *live* variety extravaganza, remains one of the seminal programs in television history. Created out of the *Admiral Broadway Revue* of the late 1940s that had teamed Borscht Belt monologist and dialectician (and Coast Guard saxophone star) Sid Caesar with vaudeville and Broadway comedienne Imogene Coca, the new show cast the now-legendary, perfectly matched duo in howlingly funny sketches with brilliant second bananas Carl Reiner and Howard Morris. The four comprised, in effect, a four-person repertory company, but the show also featured a large corps of singers and dancers, as well as top-name

The brilliant Sid Caesar as The Professor clowning with sidekick Imogene Coca on *Your Show of Shows*. Both Caesar and Coca won Emmys for acting in 1951. COURTESY OF PERSONALITY PHOTOS, INC.

guests. With excerpts from ballet and grand opera, this was a class program in which the performers entertained live on TV thirty-nine weeks a year for four remarkable years.

The highlights of *Your Show of Shows* were the parodies of hit movies, most notably "From Here to Obscurity," with Sid and Imogene spoofing the beach clinch of Burt Lancaster and Deborah Kerr in *From Here to Eternity.* But the show also presented a wide range of sketches and gags: Sid's know-it-all German professor routine, in which he is interviewed by reporter Carl Reiner ("Tell me, professor, what do you do if you happen to topple off a mountain?" "You flap your arms as fast as you can and scream all the way down."); grand opera send-ups with Sid mouthing hilariously garbled linguistics; broad pantomimes of silent films with Sid, Imogene, Carl, and Howard outrageously overacting; Sid and Imogene playing lifelike musical Swiss mantle clock figures that have gone haywire; and Caesar, Reiner, and Morris in glitter jackets and foot-high pompadours as the rock 'n roll trio, The Three Haircuts, performing "You Are So Rare"—which actually was a hit record for them at the time on RCA Victor.

And then there was perhaps the best remembered satirical sketch of them all: *Your Show of Show*'s rib-tickling version of another popular program of the time, *This Is Your Life,* with Reiner the host (à la Ralph Edwards) and Caesar the extremely reluctant subject plucked out of the audience. Morris plays a long-lost relative so overcome with emotion at again meeting Caesar that he falls to the floor and clings lovingly to the latter's leg, being dragged along as the weepy honoree makes his way across the stage to greet others who have shown up for the occasion. This particular routine was the centerpiece of the feature-length *Ten From Your Show of Shows,* compiled from beautifully restored kinescopes and released theatrically in 1973.

Saturday night special

This amazing weekly potpourri was not entirely comedy, of course. Surrounding the sketches were elaborate music productions featuring Bill Hayes, Jack Russell, Judy Johnson and the Billy Williams Quartet to satisfy pop fans, and Robert Merrill and Marguerite Piazza for the classical devotees. For dance aficionados there were creative, often avant-garde Mata and Hari, the romantic team of Bambi Lynn and Rod Alexander, the agile James Starbuck, and a corps de ballet. Regrettably, since the show was done live, only snippets of their work survive on not especially well-preserved kinescopes.

Your Show of Shows also became famous for the formidable writing talent it nurtured, most of whom went on to prodigious careers in comedy: Neil Simon, who became the foremost comedy writer on the American stage and later had a Broadway theater named after him, and in 1993 wrote the stage hit *Laughter on the 23rd Floor,* based on his reminiscences of working with Caesar and company; Woody Allen, a mere adolescent when he began writing jokes and then comedy sketches for the show, and today is considered by many to be the greatest comic writer/director of our time; Mel Brooks, whose hugely successful writing/directing/performing career also included a series of "1000-Year-Old Man" albums, a TV special or two with Carl Reiner, and of course several brilliant film comedies, including *The Producers, Blazing Saddles,* and *Young Frankenstein;* Larry Gelbart, who was later responsible for *M*A*S*H* on TV, was Oscar-nominated for *Oh God!* and *Tootsie* on the screen and received Tonys for *A Funny Thing Happened on the Way to the Forum* and *City of Angels* on stage; Bill Persky and Sam Denoff, who later did *The Dick Van Dyke Show* with Reiner and created Marlo Thomas's *That Girl* and other series; and Mel Tolkin, who continued working with Caesar on a string of subsequent shows.

In the world of variety television, *Your Show of Shows,* despite being done under what would now be considered almost primitive conditions, retains a permanent position at the very top.

VIDEO AVAILABILITY

About a dozen cassettes featuring comedy sketches from *Your Show of Shows,* some running about thirty minutes and others between fifty and sixty-seven minutes, are available at certain tape outlets. In addition, there are several tapes from Sid Caesar's follow-up show, *Caesar's*

Many fans of *Your Show of Shows* most fondly recall the program's hilarious movie spoofs, penned by young comedy writers such as Mel Brooks, Neil Simon, Woody Allen, and Larry Gelbart. Here Sid Caesar and Imogene Coca are featured in a sidesplitting spoof of the famous beach scene in *From Here to Eternity.* COURTESY OF PERSONALITY PHOTOS, INC.

Hour, with Nanette Fabray, Carl Reiner, and Howard Morris, plus *The Best of Sid Caesar,* with Caesar-Coca excerpts from the *1949 Admiral Broadway Revue.*

EMMY AWARDS

1951 Best Variety Show
Sid Caesar, Best Actor
Imogene Coca, Best Actress
1952 Best Variety Program

TRIVIA TIDBITS

- In addition to being credited with discovering Sid Caesar (and earlier, Danny Kaye), creator Max Liebman is known for coining the word "special" for television events.
- Sid Caesar's 1982 autobiography, *Where Have I Been,* painted a dark side to his life during the *Your Show of Shows* days; Imogene Coca rejoined Sid Caesar occasionally through the years on television, has guest-starred in assorted sitcoms, made an appearance as Grandma in *National Lampoon's Vacation* (1983), and played Granny Clampett's 100-year-old maw in *The Return of the Beverly Hillbillies* in 1981; Carl Reiner, of course, became a major comedy director in TV and films and author of several hilarious books on show business; Howard Morris also became a noted director on TV sitcoms and has taken once-in-a-while acting jobs, most memorably as irrepressible mountain man Ernest T. Bass on *The Andy Griffith Show* (see separate entry).
- Singer Bill Hayes had a hit record with "The Ballad of Davy Crockett," starred in a number of TV musical specials, and since 1970 has played Doug Williams on the NBC soap *Days of Our Lives* opposite real-life wife Susan Seaforth; Robert Merrill continued on as one of America's premiere opera and concert baritones and, being a lifelong New York Yankees fan, recorded the version of the National Anthem that still opens every game played at Yankee Stadium; opera singer Marguerite Piazza also starred in several TV specials in the 1950s and then returned to the musical stage briefly before leaving show business; and the Billy Williams Quartet continued recording as a group through the 1950s, having a No. 1 hit in 1957 of "I'm Gonna Sit Right Down and Write Myself a Letter" (Billy died in 1972).

- Television pioneer Sylvester "Pat" Weaver, vice president of programming at NBC at the time he devised *Your Show of Shows,* is the father of contemporary film star Sigourney Weaver.
- The 1982 film *My Favorite Year* was about a fictional appearance by Errol Flynn (Peter O'Toole as "Alan Swann") on *Comedy Cavalcade* (referring to *Your Show of Shows*). Brooksfilms, Mel Brooks's company, coproduced the film.

INDEX

(Page numbers in italic type indicate photo.)